Re-imagining Political Community

Re-imagining Political Community
Studies in Cosmopolitan Democracy

Edited by

**Daniele Archibugi, David Held
and Martin Köhler**

Stanford University Press
Stanford, California
1998

Stanford University Press
Stanford, California
© 1998 Polity Press for collection
Originating publisher Polity Press, Cambridge
First published in the U.S.A. by
  Stanford University Press, 1998
Printed in Great Britain
Cloth ISBN 0-8047-3534-4
Paper ISBN 0-8047-3535-2
LC 98-60721
This book is printed on acid-free paper.

Contents

List of Contributors   vii
Acknowledgements   xii

Introduction
Daniele Archibugi, David Held and Martin Köhler   1

Part I   The Transformation of the Interstate System

 1 Democracy and Globalization
    David Held   11
 2 Governance and Democracy in a Globalizing World
    James N. Rosenau   28
 3 Human Rights as a Model for Cosmopolitan Democracy
    David Beetham   58
 4 The Global Democracy Deficit: an Essay in International
    Law and its Limits
    James Crawford and Susan Marks   72
 5 Reconceptualizing Organized Violence
    Mary Kaldor   91

Part II   Citizenship, Sovereignty and Transnational Democracy

 6   Citizenship and Sovereignty in the Post-Westphalian
     European State
     Andrew Linklater   113
 7   Citizenship in the European Union: a Paradigm for
     Transnational Democracy?
     Ulrich K. Preuß   138
 8   Between Cosmopolis and Community: Three Models of
     Rights and Democracy within the European Union
     Richard Bellamy and Dario Castiglione   152
 9   Community Identity and World Citizenship
     Janna Thompson   179
10   Principles of Cosmopolitan Democracy
     Daniele Archibugi   198

Part III   The Prospects of Cosmopolitan Democracy

11   From the National to the Cosmopolitan Public Sphere
     Martin Köhler   231
12   Global Security Problems and the Challenge to Democratic
     Process
     Gwyn Prins and Elizabeth Sellwood   252
13   Refugees: a Special Case for Cosmopolitan Citizenship?
     Pierre Hassner   273
14   Democracy in the United Nations System:
     Cosmopolitan and Communitarian Principles
     Derk Bienen, Volker Rittberger and Wolfgang Wagner   287
15   The United Nations and Cosmopolitan Democracy: Bad
     Dream, Utopian Fantasy, Political Project
     Richard Falk   309

Index   332

Contributors

Daniele Archibugi is Researcher at the Italian National Research Council in Rome. He is an adviser to the OECD, the European Union and several UN specialized agencies. He has worked at the Universities of Sussex, Roskilde, Naples and Cambridge. He has co-edited *Cosmopolitan Democracy: an Agenda for a New World Order* (1995) and a special issue on Global Democracy for *Peace Review* (1997). He has worked on the history of peace ideas and UN reform.

David Beetham is Professor of Politics and Director of the Centre for Democratisation Studies, University of Leeds, UK. He has acted as consultant on democracy to UNESCO, the Inter-Parliamentary Union and the Council of Europe. Recent works include, as editor, *Politics and Human Rights* (1995) and, with Kevin Boyle, *Introducing Democracy* (1995).

Richard Bellamy is Professor of Politics and International Relations and Head of Department at the University of Reading. Recent publications include *Liberalism and Modern Society* (1992); with Darrow Schecter, *Gramsci and the Italian State* (1993); and, as editor, *Constitutionalism, Democracy and Sovereignty* and, with Dario Castiglione,

Constitutionalism in Transformation (1996). He is currently completing a book on *Liberalism and the Challenge of Pluralism* and directing a project on European Citizenship funded by the Leverhulme Trust.

Derk Bienen is Research Associate at the Center for International Relations/Peace and Conflict Studies at the University of Tübingen. As part of a project on German Foreign Policy after Unification, he is working on German Foreign Aid Policy.

Dario Castiglione is Senior Lecturer in Political Theory at the University of Exeter. He has written on eighteenth-century political theory, on the history of civil society and constitutionalism, and recently edited with Richard Bellamy the 1996 *Political Studies* special issue on *Constitutionalism in Transformation: European and Theoretical Perspectives*. He is currently working on a monograph on David Hume's political philosophy, besides continuing his research on constitutionalism and Europe.

James Crawford is Whewell Professor of International Law and Director of the Lauterpacht Research Centre for International Law, University of Cambridge. He previously held chairs at the Universities of Adelaide and Sydney. He was a member of the Australian Law Reform Commission, where he worked on Aboriginal customary laws, admiralty and foreign state immunity. He is now a member of the United Nations International Law Commission, where he has worked on the International Criminal Court and is currently the special rapporteur on state responsibility. He has written widely on statehood and the rights of peoples, especially self-determination and democratic rights.

Richard Falk is Albert G. Milbank Professor of International Law and Practice at Princeton University. He has been a major contributor to the world order literature for more than three decades. His recent books include *On Humane Governance: Toward a New Global Politics* (1995) and *Explorations at the Edge of Time: Prospects for World Order* (1992). He is currently a member of the Independent World Commission on the Oceans.

Pierre Hassner is Research Director at the Centre d'Études et de Recherches Internationales (Paris), and teaches at the Institut d'Études Politiques (Paris) and the Johns Hopkins University European Center (Bologna). He is the author of *Violence and Peace* (1967) and of many articles and book chapters on political philosophy (mainly Rousseau, Kant, Hegel) and on international relations (mainly nationalism, totalitarianism and European security).

David Held is Professor of Politics and Sociology at the Open University. Among his recent publications are *Models of Democracy* (second edition, 1996), *Democracy and the Global Order: From the Modern State to Cosmopolitan Governance* (1995) and (as editor) *Prospects for Democracy: North, South, East, West* (1993). He has just completed (with colleagues) *Global Transformation: Concepts, Evidence and Arguments* (forthcoming 1998).

Mary Kaldor is Jean Monnet Reader in Contemporary European Studies at the University of Sussex. Her books include *The Baroque Arsenal* (1982) and *The Imaginary War: Understanding the East–West Conflict* (1991). She is Director of the UNU/WIDER project, Restructuring the Global Military Sector, and she is a consultant to the European Commission on democratization and democracy assistance to Central and Eastern Europe. She is also Co-Chair of the Helsinki Citizens Assembly, a pan-European non-governmental organization.

Martin Köhler is Researcher with the Centro de Investigacion para la Paz, Madrid, and he has been a research fellow of the Network of European Scholars working on the theme of The Political Theory of Transnational Democracy. He is freelance consultant of the Science Directorate of the European Parliament on Mediterranean Affairs. Together with Daniele Archibugi he has co-edited a special issue on Global Democracy for *Peace Review* (1997).

Andrew Linklater is Professor of International Relations at Keele University and Dean of Postgraduate Affairs. His main publications are *Men and Citizens in the Theory of International Relations* (second edition, 1990), *Beyond Realism and Marxism: Critical Theory and International Relations* (1990) and *The Transformation of Political Community: Ethical Foundations of the Post-Westphalian Era* (1998).

Susan Marks is Lecturer in the Faculty of Law, University of Cambridge. She teaches international law and human rights. She has written on international and European human rights law, and is currently completing a book on the conceptualization of democracy in international law.

Ulrich K. Preuß is Professor of Law and Politics at the Free University, Berlin. He has worked on the constitutional transition in the post-communist states of East and Central Europe, the development of a European constitution and on the relations between liberal constitutionalism and the multicultural society. Among his recent works are *Constitutional Revolution: the link between Constitutionalism and Progress* (1995); together with Jon Elster and Claus Offe, *Institutional Design in*

Post-Communist Societies: Rebuilding the Ship at Sea (forthcoming); and (as editor) *Zum Begriff der Verfassung: Die Ordnung des Politischen* (1994).

Gwyn Prins has taught history and political science at Emmanuel College, Cambridge, since 1976. Since 1997 he has been Senior Research Fellow at the Royal Institute of International Affairs at Chatham House, London. He is also Senior Fellow in the Office of the Special Adviser to the Secretary-General of NATO and Visiting Senior Fellow at the UK Centre for Defence Analysis/Defence Evaluation and Research Agency. He is General Editor of *Global Transformations* for UCL Press.

Volker Rittberger is Professor of Political Science and International Relations and Director of the Center for International Relations/Peace and Conflict Studies at the University of Tübingen. He is the editor of *Regime Theory and International Relations* (1993), author of *Internationale Organisationen: Theorie und Geschichte* (second edition, 1995) and co-author of *Vereinte Nationen und Weltordnung* (1997) and *Theories of International Regimes* (1997).

James N. Rosenau is University Professor of International Affairs at the George Washington University. A founder of international regimes theory, his more recent writings include *Along the Domestic-Foreign Frontier: Exploring Governance in a Turbulent World* (1997); *Turbulence in World Politics: a Theory of Change and Continuity* (1990); as co-author, *Thinking Theory Thoroughly: Coherent Approaches to an Incoherent World* (1995); and as co-editor, *Governance without Government: Order and Change in World Politics* (1992).

Elizabeth Sellwood is Research Assistant at the Royal Institute of International Affairs at Chatham House, London. She has worked with Gwyn Prins on projects on strategic prediction, NATO enlargement, UK force planning and preparation for joint peacekeeping operations, as well as the project reported in this volume.

Janna Thompson is Senior Lecturer in Philosophy at La Trobe University, Melbourne. She is the author of *Justice and World Order: a Philosophical Inquiry* (1992) and has recently completed a book on ethical epistemology, *Discourse and Knowledge: Defence of a Collective Procedure* (1998). She has also published articles on environmental ethics and social philosophy. She is presently working on a project on group rights and community values in a global and national context.

Wolfgang Wagner is Research Associate at the Center for International Relations/Peace and Conflict Studies at the University of Tübingen. As part of a project on German Foreign Policy after Unification, he is working on Germany's Foreign Policy towards the European Union.

Acknowledgements

The idea of discussing the notion of cosmopolitan democracy from a variety of academic perspectives originated during some rainy Cambridge evenings in the winter of 1992. At the time, one of us was working on the effects of globalization on democratic systems and another on the prospects of peaceful, democratic interstate relationships. The two research agendas converged in a number of interesting respects, but we felt that the gathering of expertise from a larger number of fields and viewpoints would enhance the discussion considerably.

We decided, therefore, to present an application to the European Commission to fund a Network of European Scholars on the theme of The Political Theory of Transnational Democracy: Citizens, Minorities and Peoples in Europe (Human Capital and Mobility Programme, Directorate-General Science, Research and Development, contract no. ERBCHRXCT940664). This grant, which lasted from January 1995 to June 1996, financed a network of colleagues and friends examining the prospect of extending democracy beyond borders. We held meetings in Rome, Italian Parliament (March 1995) and in Cambridge, Emmanuel College (April 1996). Both these meetings involved a thorough preparation and a massive follow-up exchange of written comments which overloaded the Internet and stressed contributors, but also helped to create a more cohesive and consistent outcome. Daniele Archibugi, Martin Köhler and Erminia Licitri, on the one hand, and David Held, Gwyn Prins and Elizabeth Sellwood, on the other, took care of the technicalities relating to the meetings in Rome and Cambridge.

Fabio Armao, Luigi Bonanate, Hilal Elver, Luigi Ferrajoli, Niels Petter Gleditsch, Hans Köchler, Mathias König-Archibugi, Ekkehart Krippendorff, Stephan Leibfried, Fabio Marcelli, Mario Pianta, Alberto Piris, François Rigaux, Bruce Russett and Salvatore Senese, along with the majority of the authors of this volume, participated in these meetings and provided important contributions in shaping the project. Some of us also benefited from discussions held at the Seminar on Cosmopolitan Democracy convened by Mary Kaldor at the Sussex European Institute, University of Sussex, in 1995–6.

The European Commission's grant was managed in Rome by the Lelio Basso International Foundation for the Rights and Liberation of Peoples, which provided an ideal intellectual environment for our research. We wish to thank Erminia Licitri for her patient and skilful help with the administration of the project. Linda Bimbi and her colleagues at the Basso Foundation helped to sort out several problems on our way.

Marcela Bulcu in Rome and Julia Harsant and Sue Pope in Cambridge helped considerably with the preparation of the manuscript, managing to make compatible several different types of software. We are very grateful to them. In addition, we would like to thank Ann Bone in Oxford for her invaluable assistance in the final stages of the preparation of the book.

The Editors

Introduction

Daniele Archibugi, David Held and Martin Köhler

Among the twentieth century's most important legacies to the new millennium are the accentuation of processes of globalization, the end of the Cold War and the assertion of democracy as the legitimate system of government.

The first legacy – the globalization of economic, social and cultural life – is a gradual but enduring process. It is secular in nature and involves a variety of subjects and fields whose interactions trigger multiple effects. It is not the product of a political design imposed by a restricted group of actors; on the contrary, it grows more intensive every day through the workings of firms, associations and individuals, as well as governments and international organizations. Albeit by no means a new phenomenon, globalization has increased significantly in the post-Second World War years. Future generations will have to come to terms with the processes of globalization even more than those of the past or present.

The second legacy is the ending of the Cold War. Nuclear terror, which dominated political life after the Second World War, is no longer uppermost on the political agenda. But even history-making events such as those we have witnessed since 1989 do not necessarily mark the beginning of an irreversible process. The nuclear confrontation between West and East, between capitalist democracy and Soviet communism, is a thing of the past. However, that does not mean that war is no longer used to solve controversies or that states have stopped squabbling over political hegemony. Now that almost ten years have passed since the collapse of the Berlin Wall (an event which now rivals the storming of the Bastille as a symbol of historical change), it is plain enough to see that interstate rivalries remain and often spill over into bloody conflict. The nuclear disarmament process is only just beginning and nuclear terror, albeit not as immediate as before, still exists. There is no guarantee that new and stronger conflicts will not break out between rival areas of influence. In different historical conditions, and among different geographical and political areas, forms of international conflict no less intense than those we have seen are still possible. The end of the Cold War must be seen as an opportunity for creating a more progressive, stable system of interstate relations.

The third legacy is the extension of the aspiration of peoples to be governed on the basis of democratic criteria. Peoples in the East and South have demanded and, in many cases, obtained the right to participate in the government of their communities through the medium of elected representatives, as is already the case in Western countries. Never before has the idea of democratic government been so popular. For the first time in the history of humanity, the last decade of the twentieth century is witnessing the development of a general consensus about the relative virtues of a single, specific form of government. However, democracy's victory is far from being total. Acceptance of democracy is by no means univocal and democracy itself appears in different historical forms. Over a third of the population of the world is still governed by autocratic regimes, while in countries with more consolidated democratic traditions many social and economic demands remain unmet. Over the last decade, democracy has, admittedly, won many proselytes, but it has also disappointed the expectations of some. Even though democracy has achieved significant results in the process of state governance, it still fails to be applied to the management of interstate relations over regional or global problems. So it cannot be said that democracy is destined to enjoy an irreversible success. It may develop, but it may also be replaced by different forms of power management. It too presents itself as an opportunity which may or may not be pursued.

It seems reasonable to predict that political communities in the next millennium will have to come to terms with the developing process of globalization. Accordingly, they will have to adapt and consolidate democracy as a system of power management and to develop stable peaceful relations. Peace and democracy are obviously intertwined since a peaceful international system is the prerequisite for the development of democracy both inside states and within the international system itself.

In the scenario we have sketched briefly, the structure of political communities is still very uncertain. Globalization has affected our daily lives a great deal, but political institutions continue to be designed for a society which worked on a narrower geographic scale – namely, the territorial state. Seats of power, authority and decision-making are mostly concentrated in individual states, even when political choices concern questions which extend beyond their borders.

Not that this means that states are secure in their traditional form. Although the matter is often overstated, the sovereignty and autonomy of states have been challenged and remoulded in significant ways. International law, international organizations, diplomacy, the interests of the big multinationals, the emergence of a transnational civil society, no less than the distribution of military strength across the planet, ensure that states can take fewer and fewer decisions without extensive consultation, collaboration and negotiation with other states and agencies. World politics is contested and regulated by control mechanisms with which governments have to come to terms in a number of spheres. As international regime doctrine has taught, global society is not anarchic, it is governed by a network of controls and countervailing powers – in short, an international system of 'governance without government'.

It is vital to appreciate the profound difference that exists between the ways in which domestic and international political systems have developed. Domestic political systems have evolved on the basis of projects often intentionally pursued by thinkers, leaders and political, social and cultural movements. No matter how much these political projects have gradually been shaped to fit changing historical conditions, they have nonetheless managed to alter social circumstance. Political theory and political systems have evolved, in part, in parallel, and political theory has certainly left an indelible mark on the history of political systems in the modern era. The political systems of Great Britain, France, the United States, China, Cuba and Iran have all, for good or for evil, been influenced by given theoretical models.

But if we turn our attention to the international political system, the first thing we note is that it has not been inspired by many great theoretical doctrines (although, of course, they have not been entirely absent). The international system has developed progressively under the push and pull of widely different tendencies that have rarely been deliberately designed or intentionally pursued. If we pause to consider the complexity of world society compared to the more limited ambit of single states, it is not hard to understand why political projects have had a more telling effect at the state as against the global level. But does the same phenomenon necessarily have to repeat itself in the present historical conditions?

Today the international community is desperately searching for a new global political balance. In some quarters, the ideal would be a world order in which a few hundred big companies could dictate norms designed to further their own interests to a panel of strong, powerful states. Some prefer global technocratic solutions, others even expect to see new clashes between civilizations. There is, in addition, a widely growing aspiration towards the development of a world order founded on international legality, the self-government of peoples and respect for universal rights.

Cosmopolitan democracy is a political project which aims to engender greater public accountability in the leading processes and structural alterations of the contemporary world. Not that it is the only project of its kind; many others with similar aspirations – from perpetual peace projects to the World Order Models Project – have been developed over the course of time. We have drawn and learnt a lot from these. The distinctive feature of the model discussed here, however, is that it has made democracy the primary focus and studied the conditions for its application to states, interstate relations and global issues. The essays in this book explore the potential of the cosmopolitan approach as a political project for a new world order from different perspectives.

The book is divided into three sections. The first section examines the transformation of the interstate system. David Held asks how globalization has altered democratic systems and explores the impact of changes in the spatial organization of economic, political, cultural and environmental processes on the nature and form of political community. Globalization places significant constraints on domestic democracy, which is why the renewal of democracy is not only an internal question for individual states, but a matter for international political life as well. James Rosenau paints a fresco of the many forms of collaboration in world politics, and assesses which control mechanisms regulate – despite a surface impression of anarchy – the actions of world political subjects. His essay raises two questions. Should we be satisfied with existing control mechanisms? And to what extent do they respond to the principle of democracy?

David Beetham compares the ambitions of the cosmopolitan project and the ongoing human rights regime, signalling some interesting points of convergence. He argues that the criteria which have inspired the human rights regime over the last half-century are undoubtedly universalist, although the extent of their enforcement is clearly a separate question. If the human rights regime is to be fully implemented, he continues further, political subjects other than states – be they international or non-governmental organizations – have to be granted a broader mandate. The essay by James Crawford and Susan Marks is a critical analysis of the relationship between international law and democracy. Recent developments in legal theory and practice have entrenched a certain 'right to democratic government'. However, even though this right may have a useful role to play in the process of national democratization, it remains ambiguous in relation to wider international considerations. Crawford and Marks's review of the literature shows how rarely international law attempts to arrive at democratic procedures in interstate relations and truly global issues. This is a glaring lacuna in so far as lack of democracy is a problem not only for the domestic regimes of states but also for the international community as a whole. Hence the need to review traditional legal categories to allow the concept of democracy to extend to intergovernmental decision-making processes as well as to genuinely planetary issues.

Mary Kaldor shows how the wars of the 1990s followed a very different logic from traditional ones. Basing her argument on the conflicts in the former Yugoslavia and other European regions, she identifies the typical characteristics of the collective violence of these 'new' civil wars, which the traditional interstate system has proved incapable of preventing. Speaking from a cosmopolitan perspective, Kaldor advocates more active intervention by civil society as an antidote to this type of violence, both inside and outside the areas hit by war. And she argues that such intervention can be effectively pursued if the maintenance and enforcement of human rights law is seen as a task as important as the furthering and upholding of the rules of war. For these are two sides of a regulatory system that could, in principle, circumscribe and check violence in diverse forms.

The second section of the volume presents the model of cosmopolitan democracy in the context of ongoing theoretical debate. The cosmopolitan model, argues Andrew Linklater, is inevitably at loggerheads with traditional notions of citizenship and sovereignty and demands that they be redefined. Linklater suggests we set out from a 'thin' notion of citizenship but envisage the rights and obligations of the individual independently of his or her belonging to a particular state. And he shows just how much notions of citizenship and sovereignty have changed in Europe and how the process is far from coming to an end. Ulrich Preuß also addresses the question of citizenship in his essay on the European Union's emblematic attempt to develop the idea of transnational citizenship. Although the relevant rights and duties are still limited, this is a significant example of an attempt to build a form of citizenship transcending the state.

The chapters by Richard Bellamy and Dario Castiglione and by Janna Thompson analyse the contrast between the communitarian and cosmopolitan approaches. Bellamy and Castiglione explore the implications of the debate for the European Union and other regions. They point out that the EU is effectively developing a model midway between the cosmopolitan and communitarian ideals. The idea of a variable geometry for European integration – the so-called 'Europe à la carte' – is original and deserves to be preserved. It is necessary, however, to define the optional and constitutive aspects of integration. Through a more strictly philosophical lens, Janna Thompson looks at the controversy between communitarian and cosmopolitan theorists. She criticizes the communitarians' idea that it is possible to predefine the identity of a political community, but acknowledges that they are right to remind cosmopolitans that any political community has to have an identity of its own, and that the identity of the world political community is still embryonic. The cosmopolitan project has to establish how that identity can be achieved.

Daniele Archibugi argues the need for cosmopolitan democracy to be based on three dimensions: domestic, interstate and global. Democratic procedures may be substantially different at each of these levels. Reviewing the traditional confederate and federalist models, Archibugi argues that neither has the wherewithal to meet the requirements of cosmopolitan democracy. Hence the need to come up with a different model of political community, more unified than a confederation but less centralized than a federal state.

The third section of the book contains essays on the political processes and actors at which the cosmopolitan democracy model is directed. Martin Köhler tries to establish whether the forces of civil society can become leading players in global change. Can they play an active political role in pursuance of the cosmopolitan project? The social and technical structure of the contemporary world allows for this and, in many cases, demands it. But it is also necessary to assess the relative influence of civil society in global political choices. Gwyn Prins and Elizabeth Sellwood study the specific case of the Brent Spar floating oil storage buoy, showing how an international campaign to save the environment succeeded in achieving its objective. We know of many campaigns waged by civil society which managed to obtain tangible results: historical milestones such as the collapse of the Berlin Wall and the end of apartheid, as well as more specific, local events, such as the checking of nuclear experiments in the Pacific or the controlling of the 'mad cow' trade, were achieved partly thanks to transnational public opinion. Yet it would be over-optimistic to mention only these partial and often hard-won successes without also recalling the many instances in which transnational civil society has failed to formulate alternative political projects to the ones already existing. The cosmopolitan democracy project acknowledges the weakness with which civil society addresses global political choices. It hopes, however, to help identify the objectives on which civil society is able to rally and the fields in which it is most likely to achieve tangible political results.

There are many concrete cases in which the interstate system is incapable of generating acceptable solutions. One is that of refugees, the subject of Pierre Hassner's essay. Only a small minority of the population of the planet possesses this special status, but it is large enough to trigger conflict, tensions and often violations of basic human rights. Hassner shows that the problem of refugees is handled instrumentally in interstate relations and he appeals, as a solution to a specific problem, to Kant's old yet very contemporary idea of cosmopolitan citizenship. One wonders whether, setting out from a specific, long-suffering category such as that of refugees, it might not be possible to sow the seed of a notion of citizenship independent, at least in some essential aspects, of the individual's belonging to a specific state.

The programme of research on cosmopolitan democracy explores transnational political initiatives, especially in relation to appropriate institutional centres. The most important of these is the United Nations, the most ambitious international organization in the history of humankind. The essays by Derk Bienen, Volker Rittberger and Wolfgang Wagner and by Richard Falk analyse prospects for reform at the United Nations. In the wake of the various proposals forwarded by government and non-government organizations, Bienen, Rittberger and Wagner study which reforms are needed to introduce democratic criteria into the workings of the United Nations. Who should the effective members of the United Nations be – peoples or their governments? As things stand, the answer is of course governments, but the effective democratization of the UNO demands that individuals too – at least at certain levels – enjoy political rights. Falk draws an outline of the role of the United Nations in international political affairs today, advocating the need to make the often utopian aspirations of reform projects take root in the terrain of effective power.

The notion of cosmopolitan democracy, set out and explored in this volume, recognizes our complex, interconnected world. It recognizes, of course, certain problems and policies as appropriate for local governments and national states; but it also recognizes others as appropriate for specific regions, and still others – such as the environment, global security concerns, world health questions and economic regulation – that need new institutions to address them. Deliberative and political decision-making centres beyond national territories are justified when cross-border or transnational groups are affected by a public matter, when 'lower' levels of decision-making cannot resolve the issues in question and when the issue of the accountability of a matter in hand can only itself be understood and redeemed in a transnational, cross-border context. The essays that follow seek to show that transnational political arrangements are not only a necessity but also a possibility in the light of the changing organization of regional and global processes, evolving political decision-making centres such as the European Union, and growing political demands for new forms of political deliberation, conflict resolution and negotiation. In such a world, cities, national parliaments, regional assemblies and global authorities could all have distinctive but interlinked roles within a framework of democratic accountability and public decision-making.

The fifteen studies contained in this book by no means provide an exhaustive theoretical account of cosmopolitan democracy. Still less do they say everything that might be said about its potential relevance as a notion in political activity. But they show that it is a fertile field of debate and research. It is our hope that the questions pursued will contribute to a reconsideration of the nature and form of political community in the years ahead.

Part I

The Transformation of the Interstate System

1

Democracy and Globalization

David Held

There is a striking paradox to note about the contemporary era: from Africa to Eastern Europe, Asia to Latin America, more and more nations and groups are championing the idea of democracy; but they are doing so at just that moment when the very efficacy of democracy as a national form of political organization appears open to question. As substantial areas of human activity are progressively organized on a regional or global level, the fate of democracy, and of the independent democratic nation-state in particular, is fraught with difficulty.

Throughout the world's major regions there has been a consolidation of democratic processes and procedures. In the mid-1970s, over two-thirds of all states could reasonably be called authoritarian. This percentage has fallen dramatically; less than a third of all states are now authoritarian, and the number of democracies is growing rapidly.[1] Democracy has become the fundamental standard of political legitimacy in the current era. Events such as the release of Nelson Mandela from prison and the tearing down of the Berlin Wall are symbolic of changes indicating that, in more and more countries, citizen-voters are in principle able to hold public decision-makers to account. Yet at the same time the democratic political community is increasingly challenged by regional and global pressures and problems. How can problems such as the spread of AIDS, the debt burden of many countries in the 'developing world', the flow of financial resources which escape national jurisdiction, the drugs trade and international crime be satisfactorily brought within the sphere of democracy? What kind of accountability and control can citizens of a single nation-state have over international actors, such as multinational corporations, and over international organizations, such as the World Bank? In the context of trends towards regionalization, European integration, fundamental transformations in the global economy, mass communications and information technology, how can democracy be sustained? Are new democratic institutions necessary to regulate and control the new international forces and processes? How can citizens participate as citizens in a new and more complex internationally organized world? In a world organized increasingly on regional and global lines, can democracy as we know it survive?

Of course, there is nothing new about the emergence of global problems. Although their importance has grown considerably, many have existed for decades, some for centuries. But now that the old confrontation between East and West has ended, many regional and global issues have come to assume an urgent place on the international political agenda. Nonetheless, profound ambiguity still reigns as to where, how and according to what criteria decisions about these matters can be taken.

Democratic theory's exploration of emerging regional and global problems is still in its infancy. While students of democracy have examined and debated at length the challenges to democracy that emerge from within the boundaries of the nation-state, they have not seriously questioned whether the nation-state itself can remain at the centre of democratic thought; the questions posed by the rapid growth of complex interconnections and interrelations between states and societies, and by the evident intersection of national and international forces and processes, remain largely unexplored.[2] By contrast, this chapter seeks to address these questions by, first, examining the nature of globalization and, second, laying out a novel conception of democratic options in the face of the new global circumstances.[3]

GLOBALIZATION

Globalization is a much contested word. On the one hand, there are those who claim that we live in an integrated global order. According to this view, social and economic processes operate predominantly at a global level and national political communities are inevitably 'decision-takers'.[4] This development represents a fundamental break in the organization of human affairs – a shift in the organizational principle of social life. On the other hand, there are those people who are very sceptical about the extent of globalization and who still think the national state is as integrated and robust as it ever was. They point out, for instance, that contemporary forms of international economic interaction are not without precedent and that nation-states continue to be immensely powerful, with an impressive range of political options.[5]

Both these views are misleading in significant respects. We live in a world which is changing due to processes of globalization. The interconnectedness of different peoples today is more extensive and intensive than it has ever been. But globalization is not a new phenomenon; societies have always been connected with one another to some degree. Conceptions of globalization need to be sensitive to the historical variation in forms of globalization, as well as to their variable impact on politics. It is easy to exaggerate the extent to which globalization signals 'the end of the nation-state'. Global processes should not be assumed to represent either a total eclipse of the states system or the simple emergence of a global society. Accordingly, before proceeding further, the concept of globalization needs clarification.

Globalization is best understood as a spatial phenomenon, lying on a continuum with 'the local' at one end and 'the global' at the other. It denotes a shift in the spatial form of human organization and activity to transcontinental or interregional patterns of activity, interaction and the exercise of power. It involves a stretching and deepening of social relations and institutions across space and time such that, on the one hand, day-to-day activities are increasingly influenced by events happening on the other side of the globe and, on the other, the practices and decisions of local groups or communities can have significant global reverberations.[6]

Globalization today implies at least two distinct phenomena. First, it suggests that many chains of political, economic and social activity are becoming interregional or intercontinental in scope and, secondly, it suggests that there has been an intensification of levels of interaction and interconnectedness within and between states and societies.[7] What is noteworthy about the modern global system is the stretching of social relations in and through new dimensions of activity and the chronic intensification of patterns of interconnectedness mediated by such phenomena as modern communication networks and new information technology. It is possible to distinguish different historical forms of globalization in terms of (1) the extensiveness of networks of relations and connections; (2) the intensity of flows and levels of enmeshment within the networks; and (3) the impact of these phenomena on particular communities.

Globalization is neither a singular condition nor a linear process. Rather, it is best thought of as a multidimensional phenomenon involving diverse domains of activity and interaction, including the economic, political, technological, military, legal, cultural and environmental. Each of these spheres involves different patterns of relations and activity. A general account of globalization cannot simply predict from one domain what will occur in another. It is important, therefore, to build a theory of globalization from an understanding of what is happening in each one of these areas.

The significance of globalization, of course, differs for individuals, groups and countries. The impact of various global flows on, for instance, policy-making in the economic domain will alter considerably depending on whether the country in question is the United States, Peru or Spain. For individuals and groups as well, variable enmeshment in global flows is the norm. The elites in the world of politics, law, business and science are often quite at home in the global capitals, the leading hotels, and in the major cultural centres. Their access and use of these different facilities is clearly in marked contrast to those peoples, for example villagers in sub-Saharan Africa, who live at the margins of some of the central power structures and hierarchies of the global order. But such peoples are by no means unaffected by changing processes and forms of globalization. On the contrary, they are often in the position of being profoundly influenced by these processes and forms, even if they cannot control them. What often differentiates their position from what some have called the new 'cosmopolitan elite' is differential, unequal and uneven access to the dominant organizations, institutions and processes of the new emerging global order.

At the heart of this 'differential access' is power, where power has to be conceptualized as the capacity to transform material circumstances – whether social, political or economic – and to achieve goals based on the mobilization of resources, the creation of rule systems, and the control of infrastructures and institutions. The particular form of power that is of concern to a theory of globalization is characterized by *hierarchy* and *unevenness*. Hierarchy connotes the asymmetrical access to global networks and infrastructures, while unevenness refers to the asymmetrical effects of such networks on the life chances and the well-being of peoples, classes, ethnic groupings and the sexes.[8]

In order to elaborate a theory of globalization, it is necessary to turn from a general concern with its conceptualization to an examination of the distinctive domains of activity and interaction in and through which global processes evolve. This task cannot be pursued here at any length. But some significant changes can be highlighted. An obvious starting point is the world economy and, in particular, trade, financial flows and the spread of multinational corporations.

Trade

There are those who are sceptical about the extent of the globalization of trade in the contemporary period and they sometimes point out that trade levels in the late twentieth century have only recently reached the same levels as in 1914. This sceptical view is open to doubt. First, using constant price data, it can be shown that the proportion of trade to gross domestic product (trade–GDP ratios) surpassed that of the gold standard era (that is, the period 1875–1914) by the early 1970s, and was considerably higher by the late 1970s and 1980s. In other words, trade has continued to expand as a proportion of GDP. Export- and import–GDP ratios were around 12–13 per cent for advanced industrial countries during the gold standard era but rose to 15–20 per cent – or even higher for some developed countries – from the late 1970s onwards.

In addition, if one removes government expenditure from the enquiry, and focuses on trade in relation to the size of national economic activity, it can be demonstrated that the proportion of trade to such activity has grown markedly, by as much as a third. Technological developments have made many classes of goods, particularly those in the service sector, tradeable where previously they were not.

The evidence also shows that there has not been a simple increase in intraregional trade around the world. Measures of the intensity of trade reveal sustained growth between regions as well (albeit concentrated among Europe, North America and Pacific Asia). Growth in trade within regions and growth among regions are not contradictory developments; rather, they appear to be mutually complementary.

What these points suggest is that trade has grown rapidly, especially in the postwar period, reaching unprecedented levels today. More countries are involved in trading arrangements, such as India and China, and more people and nations are affected by such trade. In the context of the lowering of tariff barriers across the world one can reasonably expect these trends to continue. Any argument that suggests that the world's three key trading blocks – the EU, NAFTA and Pacific Asia – are becoming more inward-looking and protectionist is not supported by the evidence. Although contemporary trading arrangements stop far short of a perfectly open global market, national economies are enmeshed in a pattern of increasingly dense, competitive international trade. When linked to changes in finance and the organization of production and banking, this has significant political implications.

Finance

The expansion of global financial flows around the world has been staggering in the last ten to fifteen years. Foreign exchange turnover is now over a trillion dollars a day. The volume of turnover of bonds, securities and other assets on a daily basis is also without precedent. A number of things can be said about these flows:

1   The relationship of foreign exchange turnover to trade has mushroomed from 11 dollars to 1 to over 55 dollars to 1 in the last thirteen to fourteen years; that is, for every 55 dollars turned over in the foreign exchange markets, 1 dollar is turned over in real trade.
2   A great deal of this financial activity is speculative – it generates fluctuations in values in excess of those which can be accounted for by changes in the underlying fundamentals of asset values.
3   While the *net* movement of capital relative to GDP is smaller for some countries today than in earlier periods, this has nothing to do with diminishing levels of globalization, that is, lower levels of integration of capital markets. The liberalization of capital markets in the 1980s and early 1990s has created a more integrated financial system than has ever been known.
4   The effects of global financial flows on economic policy are profound. Among the most important are:
    (a)   the increased possibility of rapid and dramatic shifts in the effective valuation of economies, as illustrated, for instance, in Mexico in January 1995;
    (b)   the increasing difficulty for countries of pursuing independent monetary policies and independent exchange rate strategies in the face of the current volume of international turnover in currencies and bonds;
    (c)   the erosion of the option to pursue Keynesian reflationary strategies in a single country – the costs and benefits of these strategies have shifted against the pursuit of such options in many places;
    (d)   and, finally, as can be seen in the growing macroeconomic policy convergence across political parties in the present period, a deepening acknowledgement of the decline in the economic manoeuvrability of individual governments. Recent examples of this can be found in the reshaping of economic policy among the social democratic parties of Europe. The transformation of the economic policy of the Labour Party in Britain – from policy emphasizing demand management to policy prioritizing supply-side measures (above all, in education and training) to help meet the challenges of increased competition and the greater mobility of capital – is a particular case in point.

Many of these changes might not be of concern if financial market operators had a monopoly of economic expertise, but they clearly do not. Their actions can precipitate crises and can contribute to making sound policies unworkable. In addition, they can erode the democratic quality of government. This does not necessarily lead to political impotence – although it has done so in some countries in some respects – but it creates new political questions.

Multinational corporations

The globalization of production and the globalization of financial trans-actions are organized in part, familiarly enough, by fast-growing multi-national companies (MNCs). Two central points need to be made about them. First, MNCs account for a quarter to a third of world output, 70 per cent of world trade and 80 per cent of direct international invest-ment. They are essential to the diffusion of technology. And they are key players in international money markets.

Secondly, although evidence indicates that many of the largest MNCs still generate most of their sales and profits from domestic business, this is largely due to the influence of US companies, which have, of course, a particularly large home market.[9] The proportion of sales and profits generated domestically are much lower for non-US companies and, sig-nificantly, for higher-technology companies. Moreover, although a com-pany like Ford or General Motors may well have the majority of its assets in one particular country – in these cases, the US – it would be wrong to suggest that their performance is not substantially affected by their overseas activities. Even if a minority of assets are held overseas – say 20 to 30 per cent – this still represents a significant interlocking of a company's assets with overseas market conditions and processes. Com-panies are highly vulnerable to changes in economic conditions wherever they are. Marginal decreases in demand can profoundly affect the opera-tions of a company.

Multinational corporations in general have profound effects on macroeconomic policy; they can respond to variations in interest rates by raising finance in whichever capital market is most favourable. They can shift their demand for employment to countries with much lower employ-ment costs. And in the area of industrial policy they can move their activities to where the maximum benefits accrue. Irrespective of how often MNCs actually take advantage of these opportunities, it is the fact that they could do so in principle which influences government policy and shapes economic strategies. But the impact of MNCs should not just be measured by these indicators alone. They have a significant influence on an economy even when their levels of capitalization are not particularly high. For example, in Zimbabwe, the Coca-Cola bottling plant is not a big factory by global standards, yet it has a major influence on local manage-ment practices and on aspects of economic policy more broadly.

Economic globalization has significant and discernible characteristics which alter the balance of resources, economic and political, within and across borders. Among the most important of these is the tangible growth in the enmeshment of national economies in global economic transactions (thus a growing proportion of nearly all national economies involves international economic exchanges with an increasing number of countries). This increase in the extent and intensity of economic interconnectedness has altered the relation between economic and political power. One shift has been particularly significant: 'the historic expansion of exit options for capital in financial markets relative to national capital controls, national banking regulations and national investment strategies, and the sheer volume of privately held capital relative to national reserves. Exit options for corporations making direct investments have also expanded . . . the balance of power has shifted in favour of capital *vis-à-vis* both national governments and national labour movements.'[10] As a result, the autonomy of democratically elected governments has been, and is increasingly, constrained by sources of unelected and unrepresentative economic power. These have the effect of making adjustment to the international economy (and, above all, to global financial markets) a fixed point of orientation in economic policy and of encouraging an acceptance of the 'decision signals' of its leading agents and forces as a, if not the, standard of rational decision-making. The options for political communities, and the costs and benefits of those options, ineluctably alter.

Cultural and communication trends

Interlinked changes in trade, finance and the structure of multinational corporations are somewhat easier to document and analyse – even if their implications remain controversial – than the impact of globalization in the sphere of the media and culture. Evidence of globalization in this domain is complex and somewhat uncertain. A great deal of research remains to be carried out. Nonetheless, a number of remarkable developments can be pointed to. For instance:

1   English has spread as the dominant language of elite cultures – it is the dominant language in business, computing, law, science and politics.
2   The internationalization and globalization of telecommunications has been extraordinarily rapid, as manifested in the growth of, for instance, international telephone traffic, transnational cable links, satellite links and the Internet.
3   Substantial multinational media conglomerates have developed, such as the Murdoch empire, but there are many other notable examples as well, including Viacom, Disney and Time Warner.
4   There has been a huge increase in tourism. For example, in 1960 there were 70 million international tourists, while in 1995 there were nearly 500 million.
5   And the transnationalization of television programmes and films is also striking: 60 to 90 per cent of box office receipts in Europe, for instance, come from foreign movies (although this is largely the story of American dominance).

None of these examples, or the accumulated impact of parallel instances, should be taken to imply the development of a single global, media-led culture – far from it. But taken together, these developments do indicate that many new forms of communication and media range in and across borders, linking nations and peoples in new ways. Accordingly, national political communities by no means simply determine the structure and processes of cultural life in and through which their citizens are formed. Citizens' values and judgements are now influenced by a complex web of national, international and global cultural exchange. The capacity of national political leaders to sustain a national culture has become more difficult. For example, China sought to restrict access and use of the Internet, but found it extremely difficult to do.

The environment

Contemporary environmental problems are perhaps the clearest and starkest examples of the global shift in human organization and activity, creating some of the most fundamental pressures on the efficacy of the nation-state and state-centric politics. There are three types of problems at issue. First, there are shared problems involving the global commons, that is, fundamental elements of our ecosystem. The clearest examples of the environmental commons are the atmosphere, the climate system and the oceans and seas. And among the most fundamental challenges here are global warming and ozone depletion. A second category of global environmental problems involves the interlinked challenges of demographic expansion and resource consumption. An example of the profoundest importance under this category is desertification. Other examples include questions of biodiversity and challenges to the very existence of certain species. A third category of problems is transboundary pollution of various kinds, such as acid rain or river pollutants. More dramatic examples arise from the siting and operation of nuclear power plants, for instance, Chernobyl.

In response to the progressive development of, and publicity surrounding, environmental problems, there has been an interlinked process of cultural and political globalization as illustrated by the emergence of new cultural, scientific and intellectual networks; new environmental movements with transnational organizations and transnational concerns; and new institutions and conventions like those agreed in 1992 at the Earth Summit in Brazil. Not all environmental problems are, of course, global. Such an implication would be quite false. But there has been a striking shift in the physical and environmental circumstances – that is, in the extent and intensity of environmental problems – affecting human affairs in general. These processes have moved politics dramatically away from an activity which crystallizes simply around state and interstate concerns.

It is clearer than ever that the political fortunes of communities and peoples can no longer be understood in exclusively national or territorial terms.

Politics, law and security

The sovereign state now lies at the intersection of a vast array of international regimes and organizations that have been established to manage whole areas of transnational activity (trade, the oceans, space and so on) and collective policy problems. The growth in the number of these new forms of political organization reflects the rapid expansion of transnational links, the growing interpenetration of foreign and domestic policy, and the corresponding desire by most states for some form of international governance and regulation to deal with collective policy problems. These developments can be illustrated by the following.

1 New forms of multilateral and multinational politics have been established and with them distinctive styles of collective decision-making involving governments, international governmental organizations (IGOs) and a wide variety of transnational pressure groups and international non-governmental organizations (INGOs). In 1909 there were 37 IGOs and 176 INGOs, while in 1989 there were nearly 300 IGOs and 4,624 INGOs. In the middle of the nineteenth century there were two or three conferences or congresses per annum sponsored by IGOs; today the number adds up to close to 4,000 annually. Against this background, the range and diversity of the participants at the Earth Summit in Rio de Janeiro in 1992 or the Conference on Women in Beijing in 1995 may not seem quite as remarkable as the occasions initially suggested.

2 All this has helped engender a shift away from a purely state-centred international system of 'high politics' to new and novel forms of geogovernance. Perhaps one of the most interesting examples of this can be drawn from the very heart of the idea of a sovereign state – national security and defence policy.

3 There is a documentable increase in emphasis on collective defence and cooperative security. The enormous costs, technological requirements and domestic burdens of defence are contributing to the strengthening of multilateral and collective defence arrangements as well as international military cooperation and coordination. The rising density of technological connections between states now challenges the very idea of national security and national arms procurement. Some of the most advanced weapons systems in the world today, such as fighter aircraft, depend on components which come from many countries. There has been a globalization of military technology linked to a transnationalization of defence production.

4 Moreover, the proliferation of weapons of mass destruction makes all states insecure and prolematizes the very notion of 'friends' and 'enemies'.

Even in the sphere of defence and arms production and manufacture, the notion of a singular, discrete and delimited political community appears problematic. As a result, the proper home and form of politics and of democracy becomes a puzzling matter.

RETHINKING DEMOCRACY

The developments documented above have contributed to the transformation of the nature and prospects of democratic political community in a number of distinctive ways. First, the locus of effective political power can no longer be assumed to be national governments – effective power is shared and bartered by diverse forces and agencies at national, regional and international levels. Second, the idea of a political community of fate – of a self-determining collectivity which forms its own agenda and life conditions – can no longer meaningfully be located within the boundaries of a single nation-state alone. Some of the most fundamental forces and processes which determine the nature of life chances within and across political communities are now beyond the reach of individual nation-states. The system of national political communities persists of course; but it is articulated and re-articulated today with complex economic, organizational, administrative, legal and cultural processes and structures which limit and check its efficacy. If these processes and structures are not acknowledged and brought into the political process themselves, they may bypass or circumvent the democratic state system.

Third, it is not part of my argument that national sovereignty today, even in regions with intensive overlapping and divided political and authority structures, has been wholly subverted – not at all. But it is part of my argument that the operations of states in increasingly complex global and regional systems both affect their autonomy (by changing the balance between the costs and benefits of policies) and their sovereignty (by altering the balance between national, regional and international legal frameworks and administrative practices). While massive concentrations of power remain a feature of many states, these are frequently embedded in, and articulated with, fractured domains of political authority. Against this background, it is not fanciful to imagine, as Bull once observed, the development of an international system which is a modern and secular counterpart of the kind of political organization found in Christian Europe in the Middle Ages, the essential characteristic of which was a system of overlapping authority and divided loyalties.[11]

Fourth, the late twentieth century is marked by a significant series of new types of 'boundary problem'. If it is accepted that we live in a world of overlapping communities of fate, where, in other words, the developmental trajectories of each and every country are more tightly entwined than ever before, then new types of boundary problem follow. In the past, of course, nation-states principally resolved their differences over boundary matters by pursuing reasons of state, backed, ultimately, by coercive means. But this power logic is singularly inadequate and inappropriate to resolve the many complex issues, from economic regulation to resource depletion and environmental degradation, which engender an intermeshing of 'national fortunes'. In a world where transnational actors and forces cut across the boundaries of national communities in diverse ways, and where powerful states make decisions not just for their peoples but for others as well, the questions of who should be accountable to whom, and on what basis, do not easily resolve themselves. Overlapping spheres of influence, interference and interest create dilemmas at the centre of democratic thought.

In the liberal democracies, consent to government and legitimacy for governmental action are dependent on electoral politics and the ballot box. Yet the notion that consent legitimates government, and that the ballot box is the appropriate mechanism whereby the citizen body as a whole periodically confers authority on government to enact the law and regulate economic and social life, becomes problematic as soon as the nature of a 'relevant community' is contested. What is the proper constituency, and proper realm of jurisdiction, for developing and implementing policy with respect to health issues such as AIDS or BSE (Bovine Spongiform Encephalopathy), the use of nuclear energy, the harvesting of rain forests, the use of non-renewable resources, the instability of global financial markets, and the reduction of the risks of nuclear warfare? National boundaries have traditionally demarcated the basis on which individuals are included and excluded from participation in decisions affecting their lives; but if many socioeconomic processes, and the outcomes of decisions about them, stretch beyond national frontiers, then the implications of this are serious, not only for the categories of consent and legitimacy but for all the key ideas of democracy. At issue is the nature of a constituency, the role of representation, and the proper form and scope of political participation. As fundamental processes of governance escape the categories of the nation-state, the traditional national resolutions of the key questions of democratic theory and practice are open to doubt.

Against this background, the nature and prospects of the democratic polity need re-examination. The idea of a democratic order can no longer be simply defended as an idea suitable to a particular closed political community or nation-state. We are compelled to recognize that we live in a complex interconnected world where the extensity, intensity and impact of issues (economic, political or environmental) raise questions about where those issues are most appropriately addressed. Deliberative and decision-making centres beyond national territories are appropriately situated when those significantly affected by a public matter constitute a cross-border or transnational grouping, when 'lower' levels of decision-making cannot manage and discharge satisfactorily transnational or international policy questions, and when the principle of democratic legitimacy can only be properly redeemed in a transnational context. If the most powerful geopolitical interests are not to settle many pressing matters simply in terms of their objectives and by virtue of their power, then new institutions and mechanisms of accountability need to be established.

It would be easy to be pessimistic about the future of democracy. There are plenty of reasons for pessimism; they include the fact that the essential political units of the world are still based on nation-states while some of the most powerful sociopolitical forces of the world escape the boundaries of these units. In part in reaction to this, new forms of fundamentalism have arisen along with new forms of tribalism – all asserting the *a priori* superiority of a particular religious or cultural or political identity over all others, and all asserting their sectional aims and interests. But there are other forces at work which create the basis for a more optimistic reading of democratic prospects. A historical comparison might help to provide a context for this consideration.

In the sixteenth and seventeenth centuries, Europe was marked by civil conflict, religious strife and fragmented authority; the idea of a secular state, separate from ruler and ruled, and separate from the church, seemed an unlikely prospect. Parts of Europe were tearing themselves to pieces, and yet, within 150–200 years, a new concept of politics became entrenched, based around a new concept of the state. Today, we live at another fundamental point of transition, but now to a more transnational, global world. There are forces and pressures which are engendering a reshaping of political cultures, institutions and structures. First, one must obviously note the emergence, however hesitatingly, of regional and global institutions in the twentieth century. The UN is, of course, weak in many respects, but it is a relatively recent creation and it is an innovative structure which can be built upon. It is a normative resource which provides – for all its difficulties – an enduring example of how nations might (and sometimes do) cooperate better to resolve, and resolve fairly, common problems.

In addition, the development of a powerful regional body such as the European Union is a remarkable state of affairs. Just over fifty years ago Europe was at the point of self-destruction. Since that moment Europe has created new mechanisms of collaboration and of human rights enforcement, and new political institutions in order not only to hold member states to account across a broad range of issues, but to pool aspects of their sovereignty. Furthermore, there are, of course, new regional and global transnational actors contesting the terms of globalization – not just corporations but new social movements such as the environmental movement, the women's movement and so on. These are the 'new' voices of an emergent 'transnational civil society', heard, for instance, at the Rio Conference on the Environment, the Cairo Conference on Population Control and the Beijing Conference on Women. In short, there are tendencies at work seeking to create new forms of public life and new ways of debating regional and global issues. These are, of course, all in early stages of development, and there are *no* guarantees that the balance of political contest will allow them to develop. But they point in the direction of establishing new ways of holding transnational power systems to account – that is, they help open up the possibility of a cosmopolitan democracy.

Cosmopolitan democracy involves the development of administrative capacity and independent political resources at regional and global levels as a necessary complement to those in local and national polities. At issue would be strengthening the administrative capacity and accountability of regional institutions like the EU, along with developing the administrative capacity and forms of accountability of the UN system itself. A cosmopolitan democracy would not call for a diminution *per se* of state power and capacity across the globe. Rather, it would seek to entrench and develop democratic institutions at regional and global levels as a necessary complement to those at the level of the nation-state. This conception of democracy is based on the recognition of the continuing significance of nation-states, while arguing for a layer of governance to constitute a limitation on national sovereignty.

The case for cosmopolitan democracy is the case for the creation of new political institutions which would coexist with the system of states but which would override states in clearly defined spheres of activity where those activities have demonstrable transnational and international consequences, require regional or global initiatives in the interests of effectiveness and depend on such initiatives for democratic legitimacy (see p. 22). At issue, in addition, would not merely be the formal construction of new democratic mechanisms and procedures, but also the construction, in principle, of 'broad access' avenues of civic participation at national and regional levels. Table 1.1 provides an outline of some of the constitutive features of cosmopolitan democracy.[12]

In sum

The theory of cosmopolitan democracy is one of the few political theories which examines systematically the democratic implications of the fact that nation-states are enmeshed today in complex interconnected relations. Our world is a world of *overlapping communities of fate*, where the fate of one country and that of another are more entwined than ever

Table 1.1 Cosmopolitan democracy

Principle of justification

In a world of intensifying regional and global relations, with marked overlapping 'communities of fate', democracy requires entrenchment in regional and global networks as well as in national and local polities. Without such a development, many of the most powerful regional and global forces will escape the democratic mechanisms of accountability, legitimacy and considered public intervention.

Illustrative institutional features

Short-term	*Long-term*
Polity/governance	
1 Reform of leading UN governing institutions such as the Security Council (to give developing countries a significant voice and effective decision-making capacity).	1 New Charter of Rights and Obligations locked into different domains of political, social and economic power.
2 Creation of a UN second chamber (following an international constitutional convention).	2 Global parliament (with limited revenue-raising capacity) connected to regions, nations and localities.
3 Enhanced political regionalization (EU and beyond) and the use of transnational referenda.	3 Separation of political and economic interests; public funding of deliberative assemblies and electoral processes.
4 Creation of a new, international Human Rights Court. Compulsory submission to ICJ jurisdiction.	4 Interconnected global legal system, embracing elements of criminal and civil law.
5 Establishment of an effective, accountable, international military force.	5 Permanent shift of a growing proportion of a nation-state's coercive capability to regional and global institutions.
Economy/civil society	
1 Enhancement of non-state, non-market solutions in the organization of civil society.	1 Creation of a diversity of self-regulating associations and groups in civil society.
2 Systematic experimentation with different democratic organizational forms in the economy.	2 Multisectoral economy and pluralization of patterns of ownership and possession.
3 Provision of resources to those in the most vulnerable social positions to defend and articulate their interests.	3 Social framework investment priorities set through public deliberation and government decision, but extensive market regulation of goods and labour remain.

Continued

Table 1.1 *Continued*

General conditions

1 Continuing development of regional, international and global flows of resources and networks of interaction.

2 Recognition by growing numbers of peoples of increasing interconnectedness of political communities in diverse domains including the social, cultural, economic and environmental.

3 Development of an understanding of overlapping 'collective fortunes' which require collective democratic solutions – locally, nationally, regionally and globally.

4 Enhanced entrenchment of democratic rights and obligations in the making and enforcement of national, regional and international law.

5 Transfer of increasing proportion of a nation's military coercive capability to transnational agencies and institutions with the ultimate aim of demilitarization and the transcendence of the states' war system as a means of resolving conflicts of national interest.

before. In this world, there are many issues which stretch beyond the borders of countries and challenge the relevance of those borders in key respects. Many of these issues have already been referred to – pollutants, resource use questions, the regulation of global networks of trade, finance, etc. Can these be brought within the sphere of democracy? The theory of cosmopolitan democracy suggests this is not only a necessity, but also a real possibility.

NOTES

I should like to thank Daniele Archibugi, Martin Köhler, Joel Krieger and Craig Murphy for comments on this chapter. A version was previously published in *Global Governance*, 3.3 (1997), pp. 251–67.

1 See D. Potter, D. Goldblatt, M. Kiloh and P. Lewis (eds), *Democratization* (Cambridge: Polity Press, 1997).

2 For an elaboration of this theme, see my *Democracy and the Global Order: From the Modern State to Cosmopolitan Governance* (Cambridge: Polity Press, 1995).

3 In focusing on processes of globalization I would like to acknowledge my debt to David Goldblatt, Anthony McGrew and Jonathan Perraton, with whom I have collaborated over the last four years on a research project investigating the changing enmeshment of states in global flows and trans-formations. The conception of globalization along with many of the

examples in the following section are drawn from our joint work. See D. Goldblatt, D. Held, A. McGrew and J. Perraton, *Global Transformations: Concepts, Evidence and Arguments* (Cambridge: Polity Press, 1998).

4   See, for example, K. Ohmae, *The Borderless World* (London: Collins, 1990); and R. Reich, *The Work of Nations* (New York: Simon and Schuster, 1991).

5   See P. Hirst and G. Thompson, *Globalization in Question* (Cambridge: Polity Press, 1996).

6   See A. Giddens, *The Consequences of Modernity* (Cambridge: Polity Press, 1990).

7   See A. G. McGrew, 'Conceptualizing global politics', in A. G. McGrew and P. G. Lewis (eds), *Global Politics: Globalization and the Nation-State* (Cambridge: Polity Press, 1992).

8   See R. Falk, *On Humane Governance: Toward a New Global Politics* (Cambridge: Polity Press, 1995).

9   For a fuller account of these points see J. Perraton, D. Goldblatt, D. Held and A. McGrew, 'The globalization of economic activity', *New Political Economy*, 2.2 (July 1997). I am particular grateful for Jonathan Perraton's guidance on these matters.

10   D. Goldblatt, D. Held, A. McGrew and J. Perraton, 'Economic globalization and the nation-state: shifting balances of power', *Alternatives*, 22.3 (1997), p. 281.

11   H. Bull, *The Anarchical Society* (London: Macmillan, 1977), pp. 254–5.

12   For further discussion and elaboration of these and related features, see Daniele Archibugi and David Held (eds), *Cosmopolitan Democracy: an Agenda for a New World Order* (Cambridge: Polity Press, 1995) and Held, *Democracy and the Global Order*.

2

Governance and Democracy in a Globalizing World

James N. Rosenau

We live in a world where markets are not less important than countries and where multinational companies are not less important than governments.

Shimon Peres

As this comment by a former Israeli prime minister implies, to anticipate the prospects for increasingly democratic forms of global governance in the decades ahead is to discern powerful tensions, profound contradictions and perplexing paradoxes. It is to search for order in disorder, for coherence in contradiction and for continuity in change. It is to confront processes that mask both growth and decay. It is to look for authorities that are obscure, boundaries that are in flux and systems of rule that are emergent. And it is to experience hope embedded in despair.

This is not to imply the task is impossible. Quite to the contrary, one can discern patterns of governance that are likely to proliferate, others that are likely to attenuate and still others that are likely to endure as they always have. No, the task is not so much impossible as it is a challenge to one's appreciation of nuance and one's tolerance of ambiguity.

CONCEPTUAL NUANCES

In order to grasp the complexities that pervade world politics, we need to start by drawing a nuanced set of distinctions among the numerous processes and structures that fall within the purview of global governance. Perhaps most importantly, it is necessary to clarify that global governance does not refer only to the formal institutions and organizations through which the management of international affairs is or is not sustained. The United Nations system and national governments are surely central to the conduct of global governance, but they are only part of the full picture. Consequently, in the ensuing analysis global governance is conceived to include systems of rule at all levels of human activity – from the family to the international organization – in which the pursuit of goals through the exercise of control has transnational repercussions. The reason for this broad formulation is simple: in an ever more interdependent world where what happens in one corner or at one level may have consequences for what occurs at every other corner and level, it seems a mistake to adhere to a narrow definition in which only formal institutions at the national and international levels are considered relevant. In the words of the Council of Rome,

We use the term governance to denote the *command* mechanism of a social system and its actions that endeavor to provide security, prosperity, coherence, order and continuity to the system . . . Taken broadly, the concept of governance should not be restricted to the national and international systems but should be used in relation to regional, provincial and local governments as well as to other social systems such as education and the military, to private enterprises and even to the microcosm of the family.[1]

Governance, in other words, encompasses the activities of governments, but it also includes the many other channels through which 'commands' flow in the form of goals framed, directives issued and policies pursued.

Command and control

But the concept of commands can be misleading. It implies that hierarchy, and perhaps even authoritarian rule, characterize governance systems. Such an implication may be descriptive of many forms of governance, but hierarchy is certainly not a necessary prerequisite to the framing of goals, the issuing of directives and the pursuit of policies. Indeed, a central theme of the ensuing analysis is that often the practices and institutions of governance can and do evolve in such a way as to be minimally dependent on hierarchical, command-based arrangements. Accordingly, while preserving the core of the Council of Rome formulation, here we shall replace the notion of command mechanisms with the concept of *control* or *steering* mechanisms, terms that highlight the purposeful nature of governance without presuming the presence of hierarchy. These terms, moreover, are informed by the etymological roots of 'governance': the term 'derives from the Greek "kybenan" and "kybernetes" which means "to steer" and "pilot or helmsman" respectively (the same Greek root from which "cybernetics" is derived). The process of governance is the process whereby an organization or society steers itself, and the dynamics of communication and control are central to that process.'[2]

To grasp the concept of control one has to appreciate that it consists of relational phenomena which, taken holistically, comprise systems of rule. Some actors, the controllers, seek to modify the behaviour and/or orientations of other actors, the controllees, and the resulting patterns of interaction between the former and the latter can properly be viewed as a system of rule sustained by one or another form of control. It does not matter whether the controllees resist or comply with the efforts of controllers; in either event, attempts at control have been undertaken. But it is not until the attempts become increasingly successful and compliance with them increasingly patterned that a system of rule founded on mechanisms of control can be said to have evolved. Rule systems and control mechanisms, in other words, are founded on a modicum of regularity, a form of recurrent behaviour that systematically links the efforts of controllers to the compliance of controllees through either formal or informal channels.[3]

It follows that systems of rule can be maintained and their controls successfully and consistently exerted even in the absence of established legal or political authority. The evolution of intersubjective consensuses based on shared fates and common histories, the possession of information and knowledge, the pressure of active or mobilizable publics, and/or the use of careful planning, good timing, clever manipulation and hard bargaining can – either separately or in combination – foster control mechanisms that sustain governance without government.[4]

Interdependence and proliferation

Implicit in the broad conception of governance as control mechanisms is a premise that interdependence not only involves flows of control, consequence and causation within systems, but that it also sustains flows across systems. These micro-macro processes – the dynamics whereby values and behaviours at one level get converted into outcomes at more encompassing levels, outcomes which in turn get converted into still other consequences at still more encompassing levels – suggest that global governance knows no boundaries, geographic, social, cultural, economic or political. If major changes occur in the structure of families, if individual greed proliferates at the expense of social consciences, if people become more analytically skilful, if crime grips neighbourhoods, if schools fail to provoke the curiosity of children, if racial or religious prejudices become pervasive, if the drug trade starts distributing its illicit goods through licit channels, if defiance comes to vie with compliance as characteristic responses to authority, if new trading partners are established, if labour and environmental groups in different countries form cross-border coalitions, if cities begin to conduct their own foreign commercial policies – to mention only some of the more conspicuous present-day dynamics – then the consequences of such developments will ripple across and fan out at provincial, regional, national and international levels as well as across and within local communities. Such is the crazy-quilt nature of modern interdependence. And such is the staggering challenge of global governance.

And the challenge continues to intensify as control mechanisms proliferate at a breathtaking rate. For not only has the number of UN members risen from 51 in 1945 to 185 a half-century later, but the density of non-governmental organizations (NGOs) has increased at a comparable pace. More accurately, it has increased at a rate comparable to the continuing growth of the world's population beyond 5 billion and a projected 8 billion in 2025. More and more people, that is, need to concert their actions to cope with the challenges and opportunities of daily life, thus giving rise to more and more organizations to satisfy their needs and wants. Indeed, since the needs and wants of people are most effectively expressed through organized action, the organizational explosion of our time is no less consequential than the population explosion. Hastened by dynamic technologies that have shrunk social, economic, political and geographic distances and thereby rendered the world ever more interdependent, expanded by the advent of new global challenges such as those posed by a deteriorating environment, an AIDS epidemic and drug trafficking, and further stimulated by widespread authority crises within existing governance mechanisms,[5] the proliferation of organizations is pervasive at and across all levels of human activity – from neighbourhood organizations, community groups, regional networks, national states and transnational regimes to international systems.[6]

Not only is global life marked by a density of populations, in other words; it is also dense with organized activities, thereby complicating and extending the processes of global governance. For while organizations provide decision points through which the steering mechanisms of governance can be carried forward, so may they operate as sources of opposition to any institutions and policies designed to facilitate governance. Put in still another way, if it is the case, as many (and this author) argue,[7] that global life late in the twentieth century is more complex than ever before in history, it is partly because the world is host to ever greater numbers of organizations in all walks of life and in every corner of every continent. And it is this complexity, along with the competitive impulses which lead some organizations to defy steerage and resort to violence, that make the tasks of governance at once so difficult and so daunting.

Disaggregation and innovation

An obvious but major conceptual premise follows from the foregoing: namely, there is no single organizing principle on which global governance rests, no emergent order around which communities and nations are likely to converge. Global governance is the sum of myriad – literally millions – of control mechanisms driven by different histories, goals, structures and processes. Perhaps every mechanism shares a history, culture and structure with a few others, but there are no characteristics or attributes common to all mechanisms. This means that any attempt to assess the dynamics of global governance will perforce have multiple dimensions, that any effort to trace a hierarchical structure of authority which loosely links disparate sources of governance to each other is bound to fail. In terms of governance, the world is too disaggregated for grand logics that postulate a measure of global coherence.

Put differently, the continuing disaggregation that has followed the end of the Cold War suggests a further extension of the anarchic structures that have long pervaded world politics. If it was possible to presume that the absence of hierarchy and an ultimate authority signified the presence of anarchy during the era of hegemonic leadership and superpower competition, such a characterization of global governance is all the more pertinent today. Indeed, it might well be observed that a new form of anarchy has evolved in the current period – one that involves not only the absence of a highest authority, but that also encompasses such an extensive disaggregation of authority as to allow for much greater flexibility, innovation and experimentation in the development and application of new control mechanisms.

Stated in terms of a rough quantitative measure, it is perhaps suggestive of the scale of disaggregative dynamics and the shift of authority away from governments that in the United States even the police function is in relative decline: whereas people once relied on public authorities to protect them from crime, in recent years they have turned to hiring their own police. The number of publicly authorized police on duty throughout the country has remained roughly at half a million since 1980, but during the same period the number of private security guards has risen more than 600000 (to 1.6 million)[8] and expenditures to maintain them are roughly double the amount spent on public police protection.[9] In sum, while politicians and pundits may speak confidently or longingly about establishing a new world order, such a concept is only meaningful as it relates to the prevention or containment of large-scale violence and war. It is not a concept that can be used synonomously with global governance if by the latter is meant the vast numbers of rule systems that have been caught up in the proliferating networks of an ever more interdependent world.

Emergence and evolution

Underlying the growing complexity and continuing disaggregation of modern governance are the obvious but often ignored dynamics of change wherein control mechanisms emerge out of path-dependent conditions and then pass through lengthy processes of either evolution and maturation or decline and demise. In order to acquire the legitimacy and support they need to endure, successful mechanisms of governance are more likely to evolve out of bottom-up than top-down processes. As such, as mechanisms that manage to evoke the consent of the governed, they are self-organizing systems, steering arrangements that develop through the shared needs of groups and the presence of developments that conduce to the generation and acceptance of shared instruments of control.

But there is no magic in the dynamics of self-organization. Governance does not just suddenly happen. Circumstances have to be suitable, people have to be amenable to collective decisions being made, tendencies towards organization have to develop, habits of cooperation have to evolve, and a readiness not to impede the processes of emergence and evolution has to persist. The proliferation of organizations and their ever greater interdependence may stimulate felt needs for new forms of governance, but the transformation of these needs into established and institutionalized control mechanisms is never automatic and can be marked by a volatility that consumes long stretches of time. Yet, at each stage of the transformation, some form of governance can be said to exist, with a preponderance of the control mechanisms at any moment in time evolving somewhere in the middle of a continuum that runs from nascent to fully institutionalized mechanisms, from informal modes of framing goals, issuing directives and pursuing policies to formal instruments of decision-making, conflict resolution and resource allocation.

No matter how institutionalized rule systems may be, in other words, governance is not a constant in these turbulent and disaggregated times. It is, rather, in a continuous process of evolution, a becoming that fluctuates between order and disorder as conditions change and emergent properties consolidate and solidify. To analyse governance by freezing it in time is to ensure failure in comprehending its nature and vagaries.

THE RELOCATION OF AUTHORITY

Notwithstanding the evolutionary dynamics of control mechanisms and the absence of an overall structural order, it is possible to identify pockets of coherence operating at different levels and in different parts of the world that can serve as bases for assessing the contours of global governance in the future. It may be the case that 'processes of governance at the global level are inherently more fragile, contingent, and unevenly experienced than is the case within most national political systems,'[10] but this is not to deny the presence of central tendencies. One such tendency involves an 'upsurge in the collective capacity to govern': despite the rapid pace of ever greater complexity and decentralization – and to some extent because of their exponential dynamics – the world is undergoing 'a remarkable expansion of collective power', an expansion that is highly disaggregated and unfolds unevenly but that nevertheless amounts to a development of rule systems 'that have become (1) more intensive in their permeation of daily life, (2) more permanent over time, (3) more extensive over space, (4) larger in size, (5) wider in functional scope, (6) more constitutionally differentiated, and (7) more bureaucratic'.[11] Global governance in the coming decades may not take the form of a single world order, but it will not be lacking in activities designed to bring a measure of coherence to the multitude of jurisdictions that are proliferating on the world stage.

Perhaps even more important, a pervasive tendency can be identified in which major shifts in the location of authority and the site of control mechanisms are underway on every continent and in every country, shifts that are as pronounced in economic and social systems as they are in political systems. Indeed, in some cases the shifts have transferred authority away from the political realm and into the economic and social realms even as in still other instances the shift occurs in the opposite direction.

Partly these shifts have been facilitated by the end of the Cold War and the lifting of the constraints inherent in its bipolar global structure of superpower competition. Partly they have been driven by a search for new, more effective forms of political organization better suited to the turbulent circumstances that have evolved with the shrinking of the world by dynamic technologies.[12] Partly they have been driven by the skill revolution that has enabled citizens to identify their needs and wants more clearly as well as to be more thoroughly empowered to engage in collective action.[13] Partly they have been stimulated and sustained by subgroupism – the fragmenting and coalescing of groups into new organizational entities – that has created innumerable new sites from which authority can emerge and towards which it can gravitate.[14] Partly they have been driven by the continuing globalization of national and local economies that has undermined long-established ways of sustaining commercial and financial relations.[15] And, no less, the shifts have been accelerated by the advent of interdependence issues – such as environmental pollution, AIDS, monetary crises and the drug trade – that have fostered new and intensified forms of transnational collaboration as well as new social movements that are serving as transnational voices for change.[16]

In short, the numerous shifts in the loci of governance stem from interactive tensions whereby processes of globalization and localization are simultaneously unfolding on a worldwide scale. In some situations the foregoing dynamics are fostering control mechanisms that extend beyond national boundaries and in others the need for the psychic comfort of neighbourhood or ethnic attachments is leading to the diminution of national entities and the formation or extension of local mechanisms. The combined effect of the simultaneity of these contradictory trends is that of lessening the capacities for governance located at the level of sovereign states and national societies.[17] Much governance will doubtless continue to be sustained by states and their governments initiating and implementing policies in the context of their legal frameworks – and in some instances national governments are likely to work out arrangements for joint governance with rule systems at other levels – but the effectiveness of their policies is likely to be undermined by the proliferation of emergent control mechanisms both within and outside their jurisdictions.[18] In the words of one analyst, 'the very high levels of interdependence and vulnerability stimulated by technological change now necessitate new forms of global political authority and even governance.'[19]

Put more emphatically, perhaps the most significant pattern discernible in the criss-crossing flow of transformed authority involves processes of bifurcation whereby control mechanisms at national levels are, in varying degrees, yielding space both to more encompassing forms of governance and to narrower, less comprehensive forms. For analytic purposes, we shall refer to the former as transnational governance mechanisms and the latter as subnational governance mechanisms, terms that do not preclude institutionalized governmental mechanisms but that allow for the large degree to which our concern is with dynamic and evolving processes rather than with the routinized procedures of national governments.

While transnational and subnational mechanisms differ in the extent of their links across national boundaries – all the former are by definition boundary-spanning forms of control, while some of the latter may not extend beyond the jurisdiction of their states – both types must face the same challenges to governance. Both must deal with a rapidly changing, ever more complex world in which people, information, goods and ideas are in continuous motion and, thus, endlessly reconfiguring social, economic and political horizons. Both are confronted with the instabilities and disorder that derive from resources shortages, budgetary constraints, ethnic rivalries, unemployment and incipient or real inflation. Both need to contend with the ever greater relevance of scientific findings and the epistemic communities that form around the findings. Both are subject to the continuous tensions that spring from the inroads of corrupt practices, organized crime and restless publics that have little use for politics and politicians. Both must cope with pressures for further fragmentation of subgroups on the one hand and for more extensive transnational links on the other. Both types of mechanisms, in short, have severe adaptive problems and, given the fragility of their legal status and the lack of long-standing habits of support for them, many of both types may fail to maintain their essential structures intact.[20] Global governance, it seems reasonable to anticipate, is likely to consist of proliferating mechanisms that fluctuate between bare survival and increasing institutionalization, between considerable chaos and widening degrees of order.

MECHANISMS OF GLOBAL GOVERNANCE

Steering mechanisms are spurred into existence through several channels: through the sponsorship of states, through the efforts of actors other than states at the transnational or subnational levels, or through states and other types of actors jointly sponsoring the formation of rule systems. They can also be differentiated by their location on the afore-mentioned continuum that ranges from full institutionalization on the one hand to nascent processes of rule-making and compliance on the other. Although extremes on a continuum, the institutionalized and nascent types of control mechanisms can be causally linked through evolutionary processes. It is possible to trace at least two generic routes that link the degree to which transnational governance mechanisms are institutionalized and the sources that sponsor these developments. One route is the direct, top-down process wherein states create new institutional structures and impose them on the course of events. A second is much more circuitous and involves an indirect, bottom-up process of evolutionary stages wherein nascent dynamics of rule-making are sponsored by publics or economies that experience a need for repeated interactions that foster habits and attitudes of cooperation which, in turn, generate organizational activities that eventually get transformed into institutionalized control mechanisms.[21] Stated more generally, whatever their sponsorship, the institutionalized mechanisms tend to be marked by explicit hierarchical structures, whereas those at the nascent end of the continuum develop more subtly as a consequence of emergent interaction patterns which, unintentionally and without prior planning, culminate in fledgling control mechanisms for newly formed or transformed systems.

Table 2.1 offers examples of the rule systems derivable from a combination of the several types of sponsors and the two extremes on the continuum, a matrix that suggests the considerable variety and complexity out of which the processes of global governance evolve. In the table, moreover, there are hints of the developmental processes whereby nascent mechanisms become institutionalized: as indicated by the arrows, some of the control mechanisms located in the right-hand cells have their origins in left-hand cells as interdependence issues that generate pressures from the non-governmental world for intergovernmental cooperation which, in turn, leads to the formation of issue-based transnational institutions. The history of more than a few control mechanisms charged with addressing environmental problems exemplifies how this subtle evolutionary path can be traversed.

However they originate, and at whatever pace they evolve, transnational governance mechanisms tend to be essentially forward

Table 2.1 The sponsorship and institutionalization of control mechanisms

		Nascent	*Institutionalized*
Not state-sponsored	Transnational	• non-governmental organizations • social movements • epistemic communities • multinational corporations	• Internet • European Environmental Bureau • credit-rating agencies
	Subnational	• ethnic minorities • micro regions • cities	• American Jewish Congress • the Greek lobby • crime syndicates
State-sponsored		• macro regions • European community • GATT	• United Nations system • European Union • World Trade Organization
Jointly sponsored		• cross-border coalitions • issue regimes	• election monitoring • human rights regime

looking. They may be propelled by dissatisfactions over existing (national or subnational) arrangements, but their evolution is likely to be marked less by despair over the past and present and more by hope for the future, by expectations that an expansion beyond existing boundaries will draw on cooperative impulses which may serve to meet challenges and fill lacunae that would otherwise be left unattended. To be sure, globalizing dynamics tend to create resistance and opposition, since any expansion of governance is bound to be detrimental to those who have a stake in the status quo. Whether they are explicitly and formally designed or subtly and informally constructed, however, on balance transnational systems of governance tend to evolve in a context of hope and progress, a sense of breakthrough, an appreciation that old problems can be circumvented and moved towards either the verge of resolution or the edge of obsolescence.

Relatively speaking, on the other hand, subnational mechanisms are usually (though not always) energized by despair, by frustration with existing systems that seems best offset by contracting the scope of governance, by a sense that large-scale cooperation has not worked and that new subgroup arrangements are bound to be more satisfying. This distinction between transnational and subnational governance mechanisms can, of course, be overstated, but it does suggest that the delicacies of global governance at subnational levels may be greater than those at transnational levels.

THE PROSPECTS FOR DEMOCRACY

A detailed analysis of the examples set forth in table 2.1 reveals even more fully the high probability that global governance will become increasingly pervasive, complex and disaggregated in the years ahead. However, elaboration along these lines has been undertaken elsewhere and need not detain us here.[22] Rather, we need to confront the overriding normative question of what a decentralized world of diverse and multiple rule systems portends for the evolution and preservation of democratic practices. To what extent are the nascent control mechanisms now emerging in the new political spaces – what elsewhere I have varyingly referred to as Globalized Space[23] or the domestic-foreign Frontier,[24] using capital letters to emphasize their non-territorial foundations – created by the lessened governance capacity of states and the growing porosity of the boundaries separating local, national and international affairs likely to evolve just and open policy-making institutions? Is the continuing proliferation of transnational and subnational rule systems likely to enhance the participation of individuals and groups in the processes that affect their interests and values? Does the relocation of authority on a huge scale mean that democratic methods for assuring representative, accountable and responsible governance in Globalized Space are likely to undergo diminution, or at least suspension, as the new rule systems struggle to establish their legitimacy, settle into place, adapt to each other and learn the limits of their ability to evoke compliance?

Clear-cut answers to these questions are not presently available. The circumstances wherein government by states is yielding to disaggregated forms of global governance are too recent for unmistakable, or at least discernible, institutions expressive of the prospects for democratic practices to evolve. Indeed, it could be argued that with the Cold War having receded into obscurity, the world has entered a crucial turning point, one in which the practices adopted today will determine the likelihood of democratic commitments becoming solidified tomorrow. Much remains fluid as people and groups become increasingly conscious of the myriad uncertainties that mark politics at the turn of the century. To be sure, increasing numbers of countries are adopting democratic procedures, but such a pattern offers little guidance with respect to the widening of Globalized Space wherein the authority of national governments is no longer operative. How, for example, will the multinational corporations that occupy key command posts in Globalized Space be held accountable for their decisions? What mechanisms are available to ensure that the decision-making processes of NGOs are transparent and open to inputs from people affected by them? How do new rule systems acquire legitimacy and the right to engage in governance? Where jurisdictions in Globalized Space are contested, what judicial bodies or adjudication procedures can be used to authoritatively resolve the disputes? How can the dynamics of globalization and localization be brought under democratic control? In short, whatever the chances of effective governance in Globalized Space, how can its quality begin to approach democratic ideals?

Responses to such questions are bound to be elusive. Democracy as we know it within countries does not exist in Globalized Space. More accurately, to the extent that Globalized Space is marked by conventional democratic procedures, these are ad hoc, non-systematic, irregular and fragile. They lack the constituencies, scope and support that are necessary to provide Globalized Space's diverse forces with adequate equity and voice. Globalized Space is not chaotic; it does have some established patterns and others that are coming into being; and it also has pockets (such as externally monitored elections) wherein open democratic procedures are practised; but at the same time neither the patterns nor the pockets are sufficient to suffuse the politics of Globalized Space with accountability and responsibility.

Thus questions of implementation arise. How, then, to foster the authority and institutions that would bring greater degrees of democracy to governance in Globalized Space? How to subject its decision-makers to a modicum of accountability and responsibility? How to ensure the liberties of individuals who roam around, voluntarily or otherwise, in this widening domain? And equally important, how to begin to answer these questions without appearing hopelessly naive, idealistic or otherwise out of touch with the realities of politics in Globalized Space?

The clearest response to these queries involves the necessity of not pondering them in the context of democratic notions appropriate to territorial polities. It is the very nature of Globalized Space that territoriality is not a central organizing premise for actions and interactions. Hence, concepts of representation and accountability based on long-established territorial democracies in countries, provinces or cities ought not to serve as the basis for pondering the foregoing questions. For, in the absence of fixed boundaries in Globalized Space, processes of representation and responsibility normally associated with democratic institutions are of limited relevance. Rather, imagination and flexibility are needed if the dynamics that sustain the politics of this emergent domain are to be assessed in terms of their susceptibility to democratic control. What is needed is a capacity for discerning how functional equivalents of the basic precepts of territorial democracy might evolve in Globalized Space.

Disaggregation as a functional equivalent

In a circuitous way, the very processes of disaggregation have embedded within them one major functional equivalent of democracy. The decentralization of rule systems in disparate and localized sites has greatly inhibited the coalescence of hierarchical and autocratic centres of power. It is as if the politics of Globalized Space, through having both integrative and fragmented components, mimics the global market with its shifting loci of limited decision-making authority and its subservience to macro tides of inflation, currency swings and productivity breakthroughs.[25] None of the rule systems in Globalized Space can exercise extensive control over people and policies outside their own limited jurisdictions. To be sure, numerous control mechanisms, especially transnational corporations, are hierarchically organized and all too often make decisions without concern for whether they disempower people or do ecological harm.[26] In 1992 it was estimated that the number of transnational corporations exceeded 35,000 and that, in turn, these had over 200,000 subsidiaries.[27] While these figures indicate that sizeable areas of global life rest on a form of governance that lacks democratic accountability, they also suggest that the dispersal of authority in Globalized Space is so widespread that severe violations of democratic values cannot be readily concentrated in hegemonic hands. Put differently, although markets are not democratic in their functioning and are impervious to any damage they may do, so are they not systematic in any harm they may cause, all of which can also be said about the dynamics that underlie the disaggregation of rule systems in Globalized Space.

Stated in more negative terms, authority is so widely dispersed that neither tyrannical majorities nor autocratic leaders are likely to gain much of a foothold in this emergent domain and, if they do, the constraints against their tyranny are likely to be too numerous and resistant for them to expand the scope of their power. Viewed in this way, the functional equivalent of democracy is achieved through the absence of absolutist rule as a viable control mechanism, hardly the same as the maintenance of democratic procedures and yet not a trivial dimension of governance in Globalized Space.

Non-governmental organizations as functional equivalents

Nor need all the functional equivalents be cast in negative terms. Irrespective of whether they are volunteer or profit-making organizations, and quite apart from whether their structures are confined to one country or span several, more than a few transnational nascent control mechanisms evidence an awarenesss of their potential role in the evolution of democratic procedures of global governance. They appear to appreciate that in an ever more interdependent world the need for control mechanisms outstrips the capacity or readiness of national governments to provide them, that there are a variety of types of situations where governments are unwelcome, or where they fear involvement will be counterproductive, or where they lack the will or ability to intrude their presence. Hence, just as at the local level 'community associations are taking over more of the functions of municipal governments,'[28] and just as in diplomatic situations distinguished individuals from the private sector are called upon when assessments are made which assert, in effect, that 'I don't think any governments wanted to get involved in this,'[29] so are diverse private organizations of all kinds to be found as the central actors in the deliberations of control mechanisms relevant to their spheres of activity. Whether the deliberations involve the generation and allocation of relief supplies in disaster situations around the world or the framing of norms of conduct for trade relationships – to mention only two of the more conspicuous spheres in which transnational governance occurs – volunteer associations or business corporations may make the crucial decisions. In the case of alliances fashioned within and among multinational corporations, for example, it has been found that 'transnational actors, unlike purely domestic ones, have the organizational and informational resources necessary to construct private alternatives to governmental accords.'[30]

That both volunteer and profit-making organizations are not unmindful that their role as nascent control mechanisms can contribute to the development of democratic institutions can be discerned in the charters of the former and in the public pronouncements of the latter. An especially clear-cut expression along this line was made by the chairman and chief executive officer of the Coca-Cola Company, who contended that

four prevailing forces – the preeminence of democratic capitalism, the desire for self-determination, the shift in influence from regulation to investment, and the success of institutions which meet the needs of people – reinforced by today's worldwide communications and dramatic television images . . . all point to a fundamental shift in global power. To be candid, I believe this shift will lead to a future in which the institutions with the most influence by-and-large will be businesses.[31]

Much the same can be said about non-profit NGOs. While some of them maintain decision-making processes that are not fully open to external controls, many – perhaps even most – do exert pressures within Globalized Space for greater transparency and access to be provided by hierarchical organizations, pressures that are in some respects functional equivalents of the various electoral, legislative and journalistic checks that sustain a modicum of democracy in territorial polities. Indeed, the rule systems of NGOs face the danger of too much democracy, of multiple accountabilities – ' "downward" to their partners, beneficiaries, staff, and supporters; and "upward" to their trustees, donors, and host governments'[32] – that foster inefficiencies and indecisive policy-making.

Social movements as functional equivalents

Although much less structured, social movements also serve as functional equivalents of important aspects of territorial democracies. Indeed, they have evolved as well-springs of global governance in recent decades and are perhaps the quintessential case of nascent control mechanisms that have the potential of developing into institutionalized instruments of democratic governance. Their nascency is conspicuous: they have no definite memberships or authority structures; they consist of as many people, as much territory and as many issues as seem appropriate to the people involved; they have no central headquarters and are spread across numerous locales; and they are all-inclusive, excluding no one and embracing anyone who wishes to be part of the movement. More often than not, social movements are organized around a salient set of issues – like those that highlight the concerns of feminists, environmentalists or peace activists – and as such they serve transnational needs that cannot be filled by national governments, organized domestic groups or private firms. Social movements are thus constituent parts of the globalizing process. They contribute importantly to the non-economic fabric of ties facilitated by the new communications and transportation technologies. They pick up the pieces, so to speak, that states and businesses leave in their wake by their boundary-crossing activities: just as the peace movement focuses on the consequences of state interactions, for example, so has the ecological movement become preoccupied with the developmental excesses of transnational corporations. Put even more strongly, 'The point about these antisystemic movements is that they often elude the traditional categories of nation, state, and class. They articulate new ways of experiencing life, a new attitude to time and space, a new sense of history and identity.'[33]

The broad-based effort of publics in various countries to bring apartheid in South Africa to an end through a disinvestment campaign designed to get corporations to cease their operations in that country offers a classic illustration of how a social movement can serve to constrain the authority of national governments. An even more recent example is provided by the effort of Greenpeace to mobilize support to get France to cease nuclear testing in the South Pacific. Bundles of petitions weighing nearly three tons and containing more than 7 million signatures from people in some thirty countries flooded (and momentarily paralysed) the French postal system[34] and may have been one of the factors that contributed to the French government's decision to cut back the number of projected tests from eight to six.

Despite the lack of structural constraints which allows for their uninhibited growth, however, social movements may not remain permanently inchoate and nascent. At those times when the issues of concern to their members climb high on the global agenda, they may begin to evolve at least temporary organizational arrangements through which to move towards their goals. The International Nestlé Boycott Committee is illustrative in this regard: it organized a seven-year international boycott of Nestlé products and then was dismantled when the Nestlé Company complied with its demands.[35] In some instances, moreover, the organizational expression of a movement's aspirations can develop enduring features. Fearful that the development of organizational structures might curb their spontaneity, some movement members might be aghast at the prospect of formalized procedures, explicit rules and specific role assignments, but clearly the march towards goals requires organizational coherence at some point. Thus have organizations representing transnational social movements begun to dot the global landscape.[36] Oxfam and Amnesty International are two examples among many that could be cited of movement spin-offs that have evolved towards the institutionalized extreme of the continuum.

Cities and micro regions as functional equivalents

The concept of regions, both the macro and micro variety, has become increasingly relevant to the processes of global governance. Although originally connotative of territorial space, it is a concept that has evolved as a residual category encompassing those new patterns of interaction that span established political boundaries and at the same time remain within a delimited geographic space. If that space embraces two or more national economies, it can be called a macro region, whereas a space that spans two or more subnational economies constitutes a micro region.[37] As can be inferred from table 2.1, both types of regions can emerge out of bottom-up processes and thus can evolve out of economic foundations into political constraints that may enhance democratic procedures in Globalized Space. This evolutionary potential makes it 'difficult to work with precise definitions. We cannot define regions because they define themselves by evolving from objective, but dormant, to subjective, active existence.'[38]

Abstract and elusive as it may be, however, the notion of micro and macro regions as residual categories for control mechanisms that span conventional boundaries serves to highlight important features of transnational governance. In the case of micro regions, it calls attention to the emergent role of certain cities and 'natural' economic zones as subtle and nascent forms of transnational rule systems that are not sponsored by states and that, instead, emerge out of the activities of other types of actors which at least initially may foster a relocation of authority from the political to the economic realm. To be sure, some micro regions may span conventional boundaries within a single state and thus be more logically treated as instances of subnational control mechanisms, but such a distinction need not be drawn because many such regions are, as noted in the ensuing paragraphs, transnational in scope. Indeed, since they 'are interlinked processes',[39] it is conceivable that the evolution of micro regions contributes to the emergence of macro regions, and vice versa.

An insightful example along these lines is provided by the developments that have flowed from the success of a cooperation pact signed in 1988 by Lyons, Milan, Stuttgart and Barcelona, developments that have led one analyst to observe that 'a resurrection of "city states" and regions is quietly transforming Europe's political and economic landscape, diminishing the influence of national governments and redrawing the continental map of power for the 21st century.'[40] All four cities and their surrounding regions have an infrastructure and location that is more suited to the changes at work in Europe.[41] They are attracting huge investments and enjoying a prosperity that has led to new demands for greater autonomy. Some argue that, as a result, the emerging urban centres and economies are fostering 'a new historical dynamism that will ultimately transform the political structure of Europe by creating a new kind of "Hanseatic League" that consists of thriving city-states'.[42] One specialist forecasts that there will be nineteen cities with at least 20 million people in the greater metropolitan area by the year 2000, with the result that 'cities, not nations, will become the principal identity for most people in the world.'[43] Others offer similar interpretations, anticipating that these identity shifts will have profound implications for democratic practices as well as for nationhood and traditional state boundaries.[44]

And what unit is evolving in the place of the nation-state as a natural unit for organizing activity within the economic realm? Again the data point to the emergence of control mechanisms that are regional in scope. These regional control mechanisms are not governmentally imposed but 'are drawn by the deft but invisible hand of the global market for goods and services'.[45] This is not to say, however, that regional rule systems are lacking in structure. On the contrary, since they make 'effective points of entry into the global economy . . . the very characteristics that define them are shaped by the demands of that economy,' which is another way of reiterating that while markets are at best disaggregative mechanisms, their democratic foundations are bound to be ad hoc and variable. This is especially so in as much as the boundaries of regional control mechanisms are determined by the 'naturalness' of their economic zones and thus rarely coincide with the borders of geographic political units. The clash between the incentives induced by markets and the authority of governments is thus central to the emergence of transnational governance mechanisms. Indeed, it is arguable that a prime change at work in world politics today is a shift in the balance between these two forces, with political authorities finding it increasingly expedient to yield to economic realities. In some instances, moreover, political authorities do not even get to choose to yield, as 'regional economic interdependencies are now more important than political boundaries.'[46] Put differently, the implications of these regional rule systems 'are not welcome news to established seats of political power, be they politicians or lobbyists. Nation states by definition require a domestic political focus, while [regional systems] are ensconced in the global economy.'[47]

This potential clash, however, need not necessarily turn adversarial. Much depends on whether the political authorities welcome and encourage foreign capital investment or whether they insist on protecting their non-competitive local industries. If they are open to foreign inputs, their economies are more likely to prosper than if they insist on a rigorous maintenance of their political autonomy. But if they do insist on drawing tight lines around their authoritative realms, they are likely to lose out.

It seems clear, in short, that cities and micro regions are likely to be major control mechanisms in the world politics of the future and, as such, they will surely enrich the degree to which Globalized Space is marked by disaggregation. Even if the various expectations that they replace states as centres of power prove to be exaggerated, they seem destined to emerge as either partners or adversaries of states as their crucial role becomes more widely recognized and they thereby move from an objective to an intersubjective existence.

Electronic technologies as functional equivalents

Although a stretch of the imagination is required to appreciate its functional equivalency, the widespread growth of the Internet, the World Wide Web and the other electronic technologies that are shrinking the world offers considerable potential as a source of democracy. More accurately, by facilitating the continued proliferation of networks that know no boundaries, these technologies have introduced a horizontal dimension to the politics of Globalized Space. They enable like-minded people in distant places to converge, share perspectives, protest abuses, provide information and mobilize resources – dynamics that seem bound to constrain the vertical structures that sustain governments, corporations and any other hierarchical organizations. As one observer put it, 'Anyone with a modem is potentially a global pamphleteer,'[48] while another admitted finding 'electrons more fascinating than elections'.[49]

Many examples could be cited to illustrate the potential of the Internet as a creator of non-territorial communities of like-minded people who may converge in cyberspace for political purposes that constrain the alternatives open to organizations in the 'real' world. A hint of this potential is evident in the thousands of messages received from all over the world by people in Montoursville, Pennsylvania, after twenty-one of its residents lost their lives in the explosion of TWA Flight 800. 'Because of that common spirit,' said the Rev. Michael Cooper at one funeral, referring to the e-mail messages, 'something in us unites together.'[50] Or more immediately relevant, consider how democratic constraints may eventually flow from postings such as the following that appeared on 28 July 1996 in several folders of the 'Politics' message board on America On-line:

InterActivism is a pioneering organization promoting on-line activism to support many progressive issues and causes. Its web site regularly highlights actions that net citizens can take part in. InterActivism is now raising funds to rebuild the burnt Black Churches and also to support NARAL. Visitors to InterActivism can use a free fax service to call on leaders in Washington, DC, to cut back defense spending and increase services to the nation's children. Many more actions like these are in the pipeline. Take a look at the innovative use of cyberspace at url: http://www.interactivism.com.

In sum, since these new microelectronic technologies have the potential 'of bringing information directly into our homes any time we want it', they could render 'political institutions (*all institutions*) . . . far less important. . . . Computers could displace schools, offices, newspapers, scheduled television and banks . . . Government's regulatory functions could weaken, or vanish. It's already a cinch on the Internet to get around the rules; censorship, telecommunications restrictions and patent laws are easily evaded.'[51]

Nor can it be argued that this line of reasoning is misguided because the computer is available only to a relatively small stratum of the world's population. To be sure, large numbers of people still do not have access to computer networks, but this circumstance seems likely to be dramatically altered as 'computers keep getting faster, cheaper, and smaller.'[52] Indeed, the decline in the cost of computer equipment is matched only by the acceleration of its power to process information: 'The number of components that engineers could squeeze onto a microchip has doubled every year since 1959 [with the result that] twenty years from now, a computer will do in 30 seconds what one of today's computers takes a year to do.'[53] Accordingly, it is hardly surprising – to cite but two of myriad examples – that geographically remote Mongolia is now wired into the Internet[54] and that its use is spreading so rapidly in China that the Internet 'can be accessed in 700 cities via local dial-up calls'.[55]

ALTERNATIVE SYSTEMS OF CONSTRAINT

In short, the multicentric world of diverse non-governmental actors is increasingly pervaded with checks and balances. These constraints are not formalized as they are in territorial polities, and they operate unevenly in the various segments of the multicentric world, but more often than not they tend to inhibit unrestrained exercises of power and to subject unfair or criminal practices to the glare of publicity. In a few rule systems, such as credit-rating agencies, the authority of the constraints is rooted in a reputation for even-handedness; in some systems, such as professional or epistemic communities, the constraints derive from the dissemination of authoritative knowledge about problems and issues on Globalized Space's agenda; in other systems, such as those active with respect to human rights, checks and balances are served through moral authority; in still other systems, such as cross-border coalitions among consumer activists or environmentalists, the capacity to restrain excesses stems from the kind of organizational work that suffuses demands and protests with a ring of authority. In many rule systems constraints arise out of coalitions of governmental and non-governmental actors that preside over issue regimes; occasionally, in issue-specific systems, social movements can initiate changes in the diplomatic chambers of the state-centric system by aggregating individuals to boycott the products of companies doing business with pariah states.[56] And so on through all the domains wherein governance occurs in Globalized Space.

There is one control mechanism, however, where the constraints are more nascent than active. The global market is unregulated and presently beyond the capacity of any rule system to direct. Unwilling to protect their industries and labour forces, states allow the global market to prevail and it, in turn, unfolds by economic rules that amount to arbitrary rather than democratic governance. Considered from a long-run perspective, however, the global market is no less subject to decentralizing dynamics than any other realm of global governance. Most notably, if free trade agreements lead to excesses in which only the wealthy participate, other groups in societies may eventually become active in Globalized Space and demand that the excesses be brought under control. The uprising of Mayan Indians in Chiapas and the 1996 presidential candidacy of Patrick Buchanan in the USA were both partly reactions to the North Atlantic Free Trade Agreement (NAFTA) and, as such, are illustrative of how the unregulated system known as the global economy subsumes nascent constraints capable of becoming major political forces. Whether the activation of these forces will expand the democratic dimensions of Globalized Space is questionable. More accurately, democracy will be served if the upheavals like those in Chiapas result in greater autonomy for local populations, whereas it may well be set back if xenophobic politicians in industrial countries successfully persuade populations that their future lies in repressive measures designed to control the flow of goods and ideas.

Another way to formulate this problem of how to achieve democratic practices under conditions wherein state authority has been diffused is to focus on those dimensions of the diffusion that cannot be readily traced, those issues that have 'leaked away . . . gone nowhere, just evaporated'.[57] That is, while it is possible to discern accountability in the upward diffusion of authority to supranational organizations such as the UN, the International Monetary Fund, and NGOs like Greenpeace, and while the shift of responsibilities downwards to provincial and local governments can also be easily appraised, it is perplexing to assess the shift of authority with respect to those economic, labour and welfare matters from which states have retreated and where they have been superseded by the anarchy of global markets. Assuming that the notion of continued economic growth keeping capricious markets in check is illusory – as continued growth is by no means assured – the question remains of what control mechanisms will evolve and 'how much in the way of rules, supervision, and intervention [will they need] for the system's continued stability, equity, and prosperity . . . What, in other words, is the sine qua non of political management for a capitalist market-oriented, credit-dependent economic system of production, trade, and investment?'[58]

The answer to this important question is complex. On the one hand, it can be reasoned that 'just as experience and the record of history have clearly shown that society can tolerate a certain measure of violence and insecurity, [so] economies can carry on despite a certain degree of inflation in the value of money, a measure of financial instability'; but on the other hand, 'the answer to the question, "How much anarchy is too much?" is by no means clear. To put the question another way, how much does it matter to the system, to the people living in and by it, that half of Africa and certain parts of Latin America and Asia remain sunk in political chaos, economic stagnation, and recurrent famine, endemic disease, and internecine warfare?'[59]

It follows that the diverse checks and balances embedded in different types of rule systems offer a mixed picture in so far as being reliable instruments of democratic governance is concerned. There remain pockets, even large gaps, wherein democratic principles are systematically ignored, grossly violated or paid only superficial lip service. Yet the same sentence could be written about territorial polities regarded as democratic systems; they too are not lacking in distortions and assertions of democratic ideals that are not honoured in practice. Besides, and to repeat, the test of whether democracy is evolving in Globalized Space is not whether the institutions of representation and responsibility conform to those to be found in territorial polities; rather, the test lies in the degree to which ad hoc control mechanisms evolve to steer the politics of this emergent domain in the direction of more checks on the excesses of power, more opportunities for interests to be heard and heeded, and more balanced constraints among the multiplicity of actors that seek to extend their command of issue areas. Viewed in this way, it seems reasonable to conclude that the more densely populated Globalized Space becomes, thus promoting a greater sense of connectivity among widely separated peoples and groups, the more will its governance exhibit democratic tendencies.

Furthermore, it is likely that the more densely populated Globalized Space becomes, the more will states be under pressure to 'provide new vehicles for democratic expression at the national level that also provide national democratic access to supranational decision-making'.[60] This is another way of saying that in addition to the control mechanisms that evolve within Globalized Space, others exist (or are being nursed into being) through collaboration between state-centric and multicentric actors. When agencies of the UN collaborate with volunteer groups over issues of population growth, health and environmental sustainability, when governments that maintain foreign aid programmes in the developing world work with local specialists to frame and administer programme goals, when representatives of the two worlds simultaneously hold adjacent summit meetings to consider progress in particular issue areas, when provincial governments seek to promote new trading partners abroad, when local communities engage in exchanges with twinned cities – all these (and doubtless many other) ad hoc mechanisms for superseding or bypassing domestic-foreign boundaries can quickly become institutionalized and thereby sustain rule systems that enlarge governance in Globalized Space. To be sure, it has become commonplace to conclude that 'the current state of NGO . . . accountability is unsatisfactory,'[61] but few would deny that the standards for assessing organizational performance have steadily risen and that what are judged to be unsatisfactory today would earlier have seemed like worthy goals on the road to more extensive democracy.

While some analysts treat the emergence of Globalized Space's numerous, diverse and collaborative rule systems, and the ways in which they may check and balance each other, as amounting to democracy in the sense that the result is an empowering of communities,[62] others envisage its politics as leading to 'cosmopolitan democracy'.[63] The latter argue that

democracy can only be fully sustained in and through the agencies and organizations which form an element of and yet cut across the territorial boundaries of the nation-state. The possibility of democracy today must . . . be linked to an expanding framework of democratic states and agencies. . . . [This framework is] 'the cosmopolitan model of democracy', by which [is meant] a system of governance which arises from and is adapted to the diverse conditions and interconnections of different peoples and nations.[64]

Those who discern empowered communities and cosmopolitan forms of transnational governance recognize that these control mechanisms are still very far from mature institutions and that numerous obstacles must still be overcome if they are to become firmly embedded as features of Globalized Space. Yet they perceive in the underpinnings of global governance – in the overlapping of peoples, the shrinking of distances and the emergence of shared norms – hope that progress towards democratic forms of governance can be sustained.

Is the hope justified? Or are there reasons to fear that the bottom-line orientations of profit-making organizations and the self-serving tendencies of non-profit actors are too extensive for the nascent structures of Globalized Space to become the functional equivalents of democratic polities? Perhaps the only plausible answer is that 'the jury is still out regarding the [liberalized new world order's] effects on global democracy and government generally'[65] and that thus both the hopes and the fears are warranted. So much change is at work that one can readily construct scenarios in which the politics of this emergent domain becomes increasingly democratic, just as contrary scenarios are not far-fetched. Stated more positively, given a continuing skill revolution and proliferation of networks that link diverse and distant individuals, there is certainly no reason to abandon hope if one's concept of democracy allows for the growth of institutions unique to transnational rather than territorial political spaces.

POLYARCHY VERSUS POLLYANNA

Not to abandon hope, however, is hardly a satisfying conclusion. It may well leave the reader, like the author, feeling let down, as if it ought to be possible to write an upbeat final chapter of this story of democratic development in a disaggregated and fragmenting global system of governance. It is an unfinished story, one's need for closure would assert. It needs a drawing together of the 'big picture', a sweeping assessment which offers a basis for believing that somehow the world can muddle through and evolve techniques of cooperation that will bridge its multitude of disaggregated parts and achieve a measure of coherence which enables future generations to live in peace and maintain a modicum of democratic order. You need to assess the overall balance, one's training cries out, show how the various emergent centres of authority form a multipolar system that can cope with violence within and among its members. Yes, that's it, depict the overall system as polyarchical and indicate how such an arrangement can generate multilateral institutions of democratic control that effectively address the huge issues which clutter the global agenda. Or, perhaps better, indicate how a liberal hegemon will emerge out of the disaggregation and have enough clout to foster democracy as well as progress and stability. At the very least, one's normative impulses demand, suggest how worldwide tendencies towards disaggregation and localization may be offset by no less powerful tendencies towards aggregation and globalization, thus resulting in a complex system of constraints that begin to approach the functional equivalent of democratic practices.

Compelling as these alternative interpretations may be, however, they do not quell a sense that it is only a short step from polyarchy to Pollyanna and that one's commitment to responsible analysis must be served by not taking that step. The world is on a path-dependent course, to be sure, and some of its present outlines can be discerned if, as noted at the outset, allowance is made for nuance and ambiguity. Still, in this time of continuing and profound transformations too much remains murky to project beyond the immediate present and anticipate long-term trajectories. All one can conclude with confidence is that in the next century the paths to governance will lead in many directions, some that will emerge into sunlit clearings and others that will descend into dense jungles.

NOTES

Parts of this essay have been adapted from J. N. Rosenau, 'Governance in the twenty-first century', *Global Governance: a Review of Multilateralism and International Organizations*, 1.1 (Winter 1995), pp. 23–38, © 1995 by Lynne Rienner

Publishers Inc., used with permission, and J. N. Rosenau, *Along the Domestic-Foreign Frontier: Exploring Governance in a Turbulent World* (Cambridge: Cambridge University Press, 1997), ch. 21.

Epigraph from A. D. Marcus, 'Peres presses for his version of peace to maintain his political clout in Israel', *Wall Street Journal*, 16 Aug. 1996, p. A4.

1   A. King and B. Schneider, *The First Global Revolution: a Report of the Council of Rome* (New York: Pantheon, 1991), pp. 181–2 (emphasis added). For other inquiries that support the inclusion of small, seemingly local systems of rule in a broad analytic framework, see J. Friedmann, *Empowerment: the Politics of Alternative Development* (Oxford: Blackwell, 1992); and R. Huckfeldt, E. Plutzer and J. Sprague, 'Alternative contexts of political behavior: churches, neighborhoods, and individuals', *Journal of Politics*, 55 (May 1993), pp. 365–81.

2   S. A. Rosell et al., *Governing in an Information Society* (Montreal: Institute for Research on Public Policy, 1992), p. 21.

3   Rule systems have much in common with what has come to be called the 'new institutionalism'. See, for example, R. O. Keohane, 'International institutions: two approaches', *International Studies Quarterly*, 32 (Dec. 1988), pp. 379–96; J. G. March and J. P. Olsen, 'The new institutionalism: organizational factors in political life', *American Political Science Review*, 78 (Sept. 1984), pp. 734–49; and O. R. Young, 'International regimes: toward a new theory of institutions', *World Politics*, 39 (Oct. 1986), pp. 104–22. For an extended discussion of how the concept of control is especially suitable to the analysis of both formal and informal political phenomena, see J. N. Rosenau, *Calculated Control as a Unifying Concept in the Study of International Politics and Foreign Policy*, Research Monograph 15, Center of International Studies (Princeton: Princeton University, 1963).

4   Cf. J. N. Rosenau and E.-O. Czempiel (eds), *Governance without Government: Order and Change in World Politics* (Cambridge: Cambridge University Press, 1992). Also see the formulations in P. Mayer, V. Rittberger and M. Zuern, 'Regime theory: state of the art and perspectives', in V. Rittberger (ed.), *Regime Theory and International Relations* (Oxford: Oxford University Press, 1993); and T. J. Sinclair, 'Financial knowledge as governance', paper presented at the annual meeting of the International Studies Association, Acapulco, 23–7 Mar. 1993.

5   For a discussion of the breadth and depth of the world's authority crises, see J. N. Rosenau, 'The relocation of authority in a shrinking world', *Comparative Politics*, 24 (Apr. 1992), pp. 253–72.

6   A vivid picture of the organizational explosion in the non-governmental world is presented in L. M. Salamon, 'The global associational revolution: the rise of the third sector on the world scene', *Foreign Affairs* (July–Aug. 1994), p. 109. As for the world of governments, in addition to the new states that have recently swollen the ranks of the international system, a measure of the extraordinary organizational density that has evolved can be extrapolated – assuming the pattern is global in scale – from the following description of the United States some three decades ago:

It has been estimated that there are over 8,000 multifunctional and autonomous local governments, including over 3,000 counties and more than that number of urban governments for the thousands of incorporated municipalities which speckle the map. The mesh is made still finer by the number of special-purpose districts which have been mushrooming over the past decades, particularly in the major metropolitan regions. From 1942 to 1962 the number of special districts (excluding school districts) grew from 8,300 to over 18,000. When school districts are added, the result in 1962 was an astonishing total of over 63,000 local governments with some autonomous authority over specific parcels of U.S. space. . . . Emerging from this complex geopolitical web are thousands of discrete units of territorial identity and exclusion – cities and suburbs, townships and counties, school districts and whole metropolitan regions – which instill a sense of community and apartness usually surpassed only at the national and family levels.

See E. W. Soja, *The Political Organization of Space*, Resource Paper 8 (Washington, D.C.: Association of American Geographers, 1971), p. 45.

7   For an extended discussion of why the changes at work in the world today involve differences in kind rather than degree, see J. N. Rosenau, *Along the Domestic-Foreign Frontier: Exploring Governance in a Turbulent World* (Cambridge: Cambridge University Press, 1997) ch. 2.

8   J. P. Pinkerton, *What Comes Next: the End of Big Government – and the New Paradigm Ahead* (New York: Hyperion, 1995), p. 43.

9   K. Phillips, *Boiling Point: Republicans, Democrats, and the Decline of Middle-Class Prosperity* (New York: Random House, 1993), p. 141.

10 A. G. McGrew, 'Global politics in a transitional era', in A. G. McGrew, P. G. Lewis et al., *Global Politics: Globalization and the Nation-State* (Cambridge: Polity Press, 1992), p. 318.

11 M. Hewson, 'The media of political globalization', paper presented at the annual meeting of the International Studies Association, Washington, D.C., Mar. 1994, p. 2.

12 For cogent analyses of the bases of political organization, see E. Adler, 'Imagined (security) communities', paper presented at the annual meeting of the American Political Science Association, New York, 1–4 Sept. 1994; D. Ronfeldt, 'Tribes, institutions, markets, networks: a framework about societal evolution', Rand Corporation, Santa Monica, 1996; and Soja, *The Political Organization of Space*.

13 The skill revolution is outlined in J. N. Rosenau, *Turbulence in World Politics: a Theory of Change and Continuity* (Princeton: Princeton University Press, 1990), ch. 13. An analysis of how the skill revolution has empowered people to engage more effectively in collective action can be found in Rosenau, 'The relocation of authority in a shrinking world', pp. 253–72. Systematic data tracing skills across sixty years and supporting the proposition that they have expanded, at least among diverse types of elites, are presented in J. N. Rosenau and W. M. Fagen, 'Increasingly skillful citizens: a new dynamism in world politics?', *International Studies Quarterly*, 41 (Dec. 1997), pp. 655–86.

14   The dynamics of subgroupism are set forth in Rosenau, *Turbulence in World Politics*, pp. 133–6, 396–8.

15   See, for example, P. F. Drucker, *Post-Capitalist Society* (New York: HarperCollins, 1993).

16   A discussion of the impact of new interdependence issues is offered in Rosenau, *Turbulence in World Politics*, pp. 429–30. The emergent role of new social movements is assessed in R. B. J. Walker, *One World, Many Worlds: Struggles for a Just World Peace* (Boulder: Lynne Rienner, 1988); and L. P. Thiele, 'Making democracy safe for the world: social movements and global politics', *Alternatives*, 18 (1993), pp. 273–305.

17   For analyses of these contradictory trends, see J. N. Rosenau, 'The person, the household, the community, and the globe: notes for a theory of multilateralism in a turbulent world', in Robert W. Cox (ed.), *The New Realism: Perspectives on Multilateralism and World Order* (Houndsmills: Macmillan, 1997), pp. 57–80.

18   None of this is to imply, of course, that the shifts in the loci of authority occur easily, with a minimum of commotion and a maximum of clarity. Far from it: the shifts derive from delicate bargaining, and usually they must overcome extensive opposition. As a result:

> Transfer of authority is a complicated process and it seems there no longer is one single identifiable sovereign, but a multitude of authorities at different levels of aggregation and several centres with differing degrees of coercive power (not all of them public and governmental!) . . . it becomes increasingly difficult to differentiate between public and private institutions, the State and Civil Society, domestic and international.

See K. Lahteenmaki and J. Kakonen, 'Regionalization and its impact on the theory of international relations', paper presented at the annual meeting of the International Studies Association, Washington, D.C., Mar. 1994, pp. 32–3.

19   J. Vogler, 'Regimes and the global commons: space, atmosphere and oceans', in McGrew and Lewis, *Global Politics*, p. 118.

20   For a conception of political adaptation in which adaptive systems are posited as being able to keep fluctuations in their essential structures within acceptable limits, see J. N. Rosenau, *The Study of Political Adaptation* (London: Frances Pinter, 1981).

21   For a cogent analysis in which this bottom-up process is posited as passing through five distinct stages, see B. Hettne, 'The new regionalism: implications for development and peace', in B. Hettne and A. Inotai, *The New Regionalism: Implications for Global Development and International Security* (Helsinki: UNU World Institute for Development Economics Research, 1994), pp. 7–8.

22   The elaboration of these examples is provided in J. N. Rosenau, 'Governance in the twenty-first century', *Global Governance*, 1 (Winter 1995), pp. 23–38.

23   J. N. Rosenau, 'Material and imagined communities in globalized space', in Donald H. McMillen (ed.), *Globalization and Regional Communities:*

Geoeconomic, Sociocultural and Security Implications for Australia (Too-womba: USQ Press, 1997), pp. 24–40.

24 Rosenau, *Along the Domestic-Foreign Frontier*, ch. 1.

25 For an elaboration of the notion that world politics may mimic the global marketplace, see J. Agnew and S. Corbridge, *Mastering Space: Hegemony, Territory and International Political Economy* (New York: Routledge, 1995), p. 207.

26 The role of corporations as control mechanisms is essayed in C. Cutler, V. Haufler and T. Porter, 'Private authority and international regimes', draft of a paper for a workshop at the annual meeting of the International Studies Association, San Diego, 16 Apr. 1996; and D. C. Korten, *When Corporations Rule the World* (West Hartford, Conn.: Kumarian Press, 1995).

27 R. Boyer and D. Drache, 'Introduction', in R. Boyer and D. Drache (eds), *States against Markets: the Limits of Globalization* (London: Routledge, 1996), p. 7.

28 D. J. Schemo, 'Rebuilding of suburban dreams', *New York Times*, 4 May 1994, p. A11.

29 S. Greenhouse, 'Kissinger will help mediate dispute over Zulu homeland', *New York Times*, 12 Apr. 1994, p. A8.

30 P. B. Evans, 'Building an integrative approach to international and domestic politics: reflections and projections', in P. B. Evans, H. K. Jacobson and R. D. Putnam (eds), *Double-Edged Diplomacy: International Bargaining and Domestic Politics* (Berkeley: University of California Press, 1993), p. 419. For interesting accounts of how multinational corporations are increasingly inclined to form transnational alliances, see 'The global firm: R.I.P.', *The Economist*, 6 Feb. 1993, p. 69; and 'The fall of big business', *The Economist*, 17 Apr. 1993, p. 13.

31 R. C. Goizueta, 'The challenges of getting what you wished for', remarks presented to the Arthur Page Society, Amelia Island, Florida, 21 Sept. 1992.

32 M. Edwards and D. Hulme, 'NGO performance and accountability', in M. Edwards and D. Hulme (eds), *Beyond the Magic Bullet: NGO Performance and Accountability in the Post-Cold War World* (West Hartford, Conn.: Kumarian Press, 1996), p. 8.

33 J. A. Camilleri, 'Rethinking sovereignty in a shrinking, fragmented world', in R. B. J. Walker and S. H. Mendlovitz (eds), *Contending Sovereignties: Redefining Political Community* (Boulder: Lynne Rienner, 1990), p. 35.

34 'Protests swamp Paris Post Office', *Washington Post*, 29 Oct. 1995, p. A34.

35 K. Sikkink, 'Codes of conduct for transnational corporations: the case of the UWH/UNICEF code', *International Organization*, 40 (Autumn 1986), pp. 815–40.

36 J. Leatherman, R. Pagnucco and J. Smith, 'International institutions and transnational social movement organizations: challenging the state in a three-level game of global transformation', paper presented at the annual meeting of the International Studies Association, Washington, D.C., Mar. 1994.

37 R. W. Cox, 'Global perestroika', in R. Milband and L. Panitch (eds), *Socialist Register* (London: Merlin Press, 1992), p. 34.

38 Hettne, 'The new regionalism', p. 2.

39 Ibid., p. 6.

40   W. Drozdiak, 'Revving up Europe's "four motors"', *Washington Post*, 27 Mar. 1994, p. C3.

41   For an analysis which conceives of these 'four motors' of Europe in terms of micro regions rather than as cities – the Rhone Alps instead of Lyons, Lombardy instead of Milan, Baden-Wurttemberg instead of Stuttgart, and Catalonia instead of Barcelona – see Lahteenmaki and Kakonen, 'Regionalization and its impact on the theory of international relations', p. 15.

42   Drozdiak, 'Revving up Europe's "four motors"', p. C3.

43   P. Maragall, quoted in ibid. For extensive inquiries that posit the transnational roles of cities as increasingly central to the processes of global governance, see S. Sassen, *The Global City: New York, London, Tokyo* (Princeton: Princeton University Press, 1991); and E. H. Fry, L. H. Radebaugh and P. Soldatos (eds), *The New International Cities Era: the Global Activities of North American Municipal Governments* (Provo, Utah: Brigham Young University Press, 1989).

44   See, for example, T. P. Rohlem, 'Cosmopolitan cities and nation states: a "Mediterranean" model for Asian regionalism', paper presented at the Conference on Asian Regionalism, Maui, 17–19 Dec. 1993; and K. Ohmae, 'The Rise of the Region State', *Foreign Affairs*, 72 (Spring 1993).

45   Ohmae, 'The rise of the region state', pp. 78–9.

46   M. Clough and D. Doerge, *Global Changes and Domestic Transformations: New Possibilities for American Foreign Policy. Report of a Vantage Conference* (Muscatine, Iowa: Stanley Foundation, 1992), p. 9. For indicators that a similar process is occurring in the American south-west without the approval of Washington, D.C., or Mexico City, see C. L. Thorup, *Redefining Governance in North America: the Impact of Cross-Border Networks and Coalitions on Mexican Immigration into the United States* (Santa Monica: Rand Corporation, 1993). Although using a different label ('tribes'), a broader discussion of regional control mechanisms can be found in J. Kotkin, *Tribes: How Race, Religion and Identity Determine Success in the New Global Economy* (New York: Random House, 1993).

47   Ohmae, 'The rise of the region state', p. 83.

48   J. Markoff, 'If medium is the message, the message is the Web', *New York Times*, 20 Nov. 1995, p. A1.

49   J. K. Glassman, 'Brave New Cyberworld', *Washington Post*, 29 Aug. 1995, p. A19.

50   R. Meredith, 'Global village comforts a tiny town', *New York Times*, 29 July 1996, p. B4.

51   Glassman, 'Brave New Cyberworld,' p. A19 (emphasis in the original).

52   Ibid.

53   Ibid.

54   E. Corcoran, 'How the "butter fund" spread the Internet to Mongolia', *Washington Post*, 1 Mar. 1996, p. A1.

55   'Internet thrives in nation starved of information', *Eastern Express* (Hong Kong), 6 Apr. 1995, p. 9.

56   Perhaps because the disinvestment campaign against apartheid in South Africa was so successful, this pattern appears to be recurring with greater frequency. Recently, for example, pressures have been successfully launched

against companies to withdraw from Myanmar until its military rulers step down: 'The Carlsberg and Heineken breweries both announced earlier this month they were ending business dealings there after pro-democracy groups called for a boycott of the companies' products.' *New York Times*, 19 July 1996, p. A4.

57 S. Strange, 'The defective state', *Daedalus*, 124 (Spring 1995), p. 56.
58 Ibid., p. 71.
59 Ibid., pp. 71–2. For a similar analysis that poses, in effect, this question, see R. Petrella, 'Globalization and internationalization: the dynamics of the emerging world order', in Boyer and Drache, *States against Markets*, p. 81.
60 V. A. Schmidt, 'The New World Order, Incorporated: the rise of business and the decline of the nation-state', *Daedalus*, 124 (Spring 1995), p. 77.
61 M. Edwards and D. Hulme, 'Beyond the magic bullet? Lessons and conclusions', in Edwards and Hulme, *Beyond the Magic Bullet*, p. 257.
62 Agnew and Corbridge, *Mastering Space*, ch. 8.
63 D. Archibugi and D. Held (eds), *Cosmopolitan Democracy: an Agenda for a New World Order* (Cambridge: Polity Press, 1995).
64 D. Held, 'Democracy and the new international order,' in ibid., p. 106.
65 Schmidt, 'The New World Order, Incorporated', p. 76.

3

Human Rights as a Model for Cosmopolitan Democracy

David Beetham

The aim of this paper is to explore what the human rights 'regime', to use that term in its broadest sense, has to offer as a model for the project of cosmopolitan democracy. The paper is in three parts. The first part has a positive story to tell about the universalist impetus of the post-1945 human rights regime – as a philosophy, a body of international law, a set of institutions for monitoring and implementation, and as an important component, and legitimator, of an emergent global civil society. The second part explores some of the contradictions to which this regime is subject due to its insertion in a world of still sovereign (in important senses) nation-states and of structured global inequalities, such that states are at one and the same time the necessary agents for the implementation of human rights, and also among their chief violators, or at least colluders in their violation. The final part uses the criteria of cosmopolitan democracy to attempt some overall assessment of the human rights regime, viewed not only as achievement or utopian project, but for its dynamic potential for contributing to progressive change.

In discussing human rights in the paper, I include both sets of rights of the International Bill of Rights, economic, social and cultural as well as civil and political, despite the fact that to do so complicates the story considerably.[1] Philosophically, some may doubt whether economic rights properly count as human rights, while, at the institutional level, many of the international organizations devoted to protecting people's capacity for physical or economic survival are not usually categorized as human rights organizations; and the boundaries of the subject thus become not only considerably enlarged, but also less clear-cut.[2] However, it seems to me incontestable that the 'right to life' entails the right to the means to life, and that the 'right to liberty' entails the right to the means of exercising liberty; and that our duties to others cannot therefore be exhausted by the negative duty of refraining from harming or obstructing them.[3] Admittedly, there may be sound practical and political reasons for preserving a narrow focus, and a mutual division of labour, in human rights campaigning (Amnesty here, Oxfam there, etc.). But writers on human rights have a responsibility to insist on an inclusive conception of these rights. Otherwise they invite the justifiable charge of endorsing a narrowly liberal and Western preoccupation with civil and political rights alone.[4]

UNIVERSALISM

In the context of a project for cosmopolitan democracy there is some ground for arguing that human rights are more consistently universalist, and more readily identifiable with a global politics, than the idea of democracy has been. To be sure, democracy embodies the universalist assumption that all adults are capable of making reflective choices about collective priorities, given the relevant information; and there is no reason why this assumption should stop short at national boundaries. In this respect democracy shares a similar philosophical grounding to that of human rights.[5] However, in the context of the modern state and a world of differentiated peoples, the *demos* which is democracy's subject has come to be defined almost exclusively in national terms, and the scope of democratic rights has been limited to the bounds of the nation-state. In this sense, extending the concept of the *demos*, and the range of democracy's operation, from the nation to humankind as a whole involves the same leap of imagination as it took in the eighteenth century to extend democracy from the town meeting to the level of the state.[6] And, arguably, it will require a similar institutional innovation to that of political representation, which in the eighteenth century enabled the spatial limitation of the direct assembly to be transcended, if democracy is to be made effective at the global level.

The idea of human rights, in contrast, has from the outset been universalist in aspiration and global in its scope of operation. As the term 'human' indicates, these are entitlements ascribed to human beings everywhere; and the institutions involved in their implementation, both formal and informal or civic, proceed from the international to the national and local levels, rather than vice versa as is the case with democracy. In support of this assertion I shall consider first the normative basis of the human rights agenda, and then the regime of human rights implementation.

There are three separate assumptions entailed in the normative foundation of human rights claims, derived from considerations of common humanity, shared threats and minimum obligations respectively.

1   Despite all differences of culture, social position or circumstance, all humans share certain common needs and capacities: the need for subsistence, security and respect; the capacity for reflective individual and collective choice and ingenuity in meeting their needs.[7] To insist on human equality in these respects is not to deny difference. Indeed, the capacity for difference, and the need to have one's difference recognized and respected, is itself distinctively human, and is acknowledged in such human rights instruments as the UN Resolution on Minorities. Critics of human rights universalism typically appeal to the equal respect due to other cultures, but it is difficult to see how such respect can be justified except in terms of the equal respect due to other people *qua* human. Much of the currently fashionable 'politics of difference' presupposes an Enlightenment-derived argument for equality, despite all the criticism of the 'Enlightenment project' for its supposed bankruptcy.[8]

2   In the conditions of the modern world there are some minimum necessary means all require to meet their needs and realize their capacities, whatever their goals or forms of life; and certain standard threats to which all are likewise exposed. Reference to these determines the content of the human rights agenda. Some of these threats have always existed (physical violence, disease, malnutrition), others are distinctively modern (unbridled state power, unfettered market forces, the pollution of air and water), as also are the means of protection against them. The changing historical character of such threats and the means of protection against them is recognized in the replacement of the term 'natural' by 'human' rights, indicating that their universality is a spatial not a temporal one (applicable to all alive now, not in the past); and that the human rights agenda is itself subject to evolution. Yet it is as much the exposure to common threats as the sharing in a common humanity that justifies the claim that the human rights agenda is universal.

3   There are minimum duties to strangers that we all owe, which include not merely refraining from damaging the means to the fulfilment of their basic needs and capacities, but assisting their realization. In the contemporary world such duties are typically met through impersonal institutions of taxation and provision, rather than personally and directly. As Henry Shue has shown, these duties involve minimal rather than unlimited cost, but their acknowledgement is logically entailed in the idea of human rights; that is to say, the individualism of rights claims is necessarily complemented by the solidarity which accompanies duties.[9]

If rights have come to be emphasized at the expense of duties, this is partly because we have failed to acknowledge the state's role as implementor of the responsibilities we owe to one another.

Neoliberals and other egoists reject any non-contractual duties to others going beyond the negative duty of restraint from inflicting harm. Such a view depends on a contestable definition of what counts as 'harming' others, and a contestable theory of property as a 'natural right' rather than a social institution whose justifiability itself depends on a wider framework of rights and obligations.[10] It also overlooks the evidence about the sort of society which emerges where no positive duties to others are acknowledged, and the 'contented' are forced to construct increasingly expensive forms of defence against the exigencies of the impoverished.[11] Admittedly, both these counter-arguments still carry more conviction at the national than the global level. Yet the increasing evidence of global interdependence (consequences of population growth, environmental degradation, pressures for migration, 'social dumping', etc.) indicates that the costs of human rights denials are increasingly exported, not just experienced by their immediate victims. Such interdependencies combine with the processes of global shrinking and the internationalization of the media to expand our definition of the stranger who merits our concern.[12]

The above propositions can be defended independently of the fact that each of the main human rights covenants has been ratified by 140 out of 185 or so states, and that more states continue to ratify them. Yet they are also powerfully reinforced by that fact. In particular, the assumption by states of duties of protection and provision, as well as of restraint, is evidence that such duties are in practice widely acknowledged. And the existence of institutions at the international level to monitor their implementation not only presupposes, but also serves to consolidate, the common moral foundation on which they are premised.

The international regime of human rights implementation

The international human rights regime comprises both formal institutions (UN and regional bodies) and informal ones (NGOs), which are together involved in the processes of standard setting, monitoring and enforcement (or 'implementation' in the narrow sense). To take the formal level first, the basis of the UN's authority in the human rights field lies in the two international covenants, with their implementation procedures, and the subsequent specific conventions (against torture, discrimination against women, on the rights of the child, minority rights, etc.).[13] Although these covenants have the status of an intergovernmental treaty, once a state has ratified them it in effect acknowledges the right of a supranational body to investigate and pass judgement on its record. How a state treats its own citizens, and even what legal and constitutional arrangements it has, can thus no longer be regarded as a purely internal matter for the government concerned.[14]

The committees of experts which are charged with monitoring compliance with the respective covenants are genuinely supranational rather than intergovernmental in character (for example, members serve in an individual capacity). In interpreting the texts of the treaties they are directly engaged in an evolving process of standard setting of a quasi-judicial kind. For example, to overcome the excuse of inadequate resources as a reason for non-compliance, the Committee on Economic, Social and Cultural Rights under Philip Alston set itself the task of defining a 'minimum core' of these rights, and 'an absolute minimum entitlement, in the absence of which a state party is to be considered in violation of its obligations'.[15] Although the basic mechanism for monitoring compliance of all the covenants and conventions is reports submitted by the states themselves, these are now typically supplemented by independent evidence supplied by local and international NGOs.[16] And there is evidence of the practice of on-site inspection developed in arms control monitoring being extended to the human rights field, for instance in the investigation of torture.[17] In these different respects the human rights regime is increasingly taking on the character of an independent jurisdiction.

The weak point in this regime of course remains that of enforcement. Since the UN has no independent enforcement machinery or taxation powers of its own, it is dependent on intergovernmental agreement for the use of sanctions in even the most extreme cases of human rights violation; and their use tends to be skewed by the historical structure of the Security Council, and the economic and strategic interests of major powers.[18] The implications of this deficiency will be considered more fully below. It leaves the UN bodies largely reliant on moral persuasion, and on the wider consequences of public exposure and condemnation in an increasingly interdependent world. Such pressures are not, however, to be underestimated. Nor should we overlook the positive effects of UN agencies in the economic and social field (WHO, UNICEF, UNHCR, UNDP, etc.), whose work in cooperation with governments has had a long-term impact in reducing the incidence of disease, child mortality and so forth. Although not defined as human rights agencies, these can properly be seen as assisting governments to implement a human rights agenda.

The limits to human rights enforcement considered above apply to the world beyond Europe. Europe has what is generally regarded as a model of human rights enforcement in the European Court of Human Rights, which acts as final arbiter of the European Convention, and to which individuals have the rights of appeal against their domestic courts. If we add to this the role of the European Court at Luxembourg in the field of employment rights, the two together comprise a wide-ranging regional human rights jurisdiction.[19] The limitations this jurisdiction imposes on national sovereignty can be demonstrated from the case of the UK. Despite all the huffing and puffing about unfavourable rulings at Strasbourg, the UK government felt unable to rescind the individual right of appeal to the Court when it came up for renewal in January 1996. And despite the Conservative opt-out from the social chapter of the Maastricht Treaty, the Luxembourg Court imposed some of the same provisions through existing health and safety legislation; and there were few who seriously believed that such an opt-out was sustainable over time in a European Union committed to a level playing field in economic competition. These examples neatly illustrate the dynamic processes inherent in much international jurisdiction; what start out as intergovernmental treaties take on a supranational dynamic which drags member states along even despite themselves.

The informal regime

The proliferation of networks of NGOs, linking local with international levels, is one of the most striking developments of the human rights regime since 1948. They are involved in all three functions of standard setting, monitoring and implementation.[20] NGOs have played an active role in the development of a number of the UN conventions. Thus it is possible to trace the influence of the international women's movement on the progressive evolution of standards for the human rights of women from the simple anti-discrimination clauses of the two 1966 covenants, to the legitimation of affirmative action policies and positive education programmes in the 1979 Convention on the Elimination of All Forms of Discrimination against Women, and the 1992 draft Declaration on Violence against Women, which identifies men in civil society as well as state personnel as the potential violators of human rights.[21] Amnesty International and the International Commission of Jurists made a decisive input into the UN Declaration and Convention against Torture. The imprint of the NGO group involved in the drafting of the 1989 Convention on the Rights of the Child 'can be found in almost every article'.[22] It was local civic groups that developed and campaigned for the idea of a truth commission for the identification of human rights violators in countries emerging from dictatorship in Latin America.[23] And so on. The most visible recent manifestations of this influence have been the NGO forums held in parallel to the UN World Conferences at Vienna and Beijing, which have been regarded as of equal importance to the official assemblies of state representatives.[24]

NGO influence has been equally evident at the levels of monitoring and implementation. As already noted, it is now standard practice for

NGOs to submit evidence and informed comment to the relevant UN committees in their regular reviews of state compliance under the two covenants. NGOs are involved in obtaining evidence to support human rights cases in national and international courts, and in providing financial and legal support for victims. They are involved in public exposure of human rights abuses, and in bringing international pressure to bear on offending regimes which governments may be more chary of doing.[25] And again, if we extend our view to economic and social rights, there is the enormous contribution of NGOs to the work of economic development, famine relief, refugee support and so on.

As many commentators have noted, what we have here is an already developed international civil society, with strong linkages both at the global level and mediating between global and local actors.[26] Its component elements are the NGOs themselves, networks of human rights lawyers, citizen assemblies and national and international media operating independently of governments. It is not far-fetched to talk of an international public opinion to which governments in all regions are seen to be accountable, even though they may not acknowledge such accountability themselves. Such a global civil society is not, however, independent of the formal human rights regime, which provides both a focus for its influence, and, perhaps more importantly, a legitimation for its activities on the territory of supposedly sovereign states. As the theory of civil society at the national level insists, the development of self-organizing associations of a civil nature depends on a political regime providing the framework for their operation.[27] This reciprocal relationship between formal and informal institutions is also evident at the international level in the human rights regime.

COUNTERVAILING LOGICS

The story so far is one which sounds very positive from a cosmopolitan standpoint, whether we consider human rights as a minimum universal morality, or as a supranational regime of implementation involving formal and informal institutions. However, as already noted, the weak point of this regime is that of enforcement. Here, the global aspiration remains constrained by the system of sovereignty-claiming states, on which it is dependent for enforcement, and to whose assertion of power interests, or to whose powerlessness, it is continually vulnerable.[28]

The catalogue of serious human rights failures is only too familiar. There are states which are powerful and immune to external pressure to moderate internal repression (China in Tibet, Indonesia in East Timor). There are states which are so disabled in the face of civil war that they are unable to protect their peoples from genocide, in which they may also be complicit (Bosnia-Herzegovina, Rwanda, Somalia). There are states which are able to deflect international sanctions on to the most vulnerable sections of the population, so that the human rights situation is as bad as, or worse than, it would have been without them (Iraq). There are powerful states which have undertaken a surrogate UN role of policing human rights performance through so-called aid conditionality (USA, UK), where the conditions are dropped as soon as they conflict with significant trading or strategic interests (in China, Nigeria).[29] The impartiality of the UN is compromised by acting as a fig-leaf for particular US interests. And its own effectiveness in human rights protection is undermined by the unwillingness of member states to fund its operations, or to sacrifice their citizens' lives to protect the nationals of another country from human rights violations.

It would be easy to conclude from this sorry catalogue that internationalism is good, nation-statism is bad; or that the deficiencies of the human rights regime derive entirely from its insertion in the system of sovereignty-claiming states. However, such a conclusion requires qualification in two respects. First, nation-states remain for the foreseeable future the necessary instruments for the provision of security and welfare for their citizens. It is inconceivable that any supranational authority, even at the regional level, could possibly provide the administration necessary to guarantee the human rights of their peoples. The most they can do is provide a set of common minimum standards for states or substate authorities within their jurisdiction to observe, and some system of resource redistribution to enable the weakest to attain these standards. Such administrations will inevitably seek to buttress themselves with national loyalties, and to maintain local forms of distinctiveness, which will stand in some tension with any supranational regime.

Second, deficiencies in the implementation of human rights derive as much from the systematic inequalities between states and regions in their ability to guarantee subsistence, security and respect, as they do from the particularism of the nation-state *per se*. In other words, it is the structuring of the global system itself into developed and underdeveloped economies, zones of security and insecurity, hegemonic and subordinate cultures, as well as the reproduction of these inequalities within states, that is a major source of problems in human rights implementation.[30] If, *per impossibile*, the boundaries of nation-states were to evaporate and their functions were to be taken over by regional bodies such as the EU, these inequalities would still persist. From this perspective, the state is a site of conflicting forces, external and internal, and an enormously variable capacity to manage these in a manner consistent with the protection of human rights. The tension is thus not one between universalism and particularism, but one between a strategy for minimal global equality on the one hand, and the systematic reproduction of global inequalities on the other.[31]

ASSESSMENT

How, then, should we evaluate the human rights regime from the stand-point of cosmopolitan democracy? Three different criteria suggest them-selves. How cosmopolitan is it? How democratic? How should we assess it, not so much as an achievement, or as a future end state, but for its capacity to contribute to a *process* of change, that is for its progressive potential?

As to the first criterion, I have argued that, at the level of standard setting and monitoring, the human rights regime is genuinely universalist, both in its philosophy and in the institutionalization of its practice. In signing the UN conventions, states submit themselves to a supranational regime for evolving and monitoring human rights standards, and to the judgement of an alert and active international public opinion, whose scope now reaches beyond the list of signatory states. These standards claim minimum entitlements for all people everywhere on the basis of their shared human needs and capacities.

In respect of implementation, however, the human rights regime is almost wholly dependent on the governments of individual states, and their capacity and willingness to protect them in the context of compet-ing priorities and conflicting forces. In this respect the professed universalism is still embedded in the old structure of nation-states. This is no easy conjunction of overlapping jurisdictions, however (as in Bull's scenario quoted by Andrew Linklater in chapter 6 below), nor yet an unproblematic tiering of political allegiancies at different spatial levels. It is a relationship that is full of contradictions. We are talking about a quasi-legal regime whose proclaimed standards are deeply compromised by the failure to guarantee their implementation, through lack of control over the implementation process. We do not have to accept a fully Hobbesian world-view to see the force of the proposition that 'covenants without the sword' are ineffective. This is not merely a matter of a supranational enforcement mechanism (UN police force or whatever), but of institutions at the international level which could modify the systematic global inequalities that lie at the root of much human rights abuse. In this regard the aims of cosmopolitanism have to be more ambitious than anything realized to date.

As to the democratic criterion, the aspects of the human rights regime that are clearly universalist – standard setting and monitoring – have good claim to be also democratic in both content and procedure, how-ever far short they may fall of a thorough democratization of the inter-national sphere. As to *content*, the agenda of the human rights covenants taken together provides much of what is required for the foundation of a global democratic citizenship. If we compare this agenda with the list of democratic rights proposed in David Held's *Democracy and the Global Order*, we will find a considerable degree of overlap between them.[32] Such difference as there is is largely one of status. For David Held these have a conditional status for those who *choose* democracy, whereas the list of human rights represents both a claim to universality and an actual commitment by the vast majority of states which have signed up for them.

In terms of *procedure*, the arrangements for human rights standard setting and monitoring (if not enforcement) now have clear democratic components, once one accepts that, historically, later signatories have had to accept covenants whose content has been determined by others.[33] There may be no direct electoral authorization or accountability. Yet there is evident representativeness, both in the UN assembly itself and in the committees of experts, which are carefully balanced between regions and types of country. And the procedures are open to public inspection and to NGO influence in both standard setting and monitoring. We may question the internal representativeness of human rights NGOs, but the same point could be made about the associations of civil society at the national level. If we use Habermasian criteria of deliberative democracy – the absence of exclusion or power distortion – then the international procedures for human rights standard setting and monitoring, if not enforcement, must be judged relatively democratic.

What, finally, are the prospects that these cosmopolitan and democratic features of human rights procedure in the field of standard setting and monitoring might be extended to the much more contested arena of enforcement? Here the task is not so much to define a programme of action or sketch out an institutional end product as to identify the elements at work in the human rights regime which have provided its developmental impetus to date, and which might plausibly continue to do so in the future.

What are we looking for here? If we consider the EU as the most successful example to date of a dynamic process for the development of cosmopolitan democracy, for all its limitations, we can identify a number of elements that have contributed.[34] There is the existence of an independent supranational body alongside the intergovernmental ones. There are political elites in most countries committed to a European ideal, with just enough popular support to give them legitimacy. There are the 'spillover effects', whereby developing a common regime in one area of policy proves unstable unless it is extended to others. Then the assumption of new powers in turn exposes a 'democratic deficit', which provokes demands for greater accountability.[35]

There is nothing to say that these elements will have the same dynamic force elsewhere. As other attempts at regional economic integration have shown, it may well require relatively equal levels of development to provide a sufficient base for common interests to begin with. Yet it is at least possible to identify some of the same elements at work in the human rights regime. At the level of institutions, a strong supranational element has been institutionalized alongside the intergovernmental ones. Although there is currently a worrying dearth of political leadership at the highest level committed to any international ideal, there is a strong cosmopolitan elite in both the formal and informal sectors committed to the greater effectiveness of the human rights regime. A distinctive feature of this elite is its ability to forge links with popular struggles at the most local level anywhere in the world. It is often explicitly in the language of human rights that such struggles are conducted and legitimated. In the political sphere this language is more potent than that of democracy; in the economic sphere it has largely replaced the language of socialism. So there exists some plausible account of social and political agency, even if it may be a fluctuating one.

Finally, there is the contradiction within the human rights regime between the principles to which states are explicitly committed and the all too evident failures of implementation. A pessimistic response to these failures is to say 'I told you so.' An optimistic one is to see these very failures as themselves providing the dynamic to extend and consolidate the human rights regime. Since 1945 this extension and consolidation has been gradual and cumulative, if often unremarked. The human rights failures, by contrast, have been sudden and shocking.[36] What is also remarkable, however, is the way in which human rights campaigners pick themselves up after each setback, and try to devise ways to strengthen the human rights regime against future repetition. There is no ground for thinking that this dynamic process will not continue.

NOTES

1   For the texts of the two international covenants see I. Brownlie (ed.), *Basic Documents on Human Rights*, 3rd edn (Oxford: Oxford University Press, 1992), pp. 114–43.
2   For a classic criticism of economic and social rights as human rights see M. Cranston, 'Human rights, real and supposed', in D. D. Raphael (ed.), *Political Theory and the Rights of Man* (London: Macmillan, 1967), pp. 43–52. More recent objections are summarized and answered in P. Alston and G. Quinn, 'The nature and scope of states parties' obligations under the ICESCR', *Human Rights Quarterly*, 9 (1987), pp. 157–229.
3   I have argued this at some length in D. Beetham, 'What future for economic and social rights?' in D. Beetham (ed.), *Politics and Human Rights* (Oxford: Blackwell, 1995), pp. 41–60. See also H. Shue, *Basic Rights* (Princeton: Princeton University Press, 1980); S. M. Okin, 'Liberty and welfare: some issues in human rights theory', in J. R. Pennock and J. W. Chapman (eds), *Human Rights: Nomos XXIII* (New York: New York University Press, 1981), pp. 230–56; R. Plant, 'A defence of welfare rights', in R. Beddard and D. M. Hill (eds), *Economic, Social and Cultural Rights* (Basingstoke: Macmillan, 1992), pp. 22–46.

4 How much of the non-Western objections to the human rights agenda of the West stem from its manifest selectivity, it is hard to judge. Since the end of the Cold War, at least, the 'indivisibility' of the human rights agenda has been constantly emphasized in human rights circles. See e.g. the Vienna Declaration and Programme of Action adopted by the World Conference on Human Rights, 25 June 1993, UN Doc. A/CONF.157/23.

5 The connection is explored in D. Beetham, *Human Rights and Democracy: a Multi-faceted Relationship* (Leeds: University of Leeds Centre for Democratization Studies, 1995).

6 Current disillusionment with representative democracy leads us to forget what a remarkable invention it seemed to its contemporaries, in Paine's view outrivalling even ancient Athens in democracy. T. Paine, *Rights of Man* (Oxford: Oxford University Press, 1995), part 2, ch. 3.

7 Some philosophical defences of human rights are couched in terms of the conditions for human agency, e.g. A. Gewirth, *Human Rights* (Chicago: University of Chicago Press, 1982); others in terms of human needs, e.g. L. Doyal and I. Gough, *A Theory of Human Need* (Basingstoke: Macmillan, 1991); others in terms of fundamental interests, e.g. M. Freeman, 'The philosophical foundations of human rights', *Human Rights Quarterly*, 16 (1994), pp. 491–514; yet others in terms of needs and capacities, e.g. Okin, 'Liberty and welfare'. Of these the last seems to me preferable, though it merits fuller argument than there is space for here.

8 J. Gray, *Enlightenment's Wake* (London: Routledge, 1995), ch. 10, provides a typical example of the genre. For a similar reason, attempts to provide a postmodernist defence of human rights, or even a revised Rawlsian one, give us no good reason for treating the bearers of other cultures equitably, if we can avoid doing so: see, respectively, R. Rorty, 'Human rights, rationality and sentimentality', and J. Rawls, 'The law of peoples', in S. Shute and S. Hurley (eds), *On Human Rights* (New York: Basic Books, 1993), pp. 41–82, 111–34.

9 H. Shue, 'Mediating duties', *Ethics*, 98 (1988), pp. 687–704.

10 Not only is the Nozickian idea of a pre-social right to property, based on self-ownership, problematic in itself; it notoriously fails to offer any practical method for dealing with the forcible appropriation of original holdings; see R. Nozick, *Anarchy, State and Utopia* (Oxford: Blackwell, 1974), ch. 7. Steiner's attempt to solve this, by continuous redistribution of natural resource values internationally, makes the best of a flawed theory; see H. Steiner, *An Essay on Rights* (Oxford: Blackwell, 1994), chs 7 and 8. For a critique of the self-ownership theory see G. A. Cohen, *Self-ownership, Freedom and Equality* (Cambridge: Cambridge University Press, 1995).

11 J. K. Galbraith, *The Culture of Contentment* (London: Sinclair-Stevenson, 1992), ch. 14; W. Hutton, *The State We're In* (London: Cape, 1995), ch. 7; R. Wilkinson, *Unhealthy Societies: the Afflictions of Inequality* (London: Routledge, 1996).

12 This is of course only one aspect of so-called 'globalization'; another is increased economic competition and differentiation. Both need to be kept in view.

13 The relevant texts are in Brownlie, *Basic Documents on Human Rights*.

14 A. Rosas, 'State sovereignty and human rights: towards a global constitutional project', in Beetham, *Politics and Human Rights*, pp. 61–78; R. Falk,

Human Rights and State Sovereignty (New York: Holmes and Meier, 1981);
D. P. Forsythe, *The Internationalization of Human Rights* (Lexington:
Lexington Books, 1991); J. Camilleri and J. Falk, *The End of Sovereignty?*
(Aldershot: Edward Elgar, 1992).

15   P. Alston, 'Out of the abyss: the challenge confronting the new UN Committee on Economic, Social and Cultural Rights', *Human Rights Quarterly*, 9
(1987), pp. 332–81, at p. 353.

16   For an overview of the compliance process see A. H. Robertson and
J. G. Merrills, *Human Rights in the World: an Introduction to the Study
of the International Protection of Human Rights*, 3rd edn (Manchester:
Manchester University Press, 1992).

17   Rosas, 'State sovereignty and human rights', p. 72.

18   See D. Held, *Democracy and the Global Order* (Cambridge: Polity Press,
1995), ch. 4.

19   H. Storey, 'Human rights and the new Europe', in Beetham, *Politics and
Human Rights*, pp. 131–51; A. H. Robertson and J. G. Merrills, *Human
Rights in Europe*, 3rd edn (Manchester: Manchester University Press, 1993).

20   N. Rodley, 'The work of non-governmental organizations in the world-wide
promotion and protection of human rights', *Bulletin of Human Rights*, 90
(1991), pp. 84–93; R. Brett, 'The role and limits of human rights NGOs at
the United Nations', in Beetham, *Politics and Human Rights*, pp. 96–
110.

21   Cf. Brownlie, *Basic Documents on Human Rights*, pp. 115 and 172. For the
role of women's groups in the Vienna World Conference see K. Boyle,
'Stock-taking on human rights: the World Conference on Human Rights,
Vienna 1993', in Beetham, *Politics and Human Rights*, pp. 79–95, esp. pp.
91–2.

22   Brett, 'The role and limits of human rights NGOs at the United Nations', pp.
100–1.

23   D. Garcia-Sayan, 'NGOs and the human rights movement in Latin
America', *Bulletin of Human Rights*, 90 (1991), pp. 31–41; F. Panizza,
'Human rights in the processes of transition and consolidation of democracy in Latin America', in Beetham, *Politics and Human Rights*, pp.
168–88.

24   M. Novak and I. Schwartz, 'Introduction: the contribution of non-
governmental organizations', in M. Novak (ed.), *World Conference on
Human Rights* (Vienna: Manz, 1994), pp. 1–11.

25   Brett, 'The role and limits of human rights NGOs at the United Nations', pp.
101–4.

26   P. Willetts (ed.), *Pressure Groups in the Global System* (London: Pinter,
1982); M. Shaw, 'Global society and global responsibility: the emergence of
global civil society', *Millennium*, 21 (1992), pp. 421–34.

27   See, e.g. P. Schmitter, *Some Propositions about Civil Society and the
Consolidation of Democracy* (Vienna: Institute for Advanced Studies,
1993), p. 11: civil society's 'emergence requires explicit policies by public
authorities'.

28   R. J. Vincent, *Human Rights and International Relations* (Cambridge:
Cambridge University Press, 1986), esp. ch. 8; D. P. Forsythe (ed.), *Human
Rights in World Politics* (Lincoln: University of Nebraska Press, 1989).

29 For an assessment of the competing elements in US foreign policy see D. P. Forsythe, 'Human rights and US foreign policy: two levels, two worlds', in Beetham, *Politics and Human Rights*, pp. 111–30.

30 For a recent survey of economic inequalities at the global level, and their reproduction within countries, see UNDP, *Human Development Report 1996* (Oxford: Oxford University Press, 1996). These inequalities are of course also reflected in the structure and policy of the international financial institutions (IFIs). For the argument that wars are now largely conducted within states, rather than between them, see Mary Kaldor, chapter 5 below. For the reproduction of inequalities between cultures, see especially the work of Edward Said.

31 The human rights agenda, it should be emphasized, would not bring the end of inequality, merely its marginal modification, albeit one that would make an enormous difference to the lives of those now subject to human rights denials. From the standpoint of a theory of justice, whether national or international, its demands are very modest.

32 Held, *Democracy and the Global Order*, pp. 190–4.

33 I am indebted to Richard Falk for this important qualification.

34 For a fuller discussion of the EU in this context see Ulrich Preuss, chapter 7 below.

35 The 'neofunctionalist' undertone of this account is contestable, though it would take more space than is available here to defend it in the context of the enormous literature on European integration. For recent surveys see J. A. Caporaso, 'The European Union and forms of state: Westphalian, regulatory or post-modern?', *Journal of Common Market Studies*, 34 (1996), pp. 29–52; S. Hix, 'The study of the European Community: the challenge to comparative politics', *West European Politics*, 17 (1994), pp. 1–30; T. Risse-Kappen, 'Exploring the nature of the beast: international relations theory and comparative policy analysis meet the European Union', *Journal of Common Market Studies*, 34 (1996), pp. 53–80; J. H. H. Weiler, U. H. Haltern and F. C. Mayer, 'European democracy and its critique', *West European Politics*, 18 (1995), pp. 4–39.

36 For a balanced survey see D. P. Forsythe, 'The UN and human rights at fifty: an incremental but incomplete revolution', *Global Governance*, 1 (1995), pp. 297–318.

4

The Global Democracy Deficit: an Essay in International Law and its Limits

James Crawford and Susan Marks

If international law started as a *jus gentium* or *droit des gens*, by the early nineteenth century it had become a law of and among sovereigns. Shedding ambiguities latent in the idea of a law of nations or peoples, it assumed the character of a distinctively interstate law. Territorial sovereignty, equality of states, non-intervention in domestic affairs and state consent as the basis of international legal obligation were the central doctrines of this period. Each of these doctrines focused on interstate relations. Constitutional issues concerning relations between citizens and government were for the most part set aside, allocated to national law. Thus, for instance, international law attributed to the head of state and head of government full powers to commit the state in respect of treaty rights and duties, irrespective of whether relevant national law actually conferred such powers.[1] Although this could produce incompatible obligations in international and national law, the resulting dilemma was not seen as problematic.

One corollary of these doctrines was that international law maintained an attitude of official indifference with respect to national political organization. It adopted a *de facto* approach to statehood and government, an approach which followed the facts of political power and made few enquiries into how that power was established. A republic was as legitimate in the eyes of international law as a monarchy, a liberal state as legitimate as a theocratic state. Another corollary was that the organization of national affairs was detached from the relative disorganization of international affairs. Efforts to establish the administration of international posts, telegraphs, watercourses, etc., beginning in the late nineteenth and early twentieth centuries, only served to highlight the depth of disorganization in other spheres of transnational interaction.

These two general corollaries are sufficient to indicate how international law seemed to stand with respect to democracy. As regards arrangements within nation-states, international law held itself to be neutral. Any deficits of democracy could not be its concern, for it had no brief for democratic politics in the first place. At the international level, political society was at most embryonic. There could hardly be a democratic deficit at that level, for there was little, so to speak, to have a deficit from.

Things changed, no doubt, after the First World War, and especially after the Second World War. But how much? To what extent has human rights law, among other international legal developments, given normative underpinnings to democratic politics? To what extent has international law come to support the application of democratic ideas not only to national political life but also to international decision-making? In the next section we highlight some areas of doctrine and institutional activity through which international law might be seen to contribute to extending democracy's purchase. In the following section we call attention to certain of the limits of that contribution. In the final section we conclude that, while international law may no longer maintain a posture of neutrality with respect to democracy, especially at the national level, there remain significant resistances to the project of 'cosmopolitan democracy'. These resistances cannot be ignored.

INTERNATIONAL LAW AND DEMOCRACY

Democratic aspirations figured prominently in the preparations for post-1945 international law, for instance in the Atlantic Charter.[2] In the event, however, the *de facto* system proved tenacious. Though concluded in the name of 'We the peoples', the United Nations Charter was signed by representatives of governments, and contained no stipulations as to their legitimacy to speak on behalf of those peoples. Cold War tensions ensured that subsequent documents adopted within the framework of the United Nations likewise largely avoided explicit reference to a democratic criterion of legitimacy. Nonetheless, human rights instruments sponsored by the United Nations and its agencies helped to develop normative standards predicated upon at least some aspects of conventional democratic politics. Regional instruments contributed to this process; some of these, notably those elaborated within the Council of Europe and the Organization of American States, expressly defined their aims in terms of democracy.[3]

The Universal Declaration of Human Rights, adopted in 1948, is generally regarded as the first detailed articulation of democratic standards in an international instrument. Of particular significance in this regard is article 21:

1.   Everyone has the right to take part in the government of his country, directly or through freely chosen representatives.
2.   Everyone has the right of equal access to public service in his country.
3.   The will of the people shall be the basis of the authority of government; that will shall be expressed in periodic and genuine elections which shall be by universal and equal suffrage and shall be held by secret vote or by equivalent free voting procedures.

The Universal Declaration was adopted by a resolution of the United Nations General Assembly,[4] and does not have the formal status of a treaty.[5] The first treaty to include a provision along the lines of article 21 of the Universal Declaration was the First Protocol to the European Convention on Human Rights, adopted within the framework of the Council of Europe in 1952. The European Convention itself, signed in 1950, has a preambular affirmation that human rights and fundamental freedoms are 'best maintained by an effective political democracy'. To this end protection is given to a range of civil and political rights, including freedoms of expression, association and assembly. The First Protocol supplements these rights by providing for the holding of free elections.[6] Article 3 of the First Protocol states: 'The High Contracting Parties undertake to hold free elections at reasonable intervals by secret ballot, under conditions which will ensure the free expression of the people in the choice of the legislature.'

In some respects this initial treaty formulation falls short of article 21 of the Universal Declaration. While article 21 enunciates universally held rights (paras 1 and 2) and principles associated with representative government (para. 3), article 3 of the First Protocol refers weakly to state undertakings with respect to the holding of elections. It was initially uncertain whether these undertakings could be the subject of claims by individuals, on the same footing as, for instance, the guarantee of freedom of expression. However, the European Commission and Court of Human Rights resolved the uncertainty in favour of individual claimants, holding that article 3 indeed entails correlative rights of participation.[7]

Subsequent human rights treaties contain corresponding provisions, with some variations. The International Covenant on Civil and Political Rights incorporates most of the elements of article 21 of the Universal Declaration, in the context of a binding treaty. Article 25 of the Covenant provides:

Every citizen shall have the right and the opportunity, without any of the distinctions mentioned in article 2 and without unreasonable restrictions:
(a) to take part in the conduct of public affairs, directly or through freely chosen representatives;
(b) to vote and to be elected at genuine periodic elections which shall be by universal and equal suffrage and shall be held by secret ballot, guaranteeing the free expression of the will of the electors;
(c) to have access, on general terms of equality, to public service in his country.[8]

The American Convention of Human Rights, adopted within the framework of the Organization of American States, likewise echoes article 21 of the Universal Declaration. Article 23 of the Convention lays down that every citizen shall enjoy the right and opportunity to take part in the conduct of public affairs, to vote and stand for election and to have access to public service posts. Under the American Convention, as under other human rights treaties, certain rights and freedoms may be suspended in times of 'national emergency'. Reflecting the rhetorical emphasis on representative democracy that has been characteristic of the OAS since its establishment, the American Convention is unique in marking out the fundamental character of the right to take part in elections by excluding it from the scope of justified suspension.[9] The relevant treaty for the African region, the African Charter on Human and Peoples' Rights, contains a much more guarded provision with respect to elections. By article 13, the right of citizens to participate in elections is recognized only 'in accordance with the provisions of the law'.[10]

These treaties appear to resist majoritarian approaches to democracy by enjoining respect for the rights of all citizens to participate in public life on the basis of full equality, and more generally by framing democracy in terms of individual rights and freedoms. Nonetheless, case law has illustrated how the provisions can be applied in majoritarian ways. In *Mathieu-Mohin & Clerfayt v Belgium*,[11] for instance, two French-speaking Belgians challenged electoral arrangements in Belgium by reference to the First Protocol to the European Convention. The arrangements operated effectively to exclude representation of French-speaking Belgians in a regional body with extensive legislative powers over a predominantly Dutch-speaking region. French-speakers in the region could vote for French-speaking candidates but, if they did so, they would be represented not in the regional body for their own region but in another regional body for the predominantly French-speaking parts of the country. The European Court of Human Rights dismissed the challenge. It was sufficient, the Court held, that French-speakers had the formal option to vote for French-speaking candidates. It took the view that the arrangements in the region in question did not exceed the 'margin of appreciation', that is to say, the area of discretion which had to be conceded to the Belgian government in deciding how best to defuse intercommunal disputes. Relevant in this regard was that, across the country as a whole, power was shared between the two communities.

In parallel with the elaboration of individual human rights has been the development of the principle of self-determination.[12] This principle became firmly established in international law in the framework of decolonization. The right of colonial peoples to self-government is, however, applied by reference to existing territorial boundaries. The identification of subgroups within a given territory as separate 'peoples' for this purpose has been, and continues to be, discouraged. Accordingly, when non-self-governing and trust territories have become independent states or other self-governing units they have almost invariably done so as single units.[13] Outside the colonial context the principle of self-determination is likewise respectful of pre-existing boundaries. Self-determination is not generally recognized as giving rise to rights of peoples to secede from their state, but rather as according rights to participate in governance. In this non- or post-colonial context, self-determination is thus primarily seen as a right of the peoples of the various states to determine their future through constitutional processes without external interference. Indeed, it adds relatively little to the human rights provisions enunciating democratic standards (reviewed above), in combination with the classical rule of international law prohibiting external interference in the choice of government. The effect of the principle of self-determination is thus not to weaken but instead to *reinforce* state structures against challenge. In this sense self-determination serves pre-eminently to legitimize the state, while indicating certain standards of conduct within national borders.[14]

Also relevant in this context, alongside the human rights provisions mentioned and the principle of self-determination of peoples, is the recognition of rights of distinctive minority groups within states, or of persons belonging to such groups. The need to provide special protection for the rights of permanent minorities received little attention in the human rights law that developed in the aftermath of the Second World War. The experience of minorities regimes in Europe during the interwar period tended to discredit the idea of minority rights. It was assumed that universally applicable individual rights were preferable and sufficient. There was no reference to the distinct position of minorities in any of the human rights instruments mentioned above,[15] with the exception of a cautiously worded provision in the International Covenant on Civil and Political Rights. Article 27 of the International Covenant stipulates: 'In those States in which ethnic, religious or linguistic minorities exist, persons belonging to such minorities shall not be denied the right, in community with the other members of their group, to enjoy their own culture, to profess and practice their own religion, or to use their own language.'[16]

Since 1989, however, the upsurge of interethnic conflict has led to a renewed sense that specific minority protection is needed. In 1992 the

United Nations General Assembly adopted a Declaration on the Rights of Persons Belonging to National, Ethnic, Religious and Linguistic Minorities.[17] Though not legally binding, the Declaration is seen as influential, at least in terms of the future development of international law. Proclaiming that states 'shall protect the existence and national, cultural, religious and linguistic identity of minorities',[18] the Declaration sets forth rights which can be claimed by members of minorities, including the right 'to participate effectively in cultural, religious, social and public life'.[19] In institutional contexts concerned with the European region the impetus to secure protection for minority rights is particularly evident. Within the Council of Europe two treaties addressing minority rights have been elaborated, a European Charter for Regional and Minority Languages[20] and a Framework Convention for the Protection of National Minorities.[21] Opened for signature respectively in 1992 and 1995, neither has yet entered into force. The Conference on Security and Cooperation in Europe (now the Organization for Security and Cooperation in Europe) has adopted a series of instruments affirming distinct minority rights across a range of aspects of collective life.[22] The OSCE has also established the office of High Commissioner for National Minorities to provide 'early warning' and 'early action' with respect to 'tensions involving national minority issues'.[23]

Accompanying these developments with respect to human rights, self-determination and minority rights have been developments with respect to electoral processes. Earlier international involvement in the holding of plebiscites or the conduct of elections was focused either on exceptional situations where boundaries were being redrawn as part of a peace settlement,[24] or on the implementation of the principle of self-determination in the context of colonial territories.[25] But the period since 1989 has seen a growing practice of international election-monitoring and, linked with it, the repeated invocation of the 'principle of periodic and genuine elections'.[26] The United Nations Observer Mission to Verify the Electoral Process in Nicaragua in 1989 was the first occasion when an intergovernmental organization monitored an election in an independent state. Since then the United Nations and other regional organizations (alongside many international non-governmental organizations) have monitored elections in a number of countries and regions.[27] The importance attached to these functions is reflected in their speedy institutionalization. The United Nations, the OAS and the OSCE have each designated a special office to coordinate electoral assistance activities.[28] In some contexts international involvement has included helping to create the conditions for free elections and for the establishment of democratic institutions, as with the United Nations operation in Cambodia in 1991–2.[29]

In the case of Haiti, international assistance extended in 1993–4 to enforcing the results of internationally supervised elections. On the basis that Jean-Bertrand Aristide was the 'legitimately elected president' and that the military government in power constituted an 'illegal *de facto* regime', the United Nations Security Council (acting with the OAS) imposed sanctions against Haiti under chapter VII of the UN Charter.[30] The Security Council even authorized the use of force to reinstate the exiled Aristide,[31] though not without significant misgivings on the part of some governments, and efforts by the Council itself to limit the extent to which a precedent might be set.[32] In the event the military leadership was ousted without force, allowing a peaceful settlement. There have been a number of subsequent cases of United Nations involvement in election monitoring, including the December 1995 presidential election in Haiti itself, which followed the return of Aristide. Decisions to monitor elections are made by United Nations organs on a case-by-case basis.[33] It is significant, for example, that the United Nations chose not to involve itself in monitoring the Bosnian elections in September 1996, a task instead assumed by the OSCE.[34]

In his Agenda for Development, published in 1994, United Nations Secretary-General Boutros Boutros-Ghali wrote that 'democracy is a fundamental human right.'[35] He later described democracy as a 'newly recognized imperative' within the United Nations.[36] Reflecting on the evidence of international law and institutional practice, a number of commentators have similarly concluded that a 'norm of democratic governance' is emerging.[37] This would mean that international law no longer holds to a *de facto* approach to statehood and government. Mere control of the institutions of government by military force would not suffice, as often in the past. More far-reachingly, it could mean that only democratic governments are to be accepted as legitimate. Undemocratic regimes, whatever their duration or degree of effectiveness, would be regarded as having less than the full authority of legitimate governments.

The emergence of democracy as a normative condition, or at least a key criterion for legitimate government, is sometimes seen in terms of a shift in international law away from realist premises and towards a 'liberal internationalist'[38] or 'Kantian'[39] perspective. Such a perspective generally entails a commitment to representative government on the basis that this is conducive to peace among nations. According to other scholars, the assessment that a norm of democratic governance is emerging is too hasty; there is insufficient evidence to warrant the judgement that international law is beginning to control the legitimacy of governments by reference to a democratic standard. Nor is such a development always seen as desirable.[40] The prospect that international law might come to divide the world into a legitimate democratic part and an illegitimate non-democratic part raises for some the spectre of neocolonialism, with its attendant cycle of intervention and resistance. Since the norm of democratic governance would operate by exclusion (restricting the scope of legitimate actors rather than empowering substitutes in their place), it raises difficulties for the postulated universality of international law.

This debate, and the doctrinal and institutional developments which it addresses, account only for a part – the most self-conscious part – of international law's current engagement with democracy. In one sense or another, international law defines democracy's normative status through almost everything it does, and a wide range of norms and procedures could have been brought to bear in this discussion. Nonetheless, the developments briefly surveyed here are sufficient to illustrate key dimensions of international legal efforts with respect to democracy. What then are the prospects for those efforts to be pressed further?

THE LIMITS OF INTERNATIONAL LAW'S CONTRIBUTION

At this point we shift our focus, to examine the background ideas that inform the developments noted in the previous section. Specifically, we discuss three ideas: the idea that the history of democracy's status in international law is a narrative of progress; the idea that democracy is above all a matter of institutions and procedures for validating government; and the idea that democracy has its locus in the arena of national politics.[41] We contend that these ideas serve as significant constraints on international law's contribution to the global deepening of democracy, and we indicate some of the ways in which they do so.

A progress narrative

The first of the three themes surfaces in connection with enquiries into the history of international law's encounter with democracy. In Thomas Franck's influential account,[42] this history is traced in terms of three 'generations' of rule-making and rule implementation.[43] The first, associated at least in modern guise with the Versailles Peace Conference and articulated especially by President Wilson, is the principle of self-determination. The second, a product of the post-Second World War period, is the international protection of human rights, and especially of the freedoms of expression, thought, association and assembly. The third, largely a phenomenon of the post-Cold War era, is the nascent principle of periodic and genuine elections, along with the institutionalization of election monitoring. Franck is among those who argue that, with this principle and its institutional concomitants, a 'norm of democratic governance' has begun to emerge.

Casting the story in terms of 'generations' might suggest that international legal concern with electoral process has superseded international legal concern with the principle of self-determination and human rights.[44]

Of course, Franck does not intend that. Elsewhere he uses the metaphor of 'building blocks'[45] to reinforce the point that self-determination and human rights are indispensable to any 'norm of democratic governance', and must remain in place. Nonetheless, whether viewed as a story about successive generations or as a story about building blocks in a completed (or nearly completed) edifice, this is plainly a narrative of progress. International norms and procedures associated with elections are presented as the highest stage of moves in the direction of normativizing 'democratic governance'.

A preoccupation with elections is, indeed, a striking feature of international legal discussions of democracy. To raise the question of democracy in international law is largely to raise the question whether international law requires states to hold periodic and genuine elections. This in turn prompts further questions. What is required by way of periodicity? In what circumstances can an election be counted as 'genuine'? Who should have the right to vote and stand for election? Do governments have the right to intervene in other countries to help install elected governments and oust unelected or unfairly elected ones?[46] These are the issues most often associated with the question of democracy's status in international law.

Moreover, while few would seek to argue that competitive national elections are sufficient conditions for modern democracy, international lawyers frequently adopt a defensive posture in this regard. Statements of the type 'elections . . . must not end the push to a democratic society, but they are an essential first step' abound in international legal literature.[47] 'Elections', it is observed, 'are something that international institutions can be very good at monitoring and evaluating. It is much more difficult to stay in a country after elections, for the long haul, to monitor all institutions of government and attempt to secure the key elements of democracy.'[48] On the one hand, international lawyers well recognize that elections are 'underdeterminative of democracy'.[49] They appreciate that, though substantive values commonly find their legal articulation in terms of procedure, 'monitoring and evaluating' do not mark the limits of international law's ambitions. On the other hand, it is hard to avoid the conclusion that electoral processes are accorded special, even overriding, importance in these accounts. One idea which informs international law's efforts with respect to democracy is, then, the notion that international law normatively arrived at, or very close to, democracy when it began to develop principles and institutional mechanisms associated with the holding of national elections.

A liberal conception

If democracy is associated with periodic elections, it is not wholly identified with them. As Franck's history suggests, human rights also form part of international legal understandings of democracy. The following definition of 'representative democracy' by the Inter-American Commission of Human Rights is typical in this respect:

The concept of representative democracy is rooted in the principle that political sovereignty is vested in the people which, in the exercise of that sovereignty, elects its representatives to exercise political power. Besides, these representatives are elected by the citizenry to carry out specific policies, which in turn implies that the nature of the policies to be implemented has already been extensively discussed (freedom of expression) among organized political groups (freedom of association) that have been able to express themselves and meet publicly (right of assembly). This all obviously presupposes that all the other basic rights – to life, humane treatment and personal liberty, residence and movement, and so on – have been guaranteed. The effective enjoyment of these rights and freedoms requires a legal and institutional order in which the law takes precedence over the will of the rulers and some institutions have control over others in order to preserve the integrity of the popular will (the constitutional state).[50]

The Inter-American Commission points here to three elements which, in addition to the periodic recall of representatives, are commonly highlighted in international legal accounts of democracy's entailments: human rights, especially freedoms of expression, association and assembly, but also the whole range of other civil rights and freedoms; the rule of law, understood to refer not just to a state in which public authorities are obliged to act within the law, but also to a state in which citizens' rights are legally underwritten (so that, for instance, legal remedies for abuse of rights are available); and the separation of public powers, involving above all an independent judiciary.

Probing further into relevant international legal sources, these elements can be seen to rest on assumptions about democracy that (expressed in summary form) include the following propositions. First, democracy concerns the selection of governments. Once selected, governments assume the conduct of public affairs. Citizens cannot claim any right to be consulted even with respect to public decisions directly affecting them.[51] Second, democracy's primary domain is national. Thus, for instance, the partial devolution of power to regional and local levels is no necessary part of democracy, but falls within the central government's 'margin of appreciation'.[52] Third, democratic government is legitimized procedurally, through competitive elections. Legitimacy is, accordingly, an event, an original act, as distinct from a process by which power must continuously justify itself and account to civil society.[53] Fourth, democracy is a technical or instrumental issue, rather than a matter of social self-definition. While there is no single blueprint, nonetheless experts can give advice and monitor progress by reference to standard requisites.[54]

What has been sketched bears the hallmarks of a familiar account of liberal democracy. But it stands at some distance from approaches to democracy that call for the expansion of avenues by which citizens might actively participate in decision-making affecting them. It stands apart too from theories that seek the reinvigoration of a public sphere, or attach importance to a vigilant civil society. It remains largely aloof from claims that democracy must infuse the private realm of workplace, family and personal relations. And it wholly fails to consider whether the responsiveness of political authorities and the capacity of citizens to choose among options may be compromised under late capitalist conditions. In so far as the conception of democracy outlined in the foregoing paragraphs is a predicate of international legal efforts with respect to democracy, that conception is open to a wide range of challenges. On the one hand, it is open to normative challenges, judging it inadequate for orienting change towards a substantial and vigorous democratic life. On the other hand, it is open to 'realist' challenges, putting in question the extent to which it grasps actual conditions prevailing in democratic countries.

A state-centric focus

In calling attention to a third idea that informs international legal efforts with respect to democracy, we return to the proposition that the primary domain of democracy is national. Not only does this bear on democracy's significance for local and other subnational decision-making. It also bears on democracy's significance for transnational and global decision-making. David Held and others have shown how in the second half of the twentieth century intensified global interconnections have undercut many of the traditional assumptions on which democratic theory has been based.[55] The notion of the 'national community of fate' that both rules itself and should be answerable solely to itself has come under severe strain. The supposition that a symmetry holds between the governed and their elected representatives cannot account for the extent to which today people are affected by decisions taken by the governments of other countries, by international and regional organizations, and by private economic actors. Held concludes that democracy must be rethought in order to address this expanding framework of political activity. His project of 'cosmopolitan democracy' has as its objective the infusion of democratic standards wherever power resides. This includes the deepening of democracy within nation-states. But it also involves the extension of democracy to the arenas of global and transnational decision-making.

International law, with its enlarging normative scope, extending writ and growing institutionalization, exemplifies the phenomenon of globalization. Yet it has left the implications of globalization for democratic theory and practice largely unaddressed. Democracy has remained for international law an idea about the government of nation-states, with little relevance for other sites of political authority, including international ones. That said, the vastly enhanced participation in recent years of non-governmental organizations at the international level is one indication of the pressures and possibilities for democracy in global decision-making. With a view to harnessing these pressures and actualizing these possibilities, various proposals have been put forward by international legal scholars sharing Held's belief that democratic ideas are as pertinent to international and other decision-making as they are to national decision-making. Some of these proposals focus on reform of international law. Philip Allott, for instance, gives detailed consideration to how international law might be 'reconceived as a system of public law', oriented to the principle that all social power is accountable (including that which is wielded internationally).[56] Other proposals focus on reform of international political processes and institutions. Thus Richard Falk, while noting the difficulty of articulating concretely how democracy might be extended to geopolitical and market arenas, attaches great importance to the role of transnational networks of grassroots organizations as constituents of a global civil society.[57] Thomas Franck, reflecting on how decision-making in international forums might be made more 'fair', expresses support for the widely mooted idea of a second chamber – 'a forum in which people rather than governments are represented' – that might sit alongside the United Nations General Assembly.[58]

Held for his part puts forward both proposals aiming at reform of international law and proposals aiming at reform of international political processes.[59] Included in the first category are recommendations that the International Court of Justice be given compulsory jurisdiction; that United Nations General Assembly resolutions count to a greater extent than currently as sources of international law; and that the enforcement of human rights and humanitarian law be improved, perhaps through the establishment of a new international human rights court, along with a specialized international criminal court. We offer a few observations on these points.

We doubt whether making the jurisdiction of the International Court of Justice compulsory would assist greatly in realizing global democracy, whatever other advantages might flow from such a change (and leaving aside also the question of its political feasibility). The Court functions largely as a bilateral dispute settlement facility for governments. Even if every government were obliged to submit its disputes with another government to the Court, this would not necessarily mean that the Court was fulfilling the democratic, public-law role of enforcing law and safeguarding the rights of those affected by state action, for individual citizens and groups of citizens would be unable to initiate proceedings. In order for the Court to contribute significantly to global democracy, individuals and non-state groups would need to be given standing. This development would, in turn, require an exponential expansion in the size and facilities of the Court. It may be questioned whether such a far-reaching transformation of the Court's character is an appropriate goal. A more sensible, and certainly a more realistic, option might be to concentrate on enhancing the effectiveness of those forums, most notably the existing human rights courts and commissions, which already offer some measure of protection and redress to individuals and groups.

A further crucial step in enabling the Court to operate as a democratic institution would be the conferral of standing on international organizations.[60] This would help also in breaking down the bilateralism which currently serves as a severe restriction on the Court's ability to take into account the interests of all those affected by its decisions.[61] Furthermore, the Court would need to have clear jurisdiction judicially to review action of all United Nations political agencies, including the Security Council.[62] Only then could the rule of law be said to extend to international political life.

The extent to which resolutions of the United Nations General Assembly are accepted as sources of international law has been expanded in recent years. The decision in *Military and Paramilitary Activities in and against Nicaragua*[63] was perhaps the high-water mark of such acceptance in the case law of the International Court of Justice. This might be seen as a step towards the democratization of international law, given that almost all states are represented – and represented on a formally equal basis – in the General Assembly. On the other hand, it must be recalled that the General Assembly acts as an executive and not a legislative organ. Were it to become a legislative organ, the one-state-one-vote rule would – as Held and others recognize – scarcely be democratic, given asymmetries of participation in national politics, quite apart from other factors. To be sure, some General Assembly resolutions, especially in the field of human rights, are intended to take effect as 'soft law'. These resolutions are often elaborated on the initiative, and/or with the active involvement, of affected non-state groups, a practice which may enhance their democratic credentials.[64]

Buttressing the enforcement of humanitarian law and human rights guarantees would contribute positively to cosmopolitan democracy, especially if the enforcement efforts were directed not just to civil and political rights, but also to economic, social and cultural rights. The establishment of an international criminal court is currently under serious consideration within the United Nations.[65] There remain disagreements about the scope of the jurisdiction of such a court, and in particular about the extent to which it should be subject to control by the Security Council. In the sphere of human rights, two established regional human rights courts already exist: the European Court of Human Rights and the Inter-American Court of Human Rights. The Ninth Protocol to the European Convention on Human Rights (adopted on 6 November

1990)[66] gives individual applicants the right to refer cases to the Court. The Eleventh Protocol (adopted on 11 May 1994),[67] when it enters into force, will make compulsory the Court's competence to deal with individual complaints. Together these protocols mark a significant shift towards the rule of law in that regional context. At the global level the Human Rights Committee, set up under the International Covenant on Civil and Political Rights, lacks power to take binding decisions. Its jurisdiction is, moreover, far from universally accepted, despite a significant increase in participation since 1989.

CONCLUDING OBSERVATIONS

At the end of the twentieth century, each of the two corollaries of international law's establishment as an interstate law, recalled at the outset of this chapter, is open to reconsideration. The gap between national organization and international disorganization has markedly narrowed as considerable areas of action and interaction have been brought under international governance. At the same time, there is evidence that international law's *de facto* approach to sovereignty may be beginning to give way to a commitment in favour of democratic government. On the other hand, in so far as it has such a commitment, international law operates – we have noted – with a set of ideas about democracy that offers little support for efforts either to deepen democracy within nation-states or to extend democracy to transnational and global decision-making. Periodic elections, civil and political rights and the validation of national governments are the key themes. International law's enmeshment in globalizing processes, linking global, national and local settings, has been accompanied by only limited steps to pursue the implications of those processes for democracy. In calling attention to these matters, we have sought to sound a note of caution with respect to international law's role in the project of cosmopolitan democracy. Much more remains to be done if international law is to serve as a constitutional law of democratic societies, let alone of a global democratic society.

NOTES

1 For a modern statement of this rule, see Vienna Convention on the Law of Treaties 1969, arts 7(2)(a) and 27. The Vienna Convention (art. 46) creates an exception where there is a 'manifest' violation of a constitutional rule 'of fundamental importance' relating to the conclusion of treaties. So far as the authors are aware, however, this has never been applied to invalidate a treaty.

2   See Atlantic Charter, 14 Aug. 1941 ('the right of all peoples to choose the form of government under which they will live'), as endorsed by United Nations Declaration, Washington, adopted 1 Jan. 1942.

3   The account that follows draws from James Crawford, 'Democracy in international law', *British Yearbook of International Law*, 64 (1993), p. 113. See further Christina Cerna, 'Universal democracy: an international legal right or the pipe dream of the West?', *New York University Journal of International Law and Politics*, 27 (1995), p. 289; *Democracy and Human Rights, Proceedings of a Colloquy organised by the Government of Greece and the Council of Europe, Sept. 1987* (Kehl am Rhein: NP Engel, 1990); Gregory Fox and Georg Nolte, 'Intolerant democracies', *Harvard International Law Journal*, 36 (1995), p. 1; Thomas Franck, 'The emerging right to democratic governance', *American Journal of International Law*, 86 (1992), p. 46; Thomas Franck, 'Democracy as a human right', in Louis Henkin and J. Lawrence Hargrove (eds), *Human Rights: an Agenda for the Next Century* (Washington D.C.: American Society of International Law, 1994), p. 73; Karl Klare, 'Legal theory and democratic reconstruction', *University of British Columbia Law Review*, 25 (1991), p. 69; Susan Marks, 'The European Convention on Human Rights and its "democratic society"', *British Yearbook of International Law*, 66 (1995), p. 209; Panel, 'National sovereignty revisited: perspectives on the emerging norm of democracy in international law', *Proceedings of the American Society of International Law*, 86 (1992), p. 249; Allan Rosas, 'Democracy and human rights', in Allan Rosas and Jan Helgesen (eds), *Human Rights in a Changing East-West Perspective* (London and New York: Pinter, 1990), p. 17; Anne-Marie Slaughter (Burley), 'Towards an age of liberal nations', *Harvard International Law Journal*, 33 (1992), p. 393; Henry Steiner, 'Political participation as a human right', *Harvard Human Rights Yearbook* (1988), p. 77.

4   UN GA Res. 217A (III), adopted 10 Dec. 1948.

5   The Declaration has, nonetheless, been enormously influential with respect to international law and, for some commentators, must now be reckoned to express legal rights and duties. For the view that art. 21 of the Universal Declaration reflects general international law see Michael Reisman, 'Sovereignty and human rights in contemporary international law', *American Journal of International Law*, 84 (1990), p. 867.

6   One reason why provisions regarding free elections proved too controversial to be included in the Convention, and had to be left for the First Protocol, was that representatives of colonial powers were concerned about the potential for applying the provisions in non-self-governing territories. There were also concerns that provisions guaranteeing free elections might put into question established electoral arrangements in particular countries. See further Marks, 'The European Convention on Human Rights and its "democratic society"'.

7   See *Application 2728/66, X v Germany, Yearbook of the European Convention on Human Rights*, 10 (1967), p. 338; *Mathieu-Mohin & Clerfayt v Belgium*, Publications of the European Court of Human Rights, series A, no. 113.

8   For an elaboration of this which takes account of cases considered by the Human Rights Committee, see Human Rights Committee, General Comment no. 25(57), UN Doc. A/51/40 (1996).

9   See American Convention on Human Rights, art. 27. Cf. European Convention on Human Rights, art. 15, and International Covenant on Civil and Political Rights, art. 4.

10 Left somewhat ambiguous is whether the qualifying phrase 'in accordance with the provisions of the law' applies to the right to participate itself or only to the method of choice of representatives.

11 Publications of the European Court of Human Rights, series A, no. 113.

12 See James Crawford (ed.), *The Rights of Peoples* (Oxford: Clarendon Press, 1988) for a review.

13 Cf. *Case concerning the Frontier Dispute (Burkina Faso/Mali)*, International Court of Justice Reports, 1986, pp. 565–7 (paras 22, 25).

14 On non-colonial self-determination see, e.g., Antonio Cassese, *Self-Determination of Peoples* (Cambridge: Grotius, 1995); Jorri Duursma, *Fragmentation and the International Relations of Microstates: Self-Determination and Statehood* (Cambridge: Cambridge University Press, 1996).

15 The African Charter on Human and Peoples' Rights does, however, make provision for certain rights of 'peoples'. It is not clear whether these might be applied to minorities.

16 For an elaboration of this which takes account of cases considered by the Human Rights Committee, see Human Rights Committee, General Comment no. 23(50), UN Doc. CCPR/C/Rev.1/Add.5 (1994).

17 UN GA Res. 47/135, adopted 18 Dec. 1992, reprinted in *Human Rights Law Journal*, 14 (1993), p. 54.

18 Art. 1.

19 Art. 2, para. 2. Where political participation is concerned, this is subject to the significant proviso that the right of members of minorities to participate effectively in decisions affecting them, whether on the national or regional level, applies only 'in a manner not incompatible with national legislation'. See art. 2, para. 3.

20 *Human Rights Law Journal*, 14 (1993), p. 148.

21 *International Legal Materials*, 34 (1995), p. 351.

22 See CSCE, Copenhagen Document on the Human Dimension, adopted 29 June 1990, part IV, reprinted in *International Legal Materials*, 29 (1990), p. 1305.

23 On the earlier experience see, e.g., Sarah Wambaugh, *Plebiscites since the World War* (Washington, D.C.: Carnegie Foundation, 1933).

24 See James Crawford, *The Creation of States in International Law* (Oxford: Clarendon Press, 1979), pp. 367–75.

25 See CSCE, Declaration and Decisions from Helsinki Summit, adopted 10 July 1992, part I, para. 23, and part II, reprinted in *International Legal Materials*, 31 (1992), p. 1385.

26 The principle was first referred to by the General Assembly in 1988. See GA Res. 43/157, adopted 8 Dec. 1988.

27 See further Michael Reisman, 'International election observation', *Pace University School of Law Yearbook of International Law*, 4 (1992), p. 1; David Stoelting, 'The challenge of UN-monitored elections in independent nations', *Stanford Journal of International Law*, 28 (1992), p. 371.

28 The United Nations established an Electoral Assistance Unit in 1991: see UN GA Res. 46/137, adopted 17 Dec. 1991; for an overview of UN election-

monitoring activities, see also Report of the Secretary-General, UN Doc. A/47/668 (1992). The OAS established a Unit for the Promotion of Democracy in 1990: see OAS GA Res. 1063, adopted 6 June 1990. And the CSCE established an Office of Free Elections (later renamed the OSCE Office for Democratic Institutions and Human Rights) in 1990: see Supplementary Document to give effect to certain provisions contained in the Charter of Paris for a New Europe, adopted 21 Nov. 1990, part G, reprinted in *International Legal Materials*, 30 (1991), p. 209.

29   See Paris Conference on Cambodia, Agreements elaborating the framework for a comprehensive political settlement of the Cambodia conflict, concluded 23 Oct. 1991, reprinted in *International Legal Materials*, 31 (1992), p. 174.

30   See UN SC Res. 841 (1993).

31   See UN SC Res. 917 (1994); SC Res. 940 (1994); SC Res. 944 (1994); SC Res. 948 (1994).

32   See, e.g., the insistence on 'the unique character of the present situation in Haiti and its deteriorating, complex and extraordinary nature, requiring an exceptional response' in SC Res. 940 (1994), para. 2.

33   Concerning the criteria applied by the United Nations in deciding whether to provide electoral assistance, see Report of the Secretary-General on Enhancing the Effectiveness of the Principle of Periodic and Genuine Elections, UN Doc. A/47/668 (1992), esp. paras 53–63. See also Guidelines for Member States Considering the Formulation of Requests for Electoral Assistance, UN Doc. A/47/668/Add.1 (1992).

34   For the elections see *Keesing's Record of World Events* (1996), p. 41278.

35   UN Doc. A/48/935 (1994), para. 120.

36   Boutros Boutros-Ghali, 'Democracy: a newly recognized imperative', *Global Governance*, 1 (1995), p. 3.

37   See, e.g., Franck, 'The emerging right to democratic governance', p. 46.

38   See, e.g., Anne-Marie Slaughter (Burley), 'International law and international relations: a dual agenda', *American Journal of International Law*, 87 (1993), p. 205.

39   See Fernando Tesón, 'The Kantian theory of international law', *Columbia Law Review*, 92 (1992), p. 53.

40   See, e.g., Thomas Carothers, 'Empirical perspectives on the emerging norm of democracy in international law', *Proceedings of the American Society of International Law*, 86 (1992), p. 261.

41   This section draws from Susan Marks, 'The riddle of all constitutions: a study of democratic ideas in international law', PhD dissertation, University of Cambridge, 1996. For discussion of the issues raised here in relation specifically to the European Convention on Human Rights, see also Marks, 'The European Convention on Human Rights and its "democratic society"'.

42   Franck, 'The emerging right to democratic governance'. This article in revised form appears as chapter 4 of Thomas Franck, *Fairness in International Law and Institutions* (Oxford: Clarendon Press, 1995).

43   Franck, 'The emerging right to democratic governance', p. 52.

44   A parallel debate was sparked, in the context of international human rights law, by the identification of 'peoples' rights' with a third 'generation' of human rights. See Philip Alston, 'A third generation of solidarity rights:

progressive development of obfuscation of human rights law?', *Netherlands International Law Review*, 29 (1982), p. 307.

45 Franck, 'The emerging right to democratic governance', see, e.g., p. 52.

46 On these and other related questions, see Guy Goodwin-Gill, *Free and Fair Elections: International Law and Practice* (Geneva: Inter-Parliamentary Union, 1994).

47 Comments by Gregory Fox, in panel discussion, see Panel, 'National sovereignty revisited', p. 271.

48 Ibid., p. 270.

49 Carothers, 'Empirical perspectives', p. 264.

50 Inter-American Commission on Human Rights, Report on Haiti, 1990. An almost identical formulation appears in *Cases 9768, 9780 and 9828 v Mexico, Inter-American Yearbook of Human Rights* (1990), pp. 74, 90 (paras 41–2).

51 See, e.g., *Grand Chief Donald Marshall v Canada*, Views of the Human Rights Committee adopted 4 Nov. 1991, UN Doc. A/47/40 (1992), p. 213. The applicant complained of the exclusion of the Mikmaq tribal people (of whom he was Grand Chief) from certain constitutional deliberations affecting them in Canada; he argued that this violated art. 25 of the International Covenant on Civil and Political Rights. The Committee dismissed the claim on the basis that 'it is for the legal and constitutional system of the State party to provide for the modalities of . . . participation [in public affairs]' (para. 5.4).

52 See, e.g., *Edwards v UK*, Application 11377/85, European Commission of Human Rights, *European Human Rights Reports*, 8, p. 96. The applicant complained of the disbanding of, and cancellation of elections to, the Greater London Council in 1985, claiming that this violated the UK's obligations with respect to the 'choice of the legislature' under the First Protocol to the European Convention on Human Rights, art. 3. The claim failed on the ground that the GLC did not form part of the UK 'legislature'. For the Commission a body only counts as the 'legislature' if the central government opts to delegate 'primary rule-making power' to it. The European Court of Human Rights later emphasized in *Mathieu-Mohin & Clerfayt v Belgium* that the government is to be accorded a 'wide margin of appreciation' with respect to the distribution of political power.

53 See, e.g., *Cases 9768, 9780 and 9828 v Mexico*, p. 74. Members of an opposition party in Mexico complained that fraud and other irregularities in the conduct of elections violated their right under the American Convention of Human Rights to seek election in genuine elections. The Inter-American Commission characterized 'representative democracy' in terms of a 'method for naming public officials through elections' (para. 45).

54 See, e.g., 'Counselling democracy: the Centre for Human Rights and Electoral Assistance', *UN Human Rights Newsletter*, 5.1 (Apr.–July 1992), p. 11. This document discusses the activities of the UN Centre for Human Rights in relation to the 'counselling' of 'democracy'.

55 See esp., in addition to David Held, chapter 1 above, David Held, *Democracy and the Global Order* (Cambridge: Polity Press, 1995).

56 See Philip Allott, *Eunomia* (Oxford: Oxford University Press, 1990). For a

summary of Allott's proposals in this regard, see Philip Allott, 'New international law: the first lecture of academic year 20–' in Philip Allott et al., *Theory and International Law: an Introduction* (London: British Institute of International and Comparative Law, 1991), p. 105, esp. pp. 111ff.

57 See esp., in addition to Richard Falk, chapter 15 below, Richard Falk, *On Humane Governance* (Cambridge: Polity Press, 1995).

58 Franck, *Fairness in International Law and Institutions* pp. 483ff.

59 Held, *Democracy and the Global Order*, ch. 12.

60 As proposed by a study group of the British Institute of International and Comparative Law: Derek Bowett, James Crawford, Ian Sinclair and Arthur Watts, 'The International Court of Justice: efficiency of procedures and working methods', *International and Comparative Law Quarterly Supp.*, 45 (1996), pp. 24–5. See also Ignaz Seidl-Hohenveldern, 'Access of international organizations to the International Court of Justice', in A. S. Muller et al. (eds), *The International Court of Justice* (The Hague: Kluwer, 1997), p. 189.

61 The difficulties of the Court in handling disputes which go beyond the strictly bilateral context and involve third states and the United Nations may be seen from the *East Timor Case*, International Court of Justice Reports (1995), p. 90.

62 The competence of the International Court of Justice to review United Nations Security Council resolutions remains uncertain. See *Aerial Incident at Lockerbie Case (Provisional Measures)* (Libya v US and UK), International Court of Justice Reports (1992), p. 3.

63 International Court of Justice Reports (1986), p. 14.

64 Indigenous groups, for instance, have actively participated in the drafting of a proposed UN Declaration on the Rights of Indigenous Peoples, see *International Legal Materials*, 34 (1995), p. 535.

65 Based on the Draft Statute proposed by the International Law Commission, see *Yearbook of the International Law Commission*, 2, part 2 (1994), ch. 2.

66 *International Legal Materials*, 30 (1991), p. 693.

67 *International Legal Materials*, 33 (1994), p. 743.

5

Reconceptualizing Organized Violence

Mary Kaldor

The aim of this book is to 'recast' democratic theory to take account of the erosion of the autonomy of the nation-state.[1] The fundamental precondition for democracy as it evolved within the nation-state was a consensus about non-violence. That consensus was, however, confined to a historically discrete time and space. Almost every classical liberal thinker of the eighteenth and nineteenth centuries – for example, Jeremy Bentham, John Stuart Mill, Thomas Paine, the Abbé de Saint-Pierre as popularized by Rousseau, and, above all, Immanuel Kant – developed schemes for 'perpetual peace'.[2] Their preoccupation was how to extend this consensus about non-violence spatially and temporally.

In this chapter, I want to argue that any scheme for 'transnational democracy' has to take account of fundamental changes in patterns of organized violence that are associated with the erosion of the autonomy of the nation-state and, in particular, the loss of territorial control over the use of violence. Classic distinctions between 'war' and 'peace', 'internal' and 'external', 'public' and 'private', 'civil society' and 'barbarism', which are associated with the autonomy of the nation-state, seem to be breaking down. An important part of the challenge of recasting democratic theory is the problem of how to reconceptualize these terms. The implication of the argument is that a consensus about non-violence can no longer be confined in spatial terms. Hence, the reconstruction of democracy in either national or transnational terms requires a spatial extension of the consensus about non-violence, that is, perpetual peace.

The first part of the chapter presents a stylized account of conceptualizations of organized violence that derive from a nation-state centred view of the world. The second part analyses changing patterns of organized violence and the implications for ways of perceiving these issues. The last part offers some preliminary suggestions for reconceptualization.

WAR, PEACE AND THE NATION-STATE

In medieval Europe, sovereignty was typically dispersed and fragmented. Political entities ranged from city-states to principalities to kingdoms, often with overlapping political loyalties; papal authority overrode the authority of kings primarily but not only in what were considered to be spiritual matters. The rise of modern states involved a centralization and secularization of power within a given territory, together with absolutist notions of sovereignty.

The key feature of the modern state, to paraphrase Max Weber, was the monopolization of legitimate organized violence within a given territory. The rise of the modern state was intimately linked on the one hand to the growth of war-making capacities, and on the other hand to the establishment of what might be described as a domestic zone of peace.[3] The ability of monarchs to protect territory externally gave legitimacy to new forms of revenue-raising, especially taxation, as well as the growth of state activity which helped to extend the rule of law. Michael Mann has shown that in the case of England military expenditures were the main component of state expenditures up to the nineteenth century and that taxation was increased and regularized, as was state borrowing, during times of war.[4]

During the period of absolutism in Europe, roughly between the seventeenth and nineteenth centuries, private armies were gradually eliminated and professional armies were developed. In earlier periods, monarchs raised coalitions of armies from among feudal lords rather as today the UN has to raise coalitions of peace-keeping forces from member nations. The ability of monarchs to raise armies and to generate finance for wars depended on the extent to which they were perceived as representing some sense of national identity. Gradually, private armies were eliminated through a combination of factors: the superior power of the monarch's forces, the effectiveness of mercenaries, and the break-up of feudal ties.

Initially, kings employed mercenaries to replace feudal armies. However, this gave rise to considerable problems during periods of demobilization. This problem was solved by the establishment of permanent navies and armies, which in turn were linked to such military innovations as training, drill, exercises, staff colleges and so on, and the emergence of what might be described as a modern military culture. John Keegan, in particular, emphasizes the significance of the regimental system in the eighteenth century as the cornerstone of the modern army, the 'device for securing the control of armed force by the state'.[5] The soldier became the legitimate bearer of arms as opposed to the criminal. To serve in the army became a civic duty which replaced the religious duties of service to feudal superiors.

External war-making capacities grew in parallel to the process of internal pacification within the territory of the state, the latter involving the extension of the rule of law, the eventual phasing out of violent forms of punishment, for example public flogging and hanging, the introduction of monetarized relations, for example wages and rent, in place of more direct coercion, and the introduction of non-violent ways of settling domestic conflicts. Essentially taxation replaced various forms of what today would be called 'protection' – payments to local lords, highwaymen, pirates.

The nation-state, which came into being in the nineteenth century, could be said to be the organized entity through which violence was contained. It was contained geographically in that violence was pushed outwards against other states and it was contained temporally because war became a discrete activity between states when 'normal' relations broke down. The implicit contract through which a rule of law and civil society was established legitimized the state as the embodiment of an emergent national identity in exchange for domestic security and external protection. Only the state had the right to use violence in order to protect and enforce a territorial regime of non-violence. The term civil society originally referred to the establishment of a domestic zone of peace, to the existence of legal, 'civilized' non-violent ways of managing human affairs, in contrast to the barbaric war methods adopted externally, to settle affairs between states. This contrast gave rise to a whole series of parallel binary oppositions which define the way we think about war and peace. These include the distinction between public (legitimate) and private (criminal) violence, between external war and anarchy and internal or domestic civil society, between the military (external) and the police (internal), and, indeed, between war and peace itself because it became possible to distinguish war and peace both in time and space. Instead of being a more or less continous pervasive phenomenon, war occured only in certain places in certain periods.

The rise of the modern state did not happen in isolation. The emergence of a European states system is usually dated back to the Treaty of Westphalia (1648). The notion of secular sovereignty within a given territory depended both on domestic legitimacy and on mutual recognition between states. It is possible to trace the dominant traditions in international thought back through the history of the states system. On the one hand, there were the predecessors of what we, today, would call 'realists' – thinkers like Hobbes and Machiavelli – who considered that violence was endemic in human nature and that only the existence of strong states could maintain order. Since there was no European or world state, the international arena was inevitably characterized by anarchy. The price of maintaining order at home was barbarism abroad. In so far as war was not a permanent feature of international relations, this was explained by the concept of the 'balance of power', which continues to have such salience right up to the present day. The 'balance of power' was regarded as the mechanism for retaining international order; as long as no single state got too strong, some kind of more or less delicate or robust order could be preserved. War broke out when the balance of power was disturbed. In effect, in a world of absolutist states, war was inevitable from time to time, in the pursuit of national interest.

In practice, of course, sovereignty was not as absolute as was claimed. The states sytem was characterized by intense interaction. There was a range of mechanisms – treaties, congresses, diplomacy – which helped to regulate international behaviour. These mechanisms offered the potential basis for 'perpetual peace' schemes. Rousseau, in his critique of the Abbé de Saint-Pierre's peace project, asked why the states of Europe did not establish a diet of Europe as proposed in various 'perpetual peace' schemes, since this was, in fact, a more rational way of pursuing national goals in the international arena than war. Given the destructiveness of wars, it is difficult to conceive of a war that could possibly represent the most rational way of fulfilling some national objective. His answer was that rulers were less interested in national goals and more concerned about their individual power. The external pressure of war, the idea of an 'other', provided a mechanism for sustaining domestic power, for justifying authoritarianism.[6]

Both these views, the realist and the idealist, took it for granted that domestic peace was achieved at the cost of external violence. But whereas the realists regarded this as inevitable and were sceptical about ever achieving 'perpetual peace' in the international arena, the idealists considered that international peace was possible. For them, democracy was a precondition for 'perpetual peace' because wars arose from the greed and/or irrationality of absolutist rulers not from national interest. By the same token, 'perpetual peace' was a precondition for democracy since wars provide the excuse for domestic despotism.

The geographical and temporal containment of violence was associated with a weakening of the constraints on war. The means of violence were concentrated in the hands of the state, which became increasingly powerful and efficient. War became much more terrible during this period, with an extremist logic which was to become the centrepiece of

Clausewitzean thinking. Modern conceptions of war date from the emergence of the modern state. While the thinking developed by Clausewitz and other contemporary strategists was assumed to apply to all wars, in fact it was primarily relevant to the period stretching from the end of the eighteenth century to 1945. Clausewitz was a realist. For him, war was between states and the aim of war could be nothing less than the total defeat of the enemy since there was always a possibility of counterattack. He derived this extremist logic from his political assumptions, that war was fought in the national interest – 'the continuation of politics by other means' – as well as from military necessity and from the modern requirements for popular mobilization which can easily get out of hand. All that prevented the realization of what he called ideal or absolute war, which combined the all-out efforts of politicians, generals and popular sentiment, was 'friction': the muddle and fog of war. The Second World War could perhaps be described as the last spasm of Clausewitzean war. The development of modern technology and organization combined with popular mobilization to produce a total war.

It can be argued that the Cold War extended the zone of peace across Europe. For the realists, the concept of deterrence which dominated the Cold War period represented the apex of balance-of-power thinking. It was based on an anticipation of a war so terrible that no rational political objectives could justify the use of force. This 'imagined' war was drawn in Clausewitzean terms from the experience of the Second World War – a clash of wills between immensely powerful states. Even the notion that force could be proportionate to the political objective, a notion that lay behind concepts of 'limited war', carried the ever-present risk of unthinkable escalation. This idea was supposed to have insulated Europe from war. For the idealists, the construction of rigid military alliances meant that the European nation-states actually abandoned their claim to a monopoly of legitimate violence. It was the blocs, rather than the nation-states, that claimed this monopoly in the name not of nation but of ideology. Hence violence was pushed further outwards against a bloc enemy and the idea of the 'other' legitimized bloc rule.[7]

Outside Europe, there were many wars in which millions of people died but they were largely considered as secondary or even as 'limited' wars. The vast majority of these wars were subnational, with external powers intervening on one side or another. Despite the horrific nature of many of these wars, they were referred to as civil wars because they were internal, intrastate, as opposed to external, interstate. These wars were effectively incorporated into the Cold War conflict so that they appeared as part of the dominant clash of wills. There were very few classic interstate wars and most of these (India–Pakistan, Israel–Egypt, Greece–Turkey, Somalia–Ethiopia) were limited by superpower intervention. Rather, conceptions about war as primarily interstate wars were transposed into conceptualizations of interbloc war. Hence an internal civic peace within each group of nations comprising a bloc, actually the Western bloc, was contrasted with the unimaginable barbarity of external interbloc war.

CHANGING PATTERNS OF ORGANIZED VIOLENCE

Wars are generally distinguished from other forms of organized violence in terms of scale. Thus most attempts to count numbers of wars define wars in terms of the number of battle deaths in a given period.[8] Implicit in these definitions, however, are received assumptions about the distinction between public and private violence and about the nature of warfare. Wars are fought for political goals, in contrast to violent crime in which the aim is private profit. Thus the conflict in Northern Ireland is generally considered a war, even though the number of violent deaths per year is lower than in many American cities.

It is sometimes argued that the post-Cold War period is much more unstable or violent. It is certainly true that the number of wars, defined as above, has increased in the 1980s and 1990s especially in Europe and Africa. More importantly, however, the nature of wars has changed. Overall casualties and direct participation in wars tend to be much lower than in earlier wars. Moreover, Peter Wallensteen and Margareta Sollenberg suggest that there has been a significant increase in minor and intermediate armed conflicts during the 1990s, that is, of conflicts with fewer than 1,000 battle-related deaths per year.[9] Wars are not typically the killing spasms of the First or Second World Wars or even Korea and Vietnam. The Second World War cost anything between 35 and 60 million lives; in Hamburg, Dresden, Tokyo, and Hiroshima and Nagasaki, some 100–200,000 people died in a single assault. Some 3 million people died in the Korean War and some 2 million people died in the Vietnam War. These wars were essentially extreme compressions of war, outbursts of violence that were contained in time and, for the most part, ended in victory or defeat.

All wars are destructive in societal terms but this is generally considered to be a consequence or by-product of military activities; in contrast, recent wars appear to be aimed at societal destruction. The ratio of civilian to military casualties has risen dramatically, as has the number of refugees.[10] A very typical feature of the new wars is population displacement, 'ethnic cleansing', which is associated with very large numbers of refugees, and its counterpart, forcible repatriation or colonization, as in the case of Russians sent to Chechnya or Serbs sent to Kosovo. In Bosnia-Herzegovina, 250,000 people were killed, mostly civilians, and some three-quarters of the Bosnian population have been displaced, creating around 3.5 million refugees. The wars in Georgia (Abkhazia and South Ossetia) claimed some 5,000 casualties and created around half a million refugees. Physical destruction of homes, economic centres such as factories and power stations, and cultural buildings, especially historical and religious monuments, is often widespread.

The wars of the 1980s and 1990s tend to be longer and less decisive than earlier wars. Unlike earlier wars, which were contained in time and tended to end in victory or defeat, few recent wars have had decisive endings; even where cease-fires are declared, they tend to usher in uneasy periods of low-level violence, neither war nor peace.

Table 5.1 provides an overview of the differences between two ideal-types of warfare: what I call Clausewitzean wars, that is, national or bloc wars, and new wars. Of course, both these types of war exist, and existed, side by side. Thus many of the wars outside Europe, and indeed in Northern Ireland, before 1989 had many of the characteristics of new wars, but their character was obscured by the overbearing nature of the Cold War. On the other hand, the 1991 Gulf War is probably best described as a Clausewitzean war. The point is about tendencies and trajectories. The trajectory of Clausewitzean warfare is reaching its end,

Table 5.1 Clausewitzean wars and new wars

	National or bloc wars	*New wars*
Actors	National armies Bloc alliances	Paramilitary groups Organized crime groups Mercenaries Parts of national armies
Goals	National or bloc interest	Identity politics Ethnic exclusion
Mode of warfare	Vertical, hierarchical command Importance of battle Extremist tendencies Advanced military technology	Dispersed, fragmented Directed against civilians Use of atrocities: rape, famine, sieges Use of light weapons, communications, land mines
War economy	Centralizing, autarkic, totalizing Full employment High production	Open, decentralized, low participation Humanitarian assistance plus underground economy High unemployment Low production
External support	Allies, imperialism Superpower patrons	Diaspora Transnational mafia Mercenaries Regional powers

to be replaced by new forms of violence whose trajectory is, as yet, less easy to anticipate.

The first difference between the two types of war has to do with the nature of the actors. Recent wars have tended to arise from the disintegration or erosion of state structures. This is characterized by a loss of legitimacy for a variety of reasons: disillusion with centralized states and state-led policies; the end of the Cold War and the collapse of socialism; disappointment with post-colonial nationalist regimes; despotism and/or widespread corruption; the inability of governments to implement promises. And, connectedly, it also involves the break-up of the monopoly of organized violence: the fragmentation of armies and police forces; the growth of organized crime and paramilitary groups; the ready availability of weapons and mercenaries. Many commentators talk about the role of non-state actors in the new wars. But it is increasingly difficult to distinguish between state and non-state actors since remnants of the state or break-away parts of the state may be contending parties and since what the international community recognizes as the state may be unable to command any more domestic legitimacy than any other organized group. Consequently, command systems no longer function. In August 1992 Shevardnadze, who had just been established as President of Georgia, ordered his troops to protect the railway from Tbilisi to Sukhumi against the secessionist Abkhaz forces who were, incidentally, supported by remnants of the Russian armed forces, in what was supposed to be a limited military operation. However, the troops represented only one of a number of military groups controlled by different political parties and ministries; they disobeyed Shevardnadze's orders and went on to attack Sukhumi even though they were few in number (and were in the event defeated).

A second difference concerns the goals of warfare. The political goals of contemporary warring parties generally have to do with identity politics – the capture of power by particular groups defined in terms of identity (racial, ethnic, religious, tribal, linguistic, etc.) and/or the exclusion or expulsion of other groups. Earlier wars, even national wars, tended to be justified either in terms of geopolitical interest or in terms of some universalizing mission. In this sense, the new warfare is not so different from gang warfare or racial violence. More importantly, perhaps, the various parties to the new wars engage in organized crime in order to finance themselves. These crimes can include robbery, kidnapping for ransom, illegal trading in drugs and arms, counterfeiting money, protection rackets and running unlicensed bars and casinos.[11] At the same time, organized crime groups may adopt political labels in order to legitimize themselves or may engage in warfare to create a situation more favourable to criminal activities. It is often rumoured for example that mafia groups are fomenting conflict in the Black Sea region in order to control tourist resorts, especially gambling.

In these circumstances, the difference between paramilitary groups and organized crime groups is often blurred. A good example of the breakdown of the distinction between political and criminal groups is the two notorious paramilitary groups among the Bosnian Serbs – Arkan's Tigers and Seselj's Chetniks. Arkan was a well-known figure from the Belgrade underground. He ran a chain of ice-cream parlours which were supposedly covers for drug dealing. Reportedly, he was hired by the Yugoslav security services in the 1980s to assassinate emigrés. His Tigers were recruited from the fan club of the Belgrade football club which Arkan owned. They were said to be well trained, well armed and disciplined. In contrast, Seselj was an extreme nationalist. He had been a professor at the University of Sarajevo and had studied at the University of Michigan. He was jailed in the 1980s for his dissident writings. His Chetniks (the same name as the wartime Serbian royalists) were the paramilitary wing of his party – the Serbian Radical Party – which was the most extreme nationalist party and which won 20 per cent of the votes in the 1992 elections during the war. Unlike the Tigers, the Chetniks were often drunk and recruited week-end fighters. Both groups were responsible for the worst atrocities of the war and both seem to have been financed through loot. Arkan is supposed to have had lists of rich Muslims, who were robbed and executed.[12]

A third difference between the two types of war has to do with the mode of warfare. Clausewitzean wars were fought by centralized national armies, recruited professionally or through conscription, with very clear vertical lines of command. The aim was to disarm the opponent and to inflict maximum violence on opposing forces. No expense was spared in developing weapons with increased accuracy, mobility and destructiveness, culminating in the Second World War with the widespread use of aircraft, tanks and heavy artillery and the development of weapons of mass destruction. At the same time, the soldier was supposed to follow clear rules about military behaviour. 'War is hell' and all wars involve looting and pillage and atrocities of various kinds, including rape. But, for the most part, these were considered to be side-effects, something commanders were supposed to minimize. The term 'collateral damage' to describe damage to civilian targets as an unintended consequence of aiming at military targets implies that, at least in theory, hitting civilian targets is proscribed.

Because the aim is often destabilization and population displacement rather than destruction of a clearly defined opponent, what were side-effects have become central to the mode of fighting. Conspicuous atrocity, systematic rape, hostage-taking, forced starvation and siege, destruction of religious and historic monuments, the use of shells and rockets against civilian targets, especially homes, hospitals or crowded places like markets or water sources, the use of land mines to make large areas uninhabitable: all are deliberate components of military strategy.

The aim is to sow fear and discord, to instil unbearable memories of what was once home, to desecrate whatever has social meaning. Often there is cooperation between warring factions, and battles, which were the centrepiece of Clausewitzean warfare, are rare. Hence the very high numbers of civilian casualties, especially in relation to military casualties. It is sometimes said that the new wars are a reversion to primitivism. But primitive wars were highly ritualistic and hedged in by social constraints. These wars are rational, in the sense that they apply rational thinking to the aims of war and reject normative constraints.

A fourth difference between the two types of war concerns the character of the war economy. The typical new war economy represents an extreme expression of the type of economy that characterizes large parts of Eastern Europe and the Third World and even inner cities in the advanced industrial world. The economy of the Second World War was autarkic, self-sufficient and involved total mobilization. In the new war zones, the formal economy is largely destroyed, either physically or economically, through the loss of markets, loss of import protection, embargoes, difficulties in acquiring spare parts or raw materials, inadequate or non-existent infrastructure, particularly communications, energy and transport, or loss of specialists. Local production of food, basic necessities or weapons may take place but both survival and the war effort depend on outside humanitarian assistance and/or imports paid for with savings, remittances from abroad, or earnings from the black market. Unlike the Second World War, participation in the war is partial, and unemployment is widespread. In many cases, joining a paramilitary group or becoming a criminal are the only sources of work or income. Humanitarian assistance is 'taxed' to finance the war effort. Often the difference between a functioning and non-functioning administration depends on whether the tax is spent by the administration for publicly defined purposes, including the war, or whether it simply stays in the hands of those responsible for 'collecting' the tax. Whereas the wars of the Clausewitzean era helped to consolidate the state by generating an enhanced capacity for revenue collection, the new wars tend to destroy or fragment existing administrative mechanisms. In so far as there is a system of revenue collection, it is generally very local, with huge differences in the effectiveness of local administration. In some cases, all forms of public services are destroyed. In other cases, new islands of 'good governance' are built from scratch to cope with the crisis.

There is thus not much difference between a war economy and a peacetime economy. Indeed many zones formally at peace experience widespread criminality and violence. Since the war accentuates the very economic tendencies which contributed to the outbreak of war, it generates additional reasons to continue the war. Even where exhaustion may establish the conditions for cease-fires, the failure to reverse some of these underlying tendencies means that war could easily break out again.

Hence, it is possible to talk about large parts of the global economy that are near-war, prewar or postwar economies.

Finally, the role of external support has changed. Whereas in earlier conflicts it was possible to identify outsiders in terms of foreign states, in the new wars the parties to the conflict have a range of transnational links corresponding to the range of interests engaged in the conflict. In nineteenth-century national wars, external support took the form of shifting alliances. In so far as there was outside intervention in local wars outside Europe, it could be clearly identified as colonial in nature. During the Cold War period, conflicting parties were dependent on outside patrons, either former colonial powers or superpowers. Just as the disintegration of states is central to an understanding of the new wars, so is the decline of patron states providing external support to, and a degree of external control over, the warring parties.

In the new wars, external support takes a variety of forms. First of all, there are frequently important diaspora elements. Sometimes, the diaspora lives in neighbouring states or remnants of states and indeed has the support of neighbouring states: such is the situation of Serbs in Croatia and Bosnia or Russians in Crimea, Moldova and a number of other places. Sometimes, a diaspora, many times larger, is to be found in the melting-pot nations – Canada, the United States, Australia and so on. The latter are often very influential, providing money, arms, volunteers or technology. Reconstruction in Ngorno-Karabakh, for example, has largely been financed by diaspora Armenians in North America. The IRA was for a long time sustained by the Irish community in the United States. It was Sikhs in Canada who first conceived the idea of a Sikh homeland, Khalistan, and it is Sikhs living abroad who are often the most enthusiastic advocates of the idea. It is Macedonians in the United States who have proposed the unification of Bulgaria and Macedonia and it is in Australia that actual fighting has broken out between Greeks and Macedonians. And sometimes, the diaspora consists of refugees or those who seek work abroad and who send money home to support their families. In the wars in ex-Yugoslavia, remittances from guest workers in Germany helped to finance the wars; in some cases, young men will return for short periods to fight in the army.

Secondly, a key role in external support is also played by transnational commercial networks, both those that are legal and above board and those that are more shady. Many networks, mafia groups for example, may be linked to networks based on identity. In the first three decades after the end of the Second World War, the private arms trade was negligible. And indeed, those who were private arms dealers were often fronts for various intelligence services, such as the notorious Sam Cummings. As the dominant suppliers began to charge their clients commercial rates in the 1980s and 1990s, the opportunities for bribes, kickbacks, siphoning off and so on grew. Nowadays, the private arms trade is still small in relation to official trade but it remains crucial in providing the small arms and light weapons that are used in the new wars. Moreover, it is increasingly integrated into what Naylor calls the 'global underground economy' as dealers seek services from those who are familiar with other types of black-market activities.[13] Chechen mafia groups, linked up to foreign economic activities as well as certain officials in Moscow interested in perpetuating the war and disrupting democratic processes, have effectively sustained the Chechen war effort, generating funds for arms, food and medicine.[14]

Thirdly, there is a multiplicity of other international actors both state and non-state. There are the foreign mercenaries and other 'military experts' made redundant as a result of the Cold War cuts in military budgets, seeking a role where their skills are still relevant. There are individuals and NGOs offering humanitarian, religious or conflict resolution services. There are foreign reporters and photographers responsible for the global transparency of these wars. And there are the representatives of states and international institutions.

Because recent wars are both local and global, it is difficult to distinguish between internal and external wars, international and civil wars, aggression or repression. Whether the war in Bosnia is a civil war or an international war depends not only on whether or not Bosnia is considered to be an internationally recognized state but also on whether the Bosnian Serbs are considered to be part of Bosnia or not. Moreover, these distinctions miss the point. Because we tend to be caught within a set of definitions drawn from the Clausewitzean era, we argue about whether one or other definition is the most appropriate. Those who favour outside intervention in Bosnia emphasize that Bosnia is an internationally recognized state and that the war is a war of aggression by Serbs. Those who oppose intervention generally insist that this is a civil war. The point is that ethnic cleansing against Muslims by Serbs is equally unacceptable whether it is done by outsiders or insiders, whether it is defined as aggression or repression. What we need is a new set of definitions that can guide the international response to this new type of warfare.

IMPLICATIONS FOR TRANSNATIONAL DEMOCRACY

Liberal writers of the late eighteenth and nineteenth centuries had a teleological view of history. They believed that the zone of civility would inevitably extend itself in time and space. In his book *Reflections on Violence*,[15] John Keane contrasts their optimism with the pessimism of twentieth-century writers like Zygmunt Bauman or Norbert Elias who consider that barbarism was the inevitable concomitant of civility. For these writers violence is embedded in human nature. The cost of allowing the state to monopolize violence is the terrible barbarity of twentieth-century wars and totalitarianism.

The end of the Cold War may mark the end of statist barbarism on this scale. Certainly, the threat of nuclear war, the absolute expression of twentieth-century barbarism, has receded. Does this mean that the world is reverting to pre-nation-state forms of violence, anarchy or primitivism, as some writers argue?[16] The analysis in the previous section suggests that new patterns of violence are the product of specific historical circumstances and have a logic that can be investigated provided we redefine the ways in which we think about war and peace. While groups who define themselves in terms of identity may well be backward looking in their ideology and rhetoric, nevertheless the way they engage in violence, the instruments they use, their goals and their forms of mobilization can only be explained in contemporary terms since they are profoundly influenced by new types of technology, globalization, etc.

The erosion of classic distinctions between war and peace or between civil society and anarchy does not necessarily imply that the world is moving towards a state of perpetual warfare and anarchy. On the contrary, what it means is that war and peace, civility and anarchy exist side by side. Just as it is possible to discern new patterns of violence so it is also possible to identify new tendencies for civility that could provide a basis for perpetual peace.

One tendency is the dramatic global increase in citizens' groups, social movements or NGOs, which are often transnationally connected and which constitute a form of public pressure for what John Keane calls the politics of civility. Within war zones, it is possible to find what might be termed civil enclaves. Some towns or regions or even suburbs are less violent than others and within these areas civil space opens up which helps to sustain relative peace. One such example is Tuzla, in Bosnia-Herzegovina, which elected a non-nationalist municipality in 1990 and managed to keep the fighting out of the town, defending it with the police and local volunteers. The town managed to sustain some local production and keep crime rates low. Both local and international NGOs have been active in the town.

Another tendency is the transnationalization of legitimate violence and the expansion of peacekeeping operations. The state's monopoly of violence is also being eroded from above. In Europe this began during the Cold War years, when armed forces were integrated into the two military blocs, NATO and the Warsaw Pact. No European country any longer has the capacity to fight a sustained war independently. Although there has been some renationalization of armed forces in the aftermath of the Cold War, there has also been a whole set of new arrangements – multinational peacekeeping, arms control agreements involving mutual inspection teams, joint exercises, new or renewed organizations like the Western European Union, Partnership for Peace, NATO Coordination

Council (NACC) – which constitute an intensification of transnationalization in the military sphere. Martin Shaw talks about the Global State to describe what he sees as the re-establishment of the monopoly of legitimate organized violence under the tutelage of the United States.[17] But the term state implies a degree of territorialization and centralization that is currently absent. Territorial defence, which was the classic task of the army of the nation-state, is becoming less and less relevant. Even though some organizations, such as NATO, still see territorial defence as their primary mission, in practice, peacekeeping and humanitarian intervention are likely to be their main activities.

The number of peacekeeping operations has increased in the aftermath of the Cold War quite substantially, but even more importantly the nature of peacekeeping operations is changing in response to the new type of warfare. Classic peacekeeping either involved the separation of warring parties after a cease-fire or intervention on one side, as in Korea. In recent years, all kinds of innovative approaches have been introduced, albeit inadequately and ineffectively for the most part and under pressure from public-spirited media or citizens' groups. These new approaches to peacekeeping are aimed at the protection of civilians and involve such innovations as safe havens, humanitarian corridors, international administrations, etc.

Can these tendencies be developed in such a way as to reconstruct a notion of rule of law or civil society on a transnational basis? On the one hand, this would imply a transnational consensus about non-violence in which the only legitimate use of violence would be to maintain that consensus. On the other hand, it would imply an active transnational civil society, in the sense of transnational public pressure to sustain the rule of law.

There is a body of already existing international law which deals with the abuses of armed power. Laws and customs of war which date back to early modern times were codified in the nineteenth and twentieth century; particularly important were the Geneva Conventions sponsored by the International Committee of the Red Cross and the Hague conferences of 1899 and 1907. The Nuremburg trials after the Second World War marked the first international proceedings against individuals accused of 'war crimes' or, even more significantly, 'crimes against humanity'. To what was known as international humanitarian law, human rights legislation was added in the postwar period.[18] The difference had to do with whether or not these crimes were committed in wartime. International humanitarian law was confined to abuses of power in wartime situations, in other words aggression. Human rights legislation was equally concerned with repression.[19] The violations of international norms with which both bodies of law is concerned are, in particular, those which form the core of the new mode of warfare.

The principles which guide international institutions and from which they derive legitimacy are contained in this legislation. The classic distinctions between aggression and repression are eroded by the changing pattern of violence. A war crime is simultaneously a massive violation of human rights. An effective international humanitarian regime would combine the control of warfare with implementation of human rights; this is, in effect, a requirement nowadays for perpetual peace. As David Beetham points out in chapter 3 above, there already exists a human rights regime, both informal and formal. Networks of NGOs monitor and draw attention to violations of human rights, and to a greater or lesser extent international institutions do respond, although as yet their response is confined to various forms of persuasion and pressure. The weakness of the human rights regime is enforcement. The analysis of new wars has certain implications for what can be termed humanitarian intervention and for the role of those who might become the instruments of enforcement, the international peacekeepers.

First of all, the key to enforcement is legitimacy – re-establishing the legitimacy of the enforcers as opposed to the new warring groups. At present, the dominant thinking in international institutions is largely derived from Realist assumptions about the way the world is structured. Because of the intergovernmental character of international institutions, behaviour is generally a compromise between different national interests and shaped by national ways of perceiving the world that derive from traditional Clausewitzean assumptions about warfare. The common denominator is an interest in preserving a domestic zone of stability. One response to new wars is to treat these wars as Clausewitzean wars and to assume that the warring factions represent, if not states, then proto-states, and to try to negotiate and even impose a solution 'from above': the argument is that stability is more important than justice. This is the approach that has led historically to partitions and that underlies agreements such as the Dayton or Oslo Accords. The other approach is that of non-intervention. This derives from a recognition that these wars cannot be understood in Clausewitzean terms, but the implication, from a Clausewitzean perspective, is that they are therefore ununderstandable: they are a reversion to primitivism, ancient rivalries, etc., and the best response is containment, to build a fortress against their spread. In fact, both approaches are unrealistic, precisely because of the failure to take into account the character of new wars. The first approach leads to unjust and unsustainable temporary cease-fires which undermine the legitimacy and credibility of international institutions. The warring factions are not states and cannot or do not wish to guarantee a peace. The second approach ignores the transnational character of the new wars and the impossibility of insulating states or groups of states from refugees, transnational criminals and diaspora political lobbies.

Effective humanitarian intervention has to be viewed as a collective, international responsibility and not a unilateral task. Those international institutions, such as the United Nations, the European Union, the OSCE, NATO, etc., who take responsibility for intervention have to be respected and trusted. In part, this has to do with accountability and transparency and democratic procedures – some of the considerations that are covered in other chapters of this book. But equally importantly, it has to do with the extent to which these institutions are able to offer an alternative politics and morality that can supersede the exclusive concerns of warring groups. Such a politics has to be built around the principles and norms of international behaviour, in effect around a notion of cosmopolitan right.[20] If international institutions are to retain and indeed extend their legitimacy, then they have to take responsibility for ensuring that the humanitarian regime is enforced and implemented. This involves, first and foremost, a political strategy of building up support and popular consensus for such an approach, creating alliances with those institutions and groups at local level which represent these principles. In other words, international institutions have the task of supporting and strengthening civility both politically and militarily. Whereas nation-states derived their legitimacy from the notion that they were responsible for external defence of the nation, the legitimacy of international institutions should derive from the notion that they have responsibility for the enforcement of humanitarian law.

The analysis of new wars also has implications for the way in which enforcement is carried out. Traditionally, a sharp distinction has been made between peacekeeping and war-fighting, based on Clausewitzean notions of war. Peacekeeping presupposes the existence of a political agreement of the Dayton or Oslo type and the main task of the peacekeepers is to monitor agreement, implementation being the responsibility of the parties to the agreement; hence concepts such as consent and impartiality are emphasized. War-fighting presupposes that the international community takes sides: one side is defined as the enemy or aggressor and the aim is to inflict maximum damage. It is widely assumed that these are the only possibilities, that because of the extremist logic of war and the inevitable polarization, it is impossible to use force without taking sides, without sliding into war-fighting.

The aim of peacekeeping in new wars, sometimes called 'robust peacekeeping' or 'second-generation peacekeeping', is to control violence and create the conditions for 'normalization'. Ultimately, this means the enforcement or overseeing the enforcement of international law as opposed to monitoring an agreement between states. Precisely because these are wars directed against civilians, they do not have the same extremist logic and therefore it ought to be possible to devise strategies for the protection of civilians and the capture of war criminals. Safe havens, humanitarian corridors and no-fly zones are examples of the kinds of strategies that would need to be developed. While it is impossible to implement such strategies effectively without engaging in violence, this does not imply full-scale war. Essentially, the new type of peacekeeping is policing but on a much larger scale. Unlike war-fighting, in which the aim is to maximize casualties on the other side and to minimize casualties on your own side, peacekeeping has to minimize casualties on all sides. This may mean risking the lives of peacekeepers in order to save the lives of victims.

This is perhaps the most difficult presupposition to change. International personnel are always a privileged class in the new wars. The lives of UN or other international personnel are valued over the lives of local people despite the UN claim to be founded on the principles of humanity. The argument about humanitarian intervention revolves around whether it is acceptable to sacrifice national lives for the sake of people far away. The preference of Western powers, especially the United States, for air strikes, despite the physical and psychological damage caused even with highly accurate munitions, arises from this privileging of nationals or Westerners. Modern armies are uneasy about peacekeeping also because they are organized along Clausewitzean lines and have been trained to confront other similarly organized armies. As was shown in the case of Somalia, when confronted with the challenge of new wars, they find it extremely difficult to identify a middle way between the application of massive firepower and doing nothing.

Although the United Nations Security Council has often passed resolutions supporting intervention along these lines, often under pressure from public opinion, there has up to now been considerable reluctance to follow through the logic of this approach. It is sometimes argued that this is because the UN is never provided with adequate means. To some extent, this is true. But much more important are deeply held assumptions about the nature of peacekeeping, and the Clausewitzean belief that the use of force cannot be limited and that therefore there is nothing between peacekeeping and war-fighting. Where international institutions are guided by geopolitical interests, moreover, the enforcement of international norms is not considered worth the risk of national casualties.

If political support for new peacekeeping is to be generated and hence the will to provide adequate means, it is important to rethink what peacekeeping means and to demonstrate the new approach in practice. Terms like consent and impartiality need to be redefined. It is often necessary to act without the consent of the warring parties, for example, in the delivery of humanitarian aid, the protection of safe havens, or the capture of war criminals. Even when agreements have been made, consent may be withheld. What is of crucial importance, however, is the consent of the victims. The peacekeeping effort has to mobilize local political support for its activities, even if, as may often be the case, this makes the consent of the warring parties impossible. Likewise, impartiality is not the same as neutrality. Neutrality means not taking sides. Impartiality means enforcing international norms in an impartial way. It is almost impossible to be both impartial and neutral since it is almost always the case that one side is more responsible for violations of international principles. Hence, peacekeeping forces may necessarily act in a way that is closer to one side than another.

Above all, there has to be a fundamental change in the moral precepts guiding the peacekeeper. The peacekeeper has to become the legitimate bearer of arms. He or she has to know and respect the laws of war (*jus in bellum*) and must be incorruptible. In the new wars, if peacekeepers do not have a mandate for enforcement and are not professionalized, there is a risk that they become just another faction in the war. Indeed, there have been many reported cases in which peacekeepers have engaged in black-market activities, especially, but by no means only, those who were receiving inadequate rates of pay, and have themselves perpetrated human rights abuses.[21] Such behaviour must be seriously investigated and punished. Above all, the motivation of the peacekeeper has to be incorporated into a wider notion of cosmopolitan rights. Whereas the legitimate bearer of arms, the soldier, had to be prepared to die for his country, the peacekeeper risks his or her life for humanity.

Hence any attempt to control violence on a transnational basis can only be conceived as part of a far-reaching cultural transformation in which the duties and rights of citizenship are redefined in cosmopolitan terms. I have argued that the logic of Clausewitzean warfare, based on the existence of a national monopoly of legitimate violence, is breaking down. It is eroded 'from below' through the privatization and informalization of organized violence, and 'from above' through the transnationalization of military forces. The binary oppositions that shaped our interpretations of violence, between private (criminal) and public (legitimate), or between external (international) or internal (civil), can only be applied with difficulty to the contemporary context. Indeed, the very notion of a distinction between war (as a temporal and geographical confinement of organized violence) and peace is called into question.

The optimistic view of current developments is the obsolescence of interstate war. War as we have known it for the last two centuries may, like slavery, have become an anachronism. National armies, navies and air forces may be no more than ritual vestiges of the passing nation-state. The pessimistic view is that war, like slavery, can always be reinvented, that we have entered an era of long-term low-level violence, of uncivil wars. Moreover, the capacity of formal political institutions, primarily nation-states, to regulate violence has been eroded. Which view is more realistic depends on whether the capacity for regulating violence can be reinstated in some new way on a transnational basis and whether barbarism can be checked by an alert and active cosmopolitan citizenry. How this might be done is, perhaps, the most crucial component of any attempt to theorize transnational democracy.

NOTES

1 See also D. Held, *Democracy and the Global Order* (Cambridge: Polity Press, 1995).

2 See D. Archibugi, 'Models of international organization in perpetual peace projects', *Review of International Studies*, 18 (1992), pp. 295–317.

3 See C. Tilly, *Coercion, Capital and European States AD 990–1990* (Oxford: Blackwell, 1990); A. Giddens, *The Modern State and Violence* (Cambridge: Polity Press, 1987).

4 M. Mann, 'State and society 1130–1815: an analysis of English state finances', in M. Mann, *States, War and Capitalism* (Oxford: Blackwell, 1988).

5 See J. Keegan, *A History of Warfare* (London: Hutchinson, 1993), p. 12.

6 'Again, anyone can understand that war and conquest without and the encroachments of despotism within give each other mutual support; that money and men are habitually taken at pleasure from a people of slaves, to bring others beneath the same yoke; and that conversely war furnishes a pretext for exactions of money and another, no less plausible, for keeping large armies constantly on foot, to hold people in awe. In a word, anyone can see that aggressive princes wage war at least as much on their subjects as on their enemies, and that the conquering nation is left no better off than the conquered.' Jean-Jacques Rousseau, 'Abstract and judgement of Saint-Pierre's project for perpetual peace' (1756), in S. Hoffman and D. P. Fidler (eds), *Rousseau on International Relations* (Oxford: Oxford University Press, 1991), pp. 90–1.

7 M. Kaldor, *The Imaginary War: Understanding the East–West Conflict* (Oxford: Blackwell, 1990).

8 R. L. Sivard, *World Military and Social Expenditures 1987–8* (Washington D.C.: World Priorities, 1995); Stockholm International Peace Research Institute, *SIPRI Yearbook 1995: Armaments, Disarmament and International Security* (Oxford: Oxford University Press, 1995).

9 P. Wallensteen and M. Sollenberg 'After the Cold War: emerging patterns of armed conflict 1989–94', *Journal of Peace Research*, 32.4 (1995), pp. 345–60.

10 The ratio of civilian to military casualties in wars has risen from 0:8 in the 1950s, 1:3 in the 1960s, 3:1 in the 1970s, 3:7 in the 1980s and 8:1 in the 1990s. See M. Kaldor, 'Introduction', in M. Kaldor and B. Vashee (eds), *Restructuring the Global Military Sector*, vol. 1: *New Wars* (London: Cassell/Pinter, 1997). For the increase in the number of refugees, see Pierre Hassner, chapter 13 below.

11 See R. T. Naylor, 'The insurgent economy: black market operations of guerilla organizations', *Crime, Law, and Social Change*, 20 (1993), pp. 13–51.

12   See the evidence collected by the UN Commission of Experts on War Crimes in the former Yugoslavia, *Final Report of the Commission of Experts Pursuant to Security Council Resolution 780 (1992)* S/1994/674, 27 May 1994, vol. 1, annex IV.

13   'Weapons might be sold for cash; bartered for teakwood, hostages, heroin, or religious artefacts; or counter-traded for grain and oil. The deals can be transacted by go-betweens who are equally at home in smuggling gold to India, trafficking in counterfeit computer chips to the United States, or shipping toxic waste to Somalia. The ships hauling the arms are probably registered in a flag-of-convenience country boasting commercial secrecy, low registration fees, and the opportunity for rapid name and ownership changes. The payments can move through a series of coded bank accounts in the name of a global network of ghost companies and are protected by the banking and corporate secrecy laws of one or several of many financial havens around the world.' R. T. Naylor, 'The structure and operation of the modern arms black market', in J. Boutwell, M. T. Klare and L. W. Reed (eds), *Lethal Commerce: the Global Trade in Small Arms and Light Weapons* (Cambridge, Mass.: American Academy of Arts and Sciences, 1995).

14   A. Zhilin 'The Caucasian War: The Scene in Moscow', *Prism: a Bi-Weekly on the Post-Soviet States*, The Jamestown Foundation, Vol. II, No. 6, Part 3, 22 March 1996.

15   J. Keane, *Reflections on Violence* (London: Verso, 1996).

16   See, for example, R. A. Kaplan 'The coming anarchy', *Atlantic Monthly* (Jan. 1994), or M. Van Creveld, *The Transformation of War* (New York: Free Press, 1991).

17   M. Shaw 'The state of globalization: towards a theory of state transformation', *Review of International Political Economy*, 4.3 (1997).

18   See chapter 3 above.

19   'The law of armed conflict had the purpose of restricting the uses of violence between states (and in the case of civil wars) between governments and rebels. Human rights law had (among other things) the purpose of averting and restricting the uses of violence by governments towards their subjects whether formally in rebellion or not; a field of conflict for which international law, by definition, brought no remedies.' G. Best, *War and Law since 1945* (Oxford: Clarendon Press, 1994).

20   See Daniele Archibugi, chapter 10 below.

21   There have been reports of human rights abuses by UN personnel in Cambodia, Bosnia-Herzegovina, Somalia and Mozambique. Abuses have included rape, killings and involvement in child prostitution in Mozambique. See for example, Africa Rights, 'Somalia: human rights abuses by the UN forces', London, July 1993.

Part II

Citizenship, Sovereignty and Transnational Democracy

6

Citizenship and Sovereignty in the Post-Westphalian European State

Andrew Linklater

The rise of the modern state involved 'a revolution in loyalties' in which an 'inner circle of loyalty expanded' and 'an outer circle of loyalty shrank.' Loyalties to the sovereign state replaced the inner web of loyalties to an 'immediate feudal superior' and the outer web of 'customary religious obedience to the Church under the Pope'.[1] As the present century draws to a close, the subnational revolt, the internationalization of decision-making and emergent transnational loyalties in Western Europe and its environs reveal that the processes which created and sustained sovereign states in this region are being reversed. The implications for social and political theory are steadily becoming clearer. It is well known that the transformation of political community in the sixteenth and seventeenth centuries produced the modern vocabulary of the sovereign territorial state. The conjunction of forces transforming contemporary Europe suggests that the time is ripe to engineer a further revolution in political thought, or, more accurately, to complete the Copernican revolution in political thinking which was initiated by Kant.[2] What is required are appropriate visions of the post-Westphalian state.

The idea that the time might be 'ripe for the enunciation of new concepts of universal political organization which would show how Wales, the United Kingdom and the European Community could each have some world political status while none laid claim to exclusive sovereignty' was suggested by Hedley Bull over fifteen years ago. Bull maintained that 'one reason for the vitality of the states system is the tyranny of the concepts and normative principles associated with it.'[3] He was right to do so. The absence of images of alternative forms of political community which could not be easily dismissed as utopian or facile has been a striking feature of modern political life. Nevertheless, Bull posed the question of whether there is 'a need to liberate thought and action from these confines by proclaiming new concepts and normative principles which would give shape and direction to the trends making against the present system'.[4] This question has acquired deeper significance as nation-states have become more vulnerable to the pressures summarized above. In this condition it has become essential to question the assumption that citizenship has no meaning apart from the sovereign nation-state.[5]

The social bond which has linked the members of each modern European state together but also separated them from other states and the rest of humankind is being challenged by subnational groups and eroded by the advance of regional organizations and globalization. These pressures combine to challenge the exclusionary nature of sovereignty and traditional ideas about community and citizenship.[6] Decisions to enshrine human rights in international conventions indicate that there has been modest but significant progress in Europe in building on the rights which individuals already possess as the citizens of sovereign states.[7] Equally important is the decisive shift away from 'difference-blind' citizenship to more complex conceptions which recognize the special identities of ethnic and racial minority groups.[8] With these developments in mind, this chapter makes the case for a normative vision of the post-Westphalian European state in which subnational and transnational citizenship supplement existing forms of national citizenship. It argues that one of the main purposes of the post-Westphalian state is to mediate between the different political loyalties, identities and authorities which have become inescapable in the modern world.

The argument is in five parts. The first part surveys Bull's prescient remarks about the possible transformation of political structures in Western Europe. The second part takes note of various developments in European international society in the period since Bull was writing which have improved the prospects for the radical extension of democracy not only within states but, crucially, in the broader transnational realm. Whether or not it is hopelessly utopian to envisage forms of cosmopolitan democracy 'in which citizens, wherever they are located in the world, have a voice, input and political representation in international affairs, in parallel with and independently of their governments' is considered here.[9] The third part considers these empirical developments in the light of Habermas's discourse theory of morality which provides important resources for strengthening the normative foundations of cosmopolitan democratic theory. The fourth and fifth parts argue for new modes of citizenship which weave the ideals of cosmopolitan democracy into the political structure of post-Westphalian states.

BULL ON THE EUROPEAN STATE

Bull seemed to find the vision of a post-Westphalian Europe congenial while seriously qualifying his support. Scepticism about the extent to which 'neo-medievalism' would represent significant progress beyond earlier forms of political life was mandatory. Violence had been ubiquitous in medieval times and could well be endemic in any future 'neo-medieval order of overlapping sovereignties and jurisdictions'.[10] Bull also argued that the post-Westphalian state could be a progressive development within international society. His remarks about the merits of alternative state structures resonate with contemporary discussions about the possibilities for transnational democracy in Europe.

Bull observed that it 'might . . . seem fanciful to contemplate a return to the medieval world, but it is not fanciful to imagine that there might develop a modern and secular counterpart of it that embodies its central characteristic: a system of overlapping authority and multiple loyalty'.[11] The momentous nature of this shift in political organization and loyalty was elaborated as follows:

One may imagine for example that a regional integration movement, like that in the countries of the European Community, might seek to undermine the sovereignty of its member states, yet at the same time stop short of transferring this sovereignty to any regional authority. If they were to bring about a situation in which the authorities existed both at the national and at the European level, but no one such authority claimed supremacy over others in terms of superior jurisdiction or its claims on the loyalties of individual persons, the sovereign state would have been transcended. Similarly, one may imagine that if nationalist separatist groups were content to reject the sovereignty of the states to which they are at present subject, but at the same time refrained from advancing any claims to sovereign statehood themselves, some genuine innovation in the structure of the world political system might take place.[12]

The new pattern of political organization would not supersede the state entirely but its role in world politics could be diminished to such an extent that 'there was real doubt both in theory and in reality as to whether sovereignty lay with the national governments or with the organs of the community'.[13] It would be a short step from 'a situation of protracted uncertainty about the locus of sovereignty' to the condition where 'the concept of sovereignty is recognized to be irrelevant'.[14]

For Bull, the move towards a more universal political order would not erase national and subnational loyalties but rather grant cultural differences the political recognition that had been withheld in the past. New forms of political organization would arise from the diffusion of sovereign power and the dispersal of political loyalties to several centres of political authority. What could emerge from demands upon states to shift power to various locales within the state and to an emergent regional authority would be a complex mesh of overlapping political authorities and loyalties:

We may envisage a situation in which, say, a Scottish authority in Edinburgh, a British authority in London, and a European authority in Brussels were all actors in world politics and enjoyed representation in world political organisations, together with rights and duties of various kinds in world law, but in which no one of them claimed sovereignty or supremacy over the others, and a person living in Glasgow had no exclusive or overriding loyalty to any one of them. Such an outcome would take us truly 'beyond the sovereign state' and is by no means implausible, but it is striking how little interest has been displayed in it by either the regional integrationists or the subnational 'disintegrationists'.[15]

The neglect of such future possibilities is no longer quite as evident among regional integrationists and subnational disintegrationists as it was when Bull was writing over fifteen years ago.[16] Bull's remarks on alternative state structures have a great deal of contemporary relevance given institutional and cultural developments in Europe which promise to despatch some of the powers of the state to new centres of political authority, so enhancing the prospects for transnational democracy. Powerful barriers to cosmopolitan democracy survive across Europe, but the cosmopolitan turn in democratic thinking does give expression to societal trends which run counter to the union of sovereignty, territoriality, shared nationality and citizenship which has been at the heart of modern political life.[17] Cosmopolitan democracy is not an ideal opposed to a reality which is recalcitrant to change but expresses important, but not unchallenged, trends within Europe which point towards the gradual democratization of international society.

CURRENT DEVELOPMENTS IN EUROPE

Recent developments suggest that the time may be ripe for easing the sovereign state back from its central role in world politics so that stronger subnational and transnational loyalties and authorities can develop. Past references to a Europe of the regions and the recent establishment of a Committee of the Regions in the European Union are important innovations which indicate one way in which the democratic deficit in European institutions can be overcome. The ethnic revolt in the former socialist bloc has raised the important question of how new political groups might extract themselves from the nation-states in which they hardly feel at home without bidding for absolute sovereignty. Fears that the acquisition of sovereignty will create profound insecurities for ethnic minorities within these fledgling states have prompted European states to ask whether the recognition of sovereignty should be made conditional on constitutional guarantees for minority rights. Developments within the CSCE and OSCE, and the decision in 1992 to create a High Commissioner on National Minorities reflect these concerns, as does the adoption of the European Charter of Regional or Minority Languages by the Council of Europe in the same year.[18] Despite these important developments the international protection of minority rights remains lamentably weak.

Resistance on the part of state structures and sections of their populations to the surrender of sovereignty abound, but the circumstances in which modern European states operate have altered significantly since Bull remarked on the possibility of a post-Westphalian Western Europe. In particular, the steady weakening of the old bonds linking citizens to the state creates unprecedented opportunities for new forms of political community attuned to the principles of cosmopolitan democracy and transnational citizenship.

There have been few comprehensive approaches to the nature of the social bonds which unite the members of a society but also separate them from the rest of humankind. Bull argued that Karl Deutsch's analysis of international security communities was one of the rare attempts 'to think about the distinguishing features of a community, the different sorts of community that obtain, the elements that make up the cohesion of a community, the determinants of mutual responsiveness between one people and another'.[19] The nature of the connections between the 'elements' of cohesion and the degree of 'mutual responsiveness' is an important theme which has been ignored by all but a small number of international theorists such as Deutsch, and sociologists such as Benjamin Nelson who reflected on how far the major world civilizations had developed a commitment to extending 'the rights of dialogue and citizenship to participants hitherto excluded'.[20] The main strands of modern social and political theory, which have assumed that there is a stark and immutable contrast between domestic and international politics, are woefully ill-prepared for the task of imagining new forms of community which promote the development of a transnational citizenry. Recent accounts of the problematical nature of national boundaries in the modern world suggest that this is now changing.[21]

The unifying and divisive character of the social bond which is peculiar to the modern state bears the imprint of several forces, including state-building and war, the quest for international order, systems of production and exchange, language, culture and belief. Multi-logic sociological explanations which highlight the interplay between this multiplicity of forces are evident in recent analyses of state-building and social power.[22] But similar approaches have yet to appear which explain how the boundaries of political communities expand and contract, fluctuate in their levels of particularism and vary in the extent of their commitment to open dialogue with those who have previously been excluded. A more comprehensive sociology of those dimensions of social and political life might include the following points.

Over the last few centuries the interplay between state-building, geo-politics, production and exchange, culture and identity resolved itself in a specific combination of monopoly powers which are unique to the modern state: first, the monopoly control of the instruments of violence which reveals the importance of, *inter alia*, state-building, domestic pacification and war; second, the monopoly right of taxation first claimed in order to finance the creation of state bureaucracies and standing armies, and a reminder of how the interplay between state-building, war and capitalist development has configured modern political communities;[23] third, the state's role in shaping political identity and prioritizing political obligations in the context of modern war and indus-trial production; fourth, the state's monopolistic position in determining how legal disputes between citizens will be resolved which has been interwoven with processes of domestic pacification, strategies of normali-zation and the creation of subjectivity in modern societies; and fifth, the state's exclusive right to belong to international organizations and to bind the whole political community in international law, which is a reminder of how modern states have stamped their ascendancy on the principles of international society.

In the course of acquiring these monopoly powers, states displaced alternative sites of subnational or transnational power which could chal-lenge their claims on human loyalty. Consolidated states which were less tolerant than their predecessors of cultural diversity and more aggres-sively nationalist in their dealings with outsiders reached the apogee of their development in the late nineteenth and early twentieth centuries.[24] But the growth of state power generated political resistance which invari-ably took the form of demands for the extension of citizenship rights.[25] The cultural capital which was accumulated with the development of claims for civil, political and social rights checked the growth of state monopoly power. The recent impact of globalization and fragmentation on the constitutionally stable societies in Europe suggests that the era of consolidated states may be drawing to an end.[26] The erosion of state monopoly powers has increased the possibility that alternative sites of power and competitors for human loyalty will emerge. This is the context in which the moral resources which were accumulated in the course of extending and deepening the meaning of citizenship can be harnessed to create a multi-ethnic, transnational social democracy which protects the legal, political, social and cultural rights of all members.

Much recent literature has focused on various developments which are loosening the bond between the citizen and the state and undermining tightly bound, separate political communities in many parts of the world.[27] Some authors maintain that the conditions under which the state has traditionally exercised control of the instruments of violence are changing in the post-industrial core regions of the world economy. War has long played a central role in the formation of national communities but the obsolescence of force between the major industrial powers makes close ties between citizens and the state harder to reproduce.[28] Of great importance, the pacification of core regions has been accompanied by calls for greater political representation from minority nations whose claims have long been suppressed on the grounds that national unity is essential given the reality of endemic interstate violence.

The conditions under which the state has exercised its monopoly power of taxation have been transformed by globalization, which compresses time and space.[29] Global capital markets and the internationalization of relations of production limit the state's capacity to determine national economic policy autonomously. Globalization is closely linked with interstate pacification, as Rosecrance has observed in his analysis of the rise of the trading state.[30] The conquest of territory has become a barrier to economic growth and the cult of violence hardly features in the self-image of core powers, at least in their dealings with one another if not in their relations with perceived threats in the periphery. Numerous 'evasions of sovereignty' have appeared, such as various forms of transnational economic cooperation and expanding contacts between Brussels and the domestic regions within the European Union which by-pass national governments entirely.[31] Because of globalization, ancient divisions between separate states are overlaid with new divisions between those who have the capacity to exercise citizenship and those for whom citizenship has been relegated to little more than formal rights. These differences of economic and political power are potentially more important than the traditional differences between nation-states. Globalization has exposed all citizens to the rigours of risk society but it reduces the value of national citizenship for the victims of growing economic inequalities.[32]

No less important, the conditions under which the state has regulated the identity of its citizens are being altered radically. Mass migration is transforming most societies into diverse, multi-ethnic societies. Throughout the world indigenous peoples and minority nations are the spearhead for the 'politics of recognition' which rejects national-assimilationist practices and ideologies.[33] These counter-hegemonic movements emphasize the value of cultural diversity and many assert the need for the public recognition of group-specific rights which detach 'the principle of cultural distinctness from that of statehood'.[34] All communities are locked into global communication and information networks embodying new forms of sociocultural power, with highly ambiguous results.

Groups espousing cultural closure compete with groups favouring greater openness to the outside world as a result of sharpening divisions in most societies between privileged transnational elites and what Beck has called 'the proletariat in global risk society'.[35] Globalization confronts states with difficult choices about the appropriate level of engagement with regional organizations and about the current relevance of national sovereignty. Central governments are finding it increasingly difficult to generate a commanding consensus about questions of national identity and national purpose as a result.

The context in which the state exercises its legal powers has also been transformed by globalization. Pressures to relax traditional assumptions about sovereign immunity have increased in the wake of commercial developments between states and private economic organizations. The use of international legislation to harmonize areas of national policy is pronounced, as is the development of the closer international scrutiny of the state's regard for the human rights of its citizens. Strong pressures exist in multicultural societies to interpret and apply the law sensitively in the light of cultural differences.[36] The state's claim to be the exclusive subject of international law has been eroded by the increasing visibility of the individual, subnational groups and indigenous peoples in international legal conventions. The right of the state to bind whole communities in international law is checked by the powerful notion that states are accountable to international society for their treatment of the minority cultures within their midst.[37]

The nature of the bond uniting members of the same society and separating them from the rest of humanity is being transformed across the world – most dramatically in many parts of Europe. In most societies, the character of the social bond is keenly contested, with the result that few communities are now entirely at one with themselves.[38] In these fluid conditions, the possibility of new forms of political community can no longer be dismissed as facile or utopian. The prospect of a post-Westphalian international society is already immanent within contemporary patterns of social, economic, cultural and political change, and new visions of community and citizenship have begun to appear in this context.[39] The upshot of these developments is that higher levels of universality and diversity can now be achieved by transcending the classical Westphalian sovereign state.[40]

Bull's comments about the future European state have acquired greater relevance in recent years, although it is essential to take his argument further by developing the normative and sociological analysis of the changing world of bounded communities. It is especially important to explore the relationship between critical theory, the discourse theory of morality and cosmopolitan democracy to advance the case for a transnational, multi-ethnic social democracy.

CRITICAL THEORY, MODES OF EXCLUSION
AND TRANSNATIONAL DEMOCRACY

The argument thus far is that the vision of cosmopolitan democracy does not clash with the existing order but gives expression to important but contested developments within the modern states of Europe. Although various political actors oppose shifting power to local regions and transnational structures, complex processes of social change reveal that the notion of cosmopolitan democracy is no longer fanciful. To show that this is a normatively desirable political future rather than simply an intriguing empirical possibility, it is useful to link recent discussions of cosmopolitan democracy with critical social theory and the discourse theory of morality.

There is an important parallel between Bull's remark about defending normative principles which support trends running against the present system and the method of critical social theory which examines the extent to which higher levels of political self-determination are immanent within existing forms of life. Rather like Bull's approach, critical theory argues for higher levels of universality and difference, and suggests that the important political question is how structures can be devised which strike the right balance between them.[41] Bull's position on the diffusion of sovereign power and the dispersal of political loyalties to several centres of political authority can be defended on the grounds that it will extend the democratic process, although the link with democratic governance is not as explicit in his writings as it is in critical social theory.[42] In Habermas's writings, support for the vision of multiple political authorities and loyalties in Western Europe is anchored in a conception of more dialogic forms of life which secure advances in universality and difference.[43]

A few comments on Habermas's argument about dialogic communities are warranted at this point. The discourse theory of morality which is elaborated in his writings defends the creation of dialogic relations at all levels of social and political life. This approach argues that human beings need to be reflective about the ways in which they include some in and exclude others from dialogue. It maintains that human subjects should be willing to problematize bounded communities (indeed social boundaries of every variety). It places the legitimacy of practices of exclusion in doubt whenever there is a failure to take account of their impact on the interests of subaltern groups and alien outsiders. Visions of the enlargement of dialogic encounters therefore clash with the principle of national sovereignty, which excludes such groups from participating in dialogue regarding issues which affect their vital interests.

Strong support for the normative vision of cosmopolitan democracy is evident in these claims. To consider this further, it is important to recall that the discourse theory of morality argues that norms cannot be valid unless they can command the consent of everyone whose interests stand to be affected by them.[44] A central claim is that the validity of principles can only be established through forms of dialogue which are in principle open to every human being. Starting with this premise, the discourse approach sets out the preconditions of authentic dialogue. These include the convention that no person and no moral position can be excluded from dialogue in advance. True dialogue is not a trial of strength between adversaries hell-bent on intellectual conquest, but an encounter in which human beings accept that there is no *a priori* certainty about who will learn from whom, and engage in a process of 'reciprocal critique' which is designed to create social arrangements which meet with the consent of all.[45]

An important theme in this argument is that public agreements should not be secured by effacing individual or cultural differences.[46] Habermas argues that a 'fully transparent . . . homogenized and unified society' is not his political ideal, but his claim that the aim of dialogue is to determine which principles can be generalized has been interpreted as endorsing the quest for a universal ethical consensus.[47] Fearing that differences might be cancelled by a stifling consensus, some feminist writers have argued that moral universals cannot emerge without dialogue between concrete others, and may not issue from dialogue at all.[48] These feminist approaches are not opposed to universalism as such but they reject forms of universalism which deny the importance of gender differences and threaten the survival of cultural diversity.[49] They stress that true discourse requires sympathetic engagement with the very different standpoints which may be taken by the 'other' and the recognition that all that may result from dialogue is an agreement to disagree.

Whether these developments redirect Habermasian critical theory or clarify intentions and aspirations which have long been crucial to Habermas's project need not detain us here. Suffice it to say that the upshot of these discussions is that the discourse theory of morality supports the development of communities which are simultaneously far more universalistic and far more open to difference than most modern states have been (or could have been when the danger of interstate war was high). Critical theory therefore intersects with the analysis of the post-Westphalian state developed earlier. It supports the normative commitment to modes of cosmopolitan democracy which seek to extend the boundaries of political community by institutionalizing universal moral principles which embody respect for cultural differences.[50]

The discourse approach to morality sets out the procedures which need to be followed so that individuals are equally free to express their moral positions and able to employ the force of the better argument to resolve their differences or to strike the appropriate compromise between competing views. It does not seek to provide solutions to substantive moral debates, envisage historical end-points or circulate utopian blueprints, but it is not entirely lacking in substantive content. The approach strongly criticizes structures and beliefs which obstruct open dialogue. Illustrating this theme, Cohen argues that the perspective is opposed to all forms of life which are 'based on domination, violence and systematic inequality', or which are hostile to full and open participation.[51] Cohen stresses the contribution of liberal-democratic society in this regard without assuming that Western liberal democracy is the one model of government which should apply universally. By implication, the discourse theory of morality can be institutionalized in many different systems of governance which are sensitive to the diversity of forms of life, although clearly it cannot be realized in societies which tolerate deep social inequalities. Nor can its goals be advanced in societies which jealously guard their sovereignty or assume that all citizens must share one dominant national identity.

The discourse theory of morality necessarily questions traditional notions of sovereignty and citizenship with a view to realizing possibilities for new forms of political community which already exist within modern societies. Rethinking citizenship is crucial since this concept has been central to the social bond which simultaneously unites the members of the sovereign state and sets them apart from the rest of humanity. Troubled by political structures which fail to take account of the interests of other societies, critical theory supports the widening of the moral and political boundaries of communities. But while supporting this development, it does not forget the extent to which most societies have excluded members of minority groups from full participation in collective arrangements. Recent accounts of critical theory argue that traditional ideas of statehood have possessed an assimilationist logic which indigenous peoples, minority nations and racial minorities emphatically reject.[52] As Kymlicka argues, these groups deny that the citizens of modern states must share the same identity and possess exactly the same political rights.[53] As well as advocating a new social contract with members of traditionally marginal groups, recent approaches to critical theory imagine forms of community in which outsiders have greater political representation and voice.[54] A more radical step is to argue that these two far-reaching developments should be integrated. Increasing the representation of subaltern groups in international institutions which are committed to transnational democracy is one important means of achieving unprecedented levels of universality and diversity.

In summary, the discourse approach to morality questions the social bond between the citizen and the state which perpetuates the sovereign state as a system of dual closure. The perspective challenges traditional modes of exclusion and imagines new dialogic possibilities which require that states despatch their powers in two separate but related directions: upwards in the search for greater universality, and downwards in response to claims for the public recognition of cultural differences. The sentiments which are expressed in Habermas's writings are broadly in line with the views expressed by Bull and provide one means of taking them further. Transfers of power and authority which create the conditions in which cosmopolitan democracy can flourish have profound implications for traditional understandings of citizenship and sovereignty. The next two sections consider these ramifications in more detail.

CITIZENSHIP

Supporters of cosmopolitan democracy envisage the widening of the boundaries of community so that insiders and outsiders are associated as equals within radical experiments in political participation. Enlarging the boundaries of political communities is insufficient however without measures to increase the influence of minority nations and local regions within dialogic communities. Progress in this direction involves the reconceptualization of citizenship and the commencement of a new stage in the development of citizenship rights.

T. H. Marshall's influential account of the development of citizenship in Britain shapes the argument to follow. Marshall suggested that the possibility of enlarging the rights of members was immanent within those societies which relied on the concept of citizenship to constitute the social bond. Initial commitments to the legal rights of citizens has entangled societies in manifold tensions and contradictions which arise less starkly, if they arise at all, in social systems in which citizenship does not enter into the constitution of the social bond.[55] Pressures to redefine and extend citizenship so that political, social and cultural rights were added to legal rights emerged in these societies.[56] Uncertainties about the nature and purposes of community, resistance to prevailing structures and predominant conceptions of identity and a degree of openness to future patterns of international relations have been intrinsic to societies which have been shaped by the ideals of citizenship.

Citizenship is therefore intriguing from the vantage-point of critical social theory because it has been central to the systems of inclusion and exclusion which are peculiar to modern states. It has been a means of depriving sections of the population of legal, political, social or cultural rights, but tensions between the egalitarian claims which are inherent in the language of citizenship and actual social inequalities have repeatedly generated resistance on the part of marginal groups. Restricted access to, or definitions of, citizenship have been the spur to political action which has aimed for the extension of citizenship rights for the previously excluded. The creation of new citizenship rights has been an unsurprising but far from inevitable response to deep social contradictions within modern states.

Marshall argued that demands for citizenship in the eighteenth century emphasized the rights which were necessary for individual freedom and which could be protected through the courts. In the nineteenth century, citizenship came to include the right of political participation, which required generalized access to the parliamentary process. In the twentieth century, citizenship has come to include 'the right to a modicum of economic welfare and security [and] the right to share to the full in the social heritage'.[57] A certain logic had unfolded here, which was the conclusion Marshall reached in his analysis of the development of citizenship in Britain over the last two centuries. He argued that the evolution of citizenship rights possessed its own forward momentum, with each advance creating the context for additional political claims for dismantling unjust exclusion. Marshall argued that the right to protection under the law was incomplete without the additional capacity to participate in the law-making process; in turn, the right of political participation was inadequate unless citizens had access to the social resources which make it possible for them to exercise what would otherwise remain merely formal rights. There is no reason to suppose that the development of citizenship had to unravel as if ushered along by some historical teleology, but there were good reasons why citizenship was shaped by significant 'developmental pressures'.[58] Initial steps to enlarge citizenship generated the experience of second-class citizenship and triggered additional pressures to promote full membership of the political community.

Various ambiguities and antinomies have surrounded the evolution of citizenship in the national domain, and many attempts to overcome these problems have had detrimental consequences for the society of states. As E. H. Carr argued, states in the first part of the century enlarged the meaning of citizenship to include welfare rights, but international tensions increased in the process.[59] Economic nationalism led to the demise of large-scale immigration, and rivalries between nation-states increased after the momentous decision was taken in 1919 to close national frontiers. Inflamed initially by the drift towards protectionism, nationalism after the First World War encouraged total war, and popular hatred blurred the vital distinction between military and civilian targets. Coupled with the decline of international law in the 1930s, the deportation of peoples to tidy the frontiers signalled the end of the liberal epoch in which nationalism united citizens without creating aggressively particularistic attitudes towards peoples elsewhere. International order was weakened as political communities in Europe became more tightly bound and more sharply divided from each other in this period.

The extension of citizenship in the first part of the century deepened the tension between obligations to the state and obligations to humanity in Europe. But questions surrounding the morality of war, global social justice and human rights ensured that the normative status of the civic bond which unites and separates the citizens of states remained controversial. Since then, the cosmopolitan element in European international society has ensured that arguments for treating insiders and outsiders as moral equals retain their importance for modern political communities. Conceptions of national citizenship have been challenged where they exclude moral obligations to outsiders.

One illustration is Shue's consideration of the ethics of exporting hazards. Shue argues that asbestos-producing plant in the United States was closed and subsequently exported to Sierra Leone given the incontrovertible evidence that asbestos production damaged the health of American workers.[60] Shue's contention is that there was no moral justification in this case for treating insiders and outsiders differently, and more generally, there is no ethical defence for the practice of exporting hazards to other countries. This argument lends ethical support to the idea of global citizenship defined as duties to vulnerable non-nationals. It is important, however, to extend the idea of global citizenship understood as 'duties beyond borders' to include, wherever possible, transnational democratic structures. The logic of moral equality, it will be argued, is best realized through democratic processes which bring insiders and outsiders together as transnational citizens with equal rights of participation.

Most recent accounts of global citizenship do not stretch this far: most stress moral obligations to the rest of humanity. Derek Heater argues that citizenship need not be confined exclusively to the rights and duties which individuals have as members of particular sovereign states.[61] Citizenship as a system of moral duties rather than legal rights can be associated with any geographical unit from the city to the whole of humanity. Heater refers to world social citizenship to convey the duties which the rich have to the poor in world society, and similarly, Martin Shaw argues for 'post-military citizenship' in which the classical duty of citizens to defend the state is replaced by obligations to the poor and duties to the environment.[62] These efforts to reconfigure the idea of citizenship encourage its severance from the relatively closed world of the sovereign state. As noted earlier, the relationship between the state and humanity has been a matter of dispute in the modern West given the impact of cosmopolitan ideas about the moral equality of all members of humankind. Addressing this problem, global citizenship encompasses moral duties to others which help reduce the tension between obligations to the state and obligations to the rest of humanity.[63]

Although it is an important step in carrying the principle of equality forward into the sphere of international relations, the idea of global citizenship has many weaknesses. Its emphasis is on the duty of the strong to help others, and on the need for the compassion of world citizens. But as Michael Ignatieff has argued, citizenship is generally taken to be about rights of participation rather than duties to others. Strictly speaking, citizenship is less about compassion than about 'ensuring for everyone the entitlements necessary for the exercise of their freedom'.[64] Ideas about global citizenship do not extend this far because they are principally concerned with the moral duties of citizens of the world. Heater's defence of world social citizenship leaves open the question of whether duty holders are at liberty to decide the extent of their international moral obligations. The moral duties of global citizens need not be accompanied by the notion that insiders and outsiders have the right to participate as equals in transnational democratic structures: they may not be connected with the belief that the members of different societies should have the freedom to grant or withhold their consent to decisions made in joint political arrangements. Nevertheless, the idea of global citizenship defends the realm of cosmopolitan moral duty. As such, it is an important bridge between the circumstances in which the ethical constituency is limited to co-nationals and a future condition in which universal political structures guarantee concrete social and political rights for the whole of humanity.

Developments such as the Nuremberg Convention challenged traditional conceptions of citizenship by defining the rights and duties inherent in an imagined moral community which transcends the boundaries of sovereign states. The Nuremberg Doctrine established that individuals had the right to disobey unlawful superior orders and could be brought before international courts where they might be found guilty of crimes against peace and against humanity. A nascent form of global citizenship was enshrined in the Nuremberg Convention, although the international rights and duties so defined were imperfect since the victorious powers retained their discretion over decisions about whom to bring before international courts of law.

Few images of global citizenship reach much further, and realizing the promise of more active forms of citizenship which can be regarded as immanent within cosmopolitan claims about the moral equality of all human beings remains a distant hope. However, an intermediate step between the Nuremberg Convention and forms of citizenship which typify the post-Westphalian state can be found in E. H. Carr's remarks on the desirable trajectory of European political development after the Second World War. Carr argued in *Nationalism and After* that interstate violence in the first part of the century occurred because the liberal balance between nationalism and internationalism collapsed following the state's increased role in national economic life. Carr imagined a new European polity which brought insiders and outsiders together as moral equals and protected their basic welfare rights. New transnational structures which were responsible for securing social citizenship were envisaged for Europe in the aftermath of the Second World War. Carr's observations about the future of citizenship are intriguing in the light of more recent efforts to construct notions of European citizenship for the peoples of the European Union.

In the new world of welfare internationalism, Carr argued, the interests of the people of Dusseldorf and Lille would count as much as the welfare of the inhabitants of Oldham or Jarrow. The transformation of political community was required because national citizenship could no longer secure the social benefits which had come to be expected from it. Carr's imagined transnational polity placed all citizens on the same level without disregarding their cultural differences. Rather like Bull's neo-medievalism, Carr's vision argued that 'the international community if it is to flourish must admit [a] multiplicity of authorities and diversity of loyalties.'[65] In this polity, international citizenship would no longer revolve around the benevolent act of performing duties to others who nevertheless lacked concrete entitlements. The principle of moral equality would be incorporated within a system of determinate social rights.[66]

Carr set out a major argument in support of the transition from the Westphalian to the post-Westphalian state over fifty years ago and, if anything, the case has strengthened considerably in recent years. Turner argues that 'we have a system of national citizenship in a social context which requires a new theory of internationalism and universalistic citizenship,'[67] and Balibar maintains that the 'struggle for citizenship as a struggle for equality must begin again' with the emergence of 'a cosmopolis of communications and financial transactions'.[68] These commitments invite the transcendence of the conflict between the state and humanity which was intensified in the first part of the century following the evolution of national citizenship, but what distinguishes them from global citizenship is that they move beyond the advocacy of duty and compassion to support for transnational democratic structures within a post-Westphalian society of states.

Carr argued that new political structures would need to take account of the variety of human loyalties, and his writings raised the central question of how the rights of minority nations could best be protected. It is important to recall that most states were unenthusiastic about introducing measures to protect minorities in the aftermath of the Second World War because the defence of minority rights had provided the pretext for Nazi German annexation of areas such as the Sudetenland. But at the century's end, no serious account of citizenship can proceed without recognizing that one of the main challenges to its part in preserving exclusionary communities comes from indigenous peoples and minority nations. Democratic polities have come under pressure to revise conventional understandings of citizenship in the light of the contemporary politics of cultural recognition.

Traditional conceptions of citizenship abstract from the particularity of persons to define the rights to which all individuals are entitled as equals. The politics of recognition argues that modern notions of citizenship are exclusionary because they neglect the different needs of specific groups such as minority nations and indigenous groups. A cogent defence of this point of view is provided by Phillips, who argues there is a short step between arguing that all citizens are equal despite their differences to concluding that differences do not matter at all.[69] Further, the invitation to particular groups to transcend their particularity, and to identify with the wider good, can all too easily be a summons to accept the cultural dominance of privileged groups. For these reasons assimilationist strategies have been challenged by the doctrine that other cultures should be treated as different and equal rather than regarded as deviant departures from pre-existing norms.[70] The upshot is that minority nations and indigenous peoples should be incorporated in the state consociationally rather than universally if the boundaries of the territorial state do not correspond with the boundaries of a single cultural community.[71] Disjunctions between the boundaries of cultural and political communities have intensified in the parts of Europe where the risk of interstate war is low, with important consequences for citizenship.

POST-WESTPHALIAN COMMUNITIES

Attempts to universalize citizenship by extending rights in international relations, and efforts to particularize it by recognizing special group rights, comprise two of the most important contemporary means of eradicating unjustified exclusion. Bull's references to a neo-medieval Europe indicated that a polity combining greater universality and difference would contain multiple structures of authority and patterns of loyalty which prompted the question of whether the concept of sovereignty had ceased to be relevant. The analysis of citizenship in the previous section points towards a similar conclusion. Further extensions of citizenship necessarily involve a significant break with the Westphalian principle of state sovereignty.

What is at stake is the unitarian conception of sovereignty developed by Bodin and bolstered by much subsequent political theory. Unitarianism argues that what 'makes a man a citizen [is] the mutual obligation between subject and sovereign' in which faith and obedience are exchanged for justice, counsel, assistance, encouragement and protection.[72] Four points are worth noting about the classical doctrine of sovereignty: first, no one can be the subject of more than one sovereign; second, only one sovereign power can prevail within any single territory; third, all citizens must have exactly the same status and rights; and fourth, the bond between citizen and sovereign necessarily excludes aliens.[73]

The ideals of cosmopolitan democracy and the Westphalian principles of sovereignty and citizenship are inevitably in tension. Greater universality and diversity require that citizens are free to develop subnational and transnational projects in several political arenas which are not arranged hierarchically. Cosmopolitan democracy involves the dispersal of sovereign powers rather than their aggregation in a single authority. If the social bond is transformed to recognize claims for diversity, then the rights of citizens need to have a flexible and varying content: the idea of an undifferentiated public which is subordinate to one sovereign power becomes untenable. Citizenship can then embrace individual rights of access to international bodies to seek redress against abuses of sovereign power. If the social bond is to be modified so that outsiders enjoy equal rights of access to dialogue, then the supposition that the rights of citizens must be protected by one sovereign container has to be abandoned. The upshot is new modes of citizenship in which multiple political identities and loyalties break with the unitarian conception of sovereignty.

To develop these points further it is useful to consider the thin conception of citizenship set out in the European Union Treaty and to reflect on what a thicker conception of citizenship would entail. The relevant section of the European Union Treaty (article 8), which maintains that 'every person holding the nationality of a Member State shall be a citizen of the Union', stresses the following individual legal rights or entitlements: the right of free movement within Europe and to reside in the territory of another member state; the right to petition the European Parliament or the EU Ombudsman; and the right to receive assistance from any member state while overseas. The Treaty creates a set of individual political rights: the right to vote and stand as a candidate in local elections in other countries and to vote or stand as a candidate for the European Parliament.[74]

What is established in article 8 of the Treaty is a thin conception of citizenship which is more appropriate for the development of an international civil society than for a transnational political community. A thicker conception of citizenship would include the right of appeal beyond the state to European courts of law, and participation in international organizations which institutionalize the right of individuals to engage in 'joint rule'.[75] It would rework the social bond to transcend the claim that all citizens have to share one dominant national identity and owe allegiance to one exclusive sovereign power. It would grant substate national identities and emergent transnational loyalties an unprecedented political role.

Two further aspects of the thick conception of citizenship warrant consideration. The first is suggested by Marshall's remarks that public recognition of formal rights is not enough to ensure full membership of a political community. Social and economic rights which make it possible for citizens to exercise their legal and political entitlements are vital for the reasons contained in Marshall's account. A second point is that an additional cluster of citizenship rights is necessary to respond adequately to the politics of recognition. Problems inherent in forms of citizenship which abstract from the particularity of persons were noted earlier. Fears that membership of the European Union might have the consequence of eroding the distinctive political traditions and identities of smaller countries have featured strongly in recent debates, not least in Scandinavia. These reservations about, or protests against, the widening of the boundaries of political community require that visions of cosmopolitan democracy address methods of bridging the gulf between the national or subnational loyalties of citizens and transnational political institutions. As already noted, such measures are critical if a transnational, multi-ethnic social democracy is to develop.

At least four possible ways of overcoming the distance between citizens and cosmopolitan democratic institutions exist: one, devolving political power so that citizenship can be enjoyed through participation in subnational or substate assemblies; two, ensuring that minority nations are adequately represented in transnational institutions; three, making it possible for the members of minority nations (and for racial and other minorities) to appeal to international courts which are authorized to scrutinize claims of unfair discrimination; and, four, providing subnational regions with access to adequate material resources to withstand the effects of de-industrialization on vulnerable economies and to ensure the survival of minority languages and cultures. These strategies can help overcome the problem of distance in wider political associations which transcend the sovereign state. The modes of citizenship discussed in the preceding paragraphs do not include the notion of global citizenship understood as duties to assist desperate strangers elsewhere. But this notion is important for reflecting upon the ways in which post-Westphalian societies should behave towards the rest of the world. Assuming the moral responsibilities of world citizenship is important if a post-Westphalian international society is to honour a commitment 'to not closing itself off'.[76]

What needs further discussion is the sequence of citizenship rights which is essential in the post-Westphalian era. Marshall's writings contained an implicit dialectics of citizenship relevant to the modern state. Legal rights were inadequate without rights of participation, but these had limited value where deep inequalities of power and wealth prevented large numbers of citizens from enjoying their legal and political entitlements. Taking the dialectic of citizenship further is essential for the reasons outlined in Carr's defence of welfare internationalism. It is possible to build on Carr's account not only by envisaging cosmopolitan democracy but also by arguing that the project of widening the moral and political boundaries of community should be linked with efforts to restore the rights of minority nations and to strengthen voluntary associations. What this is to anticipate is the reconfiguration of citizenship to bind complex levels of identities (subnational, national and supranational) in new forms of political community.[77] Reversing the processes which led to the formation of the modern European state is necessary to ensure that citizenship does not advance the cause of equality and simultaneously stand in its way.

It is possible to imagine citizens of a polity which is wider than the state but which is not itself a state because it does not monopolize control of the instruments of violence, exercise the sole right of taxation, single out just one identity and make this superior to all others, function as the final court of legal appeal, or claim the sole right of representation in international organizations and the exclusive power to bind the whole community in international law. Although it is not a state, this wider and deeper political community would necessarily encroach on traditional state monopoly powers and depart from the unitarian conception of sovereignty. According to this theory, as noted earlier, no one can be the subject of more than one sovereign and only one sovereign can prevail within a given territorial state. Further, all citizens have to possess the same status and identity, and the bond which links them together must exclude aliens. Citizens of the post-Westphalian state, by comparison, can come under the jurisdiction of several political authorities; they can have multiple identities; and they need not be united by social bonds which make them indifferent to, or enemies of, the rest of the human race. The form of state which has prevailed during the Westphalian era has defended national interests against outsiders, and frequently it has taken little account of matters of particular concern to the minorities within its borders; the post-Westphalian state can remove these moral deficits by reworking the relationship between subnational and other identities within the state, traditional nation-state loyalties and the wider sphere of cosmopolitan obligation.

CONCLUSION

This chapter has brought together several areas of discussion which are infrequently linked: Bull's comments on one possible future for Europe; current trends in Europe which invite further development of his schematic observations; the importance of critical theory and the discourse theory of morality for cosmopolitan democracy; and recent approaches to citizenship which question traditional understandings about political community. One central theme runs through all four areas of discussion – the possibility of remaking political communities to achieve levels of universality and diversity which modern states invariably discouraged under conditions of geopolitical rivalry and the high risk of interstate war. In the new international environment it is both possible and desirable to realize higher levels of universality and diversity by moving beyond the sovereign territorial state.

The argument in favour of reconstructing citizenship in the post-Westphalian state supports the claim that although citizenship is one of the central achievements of modern states, it is both 'too puffed up and too compressed': too puffed up because the needs of those who do not share the dominant national culture have frequently been disregarded; too compressed because the interests of outsiders have generally been ignored.[78] The argument set out here builds on the claim that modern states should 'go higher in [the] search for citizenship, but also lower and wider. Higher to the world, lower to the locality.'[79] 'Higher' forms of citizenship include rights of participation in supranational structures and the international protection of the individual's legal and welfare rights. 'Lower' forms of citizenship entail increasing the power of local communities and subnational groups. 'Higher' and 'lower' forms of citizenship can be integrated by granting subnational and substate groups the right of appeal to international bodies and parallel forms of representation in international institutions.

Europe gave birth to the ideas of sovereignty, territoriality, nationality and citizenship which were subsequently exported to the rest of the world. Whether the era in which these principles were central to political life is at an end is a matter of dispute. Some dimensions of European politics suggest that a new era may be emerging in which the principle of moral equality will underpin active citizenship within post-Westphalian arrangements.[80] The new polity which might come about would mark a momentous step forward for the peoples of Europe and might come to be regarded as a historical watershed in the evolution of international society as a whole. Various forces are loosening the grip of the nation-state so that a wider range of political identities and authorities can unfold. The normative task is to give these developments concrete expression in forms of political community which are committed to realizing the Kantian ideal of a universal kingdom of ends.

NOTES

This chapter is a revised version of a paper first published in the *European Journal of International Relations*, 2 (1996), pp. 77–103. I am grateful to the editor for permission to publish in this volume.

1   M. Wight, *Power Politics* (Leicester: Leicester University Press, 1978), p. 25.
2   W. B. Gallie, *Philosophers of Peace and War* (Cambridge: Cambridge University Press, 1978).
3   H. Bull, *The Anarchical Society: a Study of Order in World Politics* (London: Macmillan, 1977), p. 275.

4   Ibid., pp. 275–6.
5   See D. Heater, *Citizenship: the Civic Ideal in World History, Politics and Education* (London: Longman, 1991), p. 319; B. Turner, *Citizenship and Social Theory* (London: Sage, 1993), p. 15.
6   J. Camilleri and J. Falk, *The End of Sovereignty? The Politics of a Shrinking and Fragmenting World* (Aldershot: Edward Elgar, 1992).
7   David Beetham, chapter 3 above.
8   C. Taylor, *Multiculturalism and the Politics of Recognition* (Princeton: Princeton University Press, 1994); I. M. Young, *Justice and the Politics of Difference* (Princeton: Princeton University Press, 1991).
9   D. Archibugi and D. Held (eds), *Cosmopolitan Democracy: an Agenda for a New World Order* (Cambridge: Polity Press, 1995), p. 13.
10 H. Bull, 'The state's positive role in world affairs', *Daedalus*, 108 (1979), p. 114.
11 Bull, *The Anarchical Society*, p. 254.
12 Bull, 'The state's positive role in world affairs', p. 114.
13 Bull, *The Anarchical Society*, p. 266.
14 Ibid.
15 Bull, 'The state's positive role in world affairs', p. 114. As with any other order, Bull argued, the neo-medieval order might well contain the risk of violence among other ills but the real issue is how structures and principles can be put in place which minimize such risks. Bull was strongly disinclined to reflect on alternative forms of political organization on the grounds that moral and political advocacy had a corrupting influence in the social sciences.
16 See Camilleri and Falk, *The End of Sovereignty?*; E. Meehan, *Citizenship and the European Community* (London: Sage, 1993).
17 D. Held, *Democracy and the Global Order: From the Modern State to Cosmopolitan Governance* (Cambridge: Polity Press, 1995); Archibugi and Held, *Cosmopolitan Democracy*.
18 G. Biro, 'Minority rights in Eastern and Central Europe and the role of international institutions', in J. Laurenti (ed.), *Search for Moorings: East Central Europe in the International System* (New York: Sage, 1994).
19 H. Bull, 'International theory: the case for a classical approach', *World Politics*, 18 (1966), p. 365. These crucial themes are addressed in Deutsch's rather neglected work on security communities, see K. Deutsch, *Political Community at the International Level* (New York: Archon Books, 1970).
20 B. Nelson, 'Note on the notion of civilisation by Émile Durkheim and Marcel Mauss', *Social Research*, 37 (1971), pp. 808–13, and 'Civilisational complexes and inter-civilisational relations', *Sociological Analysis* (1973), pp. 79–105.
21 Camilleri and Falk, *The End of Sovereignty?*, p. 9; see also ibid., ch. 9.
22 See A. Giddens, *The Nation-State and Violence* (Cambridge: Polity Press, 1985); M. Mann, *The Sources of Social Power*, vol. 1 (Cambridge: Cambridge University Press, 1986); C. Tilly, *Coercion, Capital and European States: AD 990–1992* (Oxford: Blackwell, 1993).
23 Tilly, *Coercion, Capital and European States*, points out that the Prussian monarchy's main tax collection agency began life as the Prussian War Commissariat (p. 70).

24 C. Tilly, 'Futures of European states', *Social Research*, 58 (1992), p. 709.
25 O. Hintze, *The Historical Essays of Otto Hintze* (New York: Oxford University Press, 1975), p. 211.
26 Tilly, 'Futures of European states'.
27 W. Wallace, 'Rescue or retreat? The nation-state in Western Europe', *Political Studies*, 41 (1994), pp. 52–76.
28 J. Mueller, *Retreat from Doomsday: the Obsolescence of Major War* (New York: Basic Books, l989).
29 D. Held and A. McGrew, 'Globalization and the liberal democratic state', in Y. Sakamoto (ed.), *Global Transformation: Challenges to the State System* (New York: United Nations University Press, 1994), p. 59.
30 R. Rosecrance, *The Rise of the Trading State: Commerce and Conquest in the Modern World* (New York: Basic Books, 1986).
31 R. Falk, 'Evasions of sovereignty', in R. Walker and S. Mendlowitz (eds), *Contending Sovereignties: Redefining Political Community* (Boulder, Colo.: Lynne Reiner, 1990).
32 U. Beck, *Risk Society: Towards a New Modernity* (London: Sage, 1992).
33 Taylor, *Multiculturalism and the Politics of Recognition*.
34 Tilly, 'Futures of European states', p. 705.
35 Beck, *Risk Society*.
36 B. Parekh, 'British citizenship and cultural difference', in G. Andrews (ed.), *Citizenship* (London: Lawrence and Wishart, 1991).
37 See Beetham, chapter 3 above.
38 J. Derrida, *The Other Heading: Reflections on Today's Europe* (Bloomington: Indiana University Press, 1992), pp. 9–11.
39 W. Connolly, 'Democracy and territoriality', in M. Ringrose and A. J. Lerner (eds), *Reimagining the Nation* (Buckingham: Open University Press, 1993); D. Held, 'Democracy, from city states to a cosmopolitan order', in D. Held (ed.) *Prospects for Democracy: North, South, East, West* (Cambridge: Polity Press, 1993); W. Kymlicka, *Liberalism, Community and Culture* (Oxford: Oxford University Press, 1989); W. Kymlicka, *Multicultural Citizenship: a Liberal Theory of Minority Rights* (Oxford: Clarendon Press, 1995); A. Linklater, 'What is a good international citizen?' in P. Keal (ed.), *Ethics and Foreign Policy* (Sydney: Allen and Unwin, 1992); A. Linklater, 'The achievements of critical theory', in S. Smith, K. Booth and M. Zalewski (eds), *International Theory: Positivism and Beyond* (Cambridge: Cambridge University Press, 1996); R. B. J. Walker, *Inside/Outside: International Relations as Political Theory* (Cambridge: Cambridge University Press, 1993).
40 A. Linklater, *The Transformation of Political Community: Ethical Foundations of the Post-Westphalian Era* (Cambridge: Polity Press, 1998).
41 Ibid., ch. 3.
42 J. Habermas, *The Past as Future* (Cambridge: Polity Press, 1994).
43 'Afterword', in ibid.
44 J. Habermas, *The Theory of Communicative Action*, vol. 2: *The Critique of Functionalist Reason* (London: Heinemann, 1989), pp. 82ff.
45 J. Habermas, *Moral Consciousness and Communicative Action* (Cambridge: Polity Press, 1990), p. 26.
46 Habermas, *The Past as Future*, pp. 11–20.

47   J. Habermas, 'A philosophical-political profile', *New Left Review*, no. 151 (1985), pp. 75–105.

48   S. Benhabib, *Situating the Self: Gender, Community and Postmodernism in Contemporary Ethics* (Cambridge: Polity Press, 1993), p. 9. The argument first arose in the feminist literature, specifically in regard to the Gilligan/ Kohlberg debate. Carol Gilligan argued that Lawrence Kohlberg's claim that universal ethical orientations were the most advanced devalued what she described as the ethic of care and responsibility, an ethical orientation which is commonly central to the experience of women caring for specific others within the family. See S. Benhabib and D. Cornell (eds), *Feminism as Critique: Essays on the Politics of Gender in Late-Capitalist Societies* (Cambridge: Polity Press, 1987).

49   Benhabib, *Situating the Self*; C. Gilligan, *In a Different Voice* (Cambridge: Harvard University Press, 1993); O. O'Neill, 'Justice, gender and international boundaries', *British Journal of Political Science* (1989), pp. 439–59; Young, *Justice and the Politics of Difference*.

50   Linklater, *The Transformation of Political Community*.

51   J. Cohen, 'Discourse ethics and civil society', in H. Rasmussen (ed.), *Universalism vs Communitarianism* (Cambridge: MIT Press, 1990), pp. 71, 100.

52   Linklater, *The Transformation of Political Community*, chs 2–3.

53   Kymlicka, *Liberalism, Community and Culture*; Kymlicka, *Multicultural Citizenship*.

54   Linklater, *The Transformation of Political Community*.

55   T. H. Marshall, *Class, Citizenship and Social Development* (Westport, Conn.: Greenwood Press, 1973).

56   A. Honneth, *The Struggle for Recognition: the Moral Grammar of Social Conflicts* (Cambridge: Polity Press, 1995), pp. 115–18.

57   Marshall, *Class, Citizenship and Social Development*, pp. 71ff.

58   Honneth, *The Struggle for Recognition*, p. 115.

59   E. H. Carr, *Nationalism and After* (London: Macmillan, 1945).

60   H. Shue, 'Exporting hazards', in P. G. Brown and H. Shue (eds), *Boundaries: National Autonomy and its Limits* (Toyota, N.J.: Rowman, 1981).

61   Heater, *Citizenship*, pp. 163–4.

62   M. Shaw, *Post-Military Society: Militarism, Demilitarization and War at the End of the Twentieth Century* (Cambridge: Polity Press, 1991), p. 187.

63   R. Falk, 'The making of global citizenship', in B. Van Steenbergen (ed.), *The Condition of Citizenship* (London: Sage, 1994).

64   M. Ignatieff, 'Citizenship and moral narcissism', in Andrews, *Citizenship*, p. 34.

65   Carr, *Nationalism and After*, p. 45.

66   For further consideration of Carr's writings, see Linklater, 'The transformation of political community': E. H. Carr, 'Critical theory and international relations', *Review of International Studies*, 22 (1997).

67   B. Turner, *Citizenship and Capitalism: the Debate over Reformism* (London: Allen and Unwin, 1986), p. 140.

68   E. Balibar, 'Propositions on citizenship', *Ethics*, 98 (1988), p. 725.

69   A. Phillips, 'Citizenship and feminist theory', in Andrews, *Citizenship*, pp. 81–3.

70 See T. Todorov, *The Conquest of America* (New York: Harper, 1992) for further consideration of this theme.

71 A particularly striking example is Kymlicka's discussion of special citizenship rights which permit indigenous peoples to restrict the mobility, property and non-voting rights of non-indigenous peoples; see *Liberalism, Community and Culture*, pp. 137–8.

72 J. Bodin, *Six Books on the Commonwealth* (Oxford: Blackwell, 1967), p. 21.

73 A. James, *Sovereign Statehood: the Basis of International Society* (London: Allen and Unwin, 1986), pp. 48, 226–8.

74 M. Wise and R. Gibb, *Single Market to Social Europe: the European Community in the 1990s* (Harlow: Longman, 1993); M. Anderson, M. den Boer and G. Miller, 'European citizenship and cooperation in justice and home affairs', in A. Duff et al. (eds), *Maastricht and Beyond: Building the European Union* (London: Routledge, 1994).

75 C. Brewin, 'Liberal states and international obligations', *Millennium*, 17 (1988), pp. 321–38.

76 Derrida, *The Other Heading*, p. 29.

77 Held, *Democracy and the Global Order*, part 3.

78 A. Wright, 'The good citizen', *New Statesman and Society*, 18 May 1990, p. 32.

79 Ibid., p. 32.

80 Falk, 'The making of global citizenship', pp. 13–17.

7

Citizenship in the European Union: a Paradigm for Transnational Democracy?

Ulrich K. Preuß

In the accelerating process of globalization of economic, political, cultural and scientific relations, the European Union is largely seen as a successful model of the institutionalization of supranationality. Rather than contenting themselves with adding just one more to the manifold international treaties and organizations, the founding fathers of the European Economic Community (which, since Maastricht I, is on its way to a European Union) created more or less without being aware of it an unprecedented entity which they called 'Community'. Some analysts called this entity 'a market without a state' in order to emphasize its purely economic function. Yet, in contrast to a market, from its very beginning the Community possessed institutions which allowed it self-observation and self-evolution, and due to this institutional dowry it was able to develop in the course of a long and protracted process embryonic forms of a polity. The most evident and the most important achievements of that development have been the establishment of the principles of *direct effect* and of the *supremacy of Community law* over national law. *Direct effect* means that provisions of Community law must be applied by the national courts of the member states without prior transformation into national law through the national parliament; the principle of *supremacy* signifies that a directly effective provision of Community law always prevails over a conflicting provision of national law.[1]

The far-reaching implication of the principles of *direct effect* and *supremacy* is the creation of an immediate bond of affiliation between the citizens of the member states and the Community. They enjoy rights and are subject to duties which do not originate in their respective national parliaments, that is, in the political will of the citizenry of which they form a part. Rather, they are subject to legal provisions emanating from Community organs (the Council, the Commission and the European Parliament). Yet these organs do not articulate the will of a European *people* (or citizenry), but of the *peoples* (or citizenries) of the member states. This is also true for the European Parliament, which consists of 'representatives of the peoples of the States brought together in the Community' (article 137, EC Treaty), not of a European people or *demos*. Despite the *direct effect* and the *supremacy* principles the European Community is (still?) a Community of states, at best of peoples, not of citizens. The member states, not the people living within the territory of the European Community, are the constituent factors of the political body of the Community.

However, in the Maastricht Treaty of February 1992 the governments of the member states made a further step towards institutional integration in that they created the institution of 'Union citizenship'. According to article 8 of the amended EC Treaty 'every person holding the nationality of a Member State shall be a citizen of the Union'. Union citizens shall enjoy the rights conferred by the Treaty, including the qualified right to move and reside freely within the territory of the member states, the right of Union citizens who reside in a member state of which they are not nationals to vote and to stand as candidates at municipal elections and in elections to the European Parliament in the member state in which they reside, the right to consular or diplomatic protection by any member state, and the right to petition the European Parliament (articles 8a–8d, EC Treaty). At first glance Union citizenship is not a very impressive status; nationals of third countries are excluded, and the list of rights associated with it is quite short. Still, to be a citizen of a supranational entity is a major innovation in the history of political membership which merits closer scrutiny. Can we understand this new European institution as a major breakthrough in the institutional mastering of the goal of transnational solidarity which could eventually even entail some kind of transnational democracy?

Given the complex character of the concept of citizenship I shall start with a brief account of the broad scope of historical meanings which have been associated with the concept of citizenship in Europe since antiquity. In a second step I shall draw some tentative conclusions from this record and approach the idea of supranational citizenship. This undertaking can readily be understood as a preliminary study for the more difficult venture, namely to develop the constituents of transnational citizenship. However, this exacting objective is not part of this paper.

THE UNCLEAR MEANING OF 'EUROPEAN CITIZENSHIP'

The idea of 'European citizenship' is quite opaque. Although the concept is not entirely novel,[2] it was not until the Maastricht Treaty that the concept (although not the term) was formally established in a legal text of the Community. While the newly inserted text of articles 8 to 8e of the EC Treaty does not create excessively great obstacles to their legal interpretation, it is more difficult to predict how this new element of the EC Treaty may affect the process of European integration, Europe's political culture, and the still uncertain ideas of supranational constitutionalism and supranational democracy. The assessments of the importance of the institution 'citizenship of the Union' are vague and cautious at best. For example, Corbett speaks of a 'notable achievement' without explicating precisely what this achievement might consist of;[3] Curtin considers the insertion of the articles about Union citizenship in the EC Treaty a 'real progress', while stating at the same time that what, *inter alia*, constitutes the 'unique *sui generis* nature of the European Community, its true world-historical significance', namely the character of the Union as a 'cohesive legal unit which confers rights on *individuals*', is endangered by the serious shortfalls of the Treaty of Maastricht.[4] For Meehan, citizenship of the Union is part of a complex development from 'national citizenship to European civil society',[5] while according to a seemingly more down-to-earth statement of a lawyer (written before the conclusion of the Treaty of Maastricht), Union citizenship will at least over the medium term be hardly more than the subsumption of the single rights and duties of the individual under the label 'Union citizenship', without changing either the continuance of the intermediary role of national citizenship or its salient role in the lives of Europeans.[6]

Should the idea of European citizenship in fact materialize, it is safe to assume that its meaning and its importance for the ongoing process of integration will largely be shaped by the concepts of citizenship which have been developed in the several national member states of the Community. This is of course not to say that Union citizenship will be a kind of conglomerate of the different national concepts, in the sense of the lowest common denominator of those of all member states; the hypothesis is, rather, that the diversity of traditions which have shaped the concepts of citizenship in their respective national contexts is likely to generate different or at least differently coloured versions of one single Union citizenship. This proposition is derived from the unique legal attributes of the European Union: although, of course, the rights and duties associated with Union citizenship are rights and duties vis-à-vis the

Community, the principal addressee of the former and guarantors of the discharge of the latter are and will be the national member states, because the great bulk of Community law is implemented and enforced by them rather than by proper Community institutions and agencies.

If the national member states do indeed remain the principal actors in the areas in which citizenship is important for the daily life of the Europeans, then it seems safe to conclude that the national traditions and conceptual particularities of the several member states will have a major impact on the contours of an evolving concept of Union citizenship. It is hardly conceivable that an institution as essential for the structure of a constitutional polity as citizenship could be constructed without a thorough borrowing of ideas from the basic constitutional ideas of the constituent member states. This makes it a rewarding undertaking to dig into the richness and variety of elements which constitute the idea of citizenship throughout the member states of the Community. In all probability this would bring to light whether and to what degree the different elements of the national concepts of citizenship are sufficiently akin to and consistent with each other in order to serve as the conceptual underpinnings of a European citizenship. Of course, the result of this comparative analysis could also be that the national concepts of citizenship diverge so much that this will eventually prevent the national political actors from finding a common understanding of what European citizenship essentially means or could mean (to them and to the individuals on whom this status is conferred as well).

In the long history since its first appearance in Greek antiquity until recent times, the term 'citizenship' has covered an extremely broad scope of possible meanings. If it is at all possible to discover an invariable element in it, it is probably the notion of an individual's membership of a political community, be that the Greek city-state (*polis*), the Roman empire, the Christian medieval city or the modern territorial nation-state.[7] Evidently the implications of membership are largely determined by the character of the community to which the bonds of affiliation are tied. Given the diversity of communities which Europe has experienced in the last 2,500 years, it is not surprising to encounter a rich diversity of very disparate, if not opposite meanings.

Although the etymological roots of the term refer to the dwellers of a city, the 'city' (*polis*) signifies not so much a merely physical location but a symbolic space in which a new ethics of cooperation has emerged. In its ancient Greek origins, the city, and hence citizenship, replaces the familial and tribal bonds of the individuals and creates a mode of 'civic' cooperation. Its essence consists in the idea of the commonness of fates of individuals who are bound together by the more abstract ties of common religion[8] and, particularly, of common laws.[9] From its very origination in ancient Greece, citizenship has included a distinct status which draws symbolic boundaries not only against those who live physically outside the community, but, even more importantly, also against those who do live within the physical space of the community but who do not belong to it socially. In other words, in its original meaning the concept of citizenship is a social construction which is not only constitutive of the identity of a particular – political – community, but which at the same time defines the social identity of the individuals who in their quality as members replace their family, clan or tribal affiliation with their status in a more abstract community, the polity. Thus citizenship is a concept which is counterfactual in a twofold sense: it sharply distinguishes between the physical and the social boundaries of a society; and it transcends the boundaries of the 'natural' groups of the family, the clan and the tribe towards a *political* organization of a social group.

In fact, a common feature of the concept of citizenship throughout different historical contexts has been its polemical usage as a counterterm against other social roles: a citizen is not only different but is, in a way, the positive counter-image of a person whose defining social characteristics is his or her quality as a consumer, a producer, a client, a subject, a family member or simply a private person. This is perhaps only the consequence of a more fundamental property of citizenship rooted in its historical origin, namely its inherent bent towards a universalist perception of the individual and the ensuing refusal to tie that individual to narrow, parochial and particularistic social roles. As analysed by Max Weber in his sociology of the city,[10] citizenship is a genuinely occidental institution. It is closely associated with the development of the Western-type city and its main characteristics, namely its foundation on the corporate unity of the city dwellers, as opposed to the oriental cities, which were religious and/or clan associations and did not create a distinct sphere of corporate unity at the city level.

Abstracting from manifold historical and local differences, one prominent occurrence gave birth to a particular meaning of citizenship that was finally transplanted into the – equally occidental – concept of the modern state. Indeed the occidental medieval city, and with some qualifications the ancient Greek *polis* as well, was not the place of settlement of clans, families, tribes or other primordial communities (that is, of communities which existed *prior* to this locus) but rather the location of settlement for individuals who were alien to each other[11] and who were bound together through oaths of fraternization which affirmed a secular community. The corporate unity of the city was based on acts of association of individuals, it was the corporation of the 'burghers as such' who in this quality were subject to a law to which only they had access and which was only shared by them.[12] Membership in the corporation of the city was an original state of social embeddedness: it was neither derived from membership in a prior social community, nor did it content itself with the requirement of a merely physical affiliation to a particular place of settlement; it was a status based on *political* association which had its own meaning and relevance in that it ultimately created an autonomous sphere of social interaction, the public sphere.

However, despite the origin of the concept of citizenship in the Greek *polis*, its relevance has not been restricted to the sphere of politics. Throughout ancient Greek history citizenship was an institution which created distinctions which referred to almost all aspects of social life, not just to the area of 'politics' in the narrow sense of this term, that is, to the realm of public honour and the participation in the rule of the city. It was significant for the kind of military service and of religious worshipping that would be done by the members of the *polis*; it was of consequence for the nature of their occupation and for their legal capacity to own land; and it was relevant to sexual conduct.[13] Even less can we conceive of the *modern* concept of citizenship as a homogeneous and unvarying institution over the last three centuries and throughout the societies in which citizenship gained importance. The familiar civic-republican notion of 'active and virtuous participation' in the affairs of the community tends to be attributed to the ancient world, and its renaissance played, for instance, a prominent role in the reasoning of the founding fathers of the American constitution.[14] This notion, however, embodied only one meaning among several others which emerged in the modern age. For instance, according to recent research the British concept of citizenship never presupposed or entailed a 'deep concept of nationhood', nor did it 'embody notions of joint belonging, but was to be a purely personal and hierarchical one', namely subjecthood in the sense of mutual allegiance and protection to the Crown.[15]

Thus, both in the historical dimension and in contemporary debates, the scope of meanings covers extremely antagonistic understandings. They reach, for example, from a notion of citizenship which includes the right of the head of the family to participate in the governance within the hierarchical order of the premodern '*societas civilis sive politica*'[16] to the opposite concept according to which citizenship entails the passive status of a subject under an absolutist regime.[17] After the French Revolution, which established the principle of equal national citizenship in France,[18] this idea of an individual's status of political equality in a centralized state was challenged by the opposite claim that the idea of citizenship embodies membership in a rich diversity of predominantly local associations.[19] As a consequence, according to this latter understanding, citizenship does not primarily mean active political participation, but rather 'taking part in neighbourhood watch schemes, caring for dependents, running schools and housing estates, exercising consumer rights . . .'[20] Or, to mention another contrasting couple, some, following the famous claim of T. H. Marshall, regard citizenship as an instrument for modifying the structure of class inequality,[21] while others tend to consider it a discursive instrument for a mere rhetoric of equality, with-

out contributing to changing the reality of inequality in capitalist societies.[22] Finally, it may be mentioned that in the view of some theorists
citizenship is viewed as an instrument of political homogenization 'from
above',[23] whereas others emphasize its usage as an instrument of political, social and economic struggle 'from below'.[24]

The broad scope of potential functions and meanings of the concept of
citizenship reveals – very much like the notions of 'civil society' or
bürgerliche Gesellschaft inherently connected with it[25] – that it contains
at one and the same time economic, sociological, cultural and legal
elements which in their entirety constitute the particular connotation of
the concept. Depending on which of these dimensions is prevalent at
different times and in different societies, the idea of citizenship will
change considerably. A comprehensive historical account would certainly produce a plethora of meanings. Clearly the concept of citizenship
is deeply rooted in the distinct political cultures of the various European
countries. Yet there is an element of the concept of citizenship which
must not be overshadowed by the colourful variety of meanings it has
adopted during its long and wandering history. This is its inherent
rationale of loosening the bonds which tie a person who becomes a
citizen to the traditions and the 'parochialism' of his or her pre-political
(in most cases culturally defined) community. This is why membership in
the *polity* is an indispensable element of any concept of citizenship. The
associates of a polity need not be tied together through pre-political
bonds in order to be acknowledged as competent members of the society;
if and when they are citizens they need not be 'brothers' in order that
relations of trust and cooperation can prevail in the society. The
political status of citizenship outshines, so to speak, the pre- and extra-
political properties of individuals which may be significant in the
non-political spheres of the society.

Even so the concept of citizenship varies considerably among the
various member states of the EU; this makes it difficult to develop a
genuinely 'European' notion of citizenship, one that can be shared by all
member states without abandoning their particular political and cultural traditions. Consequently, Turner has suggested a broad definition
according to which citizenship should be understood as 'that set of
practices (juridical, political, economic and cultural) which define a
person as a competent member of society, and which as a consequence
shape the flow of resources to persons and to social groups'.[26] Citizenship
in this sense would hardly be distinguishable from the legal status of
any person who is at least physically part of the society and who by
this very reason enjoys the basic human rights which in a democratic
society are dispensed to every human being. The question is, then,
whether we can identify properties of a particularly European status of
citizenship?

THE EUROPEAN CHARACTER OF CITIZENSHIP:
THE ABOLITION OF THE 'DISABILITIES OF ALIENAGE
IN THE OTHER STATES'

The most obvious property of a European status of citizenship is its non-national character. I use the term non-national to convey sub- and supranational, trans- and international, and a cosmopolitan universe in which the concept of citizenship may well be meaningful. After all, the etymology of cosmo*politan* points to the ancient Greek world of the *polis* and its members, the *politeis*. On the other hand, contrary to our intuition which is largely shaped by the French model of citizenship – 'equal national citizenship'[27] – there is also a rich tradition where citizenship embodies 'a mere local "municipal" standing to which various minor rights and obligations attached', while 'subjecthood it seemed was the "superior political status" '.[28] Still, the prevailing understanding tends to associate the concept of citizenship with the idea of the nation, or, for that matter, of the nation-state. In other words, citizenship is regarded as a status of membership in the polity which is conceived as a solidaristic community where the mutuality of burdens and benefits is based on the particularism of the nation. On a closer look at the manifold concepts of citizenship which surface in the various European countries we are likely to discover that most of them more or less explicitly presuppose an exclusive community which defines its distinction between 'ins' and 'outs' in terms of citizenship.

However, it is doubtful whether the understanding of the concepts of nation and nation-state as delineating devices which create clear-cut in/out distinctions grasps their essential properties as they have developed in our times. It seems to overlook the experience that from the very beginning of political modernity there has been a political universe of states and, after the French Revolution, of nation-states; they have not 'existed in isolation as bounded geographical totalities, and they are better thought of as multiple overlapping networks of interaction'.[29] Of course, there is no denying that the institutions and the basic concepts in the field of political reasoning are still largely influenced by the robust presence of the nation-state. But the modern nation-state is no longer and has probably never been as impermeable as the ideal-type of closed statehood intimated. On the level of the member states of the EU the in/out division with respect to their nationals has largely blurred. This is due to the gradual transformation of the EU and its member states into a loosely coupled political multi-tier system. This is evidenced in the changes – not immediately noticeable – in the character of the addressees of the rights of member states' citizens.

Since most Community law is implemented by the administrative agencies of the member states rather than by distinct Union agencies, the

Union citizen who exercises his or her 'European' rights is mostly confronted with agencies of (national) member states. The European character of the rights conferred by the Community is rarely visible. Individuals who live in their native country will be confronted with their national government agencies, and whether they enforce national or Community law will hardly be a matter of interest to them. It is certainly more important for the citizens of member states who live in a member state other than their home state. By conventional standards they are aliens. Hence, Union citizenship could make a difference to them. True, the rights stipulated or referred to in articles 8 to 8e of the EC Treaty are not impressively numerous and cover only a small facet of the daily life of a person who lives in a member state other than their country of origin. Their status as an alien is likely to prevail over their alleged status as a fellow citizen of the European Community.

One objective of Union citizenship which goes beyond the merely symbolic could ultimately consist in making the citizens feel 'at home', as it were, in a foreign country. At least it should be possible to remove 'from the citizens of each state the disabilities of alienage in the other States'.[30] This judgement was made with reference to article 4, section 2 of the US Constitution, which stipulates that 'the citizens of each State shall be entitled to all privileges and immunities of citizens in the several States'. In another opinion issued more than a hundred years later, the US Supreme Court ruled that 'the primary purpose of this clause . . . was to help fuse into one nation a collection of independent sovereign states.'[31] A similar ruling could be found in article 3 of the constitution of the newly created German Reich of 1871.

In the American case the establishment of national citizenship served the goal to render the union the protector of individual rights which were jeopardized by the member states. The federal state had to protect the freedmen against the likely infringement of their rights particularly through the former slaveholder states; national citizenship became a harbour of safety against interferences by the states. Obviously this interpretation does not apply to the establishment of Union citizenship in the EC Treaty, because individual rights are essentially well protected within the constitutional systems of the member states. Moreover, the priority of Union law over member state law is secured by the aforementioned principle of supremacy of Community law over the law of the member states.[32] Hence the structural significance of the rights of the citizens of the Union consists basically in the creation of a sociolegal sphere of the Union which embodies the goal of the Union to diminish, perhaps even to abolish the 'disabilities of alienage in the other States'. This sociopolitical domain has two facets. It includes not only those who settle in a member state other than their own, but the resident nationals of the member state as well. They have to cope with the fact that persons who used to be aliens have become their fellow citizens in one respect –

in their quality as citizens of the Union – without becoming full members, that is, citizens in all respects of the daily life of the respective member state. What seems paradoxical at first glance would articulate the very particularity of the European Union: Union citizenship is not so much a relation of the individual vis-à-vis Community institutions, but rather a particular sociolegal status vis-à-vis national member states, which have to learn how to cope with the fact that persons who are physically and socially their citizens are acquiring a kind of legal citizenship by means of European citizenship without being their nationals.[33]

'Alienage' will probably be the hallmark of citizenship of the Union, a kind of permanent and structural cognitive and emotional dissonance which, in contrast to the American case, is not likely to be levelled in a unitary national culture in the forseeable future. Of course, the most serious obstacle is the lack of a common European language. Thus, unlike in most federal states, Community citizenship is not likely to supersede national citizenship or to make it a status of minor importance frequently verging on mere irrelevance; rather, both statuses will coexist, representing two different principles of political organization. While national citizenship uses territoriality as the basic means of integrating individuals into the society, the concept of citizenship of the Union presupposes a more abstract polity and membership of that polity has the main goal of integrating individuals into national societies who – by all standards of the traditional nation-states and their social structures – are aliens, or, as it was expressed in the *Proposals Towards a European Citizenship* submitted by the Spanish government in September 1990, 'privileged foreigners'. The Spanish government anticipated that taking the step towards Community citizenship 'will eliminate the negative effects presently accompanying the condition of foreigner for a citizen of a Member State in another Member State'.[34]

It remains to be seen whether the 'abolition of the disabilities of alienage', which may sometimes amount to the attempt to avoid a 'clash of political cultures', can be understood in terms of the distinction between *territorial federalism* and *personal federalism*.[35] In any case it seems safe to assume that the understanding of the meaning of citizenship of the Union will be shaped to a considerable extent by the prevailing concepts and the pertinent traditions of the member states, because it is the emerging dualism of national and Community citizenship which will finally determine the legal status of the European citizens.

It is possible that out of the dissonances resulting from the dualism between the more tangible national citizenship and the more abstract Community citizenship serious conflicts may arise which ultimately might thwart the goal of integration. The removal of 'the disabilities of alienage' requires the removal of 'alienage', and this in turn requires the mutual understanding of what the involved parties – migrating individuals originating in the various member states, and the hosting member states and their citizens themselves – assume when they make claim to or have to accept, respectively, the institution of Union citizenship.

There is a further possible effect of European citizenship. The right of the citizens of the member states to reside in any of the member states and to engage in economic, social, cultural, sporting and even, though in a limited way, political activities irrespective of the symbolic boundaries of the nation-states (the physical, that is territorial, boundaries have been abolished anyway) open the field to a multiplicity of social roles and loyalties which may lower the dominant role of national loyalty to just one among a bundle of social obligations. In the last instance this may entail the disconnection of three elements which have been considered inseparable for almost two centuries: nationality (represented by the passport), citizenship, and national identity.[36]

In this sense, European citizenship is more an amplified bundle of options within a physically broadened and functionally more differentiated space than a definitive legal status. Whereas in the traditional nation-state framework a citizen had to be a national, in the last instance European citizenship could even be conferred on individuals who do not possess the nationality of any of the member states. European citizenship would open the symbolic space for social activities which finally could lead to a European *societas civilis sive politica*, that is, a civil society beyond the physical boundaries of the nation-states. What is constitutive of this kind of citizenship is that, in contrast to national citizenship, it does not refer to a centralized and homogeneous sphere of political power. Thus European citizenship can be regarded as a step towards a new concept of politics inside and simultaneously beyond the framework of the traditional notion of politics defined by the nation-state.

Admittedly, it is a small step. It does not imply what Andrew Linklater in his chapter 6 above expected from the post-Westphalian era, namely 'forms of political community which are committed to realizing the Kantian ideal of a universal kingdom of ends'. It is true that, as Linklater states, 'various forces are loosening the grip of the nation-state so that a wider range of political identities and authorities can unfold.' But what the institution of EU citizenship has really brought about is the abolition of the nation-state's *monopoly* on individuals' affiliation to a polity, not of its predominant role in their lives as citizens of a political community. Among the three goods which are basically the object of political struggle – resources, rights and recognition – only recognition has found an institutional expression relatively independent of the nation-state. The idea of human rights embodies the idea of an individual's recognition as a bearer of human dignity and as a person worthy of some basic rights irrespective of his or her affiliation to a nation-state. Contrariwise, the just distribution of resources and the allocation of rights which are able to fulfil the basic needs of individuals is even in the European Union still to a large extent provided by the member states. Although the list of rights associated with the status of Union citizenship has been extended through the Maastricht Treaty, the basic needs and interests of individuals – ranging from the interest in a job to the provision of social and cultural services – are still mainly expected to be fulfilled by the nation-states. It is no accident that Union citizenship is a derivative of the status of nationality within one of the member states, not the other way round. (Here it is worth mentioning that Swiss nationality and citizenship is even derived from membership in a municipality; thus local communities decide about the distribution of a national good.)

Thus at present the duality of national and Union citizenships clearly displays the predominance of the former over the latter. But this is not a definitive state of affairs. Future political developments may enrich the status of Union citizenship such as to make it more attractive than at least some of the nation-state citizenships. The authors of the Treaty's rules about citizenship may have envisaged such a development because in article 8d, para. 4 they devised an institutional tool which makes it possible to 'strengthen or to add to the rights' of citizenship outside the regular and burdensome amendment procedure. Moreover, it is conceivable that in the forseeable future the adaptation of the member states' migration and asylum policies may entail the Community's competence to confer the status of Union citizenship on individuals who reside legally within its territory without possessing the nationality of any of its member states. The implication – the disconnection of citizenship from a nation-state's nationality – could be the starting-point for a general policy to grant individuals basic rights irrespective of their nationality. From different perspectives this idea has been suggested in this volume by Andrew Linklater, David Beetham and Pierre Hassner. Up to now the nation-states in the EU have only slightly loosened their grip on the definition of citizenship; but the EC has established the bold idea to disconnect nationality from citizenship, and this idea may well evolve to a general principle which ultimately transforms the ideal of cosmopolitan citizenship into a reality.

NOTES

1 T. C. Hartley, *The Foundations of European Community Law*, 3rd edn (Oxford: Clarendon Press, 1994), pp. 195ff., 234ff.
2 See, e.g., E. Grabitz, *Europäisches Bürgerrecht zwischen Marktbürgerschaft und Staatsbürgerschaft* (Cologne: Europa Union Verlag, 1970); R. Plender, 'An incipient form of European citizenship', in F. G. Jacobs (ed.), *European Law and the Individual* (New York: North Holland, 1976), pp. 39–53; A. Durand, 'European citizenship', *European Law Review*, 4 (1979), pp. 3–14; G. van den Berghe, *Political Rights for European Citizens* (Aldershot: Gower, 1982); A. Evans, 'European citizenship: a novel concept in EEC law', *American Journal of Comparative Law* (1984), pp. 679–715; S.

Magiera, 'Die Europäische Gemeinschaft auf dem Wege zu einem Europa der Bürger', *Die Öffentliche Verwaltung* (1987), pp. 221–31.

3 R. Corbett, *The Treaty of Maastricht. From Conception to Ratification: a Comprehensive Reference Guide* (Harlow: Longman, 1993), p. 52.

4 D. Curtin, 'The constitutional structure of the Union: a Europe of bits and pieces', *Common Market Law Review*, 30 (1993), p. 67.

5 E. Meehan, *Citizenship and the European Community* (London: Sage, 1993), pp. 16ff.

6 T. Oppermann, *Europarecht* (Munich: Beck, 1991), pp. 563ff.

7 M. Koessler, ' "Subject", "citizen", "national" and "permanent allegiance" ', *Yale Law Journal*, 56 (1946), pp. 58–76; S. Wiessner, *Die Funktion der Staatsangehörigkeit. Eine historisch-rechtsvergleichende Analyse unter besonderer Berücksichtigung der Rechtsordnung der USA, der UdSSR und der Bundesrepublik Deutschland* (Tübingen: Attempo Verlag, 1989), pp. 1ff.; B. Manville, *The Origins of Citizenship in Ancient Athens* (Princeton: Princeton University Press, 1990); P. Riesenberg, *Citizenship in the Western Tradition: Plato to Rousseau* (Chapel Hill: University of North Carolina Press, 1992); H. van Gunsteren, 'Four conceptions of citizenship', in B. van Steenbergen (ed.), *The Condition of Citizenship* (London: Sage, 1994), pp. 36–48.

8 M. Weber, *Economy and Society: an Outline of Interpretive Sociology* (Berkeley: University of California Press, 1964), p. 946.

9 Riesenberg, *Citizenship in the Western Tradition*, pp. 20ff.

10 Weber, *Economy and Society*, pp. 936ff.

11 Ibid., pp. 947ff.

12 Ibid., p. 944.

13 Riesenberg, *Citizenship in the Western Tradition*, pp. 28ff.

14 T. Pangle, 'Civic virtue: the Founders' conception and the traditional conception', in G. C. Bryner and N. B. Reynolds (eds), *Constitutionalism and Rights* (Provo, Utah: Brigham University Press, 1987), pp. 105–40.

15 M. Everson, 'Subjecthood, citizenship and allegiance: cracks in the nation', unpublished paper, Zentrum für Europäische Rechtspolitik, Bremen, 1996, p. 7.

16 M. Riedel, 'Bürger, Staatsbürger, Bürgertum', in O. Brunner with W. Conze and R. Koselleck (eds), *Geschichtliche Grundbegriffe. Historisches Lexikon zur politisch-sozialen Sprache in Deutschland*, vol. 1 (Stuttgart: Klett-Cotta, 1972), pp. 676ff.

17 M. Stolleis, 'Untertan – Bürger – Staatsbürger. Bemerkungen zur juristischen Terminologie im späten 18. Jahrhundert', in R. Vierhaus (ed.), *Bürger und Bürgerlichkeit im Zeitalter der Aufklärung* (Heidelberg: Schneider, 1981), pp. 65–99; Riesenberg, *Citizenship in the Western Tradition*, pp. 203ff.

18 G. H. Sabine, 'The two democratic traditions', *Philosophical Review*, 61 (1952), p. 462.

19 B. S. Turner, 'Outline of a theory of citizenship', in C. Mouffe (ed.), *Dimensions of Radical Democracy: Pluralism, Citizenship, Community* (London: Verso, 1992), p. 54.

20 Meehan, *Citizenship and the European Community*, p. 30.

21 T. H. Marshall, *Class, Citizenship, and Social Development* (New York: Doubleday, 1964); J. M. Barbalet, 'Citizenship, class inequality and resent-

ment', in B. S. Turner (ed.), *Citizenship and Social Theory*, (London: Sage, 1993) pp. 36–56.

22   B. Hindess, 'Citizenship in the modern West', in Turner, *Citizenship and Social Theory*, pp. 19–35.

23   M. Mann, 'Ruling class strategies and citizenship', *Sociology*, 21 (1987), pp. 339–54.

24   Turner, 'Outline of a theory of citizenship', pp. 38f.

25   R. Koselleck and K. Schreiner, 'Von der alteuropäischen zur neuzeitlichen Bürgerschaft. Ihr politisch-sozialer Wandel im Medium von Begriffs-, Wirkungs- und Rezeptionsgeschichten', in R. Koselleck and K. Schreiner (eds), *Bürgerschaft. Rezeption und Innovation der Begrifflichkeit vom Hohen Mittelalter bis ins 19. Jahrhundert* (Stuttgart: Klett-Cotta, 1994), p. 13.

26   B. S. Turner, 'Contemporary problems in the theory of citizenship', in Turner, *Citizenship and Social Theory*, p. 2; for a more restricted concept of citizenship see D. Zolo, 'Democratic citizenship in a post-communist era', in D. Held (ed.), *Prospects for Democracy: North, South, East, West* (Cambridge: Polity Press, 1993), pp. 254–68.

27   Sabine, 'The two democratic traditions'.

28   Everson, 'Subjecthood, citizenship and allegiance', p. 10.

29   D. Held, *Democracy and the Global Order: From the Modern State to Cosmopolitan Governance* (Cambridge: Polity Press, 1995), p. 225.

30   US Supreme Court, *Case Paul v Virginia*, 75 US 168, 180 (1869).

31   US Supreme Court, *Case Toomer v Witsell*, 334 US 385, 395 (1948); see L. H. Tribe, *American Constitutional Law*, 2nd edn (Mineola: Foundation Press, 1988), pp. 528ff., 548ff.

32   J. H. H. Weiler, 'The transformation of Europe', *Yale Law Journal*, 100 (1991), p. 2424.

33   See the brief remarks in J. H. H. Weiler, 'Fin-de-siècle Europe', in R. Dehousse (ed.), *Europe after Maastricht: an Ever Closer Union?* (Munich: Beck, 1994), p. 210.

34   Document in Corbett, *The Treaty of Maastricht*, pp. 156ff.

35   See T. Fleiner and L. R. Basta, 'Federalism, federal states and decentralization', in L. R. Basta and T. Fleiner (eds), *Federalism and Multiethnic States: The Case of Switzerland* (Fribourg: Institute of Federalism, 1996).

36   See H. Kleger, 'Transnationale Staatsbürgerschaft: Zur Arbeit an einem europäischen Bürgerstatus', in R. Erne et al. (eds), *Transnationale Demokratie. Impulse für ein demokratisch verfasstes Europa* (Zurich: Realotopia, 1995), pp. 34-59; U. K. Preuss, 'Problems of a concept of European citizenship', *European Law Journal*, 1 (1995), pp. 267–81.

8

Between Cosmopolis and Community: Three Models of Rights and Democracy within the European Union

Richard Bellamy and Dario Castiglione

Contemporary analytical political philosophers have tended to divide into either cosmopolitans or communitarians.[1] The first contend that we now live in a world society that ought to be governed according to universal principles of rights and justice; whereas the second advocate the claims of community and deny that moral principles carry much weight outside the specific social and political contexts that give them their particular character and force. This debate turns on rival accounts of political legitimacy more than, as is sometimes claimed, a relativist challenge to the very existence of universal moral values. Communitarians do not necessarily deny the possibility of universal principles. They differ from cosmopolitans in maintaining merely that justice alone cannot motivate us very deeply or lead us to accept the often onerous burdens that go with membership of any developed polity. They contend that we need specifically political obligations that tie us to a given group of citizens and set of social values if we are to recognize certain kinds of rights and the duties they impose upon us. These obligations are unlikely to stretch so far as to encompass the whole of humankind and so to legitimize a global state or a supranational legal order. More often than not, they stop at the borders of the national community.

This chapter looks at some practical implications of this debate by examining the respective merits of these two theoretical approaches as accounts of the nature and possible future of the European Union. We shall argue that although these two models often provide the background assumptions of pro- and anti-Europeans respectively, the New Europe challenges the normative and empirical basis of each of them. We suggest that a more satisfactory position may lie in a third position that synthesizes the two.

The character of political legitimacy lies at the heart of current political disputes and academic discussions about the European Union.[2] Consider for a moment how odd the European Union's political structure is.[3] It lacks the chief characteristics of a sovereign constitutional nation-state – namely, a congruence of territory, functional authority and identity; a monopoly of legitimate violence within its borders; exclusive control over the movement of goods and persons within its domain; a clear locus and hierarchy of authority and offices. It offers little if any democratic accountability to those affected by its decisions, and has no pre-set limits to its area of competence. The powers it has are largely loaned to it indirectly via the member states, which also offer it the main source of its legitimacy. Yet this transferral of powers does not occur in the institutionalized and consistent manner of a federal system. It is achieved in a piecemeal fashion, either through the internal dynamics of Community decision-making, or as a result of periodic pacts and treaties between the various governments concerned. *Eppur si muove!* It has a life of its own. The treaties are not simple international agreements; they offer the basis for an independent legal system. The European agencies and bureaucracies amount to more than an intergovernmental organization. They can generate and allocate revenue, regulate both public and private behaviour through legal and administrative directives, respond to pressure groups and organize elections, possess diplomatic status, and have the ability to conduct and conclude binding international negotiations on certain trade and security matters.

That an organization that is not a state can nonetheless possess so many of its salient characteristics offers a challenge to much conventional thinking about politics. Indeed, we believe that we need something like a Copernican revolution in our traditional political concepts if we are to comprehend the true nature of the European Union. In particular, the civic concepts of rights and democracy have to be related to those concepts associated with nationhood, notably state and popular sovereignty, in ways that do not assume a complete overlap or fit between the two groups. At stake is the normative underpinning of the respective claims of national and European legal and political institutions to be constitutionally superior within their distinct domains, and the issue of how far these spheres can be compartmentalized. Who has the authority to make decisions, about what, for whom, and how, have become questions that can no longer be easily avoided.[4]

In the next section, we shall show how the cosmopolitan and communitarian political moralities proposed by contemporary political theorists underlie the main positions in the debate about Europe, albeit usually in a crude and underdeveloped form.[5] Each of these broad schools of thought represent ideal-types involving distinctive accounts of democracy and rights that can be associated with different versions of federalism and nationalism respectively. In the following section we employ these two models to illuminate current disputes over citizenship and judicial competences within the European Union. In each case we identify the clash between communitarian and cosmopolitan concerns as the source of the present conflicts on these matters. These are real tensions that cannot be resolved in favour of either one or the other. Instead, the two positions have to be combined. We favour a combination of the cosmopolitan and communitarian accounts that sees elements of the first as issuing, and deriving their force from the second. We dub this synthesis cosmopolitan communitarianism. It stands in contrast to a communitarian cosmopolitanism that views cosmopolitan principles as providing a free-standing framework that is constitutive of all communities, and which sufficiently worked up might lead to the creation of a global cosmopolitan community. We conclude that when due weight is given in our preferred way to communitarian as well as cosmopolitan considerations, then a less harmonious and more pluralistic view of the Union becomes both normatively attractive and empirically plausible.

THE COMMUNITARIAN GHOST IN THE COSMOPOLITAN MACHINE

Two complementary strands run through both the cosmopolitan and the communitarian accounts of rights and democracy: the normative and the sociopolitical. We shall examine each in turn for both theories. Although the two positions need not be as opposed as they are sometimes presented, important differences of emphasis are nonetheless present that have considerable practical implications for how we think about political institutions.

Cosmopolitan globalists and federalists

The normative basis of the cosmopolitan ethical thesis rests on a theory of human rights that combines individualism, universality and generality.[6] The moral implications of these rights can be cashed out in either interactional or institutional terms – in other words, either as pertaining to the actions of individual persons and agencies, or as applying to the rules and procedures of certain institutional schemes. In a number of respects, the interactional case is practically weaker than the institutional. The perfect obligations necessary to uphold negative rights of non-interference can be conceptualized in global terms reasonably easily, since in principle at least they are costless and simply require individual forbearance. It is much harder to assign a global responsibility for positive rights to care and welfare which appear to rely on special obligations. Indeed, in the absence of any causal relation for the potential or actual harms involved, it is difficult even to justify positive action to secure negative rights worldwide, through the supply of peacekeeping forces and the like. The institutional view appears to fill this lacuna, since it potentially links us to a whole range of unknown others and provides a duty to safeguard even those negative rights we have not personally violated. The focus here is no longer on the direct relations between individuals, but on the justice of the practices and arrangements in which people are involved and for which they are jointly and severally responsible.

This institutional argument is contingent on the possible or actual existence of a global institutional scheme in which we all to some significant degree participate.[7] The sociopolitical strand of the cosmopolitan argument comes in here. Global socioeconomic forces are held to have created a greater degree of interconnectedness in the world than ever before. Technological advances have internationalized production, distribution and exchange and transformed financial markets. Multinational corporations (MNCs), even when they possess a regional or national base, are said to organize their affairs on an international scale and respond to global market pressures. This internationalization of markets is even more apparent in the financial sector, where new information technology has radically increased the mobility of economic units and to a large degree tied the world's major banking and trading centres into a single integrated network. New communications systems have also rendered ordinary people more aware of these global developments than ever before. The media, according to proponents of this thesis, have altered the 'situational geography' of social and political life by giving people direct access to distant events and creating new experiences, commonalties and frames of meaning that do not require direct physical contact – popular reactions to the repression of the demonstrators in Tiananmen Square and the plight of the Kurds in Iraq in the aftermath of the Gulf War being good examples of this phenomenon. A series of common cultural references – from the banality of soap operas through to greater popular awareness and knowledge of world events – has allegedly generated new solidarities, as evidenced in transnational social movements such as Greenpeace and Amnesty International.

The above mentioned processes are claimed to have weakened in turn the capacity of nation-states to provide for the security and welfare of their citizens, and led to the creation of a number of international power blocs, regimes and organizations to facilitate their continued ability to do so by managing various areas of transnational activity. These institutions range from collective security arrangements such as NATO, through a variety of other intergovernmental organizations of different degrees of formality aimed at controlling various aspects of economic and social policy, such as the meetings of the G7 group of economically power-ful countries, to a number of other international organizations, some more technical, like the Universal Postal Union, others more politically contentious, such as the International Monetary Fund, to clearly non-governmental structures such as the International Union of Free Syndicats. All these organizations modify to one degree or another the freedom of action of states and undercut their capacity to operate as sovereign units. Consequently, their title to act as the agents of the sovereign will of their people has been likewise eroded. Effective deci-sion-making and the sources of identification have in many cases passed elsewhere, or so at least it is alleged.

Finally, this move beyond the sovereign nation-state is reflected in the body of international law that has grown up in the wake of these developments. Here individuals are gradually coming to complement states as subjects of the law. On the one hand, it has been recognized that individuals have rights and obligations that are independent of and go beyond those duties and entitlements they have as citizens of particular states – a point made most strikingly in war crime trials. On the other hand, the legitimacy of states has come to rest as much on the justice of their rule as on their *de facto* hold on power. The postwar international declarations of rights have reinforced this shift from state to individual, as have challenges to the notions of 'immunity from jurisdiction' and 'immunity from state agencies' which have hitherto operated as central principles of international law.

This global positivization of individual moral rights brings the norma-tive and empirical strands of the cosmopolitan thesis together. At least two broad possible views of the European Union can follow from this perspective. One version holds that the forces described above have undermined the nation-state, but that a centralized federal Europe, that is itself not unlike a nation-state writ large, can fill the gap. Another, more truly cosmopolitan version, is not so much supranational as post-national in orientation,[8] viewing moves towards federalist principles as an alternative to, rather than a new form of the unitary sovereign state.[9] By and large, political scientists – especially those of a functionalist disposition – have been drawn towards the first position. They have advocated the strengthening of the Union's supranational features – particularly the European Parliament and the Commission – and the phasing out of intergovernmentalism, and have welcomed the move towards common policies in the spheres of domestic justice and foreign affairs in addition to economic and social matters.[10] Lawyers, by contrast, have been the principal advocates of the second position. They have drawn inspiration from the gradual development of a single legal framework by the European Court of Justice, noting with approval its increasing tendency to appeal to human rights and its claims of supremacy over the domestic law of member states and 'direct effect' with regard to their citizens.[11] Needless to say, the reality falls far short of either version of the cosmopolitan ideal – a fact that communitarians are not slow in pointing out.

Communitarians, nationalists and the sovereignty of states

Communitarians question both the normative and empirical aspects of the cosmopolitan thesis. With regard to the first element, they dispute the universalist and individualist rights-based starting-point of the cosmopolitan case. Rather than viewing rights as foundational principles presupposed by all legitimate societies, communitarians contend they are best conceived as components of particular forms of life and their related patterns of human flourishing.[12] Moreover, different communities are likely to prioritize different kinds and sets of rights. Indeed, even within a given conception of rights, conflicts between different sorts of rights involving incompatible and incommensurable values and interests tend to arise.[13] Such clashes can generally only be resolved by reference to the broader social picture of which they form a part. This wider social context is also important to motivate people to identify with rights and take on the burdens that upholding them usually entails. Finally, given their belief that the nature of our rights depends on the character of the society and the culture in which we live, communitarians tend to stress the priority of democracy over rights in the preservation of our liberty.[14] A link is thereby established with national sovereignty. Nationality defines a common political culture and identity, which gain political expression through being tied to a democratic state.[15]

Communitarians also contest the second, empirical, element of cosmopolitanism, questioning both the degree and the consequences of the processes of globalization and interconnectedness. It is possible to dispute, for example, the extent to which MNCs truly operate at a transnational level. As Hirst and Thompson have recently shown,[16] core capital, basic research and development, and management personnel and structures are mostly located within a main national base. The various political bodies and non-governmental agencies that have developed to cope with global problems of security and welfare tend to be international and intergovernmental rather than supranational. The UN, for

example, far from representing a nascent form of cosmopolitan governance, as is sometimes argued,[17] remains very much an instrument of the
sovereign states which compose it – not least the superpowers, whose
hold on the Security Council effectively blocks any move that might
damage their interests.[18] Indeed, the major powers' effective control over
the purse strings enables them to manipulate most important, and hence
costly, initiatives requiring interstate cooperation, and to stop those that
do not meet with their approval – witness the sabotaging of UNESCO by
Britain and the United States.[19]

Cosmopolitans also overlook the differential impact of global forces
on different countries and the imbalances in the degree and nature of the
interdependence they create. By and large the wealthier and more powerful nations are net beneficiaries from global market forces, for example,
while poorer states are either locked out of many of the networks or are
subordinate partners and often damaged by global trade, becoming
sources of cheap labour and resources, rather than developing strong
economies of their own. Global environmental, health, security and other
dangers that are no respecters of state borders are said to bind the
peoples of the world together as sharing a common fate. However, they
rarely affect all of them to an equal extent. When joint actions have
shared consequences, such as the depletion of fish stocks, then cooperative action may be possible, although here too the standard free-rider
problems that arise with all public goods and bads mean that many
countries will attempt to evade their responsibilities. Because the advantages and disadvantages are not usually mutual even with shared activities or problems, the incentives for cooperative behaviour are normally
lop-sided.[20] Even within the EU, the substantial differences in economic
performance, social standards and political interests between the member
states have rendered the formulation of common policies far from easy.
Britain's acrimonious attempts to reduce the massive financial transfers
to other EC states via the Common Agricultural Policy (CAP) reflect a
genuine problem that potentially weakens the commitment to the Union
of all the main contributors.[21]

Although nations do form blocs for certain limited purposes, it is also
important to note that these often have the goal of preserving state
autonomy rather than diminishing it. Alan Milward's account of the
European Community as a 'rescue' of the nation-state is highly pertinent
in this respect.[22] The EU emerges from this analysis as being, in part at
least, a reaction against the forces of globalization. Indeed, many of its
more 'social' corporatist and welfare elements are in a number of respects
anti-cosmopolitan – reflecting a desire to preserve the standards of member state workers against the effects of foreign competition. This feature
has been highlighted by the exclusionary character of recent moves to
create a European citizenship, discussed below.[23]

For related reasons, more homogeneous consumption patterns and a greater awareness of world affairs have not necessarily produced as much convergence in political identity among the general population as cosmopolitans assert. People distinguish a humanitarian concern with famine or other disasters in countries other than their own from the sorts of formalized responsibilities they have for co-nationals. They may support initiatives such as Band Aid or give to Oxfam, but that is a long way from condoning increased taxation to expand the development aid budget, say. Television, faster communication systems, greater job mobility and the like may have broadened people's horizons in certain respects and encouraged them to identify with a wider community, but the identification may not be so deep as the solidarities of old, based as they were on continuous, direct contact and personal involvement. Later in the chapter we shall produce some evidence from the EU to support this argument.

Just as we distinguished two different versions of the cosmopolitan ideal with regard to the EU, so two broad positions can be associated with communitarian thinking. On the one hand, there are conservative Eurosceptics of the British variety who think in terms of narrow national interests and conceive of the nation in quasi-ethnic terms, resulting in a particularly hard-line position on immigration for example. On the other hand, there are civic nationalists. These tend to be more left-wing and influenced by republican notions linking patriotism with democratic participation, as in the French tradition.[24] For different reasons, both groups will be reluctant to see a dilution of the intergovernmental character of the EU. However, while the first would dispute any shift in a federalist direction, the second merely argues that until such time as a global identity and public culture develop, moral weight has to be given to the self-determination of different peoples. Attempts to force the pace will be seen as unjustified, but certain moves of a cosmopolitan kind are possible – even if the total transcendence of the nation-state remains highly unlikely.

Two views of rights and democracy

Cosmopolitans and communitarians hold two different views of the nature of rights and democracy and the way they relate to each other. Cosmopolitans see rights as essentially self-standing. Their justification is independent of their recognition by any given society or culture and they do not rely on democratic endorsement for their validity. Their scope and application is uniform and universal, with individuals as their subjects. Citizenship and sovereignty are regarded as largely antithetical to rights, since they link them to membership of a state rather than regarding them as attributes of human beings as such. Even if democracy to some extent embodies the notion of equal rights, its procedures cannot always be counted on to uphold them. At best, it operates as a mechanism of imperfect procedural justice. Within the governmental and constitutional system, therefore, democracy has essentially instrumental uses as a means of allowing individuals to voice and protect their vital interests by controlling the decisions which affect their lives, usually indirectly via influence over the decision-makers. To the extent that those decisions have passed beyond, or in certain cases below, the nation-state, then so must democratic institutions. What defines the *demos* is largely functional, making the parcelling out of popular sovereignty theoretically unproblematic, even though there are numerous practical difficulties. In cases where democracy fails to offer the best protection for rights, or even endangers them, non-democratic mechanisms, such as judicial review or regulative agencies, are to be preferred.[25]

Communitarians regard rights as socially grounded and as oriented towards securing the participation of individuals within certain worthwhile collective practices. Democracy plays an important role in legitimizing and justifying a particular understanding and interpretation of rights within a given society. Consequently, its instrumental qualities are valued far less than its intrinsic ones. Communitarians conceive democratic decision-making more in terms of deliberation on the common good than as a mechanism for the aggregation of individual interests. Moreover, they contend that compromise and the avoidance of a purely self-regarding stance are far more likely among a people who identify reasonably strongly with each other. It is no accident in this respect that the two paradigmatic examples of constitution-making, namely France and the United States in the eighteenth century, were simultaneously instances of nation-building. For democracy implies the existence of a people who feel bound together. It is this sense of a shared fate and mutual responsibility that leads minorities to accept majority decisions, for example, and, perhaps more importantly, motivates majorities to take into account the opinions and concerns of minorities rather than excluding them altogether.[26]

Judicial review tends to play a more subordinate role in this version of democracy than that accorded it in less communitarian accounts.[27] Majority tyranny, the prevention of which offers a prime motive behind this legal protection of rights, is deemed less likely, and such judicial interference with the popular will be regarded as in any case illegitimate since the deliberations of the people provide both the rationale and the source of rights. Within this conception, democracy is itself a forum of principle that allows conflicting accounts and exercises of rights to be weighed and balanced against each other in ways that show equal concern and respect for the individual autonomy of others. There is no need, as some have argued, for judges to take on this role. Indeed, there are numerous disadvantages associated with their doing so. Politics mobilizes public support and commitment for taking on the burdens that are often entailed by granting particular rights. Moreover, the broader interests and values of diverse groups can be heard, and the defence of a particular right can be placed in the context of the whole range of policies being undertaken by the government and the wider needs and wishes of citizens. Judicial decisions tend to foreclose democratic involvement in policy-making and thereby impair the identification of citizens with the rights they imply. Focus on the litigated case can also lead judges to ignore the knock-on effects of legal intervention for other equally important programmes, overlooking the way spending in one area might withdraw resources from others.

In these ways, reliance on the courts may have the grave drawback of impairing democratic channels of communication, and risks producing unprincipled politics of the very sort that supporters of judicial review believe render it necessary. In any case, it is doubtful that the judiciary is capable of withstanding the influence of the wider community, no matter how independent it may seek to be. Like other parts of the political system, it needs a degree of popular legitimacy to be authoritative. The danger is that only highly selective pressure groups will be able to exercise such influence, so that the courts will become a prey to those very 'sinister' interests they are supposed to overcome.[28] As we shall see, these communitarian criticisms of cosmopolitan rights-based forms of constitutional democracy are highly pertinent to the debate over judicial competences in the EU.

When rights and obligations are nested within particular political communities, their cosmopolitan reach will clearly be affected. To the extent that our understanding of basic rights is coloured by the culture of our community, there are likely to be conflicts between the priorities and publicly recognized needs of different societies. State support for certain religions or languages may be important in some communities and regarded as illegitimate in others, for example. Even when the same rights are acknowledged, variations in local context may lead to them being interpreted and balanced in contrasting and not always compatible ways. In addition, there will be a feeling that 'charity begins at home' that will set limits on how much people will commit themselves to helping outsiders when that clashes with programmes, also motivated by rights considerations, of a domestic character. Thus communitarians regard it as legitimate that a more generous national social security system, say, might be established at the cost of spending less on foreign aid.[29]

Support for national sovereignty need not entail a view of international relations as an anarchic and amoral Hobbesian state of nature. Claims to self-determination for one group imply recognition that others have similar rights and are owed certain resulting duties – including non-aggression and limited aid. To the extent that global interdependence does link states within institutional networks, then they will have the sorts of obligations cosmopolitans advocate. Nonetheless, the absence of agreed metrics as to the value of resources or the relative worth of various rights and liberties will make arguments for a global redistribution of goods and services hard to cash out in practice – especially as such schemes can conflict with as well as support the autonomy of national communities. Still, it is reasonable to suppose that globalization will produce forms of interstate cooperation in those areas such as defence, the environment and the economy where the capacity of states to act in autonomous ways has been seriously impaired. However, in most cases these cooperative schemes will be regarded as mechanisms for preserving rather than undermining national interests and self-determination, with transfers of decision-making power being largely conditional on the extent to which involvement in the relevant international body makes that possible.[30]

A cosmopolitan communitarianism?

In what follows, we shall argue that these two models shed light on a number of the debates and difficulties currently besetting the European Union. We have already identified four possible approaches to Europe – the supranational and the post-national federalist stemming from the cosmopolitan camp, and the ethnic and the civic nationalist arising out of the communitarian. We wish to propose a variant of the last approach that develops the civic nationalist position in the direction of post-nationalism. Two points are worth making at this stage. First, it would be mistaken to regard the cosmopolitan and the communitarian arguments as totally at odds with each other, with the latter anti-liberal, anti-rights and anti-individualist, as certain commentators have claimed.[31] Rather, they offer contrasting but to some degree compatible accounts of how we should think about individuality, rights and their relationship to the societies that embody them. Our claim will be that cosmopolitan morality only makes sense to the extent that it is embedded within a communitarian framework: a position we dub cosmopolitan communitarianism. Second, cosmopolitanism and communitarianism are ontological rather than ideological positions. In other words, they orientate how we think about and justify policy rather than dictating its ideological coloration. Both cosmopolitan and communitarian forms of thinking can be found in all ideological camps. Thus there are New Right advocates of cosmopolitanism who associate it primarily with global markets and the removal of barriers to free trade, and socialists who see the cosmopolitan ideal as leading to a global scheme of social justice involving a massive redistribution from the wealthy to the poorest parts of the world. Similarly, in the UK, for example, there are Conservative Party advocates of communitarianism who emphasize national traditions, the importance of families and social responsibilities and the like, and socialists who stress social solidarity and welfare.[32] Thus all four of the options canvassed so far can be read in either a left-wing or right-wing manner, as can our position.

Michael Walzer has recently explored the difference between the two schools in terms of a distinction between 'thick' and 'thin' moralities.[33] In his terms, universal human rights represent a 'thin', 'minimal' morality that all societies ought to uphold. But they do so in numerous 'thick', 'maximal' ways. Moreover, the bearers of individual rights are similarly contextually defined. That is not to deny value individualism, as is sometimes implied, but it is to reject those versions of methodological individualism that ignore the social dimension of personal identity and the development of autonomy.[34] According to this thicker, more communitarian view of rights and the individual, a pure cosmopolitanism offers an inadequate account of moral agency. For the cosmopolitan universalist, agents are supposed to act on the basis of rational considerations of pure principle that abstract from their sense of identity as persons holding certain convictions and possessing particular attachments. By contrast, the cosmopolitan communitarian believes that both the principles and the moral motivations and character of those who follow them need to be fleshed out with natural sentiments and 'thick' concepts such as courage, honesty, gratitude and benevolence that arise out of specific ways of life. A pure cosmopolitanism cannot generate the full range of obligations its advocates generally wish to ascribe to it. For the proper acknowledgement of 'thin' basic rights rests on their being specified and overlaid by a 'thicker' web of special obligations.

Welfare states, for example, have typically arisen in societies where there are strong feelings of social solidarity. These reinforce the formal obligations that arise from being members of an institutionalized scheme of political cooperation as citizens of the same state. Essentially, they create a sense of identification among a given group of people between whom it comes to be felt both legitimate and plausible that collectively binding decisions about the distribution of burdens and benefits should take place. That sense of commonness does not determine what its precise implications or content should be, but it does provide the basis on which such determination takes place. It defines the *demos*, as it were, for whom a form of democratic rule appears appropriate and plausible.

Nationalism has traditionally provided the ideological glue necessary to define a relatively circumscribed group of people and unify them around a set of shared institutions and practices that were sovereign over a well-defined territory. Political loyalty, accountability and legitimacy were tied in this way to state power and authority. Indeed, nationality was typically the creation of states and political elites seeking to consolidate their hold over their populations. Cosmopolitans deny the necessity and desirability of such attachments. They may grant them a certain empirical weight, as does Thomas Pogge[35] and as do Archibugi, Thompson and Held in this volume,[36] but not any moral significance. A mixture of voluntarist and utilitarian considerations of a broadly functional kind provides the only normatively relevant considerations so far as people's obligations to any particular polity are concerned.[37] At most, cosmopolitans incline towards a communitarian cosmopolitanism that acknowledges the existence of different allegiances but wishes to subject them to some sort of normative cosmopolitan framework.

By contrast, our sketch of the communitarian argument has tried to suggest that largely unchosen commonalties of history, belief, geography and civic culture do have an ethical relevance. They supply the feelings of reciprocity, trust and commitment needed to supplement the ties of mere mutual advantage that result from individuals acting on the basis of rational self-interest alone. Such moral qualities have an important influence on the character of political life, since they increase people's willingness to engage in cooperative behaviour by raising their expectations and confidence in others. As David Miller has recently argued,[38] far from encouraging self-interested and partial behaviour, the lessening of the tension between personal and collective goals within a group is likely to make an impartial stance more acceptable. It may be objected that 'political communities have rarely – if ever – existed in isolation as bounded geographical totalities, and that they are better thought of as multiple overlapping networks of integration.'[39] We agree that the homogeneity of national communities has sometimes been exaggerated. But the fact that our identities and allegiances are multiple does not alter the basic communitarian point: namely, that political legitimacy has to be constructed from the bottom up. It cannot be provided from on high. The resolution of potential conflicts between ties of different kinds and degrees of intensity cannot be decided *a priori* as cosmopolitans contend.[40] Nevertheless, the very multiplicity of our community affiliations suggests a simple communitarianism is unsatisfactory also. Instead, we need a cosmopolitan communitarian approach that encourages us to actively negotiate between different communal attachments in ways that do justice to their varying degrees of importance for those concerned.

On this account, the normative aspect of the cosmopolitan argument will only go beyond a 'thin' humanitarian concern for others to the extent that we live in a relatively 'thick' cosmopolitan civil society with a corresponding public culture. So far as the EU is concerned, this result might be obtained in one of two ways. Either Europe itself will coalesce into a civic nation, as communitarian cosmopolitans propose, or it must operate as a union of nations involving a degree of variable geometry combined with a fair amount of consensus on central issues, and even certain elements of a common identity. We shall defend the second option below. It represents an example of the cosmopolitan communitarian position outlined earlier, whereby nations demonstrate civic attitudes not only internally but also to a greater or lesser extent externally, with basic 'thin' cosmopolitan sentiments thickening in various ways depending on the nature and degree of their interaction and involvement with other nations, and even international allegiances possibly developing in some instances. The civic nation variant of the communitarian argument is extended in this way to accommodate aspects of both the globalization thesis and a universal cosmopolitan morality, while denying the normative or empirical possibility of a European, let alone a global, civic nation. This position involves a rejection not only of an unqualified cosmopolitan globalism and universalism, but also of the centralized federalist version of the cosmopolitan argument and the Eurosceptical version of the communitarian case. The neofunctionalist federalist line greatly overestimates the integrative potential of global forces and the capacity of people to transfer their allegiances. The Eurosceptical argument underestimates the new realities of global economic competition and has xenophobic overtones of a decidedly uncivic nature. In sum, they too are neither plausible nor desirable.

WHOSE EUROPE, WHICH COMMUNITY?

The challenge of Maastricht

It is commonly claimed that the European Union currently finds itself at a crossroads. On the one hand, it operates as an intergovernmental organization and its mode of governance is likened to a form of consociational confederalism. All four of Lijphart's consociational principles of grand coalition, segmental autonomy, proportionality and minority veto have typified deliberations in the Council of Ministers and negotiations surrounding the various treaties, for example.[41] Moreover, these consociational mechanisms have had the aim and effect of rendering the integrative process consistent with the protection and, to some degree, the enhancement of national identities and interests.[42] These characteristics are basically compatible with a communitarian perspective. On the other hand, the EU embodies an extraordinary number of apparently supranational features – most particularly the European Court of Justice, and to a much smaller extent the European Parliament. The claim stemming from these bodies is that a new European constitutional order has gradually come into being possessing supremacy over national law and 'direct effect' on individuals and agencies within the national jurisdictions of member states. Increasingly the Court has justified its claims to judicial competence-competence as the authoritative interpreter of a 'higher' European law by reference to the protection of basic human rights. This development has been accompanied by calls for the European Parliament to have a greater role in the legislative process and the view that intergovernmentalism fails adequately to represent the interests of individual citizens – the so-called democratic deficit thesis.[43] These arguments draw on cosmopolitan notions to underpin them.

Up until the Maastricht Treaty on European Union the tensions between these two dimensions of European integration rarely manifested themselves in practice. The jurisdictional and legislative expansion of the Court of Justice was largely controlled – and to high degree abetted – by the member states, not least through a generous interpretation of article 235 EC to allow a significant extension of the scope and powers of the Community. The shift to majority voting, combined with certain renewed worries on the part of national courts as to the integrity of their own position as guardians of their distinctive constitutional orders, has changed this situation and made governments far more sensitive to the Court's jurisdictional boundaries.[44] These tensions are manifested in the Maastricht Treaty itself.[45] Thus, while the Common Provisions in title I, for example, emphasize the goal of an 'ever closer union of the peoples of Europe' (article A), the Final Provisions in title VII largely undercut them, not least by removing title I from the jurisdiction of the Court (article L). Another instance of this janus-faced character of the Maastricht Treaty is the way subsidiarity is defined in both a devolutionary manner, to suggest that decisions should be taken 'as closely as possible' to the citizens (articles A and B), and in a potentially neofederalist direction, as a means for allocating different areas of competence that allows the Community to act even outside its 'exclusive' sphere when 'by reason of the scale or effects of the proposed action' it can achieve certain objectives more effectively than the member states (article 3B EC).

Most significant of all are the various protocols attached to the Treaty incorporating various derogations from common policies, such as the British opt-out from the Social Charter and the possibility of opting out from European Monetary Union, the provisions for Danes to have privileged access to second homes in rural Denmark, and the protection of Irish anti-abortion law. These appear to threaten the central legal tenet of the Union, the *acquis communitaire*, and to open up the possibility of an *à la carte* Europe involving considerable variable geometry. Not surprisingly legal analysts have tended to be hostile to the Treaty, seeing it as reducing the capacity of the Court to produce a coherent legal order and denigrating the resulting constitutional structure as a patchwork of 'bits and pieces'. As one prominent legal commentator has put it, the Union displays 'more of a *bricoleur's* amateurism than a master brick-layer's strive for perfection and attention to detail'. The result, she continues, has jeopardized 'the cohesiveness and the unity and the concomitant power of a legal system painstakingly constructed over the course of some 30 odd years', threatening in the process 'the whole future and credibility of the Communities as a cohesive legal unit which confers rights on individuals and which enters into their national legal systems as an integral part of those systems'.[46]

Two issues bring out the conflicts between cosmopolitan and communitarian concerns in the post-Maastricht climate particularly well, namely, the notion of European citizenship and the debate over the jurisdictional limits of the Union highlighted by the Maastricht decision of the German Constitutional Court. Both raise matters related to the contrast between the two models of rights and democracy discussed earlier, and indicate the problems of advocating democratic procedures in the absence of a *demos* and of assigning rights protection to judicial review. We shall examine each in turn, suggesting in the conclusion that resolving the tensions they reveal may be a matter of yet more *bricolage* rather than architectural design.

European citizens in search of a nation

The establishment of Union citizenship in articles 8 to 8e of the amended EC Treaty has been taken by certain commentators as representing a first, albeit highly inadequate step towards the creation of a European *demos*. The chief criticisms from this cosmopolitan perspective have related to its limited nature and the huge anomalies that arise from its being tied to nationality as that is variously defined by the different member states – especially with respect to immigrants resident within the EU.[47] Conspicuously little thought, however, has been given to the more communitarian-minded issue of how many people actually desire this status.[48] In fact, most of the empirical evidence, such as the findings of the Eurobarometer poll, indicates a very low level of identification with Europe. Even though a majority of Europeans are broadly favourable to integration it is largely on the grounds that it is a 'good thing' for their own country (an opinion expressed by 69 per cent of those polled in 1990). Only 14 per cent in a 1989 poll said they 'frequently' felt a 'citizen of Europe', while 48 per cent responded that they 'never' did so. Indeed, the only group of people who appear to feel a higher level of European compared to national consciousness are those working in the various European institutions, who have a vested interest in fostering the European ideal.[49] More recent survey evidence shows that the former views remain strong. For example, a European Opinion study in July, September and October of 1995 revealed that a majority of Europeans (52 per cent) favoured an 'à la carte' Europe, a view held by over 70 per cent of the population in Austria, Britain, Denmark and Sweden.

These findings reinforce some of the earlier criticisms of the globalization thesis and suggest problems with the federalist version of the cosmopolitan argument, which seems to depend on the development of a strong European civic nation. In spite of a considerable degree of economic integration and a significant number of common political institutions, there has been comparatively little convergence in civic attitudes and allegiances. Although the intensification of trade, transport and communication links, greater labour mobility and an equalization of social conditions were important elements in the development of national identities in nineteenth-century Western Europe,[50] they were never sufficient in themselves. In the case of the European Union, the crucial role played by centralized political institutions in unifying the economy is also missing, since the common market has been more the product of deregulation than regulation.

Moreover, the growth of economic and social interdependence is not by any means centred solely on Europe, even if trade among the member states has increased more than commerce between them and the rest of the world. The European Union is also a remarkably open-ended project in terms of geographical scope, and potentially might include the most varied cultural and political traditions. Earlier nation-state building projects usually had reasonably well-defined territorial ambitions that were linked to certain pre-existing historical, linguistic and cultural boundaries. Although these sentiments were generally only shared by a dominant social group and had to be diffused among the rest of the population, there was nevertheless a sense of who was being united and where. No core cultural or geographical reference point seems to exist for the EU, however, beyond a vague commitment to certain unspecified 'principles of liberty, democracy and respect for human rights and fundamental freedoms and of the rule of law' (Preamble, Maastricht Treaty).

Post-nationalist cosmopolitans, of course, will regard the absence of a sense of European consciousness as highly desirable. A constitutional patriotism centred on universal liberal-democratic values ought to be enough to unite all peoples around common political institutions, and avoids the exclusionary connotations of a form of citizenship based on a territorially and culturally specific national identity.[51] Communitarians, however, contend that a high degree of identification forms a precondition for democracy. Without a sense of Europeanness, increasing the powers of the European Parliament risks making the democratic deficit more profound rather than less. Unless voters feel an institution is socially as well as formally legitimate then they will be disinclined either to take part in its decisions or to accept them.[52] As rational choice theorists have been forced to concede, self-interest alone cannot explain participation in elections since the rational voter will always stay at home. Voting is a practice involving a number of specific obligations that go with the role of citizen. I need a civic identity, in other words, to be inclined to vote, and that only comes through membership of a specific *polis* with appropriate traditions.

Likewise, unless there is a single right answer, I will only accept a decision as valid if I identify in some respect with those who make it. Given the plurality of ultimate values and the complex ways in which they interact, it is unlikely that clear-cut correct solutions can be discovered to many, if any, of the dilemmas that standardly confront governments over such matters as welfare, defence, health and education and the resources to be allocated to each of them. Rather, collectively binding solutions have to be constructed within specific contexts.[53] That entails involving those likely to be benefited or burdened by the outcome, and crucially getting those in the minority to accept the majority view. Once again, a feeling of belonging to a given community plays a vital part in legitimizing the democratic process among those involved. It binds together a people and generates reciprocal ties that foster a disposition to consider the general welfare and to compromise where necessary.

Admission to citizenship for these reasons usually involves more than signing up to a set of abstract principles. Naturalized citizens, in particular, normally have to be inducted into a certain form of social and political life and declare a willingness to undertake certain duties. Education and the normal processes of socialization provide a less formalized procedure for nationals. No such induction process exists at the European level, nor is it clear what it would entail. In this regard, it is noteworthy that in a 1989 Eurobarometer poll 59 per cent preferred the idea that the European Parliament should be organized around national criteria rather than the current political ones, even though as yet no European-wide parties, as opposed to groupings of national parties, exist. As Weiler has pertinently remarked,[54] at present there is as much reason for us to expect the Danes, say, to accept the legitimate authority of a German Bundestag to which they were given voting rights as that of the European Parliament. A European *demos*, in other words, has to build on the multiple communitarian attachments of the citizens of member states. These cannot be expected to dissolve into a homogeneous melting pot. Nor can feelings of Europeanness be expected to have the same scope or depth for all peoples. Variability will be necessary.

Deutschland über Alles? The German Maastricht ruling

Similar points emerge from the second issue to be considered, that of the respective judicial competences of the European Court of Justice and national constitutional courts.[55] Recent attention on this question has focused on the 1993 judgment of the German Constitutional Court in response to the challenge by Mr Manfred Brunner and others to the validity of Germany's accession to the Maastricht Treaty. Brunner had argued that Maastricht violated article 79, section 3, of the Basic Law, which forbids amendments affecting the role of the Lander in legislation and, via reference to articles 1 and 20, that curtail either basic rights or the 'democratic and social' character of the republic and the sovereign authority of the German people as exercised 'through elections and voting and by specific organs of the legislature, the executive power, and the judiciary'. Brunner's point was that the making of Community law through majority voting within the Council of Ministers, combined with the European Court's assertions of direct effect and the supremacy of Community over national law, effectively undercut the right of Germans to control their own affairs. The Lander were particularly affected in this respect, since in spite of all the fine talk about subsidiarity there is no real involvement of the regions in Community decision-making. Although the Constitutional Court rejected this particular challenge, it chose both to reassert the continuing sovereignty of the German people and to deny that either the European Court of Justice or any other European organ could claim competence over its own competence. In other words, it remained for the German Court alone to decide whether or not a European measure or development infringed the German constitutional order.

German popular sovereignty, it asserted, remained intact not only so long as national parliaments limited the extension of European functions but also provided that states retained 'sufficiently important spheres of activity of their own in which the peoples of each can develop and articulate in a process of political will-formation which it legitimates and controls, in order to give legal expression to what – relatively homogeneously – binds the people spiritually, socially, and politically together'.[56] Their reasoning on this point was essentially communitarian – to be more than 'merely a formal principle of accountability', democracy had to be among people who could influence each others' opinions and have an impact on those who governed them.[57] This condition, they noted, is not met by the European Union, which possesses neither a *demos* nor mechanisms for effective democratic control over its decision-makers by any of its constitutive peoples, either severally or collectively. Consequently, the sovereignty of the German people required that 'functions and powers of substantial importance must remain with the German Bundestag.'[58] To ensure that this situation persisted, the Court had to retain its prerogative to review legal instruments emanating from European institutions 'to see whether they remain within the limits of the sovereign rights conferred on them or whether they transgress those limits'. The 'Law of Accession' was conditional, therefore, on subsequent European developments continuing to be compatible with the German constitutional order as interpreted by the Court.[59]

A cosmopolitan perspective that sees national and popular sovereignty as matters of instrumental rather than intrinsic importance will tend to regard the German Court's arguments for defending a specifically German form of democracy as somewhat beside the point. The key question is whether liberal democratic values are defended, not their national location or colour. This issue might have been supposed to be resolved in the late 1960s and early 1970s, when the German and Italian constitutional courts obliged the ECJ to declare that the protection of fundamental rights formed 'an integral part of the general principles of law' it had a duty to uphold.[60] This declaration had been motivated by the European Court's desire to uphold the supremacy of European law against scrutiny by national courts for its protection of human rights – a matter they were often pledged to uphold, but that the ECJ apparently was not. Since no European Bill of Rights has been formally adopted by the Community to which the ECJ might refer, the Court said it would be guided by the rights protected in the constitutions of member states and international conventions – most particularly the European Convention on Human Rights.[61] Some commentators regarded this development as 'the most striking contribution the Court made to the development of a constitution for Europe'.[62] They have argued that 'there is hardly anything that has greater potential to foster integration than a common bill of rights, as the constitutional history of the United States has proved.'[63] They contend that it ought to be possible to draw from the various national constitutions and international conventions a 'common bill of rights' for the Community that 'by encapsulating the nature of the legal order that it underpins ... would create an integrationist *culture* of rights'.[64] Indeed, article F(2) of the Maastricht Treaty, which refers to the European Convention and common constitutional traditions as offering 'general principles of Community law', might be regarded as a step in this direction, although characteristically it sits alongside F(1) with its insistence that 'The Union shall respect the national identities of its Member States, whose systems of government are founded on principles of democracy.'

The use of the language of rights by the ECJ since 1970, however, provides ample evidence of the difficulties with this thesis, and goes some way to explaining the German Court's reassertion of its prerogatives. The key problem relates to the distinction between cosmopolitan and communitarian views of rights and democracy that we made earlier: namely, that even if all the member states endorse broadly the same set of rights and democratic principles, they have legitimately different views about their scope and their relative weighting with regard to both each other and other important values and interests that reflect valid cultural differences. The right to freedom of expression is accepted by all member states, for example, but in certain countries it is interpreted as warranting the special protection of linguistic minorities or a national language on the grounds that a people's culture provides the necessary context within which they express themselves as possessors of a specific identity. However, these protections can place restrictions on the free movement of goods, services, capital and labour which the Community is pledged to uphold. This conflict has been at the heart of a whole series of key cases: notably, Cinéthèque, Groener, Bond, ERT and Grogan. The reach of Community law has come to appear increasingly open-ended so that there has been a disturbing tendency for the ECJ both to extend the range of its jurisdiction and to interpret rights in a largely market manner that shows scant respect for national constitutional values.[65]

Set against this background, we submit that the German Maastricht decision is unsurprising and defensible. Not everyone thinks so. Weiler, for example, has suggested that it represents a declaration of cold war – a stand-off between the ECJ and national courts that, if either were to call the other's bluff, risks undermining the whole legal integrity of the Union.[66] For the decision flies in the face of the ECJ's insistence that it alone has the authority to decide whether or not a community measure is *ultra vires* (article 173 EC), and that within its sphere 'the validity of a Community measure or its effect within a Member State cannot be affected by allegations that it runs counter to either fundamental rights as formulated by the Constitution of that state or the principles of a national constitutional structure'[67] – a point emphatically reaffirmed by Grogan. However, the absolute supremacy of Community law over domestic constitutional provisions has never been accepted by all national supreme courts. In general, they have acknowledged the authority of Community law for reasons internal to the national legal order rather than, as the ECJ would have it, because of its intrinsic supremacy, and have distinguished between alterations to basic principles of the national constitution and the transfer of certain powers. This picture suggests that a pluralistic and interactive, as opposed to a monistic and hierarchical, picture of legal systems might be the most appropriate frame of analysis for understanding the relationship of EC to national law.[68]

CONCLUSION: A MIDDLE WAY?

What might be called hard-line cosmopolitans and communitarians find the European Union something of a standing contradiction. The former argue that the EU requires a framework of legally binding legitimizing constitutional principles and a system of supranational federal European political institutions that, within clearly demarcated spheres, are superior to either national or regional bodies. The latter argue that there can be no ceding of national sovereignty and that the EU has already gone too far. Both groups see the EU as a somewhat messy composite arrangement involving an uneasy mixture of national, intergovernmental and supranational elements that combine in *ad hoc* ways depending on the matter in play.

By contrast, we believe a middle way that draws on moderate versions of the cosmopolitan and communitarian arguments reveals this somewhat intermediate character of the EU to be both coherent and legitimate. From this mixed perspective, it proves perfectly possible to acknowledge both the validity of certain general norms and obligations, and the need for supranational collective action in those areas where global processes have rendered it prudent, without insisting that such acknowledgement needs to be of the same kind for all parties or requires the adoption of a totally unified political system. Rather, it emerges from within the distinctive perspectives of the various participants and the dialogue that ensues between them.

It may be that increasingly common points of view, and hence a willingness to pool sovereignty, will eventually emerge. Much more likely, however, is a continuation of the current piecemeal process whereby the Union develops through a mixture of *ad hoc* agreements, periodic major intergovernmental reviews, various indirect external and internal pressures, and certain internal dynamics of the Community itself. In keeping with the German Maastricht decision, democratic legitimacy within this set-up comes largely from national politicians, parliaments and courts – although more direct involvement of citizens would undoubtedly enhance popular identification with the decisions.[69] The chief objection, fuelled by Maastricht, is that such mechanisms lead to a fragmented *à la carte* Union of opt-outs and variable tracks. At some level, it will undoubtedly be necessary for member states to agree what is and what is not optional. However, this cannot be decided *a priori* – as we have seen, conventional notions of what is or is not required for a political organization to work are constantly challenged by the very existence of the EU. Rather, they have to be progressively negotiated. That suggests the need for political rather than legal mechanisms, that are capable of mediating between different cultural and national groups. The normative foundations of this conception of the EU can perhaps be best characterized as a cosmopolitan communitarianism, in which different communities converge on a range of compatible perspectives on common goals and endeavours, rather than a communitarian cosmopolitanism which assumes a universal consensus on principles and procedures. It suggests a civic Europe made up of different nations, rather than a homogeneous European civic nation. This approach may be more bricolage than the grand architecture desired by some commentators, but it has the great advantage of suggesting that mixed and plural forms of sovereignty involving variations in geometry, tracks and speeds may not be as unjustifiable or as unstable as many have wished us to believe.[70]

NOTES

Research for this paper was supported by an ESRC award for a project on Languages and Principles for a Constitution of Europe (R000221170). We are grateful for the comments on earlier versions by colleagues in the Western

174   *Richard Bellamy and Dario Castiglione*

Conference for the Study of Political Thought at a meeting in Bristol, audiences at the Universities of Oslo, Edinburgh, Bologna, Western Ontario, Laval and Victoria, particularly Thomas Pogge, Neil MacCormick, Paolo Pombeni, Richard Vernon, Guy LaForest and Jim Tully respectively, and for the written observations of Daniele Archibugi, Andreas Follesdal, David Held, Barry Holden, Barry Jones, Martin Köhler and Carole Lyons.

1   For an overview of the debate, see S. Mulhall and A. Swift, *Liberals and Communitarians*, 2nd edn (Oxford: Blackwell, 1996). See also Janna Thompson, Chapter 9 below.

2   See G. de Búrca, 'The quest for legitimacy in the European Union', *Modern Law Review*, 59.3 (1996), pp. 349–76; N. Walker, 'European constitutionalism and European integration', *Public Law*, 40 (1996), pp. 266–90.

3   These opening reflections are inspired by P. C. Schmitter, 'If the nation state were to wither away in Europe, what might replace it?', in S. Gustavsson and L. Lewin (eds), *The Future of the Nation-State: Essays on Cultural Pluralism and Political Integration* (Stockholm: Nerenius and Santérus, 1996), pp. 211–44, esp. p. 219.

4   See Walker, 'European constitutionalism and European integration', for a review of the growing impact of such issues in the recent legal and, to a lesser extent, political science literature on the EU.

5   For the application of these two models to international relations theory, see C. Brown, *International Relations Theory: New Normative Approaches* (Hemel Hempstead: Harvester/Wheatsheaf, 1992). We have offered a preliminary sketch of their relevance to European constitutional debates in R. Bellamy and D. Castiglione, 'The communitarian ghost in the cosmopolitan machine: constitutionalism, democracy and the reconfiguration of politics in the New Europe', in R. Bellamy (ed.), *Constitutionalism, Democracy and Sovereignty: American and European Perspectives* (Aldershot: Avebury 1996), pp. 111–29.

6   This paragraph essentially summarizes the argument of T. W. Pogge, 'Cosmopolitanism and sovereignty', in C. Brown (ed.), *Political Restructuring in Europe: Ethical Perspectives* (London and New York: Routledge, 1994), pp. 89–122.

7   The exposition of this thesis in the next three paragraphs derives from D. Held, *Democracy and the Global Order: From the Modern State to Cosmopolitan Governance* (Cambridge: Polity Press, 1995), chs 5 and 6.

8   J.-H. Ferry, 'Une "philosophie" de la communauté', in J.-H. Ferry and P. Thibaud, *Discussion sur l'Europe* (Paris: Calmann-Levy, 1992), pp. 179–89.

9   O. Beaud, 'La Fédération entre l'état et l'empire', in B. Théret (ed.), *L'État, la finance et le sociale* (Paris: La Decouverte, 1995). This second position corresponds to the conception of cosmopolitan democracy offered by Daniele Archibugi and David Held in this volume and elsewhere. Like that of Pogge, 'Cosmopolitanism and sovereignty', their view does not necessarily imply a single federal state, although it is informed by a federal spirit in the broader Kantian sense that implies a weakening of state sovereignty.

10 S. George, *Policy and Politics in the European Community*, 2nd edn (Oxford: Oxford University Press, 1991).

11   G. F. Mancini, 'The making of a constitution for Europe', *Common Market Law Review*, 26 (1989), pp. 595–614. For the contrast between the legal and political science paradigms, see J. H. H. Weiler with U. R. Haltern and F. C. Mayer, 'European democracy and its critique', in J. Haywood (ed.), *The Crisis of Representation in Europe* (London: Frank Cass, 1995), pp. 24–33; and D. Wincott, 'Political theory, law and European Union', in J. Shaw and G. More (eds), *New Legal Dynamics of European Union* (Oxford: Clarendon Press 1995), pp. 293–311.

12   M. Sandel, 'The political theory of the procedural republic', in G. Bryner and N. Reynolds (eds), *Constitutionalism and Rights* (Provo, Utah: Brigham Young University Press, 1987), pp. 141–55.

13   J. Waldron, 'Rights in conflict', *Ethics*, 99 (1989), pp. 503–19; R. Bellamy, 'The constitution of Europe: rights or democracy?', in R. Bellamy, V. Bufacchi and D. Castiglione (eds), *Democracy and Constitutional Culture in the Union of Europe* (London: Lothian Foundation Press, 1995), pp. 153–76.

14   M. Walzer, 'Philosophy and democracy', *Political Theory*, 9 (1981), pp. 379–99.

15   M. Walzer, *Spheres of Justice: a Defence of Pluralism and Equality* (Oxford: Martin Robertson, 1983); D. Miller, *On Nationality* (Oxford: Clarendon Press, 1995), ch. 4.

16   P. Hirst and G. Thompson, *Globalization in Question: the International Economy and the Possibilities of Governance* (Cambridge: Polity Press, 1996).

17   Held, *Democracy and the Global Order*, part 4.

18   D. Zolo, *Cosmopolis: La prospettiva del governo mondiale* (Milan: Feltrinelli, 1995), pp. 27–8; trans. as *Cosmopolis: Prospects for World Government* (Cambridge: Polity Press, 1997).

19   R. J. Barry Jones, 'The United Nations and the international political system', in D. Bourantonis and J. Weiner (eds), *The United Nations in the New World Order: the World Organization at Fifty* (Basingstoke: Macmillan, 1995), pp. 19–40.

20   R. J. Barry Jones, *Globalisation and Interdependence in the International Political Economy: Rhetoric and Reality* (London and New York: Pinter, 1995), pp. 75–7.

21   Hirst and Thompson, *Globalization in Question*, ch. 7; R. J. Barry Jones, 'The economic agenda', in G. Wyn Rees (ed.), *International Politics in Europe: the New Agenda* (London and New York: Routledge, 1993), pp. 87–110.

22   A. Milward, *The European Rescue of the Nation-State* (London and New York: Routledge, 1992).

23   C. Lyons, 'Citizenship in the constitution of the European Union: rhetoric or reality?', in Bellamy, *Constitutionalism, Democracy and Sovereignty*, pp. 96–110.

24   P. Thibaud, 'L'Europe par les nations (et réciproquement)', in Ferry and Thibaud, *Discussion sur l'Europe*, although see Miller, *On Nationality*, esp. ch. 6, for a British version.

25   Pogge, 'Cosmopolitanism and sovereignty'; L. Ferrajoli, 'Beyond sovereignty and citizenship: a global constitutionalism', in Bellamy, *Constitutionalism, Democracy and Sovereignty*, pp. 151–60.

26 Miller, *On Nationality*, pp. 96–9.

27 The role of judicial review in relation to rights and democracy has been extensively debated with regard to the part played by the Supreme Court in the United States. The case for has been made most forcefully by R. Dworkin, *A Matter of Principle* (Oxford: Clarendon Press, 1985), esp. pp. 70–1, and that against by C. R. Sunstein, *The Partial Constitution* (Cambridge: Harvard University Press, 1993). See R. Bellamy, 'Liberal politics and the judiciary: the Supreme Court and American democracy', *Res Publica: a Journal of Legal and Social Philosophy*, 3 (1997), pp. 91–106; and R. Bellamy and D. Castiglione, 'Constitutionalism and democracy: political theory and the American constitution', *British Journal of Political Science*, 27 (1997), pp. 595–618 (on which this paragraph draws), for a fuller examination of this debate.

28 For evidence to this effect with regard to the US Supreme Court, see R. J. Mckeever, *Raw Judicial Power? The Supreme Court and American Society*, 2nd edn (Manchester: Manchester University Press, 1995).

29 Miller, *On Nationality*, ch. 3 and pp. 100–3.

30 Ibid., pp. 104–8.

31 S. Holmes, *The Anatomy of Antiliberalism* (Cambridge: Harvard University Press, 1993).

32 The need to distinguish 'ontological' from 'advocacy' issues when considering the liberal–communitarian debate has been stressed by C. Taylor, 'Cross-purposes: the liberal–communitarian debate', in N. Rosenblum (ed.), *Liberalism and the Moral Life* (Cambridge: Harvard University Press, 1989), ch. 9. That the terminology we employ here has entered current political debate in the UK is shown by Charles Leadbeater's use of it to illuminate Conservative divisions over Europe in 'Life after death for the Tories . . .', *Observer*, 9 Feb. 1997, pp. 16–17.

33 M. Walzer, *Thick and Thin: Moral Argument at Home and Abroad* (Notre Dame: University of Notre Dame Press, 1994), esp. ch. 1.

34 See Y. Tamir, *Liberal Nationalism* (Princeton: Princeton University Press, 1993), ch. 1, for criticism of such views.

35 Pogge, 'Cosmopolitanism and sovereignty'.

36 See chapters 10, 9 and 1 respectively.

37 See e.g. A. J. Simmons, *Moral Principles and Political Obligation* (Princeton: Princeton University Press, 1979).

38 Miller, *On Nationality*, ch. 2.

39 Held, *Democracy and the Global Order*, p. 225.

40 J. Tully, *Strange Multiplicity: Constitutionalism in an Age of Diversity* (Cambridge: Cambridge University Press, 1995).

41 A. Lijphart, 'Typologies of democratic systems', *Comparative Political Studies*, 1.1 (1968), pp. 3–44.

42 D. N. Chryssochoou, 'Democracy and symbiosis in the European Union: towards a confederal consociation?', *West European Politics*, 17 (1994), pp. 1–14.

43 Mancini, 'The making of a constitution for Europe'.

44 J. H. H. Weiler, 'Journey to an unknown destination: a retrospective and prospective of the European Court of Justice in the area of political integration', *Journal of Common Market Studies*, 31 (1994), pp. 1–30.

45 D. Wincott, 'Is the Treaty of Maastricht an adequate 'constitution' for the European Union?', *Public Administration*, 72 (1994), pp. 573–90.

46 D. Curtin, 'The constitutional structure of the Union: a Europe of bits and pieces', *Common Market Law Review*, 30 (1993), pp. 17–69, at pp. 23–4, 67.

47 Lyons, 'Citizenship in the constitution of the European Union'.

48 The conspicuous exception is J. H. H. Weiler, 'European neo-constitutionalism: in search of foundations for the European constitutional order', in R. Bellamy and D. Castiglione (eds), *Constitutionalism in Transformation: European and Theoretical Perspectives* (Oxford: Blackwell, 1996), pp. 105–21.

49 N. Wilterdink, 'Where nations meet: national identities in an international organisation', EUI working paper, Florence, 1990, pp. 77–85; N. Wilterdink, 'An examination of European and national identity', *European Journal of Sociology*, 34 (1993), pp. 119–36, at pp. 119, 128–9.

50 E. Gellner, *Nations and Nationalism* (Oxford: Blackwell, 1983).

51 J. Habermas, 'Citizenship and national identity: some reflections on the future of Europe', *Praxis International*, 12 (1992), pp. 1–19.

52 J. H. H. Weiler, 'Parliamentary democracy in Europe 1992: tentative questions and answers', in D. Greenberg et al. (eds), *Constitutionalism and Democracy: Transitions in the Contemporary World* (Oxford and New York: Oxford University Press, 1993), pp. 249–63.

53 Bellamy, 'The constitution of Europe'.

54 Weiler, 'European neo-constitutionalism', p. 111.

55 The analysis here draws on N. MacCormick, 'The Maastricht-Urteil: sovereignty now', *European Law Journal*, 1 (1995), pp. 255–62; and S. Gustavsson, 'Squaring the circle? Provisional suprastatism and democratic accountability in the 1993 Maastricht verdict of the German Constitutional Court', paper presented to ECPR joint sessions, workshop 2 on the Political Theory of Constitutional Choice, Oslo, 29 Mar.–3 Apr. 1996.

56 German Federal Court 1993, C I 2 b (2).

57 Ibid., C I 2 b (1).

58 Ibid., C I 2 b (2).

59 Ibid., C I 3.

60 In case 11/70, *Internationale Handelsgesellschaft* [1970] ECR 1125, at 1134. See, too, case 29/69, *Stauder v Ulm* [1969] ECR 419, at 425, where the Court first stated that fundamental rights were 'enshrined in the general principles of Community law and protected by the Court'.

61 In case 4/73, *Nold (II)* [1974] ECR 491, 507.

62 Mancini, 'The making of a constitution for Europe', p. 611.

63 M. Cappelletti, *The Judicial Process in Comparative Perspective* (Oxford: Clarendon Press, 1989), p. 395.

64 P. Twomey, 'The European Union: three pillars without a human rights foundation', in D. O'Keeffe and P. Twomey (eds), *Legal Issues of the Maastricht Treaty* (Chichester: Chancery, 1994), p. 129.

65 B. De Witte, 'Droit communitaire et valeurs constitutionelles nationales', *Droits*, 14 (1991), pp. 87–96; and J. Coppel and A. O'Neill, 'The European Court of Justice: taking rights seriously?', *Common Market Law Review*, 29 (1992), pp. 669–92.

66 Weiler, 'European neo-constitutionalism', pp. 530–2.
67 Case 11/70, *Internationale Handelsgesellschaft* [1970] ECR 1125, at 1134; [1972] CMLR 255, at 283.
68 N. MacCormick, 'Liberalism, nationalism and the post-sovereign state', in Bellamy and Castiglione, *Constitutionalism in Transformation*, pp. 143–50.
69 Bellamy and Castiglione, 'The communitarian ghost', pp. 120–4.
70 R. Bellamy and D. Castiglione, 'Building the Union: the nature of sovereignty in the political architecture of Europe', *Law and Philosophy*, 16 (1997), pp. 421–45.

9

Community Identity and World Citizenship

Janna Thompson

The international world has become a 'world society' with a global economy, international institutions, transnational associations and federations, and this 'community' faces problems, environmental and social, which seem to require a new stage of international development: one that overcomes the limitations and dangers of a system based on sovereign national states.[1] With the ending of the Cold War, it seemed reasonable that governments, international associations and citizens of states would turn their attention to the solution of global problems, and that in doing so they would define the rights and responsibilities of world citizenship and develop political means of recognizing and carrying them out. However, instead of the triumph of cosmopolitanism, what we are witnessing are two developments which appear to be taking us down a different path. The first is the ascendancy of neoliberalism and its rejection of political measures for curbing or directing market forces. The second is the 'return to community': the resurgence of nationalism, the assertion of cultural or religious identity, and demands of indigenous peoples and ethnic minorities for autonomy and the right to preserve their own heritage and customs. Both of these developments not only impede cosmopolitan programmes, as they are usually defined. They also present a philosophical challenge to cosmopolitan ideas.

Cosmopolitanism, according to the Kantian tradition, depends on the existence of a universal moral law, and on the idea that it is possible to create, or move towards, a world society where this moral law becomes the basis of international law and world political organization, and governs relations between all individuals.[2] Contemporary cosmopolitans who are influenced by the 'welfare liberalism' of Rawls and Dworkin think that global justice consists not only of a catalogue of civil and democratic rights but also the entitlement of each individual to an adequate share of the world's resources. These entitlements are supposed to apply to individuals as individuals – regardless of their culture or national identity. They determine the meaning of world citizenship. The political aim of cosmopolitanism is to bring about a world society in which these principles and rights can be universally recognized and honoured.

Neoliberals do not abandon the idea that there is a universal moral law, but they have different ideas from most cosmopolitans about what that law is or how it should be brought into effect. Those who call themselves libertarians insist that individual rights severely limit what governments can do in the name of justice. Libertarianism is the opponent of any cosmopolitan political programme which would force individuals to sacrifice their own or their community's resources for the sake of benefits to the least well-off people of the world. It would oppose any transnational democracy which violated individual or communal 'right of property'.[3] To meet the challenge libertarians pose, cosmopolitans who favour democratic control of global resources and transnational redistribution of resources have to be prepared to defend their ideas about what rights and principles should be the foundation for law and political authority in world society. To do this successfully, as I will try to show, cosmopolitans must attend to the concerns of those who regard community as the basis for morality and politics.

Advocates of community present a more basic challenge to cosmopolitan philosophy and practice. For they are not only opposed to international organizations which seem to threaten the autonomy of their community, but many of them deny the absolute authority of a universal moral law. They argue either that the values of their community should (at least in some cases) take precedence over universal requirements, or they deny that there is any such thing as universal morality. The philosophical challenge to the foundations of cosmopolitanism sometimes takes the form of a postmodern suspicion of any kind of total morality or world-view. However, the communitarian challenge to cosmopolitanism is likely to be favoured by those who insist on the value of *their* community and want to defend it from economic and political forces, including programmes for a cosmopolitan world order.[4] (Table 9.1 shows the relationships between philosophical theories about justice.)

Table 9.1 Theories of justice

Contemporary positions	Ideas about justice	Authors and works
Welfare liberalism	Justice requires equity. Governments should distribute goods according to requirements of equity.	Rawls, *A Theory of Justice*. Dworkin, *A Matter of Principle*. Kymlicka, *Contemporary Political Philosophy*.
Libertarianism	Justice requires that individual rights of freedom and property not be violated. Governments are not entitled to redistribute goods owned by individuals or communities.	Nozick, *Anarchy, State and Utopia*. Paul (ed.), *Reading Nozick*.
Cosmopolitanism	Justice should govern relations in a peaceful, cooperative world society. (What kind of justice? What kind of society?)	Kant, *Zum ewigen Frieden*. Archibugi, 'Principles of cosmopolitan democracy'. Barry, 'Humanity and justice in a global perspective'. Doyle, 'Kant, liberal legacies and foreign affairs'. Beitz, *Political Theory and International Relations*. Held, *Democracy and the Global Order*. Thompson, *Justice and World Order*.
Communitarianism	The meaning and possibility of justice depends on the identification of individuals with their community and its values.	Sandel, *Liberalism and the Limits of Justice*. Taylor, 'Politics of recognition'.

It would be misleading to say that communitarianism is the philosophy of nationalists or libertarianism of neoliberals, or that there is any close association between philosophical or moral ideas and international developments. Nationalists and neoliberals have many motivations, some of which do not stand up to close critical examination. However, debates between liberals, libertarians and communitarians reflect disruptions in the political world: the growth of transnational associations and the resulting challenges to the authority of the state and its requirements; the revival of community and the demands for community autonomy or independence. The debate not only presents arguments that liberal philosophers have to answer, but it also draws our attention to problems which have to be dealt with by those whose concerns are more practical. Dealing with these challenges will better enable cosmopolitans to come to terms with developments which seem to be blocking progress towards a just and democratic world society, and to reassess their ideas of what their objectives mean.

The focus of this chapter is on the communitarian challenge to cosmopolitanism and how this challenge can be met. However, I will argue that communitarianism should not be treated as a philosophical enemy of cosmopolitanism to be promptly refuted and dismissed. Communitarians reveal weaknesses in the liberal position – weaknesses which are particularly evident when liberal ideas of welfare and democracy become cosmopolitan objectives. Communitarians raise the critical question of what makes a political society possible – a question that advocates of transnational democracy cannot ignore. By understanding the strengths and weaknesses of the communitarian position, cosmopolitans will be in a better position to defend their own idea of what makes political relations possible and to pursue more effectively a cosmopolitan political programme.

THE COMMUNITARIAN CHALLENGE

Communitarians present themselves as political and philosophical opponents of liberalism, and, by implication, cosmopolitanism. They oppose liberalism not by attacking the existence of universal moral principles. They argue that liberals have a mistaken or inadequate conception of the self. Michael Sandel takes Rawls to be a representative for all liberals and attacks him for treating the self as independent of its ends.[5] According to Sandel, it is this assumption which Rawls relies on when he imagines individuals choosing principles of justice independently of their knowledge of their race, class, gender, associations and idea of the good.[6] Charles Taylor thinks that liberals have an 'atomistic' conception of the individual, that they wrongly regard individuals as self-sufficient beings, and treat social relations as mere means to individual ends.[7]

Communitarians insist that the identity of an individual is constituted by his or her relation to others and to shared values and ideals of a community. In their view the community and its good are central to the ethical and political life of an individual, and they argue that the priority liberals give to principles of right over conceptions of the good has to be reversed.[8] But communitarians are not primarily interested in making moral or political recommendations. Their main focus is a metaphysical one. They think that liberals have never sufficiently come to terms with the implications of denying the existence of the Kantian noumenal self – the transcendent, rational will which is constituted independently of empirical conditions – and that they have therefore never faced the implications for political theory of a self that is merely an empirical creation, a creature of its cultural environment and social relations.

Liberals commonly deny that they depend on any metaphysical view about the nature of the self. Allen Buchanan argues that the liberal political thesis – that the state ought to enforce principles of justice, civil and political rights, and otherwise leave individuals free to pursue their own conceptions of the good – is independent of the metaphysical views that communitarians 'rightly criticize'.[9] Kymlicka thinks that liberalism rests on the value to each individual of his or her own life and the realization of his or her goals and objectives.[10] Rawls presents his liberal theory as a practical, political means of dealing with conflicts of interest and values (including community values) which exist in pluralist societies.[11]

Moreover, liberals rightly complain that many communitarian criticisms misrepresent the positions they are attacking. Rawls's attempt to imagine what principles of justice individuals would choose behind a veil of ignorance does not presuppose a pre-social identity. Nor do liberals have to suppose that individuals are atomistic, self-sufficient beings. Most contemporary liberals take it for granted that individuals value their political and social relationships, and are therefore predisposed to regard justice as the 'first virtue of a political society'. They can assume this because they are primarily concerned to determine principles of right for citizens in existing liberal democratic societies where the desire for political cooperation is already widespread.

However, it is notable that the justification and defence of liberal theories of justice or rights depend on presuppositions about the nature of social relations and the attitudes of individuals to them. What communitarian criticisms *do* accomplish is to draw our attention to these assumptions. In his recent works Rawls has accommodated his communitarian critics by explicitly presenting his theory as a view about justice for a liberal pluralist society – for those who are already predisposed to accept liberal ideas of fairness and who are prepared to subordinate themselves and their associations to the ultimate authority of a law based upon justice.[12] But this means that his theory of justice and liberal views about rights are self-evident only if, and so long as, individuals have the required relationships and values. If the political world changes, or liberalism embarks on cosmopolitan adventures, then these relationships and values can no longer be relied on.

Liberalism is in crisis as a theory and practice because modern societies are not only pluralist; they are also multicultural, and this means that disputes about the most fundamental moral and political ideals are bound to occur as soon as minority groups have some access to decision-making power. But the problem is not just that some individuals may not accept liberal moral principles. A multicultural society is a society in which people are likely to have strong allegiances to ethnic, religious and other communities. Members of these communities, faced with conflicts of interest between the demands of group loyalty and the requirements of political society, are likely to question why they should be expected to subordinate their community values to general principles of right. What gives principles of right supreme moral and political authority? What communitarians are questioning is not merely whether we *can* transcend the particularities of our situation and loyalties, but why we should be required to try to do so. By saying that justice is the first virtue of a political society, Rawls means that it should take precedence, as far as political relations are concerned, over other values and allegiances. The question remains why we should be obliged to adopt this virtue, and accept what justice requires, especially if this means sacrificing our community interests.[13]

This question can be asked about any of the principles and rights espoused by liberal philosophers. But Sandel wants to point out that Rawls's difference principle – the principle which requires that inequalities should be allowed if and only if they favour the least well-off members of a society – presupposes in an especially obvious way that individuals identify with their political society.[14] Sandel argues that there is a tension in Rawls's theory of justice. On one hand, Rawls argues that utilitarianism does not sufficiently recognize that individuals are separate entities whose particular desires and ways of living their lives deserve respect. Utilitarians, he says, subordinate individual interests and ends to the pursuit of the common good, and thus are too inclined to sacrifice individuals for the sake of the greater good. This objection is basic to Rawls's defence of his neo-Kantian theory. On the other hand, as Sandel points out, Rawls's difference principle entails that it is legitimate for a political society to require individuals to contribute to the well-being of others. That is, he allows that an individual's talents, wealth and income can be treated as public assets, things that can be used by the state for the welfare of others. So on the one hand Rawls insists that individuals should be respected as distinct beings, and on the other he requires that they put their labour and the fruits of their labour into a common pool.

Libertarians have been quick to argue that Rawls's willingness to 'exploit' individuals for the sake of others fails to demonstrate a proper respect for persons. Taxation for the sake of welfare, they say, is partial slavery, a way of exploiting the talents and efforts of individuals, an unjustified expropriation of their labour.[15] Sandel is not trying to defend libertarianism. He uses the libertarian critique to make the point that Rawls too readily assumes that a particular community, namely one's state, is entitled to redistribute wealth among its members. Rawls does not really explain why people should accept the sacrifices distributive justice imposes on them, and why it is their state rather than some other community they belong to which has the entitlement to impose this requirement.[16] The only possible moral basis for the requirements of distributive justice, Sandel argues, is a community where self-identity is an identity with others. 'If the difference principle is to avoid using some as means to others' ends, it can only be possible under circumstances where the subject of possession is a "we" rather than an "I", which circumstances imply in turn the existence of a community in the constitutive sense.'[17]

As I understand it, the debate between liberals, libertarians and communitarians is a debate about political obligation – and not about the existence of universal moral duties. A libertarian or a communitarian might believe that he as an individual has a moral duty to help the least well off. What he questions is the assumption that his state (or any state) has a right to appropriate his resources for the welfare of others and use them as its government sees fit. Both libertarianism and communitarianism, in their different ways, reintroduce into contemporary debate the classical question of political philosophy: what justifies political authority? The answer of communitarians is that this justification depends on intersubjectivity, the identification of individuals with each other and the values of their society. As I understand them, communitarians are not anti-liberal. They are not arguing that liberal political values are wrong or that there is no justification for liberal theories of right. They are advancing a thesis about the presuppositions of political society and the basis of political authority.

Communitarian criticism has focused mostly on liberal theories of justice. However, it can also be applied to another important value of contemporary liberalism: democratic citizenship. A citizen, according to many liberal conceptions, is supposed to transcend particular loyalties and personal interests and contribute to the common good. He or she must at least be prepared to accept the decision of the majority even when this requires a sacrifice of individual or group interests. Libertarians refuse to allow that such a requirement is justified except in defence of individual rights.[18] The communitarian response is once again to insist that the requirements of democracy and citizenship have to be underwritten by the commitment of individuals to community, by the existence of selves who identify with their political community and are thus willing to accept the sacrifices community entails.

What communitarians have to say about the foundations of justice and democracy is of obvious concern to cosmopolitans. Communitarians argue that the limits of community are the limits of justice and democracy. They thus suggest that attempts to expand democracy and distributive justice across the borders of states is not something that can be accomplished by an appeal to morality or reason, or even the creation of appropriate institutions. If communitarians are right, then ideas of international justice and transnational declarations of rights are always going to lack political legitimacy. People may agree with them as moral ideals, but they can reasonably refuse to sacrifice the goods and values of community for their sake. Such universal moral requirements, so far as they exist, cannot claim ultimate authority over the claims of our particular political and social relations. If communitarianism is right, there is no basis for transnational democracy. The United Nations or other international bodies could become more democratic in structure, but organizational forms by themselves cannot create a democratic society. The kind of commitment to community which democratic citizenship requires, communitarians are arguing, simply does not exist outside the borders of states.

The communitarian position suggests that even cautious, conservative ideas of international justice – views which take for granted the political status quo and commonly accepted moral ideas (as Rawls does in *A Theory of Justice*) – are inadequately founded.[19] They are not properly grounded in community and therefore cannot serve as the 'first virtue' of international society. The problem is not simply that there is no government or other power capable of enforcing international rights or principles in a reliable way. It is not merely that universal moral agreement is unlikely to be obtained in international society. The more basic problem is that without community these rights lack the overriding authority which justice is supposed to possess.

COMMUNITARIANISM CRITICIZED

By insisting that justice and citizenship depend upon identification with community, communitarianism seems to deny the possibility or desirability of cosmopolitan justice or transnational democracy. But the account that communitarians give of their crucial notion of 'self-identity' is not only vague, but seriously flawed. I will try to show that once these weaknesses are exposed, we will be closer to obtaining an idea of how individuals can be related to their communities which is more realistic, morally defensible, and also has more positive implications for cosmopolitanism.

Identity as oneness with a community

Communitarians reject the Kantian idea of the self but adopt a conception which is equally problematic. Their idea of self identity is strongly influenced by Hegel. Taylor, like Hegel, objects to moral or political duties which are an external imposition on individuals, and thinks that ethical behaviour should flow out of an individual's identification with an idea of the good, an idea which intrinsically involves his or her relations to others. The opposition between individual interests and moral and political life is ideally transcended by an identification with a community and its good,[20] This Hegelian ideal of an individual who is at one with his community and its good also influences Sandel's thesis about the nature of justice. Justice, he contends, is merely a remedial virtue for an imperfect community. The ideal against which relations of justice should be measured is a community where the identity of interests and objectives is complete and no conflicts requiring appeals to justice occur.[21]

The ideal of communitarians is thus an identity with community which transcends all self-interests and sectarian goals. As many critics of communitarianism have pointed out, this ideal is not only unrealistic but undesirable. Modern individuals, that is, people who are influenced by ideas coming from outside their communities and who are likely to be members of many different groups, are not likely to identify completely and uncritically with any community, and there is no moral reason why they should.[22] Indeed, there are good reasons for thinking that a community of total identification would place constraints on individual thought and action which would be oppressive, stultifying or corrupting (whether individuals are aware of these effects or not).

A more adequate conception of identity would not only allow that individuals do or can identify with many different communities, ethnic, religious, political and social. It would insist that this is a good thing. Individuals with a complex social identity will never be at one with themselves and their social world or free from conflicts of loyalty, but this a reasonable price to pay for the expansion of moral consciousness and the opportunities of choice that complexity provides. A complex identity is not only compatible with cosmopolitanism. It is conducive to the establishment of procedures for resolving conflicts between communities. People who regard membership in a number of communities as important to their lives will be motivated to search for and abide by such procedures.

Identity as a one-dimensional relationship

Communitarians fail to take into account or properly appreciate the plurality of communities which individuals can value. They also fail to appreciate that associations can exist on different levels and for different purposes and that individuals can be related to each other in different ways. For communitarians what counts is how tightly individuals are bound together in relations of identity. Closeness of relationship is supposed to make the difference between a society that is capable of justice and one that is not, a society in which justice is a virtue and one in which it is unnecessary. One problem with this conception is that communitarianism is unable to explain how justice is possible in a pluralist modern society. Most people probably identify much more closely with their family, their friends, their religious group, etc., than they do with their political society. They are more likely to share a common good with those near and dear than they are with other members of their nation. Because their account of community does not fit relations in a modern state, communitarians tend to lapse into a reactionary position, expressed by a distaste for modern political complexities and uncertainties and a longing for a simpler political life.[23]

A more adequate conception of political identity would have to allow that individuals' associations are not only of different kinds but also exist on different levels. A person can be a family member, belong to a religious group, etc., and also be a citizen of a country which contains families and religious groups. In some circumstances one identity takes precedence; in other circumstances another becomes more important. The problem for those concerned with political legitimacy of states or cosmopolitan structures is to explain to individuals why (and when) they ought to subordinate their family, religious or other group loyalties to the demands of political authority. But communitarianism doesn't solve this problem. It renders it unsolvable.

Community identity as a value consensus

Another problem with the conception of identity that communitarians favour is found in their insistence that the priority of the right over the good ought to be reversed. Communitarians are not merely pointing out that the acceptance of principles of right and democratic structures as the basis of political order depends on commitment to community. They also intend to question the primary role of principles of justice or political procedures as a basis for political society. Their contention is that agreement about an idea of the good is required for true community.[24]

The problem that this idea poses for cosmopolitan programmes is obvious. It seems to imply that general principles of right should not prevail over a community's idea of the good, and that this good and the political arrangements made to achieve it cannot be rightly criticized or interfered with for the sake of individual rights or universal justice. It undermines the cosmopolitan idea of a world society governed by principles and institutions which have authority over all individuals and communities regardless of their tradition, history, religion or conception of the good.

However, the idea that a community is united by its idea of the good fails once again to account for the complexities of community identity. Many citizens value their political relationship. But it is notoriously difficult to find any idea of the good which all people of a modern state share (apart from procedural goods like liberty or democracy). Moreover, an insistence on shared values is likely to be oppressive, or at least destructive of the meaning of citizenship. Taylor argues that a society which favours a particular good does not have to deny rights to those who do not accept the priority of this good.[25] But if there is a serious conflict between the individual rights of this minority and the achievement of the collective good, then it seems that communitarians are justified in overriding rights. Moreover, the question arises of how members of this minority could be citizens, in a true sense, of a society which is dedicated to achieving a good that they do not accept.

Any reasonable theory of identity for a modern society must allow that people can value their society and relationships and yet disagree not only about ideas of the good, but about justice and right. What values, moral or political, are capable of being a source of identity in multicultural societies is something that a cosmopolitan needs to investigate.[26] In some cases it may be a common history, or institutions which all groups have had some role in creating, or an appreciation of what each culture contributes to the character of the society, or simply the valuing of a particular system of interlocking relationships.[27] But there is no reason in principle why people cannot come to identify sufficiently with transnational institutions to regard them as having the authority to make laws of a certain kind.

Identity as fate

The social relations which truly constitute the identity of the individual, communitarians say, are those that individuals possess by virtue of birth or heritage – relationships that a person does not choose. Sandel makes a distinction between relations I enter into voluntarily for preconceived ends of my own and relations which constitute me as a person and thus have to precede my voluntary choices.[28] Taylor claims that cultural communities of origin play a fundamental role in the formation of individual identity.[29] Liberals and cosmopolitans are thus criticized for supposing that all social relations can be treated or justified as if they were voluntary.

Let us grant that there is a difference between being a member of an association in order to promote preconceived ends and being part of a relationship which defines who I am and what my ends are. However, the distinction Sandel makes between voluntary and constitutive relations is confused and it does not justify the conclusions he wants to reach. Both

Sandel and Taylor systematically confuse social influences which form a personality with the social relations which a person values or identifies with. The character of a person who grows up in a particular culture is bound to be profoundly affected by the behaviour and relationships it encourages. But this doesn't mean that the person will necessarily identify *with* her culture or adopt as her good the good of the community she comes from. Nor can it be required that she does so. She may have very good reasons for repudiating her community of origin. Constitutive relations must thus be distinguished from relations which are valued or valuable.

Moreover, individual identity is not fixed or complete once and for all. Identity is constantly under construction, and there seems no reason why relationships which individuals choose cannot also affect their development as persons and come to influence their choice of ends.[30] Chosen relations may for some individuals be more important to their identity than membership in a community of birth. An adequate conception of identity must therefore recognize that an identity is not fixed by fate, and it must allow that a person can become critical of her community. This means that we are not stuck with the conservatism inherent in a position which gives special moral and political status to communities of birth. And it means that cosmopolitan attempts to envision and establish a new world order are not undermined from the start by requirements that rule out new identifications and commitments.

Communitarianism, I have argued, is best understood as a theory of political legitimacy which holds that the authority of principles of justice and political institutions, including democratic institutions, depends on an identity of individuals with their political society. The communitarian conception of identity is faulty and needs to be replaced with one that is empirically and morally more adequate. But communitarian criticisms of liberal assumptions deserve to be taken seriously and they have obvious implications for cosmopolitan theory and practice. If communitarians are right in their criticisms of liberalism then two common approaches to cosmopolitanism are inadequate. An approach which takes for granted general moral principles and insists that world society should order itself in accordance with these principles is unsatisfactory. For principles, however rational, however widely accepted as moral ideals, will not necessarily be acceptable as the basis for transnational political authority if individuals have loyalties and interests which are threatened by the exercise of this authority. Equally unsatisfactory is a theory which concentrates on defining the political institutions which should be adopted by a cosmopolitan society.[31] For institutions are empty shells without the motivations which underwrite their authority. World citizenship requires the creation of a new political identity, and cosmopolitanism must concern itself with how this identity might be constructed.

COSMOPOLITAN THEORY RECONSTRUCTED

How should the cosmopolitan project be pursued in the light of communitarian criticisms? Communitarians give us no reason to think that a post-Kantian moral philosophy has to give up hope of justifying and promoting universal moral ideals. Their objections to liberalism are not objections to the basic idea behind liberal morality – that individuals are of intrinsic value and have equal moral worth – or to theories of right or justice. What their criticisms imply is that more attention has to be given to the question of how these liberal ideals can be realized in a world society where individuals not only have self-interests but also commitments to community. This means that the nature of cosmopolitan justice is going to depend on how these commitments can develop and change.

Cosmopolitanism must somehow take into account the particular situation and loyalties of individuals, as well as the contingencies of political struggle. However, cosmopolitanism is founded on moral ideals. It depends on the notion that there are values which everyone in the world ought to accept, whatever their personal interests or community loyalties. I suggest that these universal cosmopolitan ideals will include the following.

1 *Peace and security* Individuals and their communities should not be threatened by war, oppression or other serious harms, and there should be peaceful, mutually acceptable means of settling disputes.
2 *Self-determination of communities* Individuals should be able to preserve and maintain communities that are important to their identity and well-being. This ideal does not, however, give individuals an entitlement to preserve whatever communities they now have or to regard self-determination as overriding all other values. Nevertheless, it encompasses the communitarian perception that communities are of great importance to the way individuals understand themselves and live their lives.
3 *Freedom of individuals* Individuals should be able to make their own life choices and associate with whomever they please. I am assuming that individuals who live in modern communities which contain many kinds of associations and opportunities will generally value individual freedom, though they may have different ideas about what it means or how it should be made compatible with other values.
4 *Individual well-being* Everyone should have access to resources, material and social, which enable them to make meaningful choices and enable their communities to flourish.

To justify these values a post-Kantian cosmopolitan philosopher would have to make a case for saying that all reasonable people would agree to accept them.[32] I will make no attempt to give a systematic account of how this justification would proceed. Nevertheless, it is reasonable to believe that most people, including many non-cosmopolitans, would agree that peace, freedom, community, and individual well-being are of value. One reason why widespread agreement can be expected is that these ideals are often appealed to in political debates, not just by people in the Western world, but increasingly by people in non-Western countries. They are also recognized in one form or another by United Nations declarations. Another reason why it is reasonable for cosmopolitans to assume that these ideals are universal is that most political philosophies recognize them as values, even though theorists often have different ideas about what they mean, how they should be realized and which should take priority. Cosmopolitan values could thus be thought of as constituting what Rawls calls an 'overlapping consensus' among individuals who not only have different interests but also different, and sometimes contrary, political philosophies.[33]

However, these ideals cannot be regarded as moral or political *principles*. This means that they cannot by themselves make specific demands on individuals or societies. They cannot be regarded as principles of justice which world society is committed to upholding or as rights which must always be acted on. One reason why cosmopolitan ideals do not have the force of moral principles is because of the disagreement that clearly exists among people of the world about what they mean and how they should be applied or made compatible with other values. Another reason is that their application depends on what political programme cosmopolitans regard as realizable. Global justice in the framework of a centralized world state would impose different requirements on communities and individuals than justice administered in a system of overlapping, semi-autonomous associations. But the main reason why ideals cannot automatically be translated into prescriptions for action, and the reason most relevant to the communitarian critique, is that it is not clear, given political realities, community identities and conflicts of value, whether and how individuals or communities can be held responsible for ensuring that these ideals are realized. In world society as it is, the political will required to put these norms into practice in a systematic way does not exist, and cosmopolitans must thus concern themselves with the question of how it can come into existence. This is why a cosmopolitan programme has to take the views of communitarians seriously.

Cosmopolitan ideals *do* serve as a standard for judging the political status quo and a motivation for cosmopolitan programmes. The fact that individuals and communities are oppressed or under threat, and that many people in the world do not have sufficient resources for a decent life are reasons for being dissatisfied with the present global structure and for trying to find a political solution. But whether a solution exists is going to depend on what kinds of community identities individuals are able and willing to construct. Cosmopolitans cannot be content with putting forward a moral position or with constructing blueprints for a cosmopolitan society. They must turn their attention to the creation of community.

If, for example, cosmopolitans propose that the United Nations should become a body capable of legislating in a democratic way for the people of the world and of imposing principles of justice on world society, then they have to consider what social development could make individuals into world citizens prepared to obey the law and accept the rule of the majority, even at the expense of personal objectives and the communities that they value. Whatever form it takes, the political realization of cosmopolitan values will require that individuals come to identify with transnational communities in a way that so far has not happened. This does not mean that existing social commitments will have to wither away, but it requires that these other allegiances sometimes take a subordinate place in a global framework in which new loci of political authority become more prominent and are able to command support on crucial issues.

How is cosmopolitan reasoning informed by communitarian criticism related to the promotion of transnational democracy? Once we abandon the mythical views of communitarians about self-identity and allow that individuals can construct their own identity, it becomes reasonable to suppose that democracy will play a central role in a cosmopolitan account of how commitments to transnational communities are forged. Participation of individuals in the practice of democracy encourages them to think as citizens and to take responsibility for the decisions that they have collectively made. Democracy is a means of constructing a community identity.

However, the idea that a transnational political order can be constructed by democratic participation is vulnerable to the same objection that communitarians make to liberal contract theory. Democracy, they convincingly argue, presupposes the existence of an identity with community. If this identity does not exist then there is no reason why individuals should feel that they are obligated to accept the decisions made by a political authority, whether democratic or not. How then can democracy bring about a commitment to community?

One of the problems with the communitarian view of identity, I have argued, is that it has no resources for understanding social change. According to the communitarian view, individuals have the identity that they are fated to have; either they identify with a community or they do not. And if they do not, then there is no way of understanding why they should come to do so – whether by democratic or other means. This position is clearly inadequate. But what it does point out is that identity with community cannot be represented as a rational choice from pre-existing ends. An account of the development of community also requires an account of the development of individuals – how they come to have new objectives, values and relationships. What cosmopolitanism requires is a story (or a number of stories) about how social changes and problems in world society or within states could affect individual self-understandings, thus encouraging new practices and relationships, and how these in turn could provide the motivation for new political formations.

One of the most promising directions is that taken by David Held and others who consider how global developments could encourage the development of an interlocking system of transnational associations.[34] These associations, Held argues, could become the basis of a democratic global system which enables individuals to deal collectively with transnational problems within a framework of law. What needs to be added to this account is how global problems and opportunities to develop transnational associations affect individual consciousness, and how these associations can become part of individuals' understanding of who they are. In this account of the evolution of individuals and society, the meaning of democracy and what it can accomplish will also change. Transnational democracy is likely to be conceived at the beginning as a last resort, as a means of resolving issues that cannot adequately be dealt with by what people regard as their 'true' communities. However, if transnational democracy under law is to become a stable, effective basis for global governance, then it will have to become something more than an occasional occurrence or a necessary evil. Democratic practice and the civil rights which underwrite it will themselves have to become a focus for community identity across borders.

NOTES

1 'World society' is a contentious notion, rejected by those who think it a mistake to draw analogies between domestic and global politics. Though it is clear that the international world lacks important features of a society (such as reliable institutions for making and enforcing law), nevertheless the existence of international institutions, both governmental and non-governmental, the widespread acceptance of common ideals and conventions (see below), the growth of a world economy and the recognition of the need for a cooperative approach to global problems justify the use of this term (at least in scare quotes). However, to talk of world society is also to issue a promissory note which requires the realization of a cosmopolitan programme. One of the purposes of this chapter is to consider how 'world society' can become truly a world society.

2 The classic statement of the cosmopolitan position is in Kant's *Zum ewigen Frieden* (see *Kant on History*, trans. L. W. Beck (New York: Bobbs-Merrill, 1974)). For a contemporary revision of Kant's position see Daniele Archibugi, 'Principles of cosmopolitan democracy', chapter 10 below. Contemporary philosophical proponents of cosmopolitanism also include C. Beitz, *Political Theory and International Relations* (Princeton: Princeton University Press, 1979); M. W. Doyle, 'Kant, liberal legacies and foreign affairs', parts 1 and 2, *Philosophy and Public Affairs*, 12.3 and 12.4 (1983); B. Barry, 'Humanity and justice in a global perspective', in B. Barry, *Democracy, Power and Justice: Essays in Political Theory* (Oxford: Clarendon Press, 1989), pp. 434–62; D. Held, *Democracy and the Global Order* (Cambridge: Polity Press, 1995); J. Thompson, *Justice and World Order* (London and New York: Routledge, 1992).

3 A well-known philosophical presentation of the libertarian position is found in R. Nozick, *Anarchy, State and Utopia* (New York: Basic Books, 1974). Not all neoliberals are libertarians. There are some (the economic rationalists) who are utilitarians in their moral philosophy and insist that the free market will eventually bring about the best possible results for everyone. The refutation of this kind of neoliberalism would take the familiar form of showing that this belief is mistaken or that its implementation would not have the desired results. Liberal and socialist critics of libertarianism have been mainly concerned with libertarianism as a theory of justice for domestic society. For criticisms see G. A. Cohen, 'Self-ownership, world ownership and equality, Part II', *Social Philosophy and Policy,* 3.2 (1986), and contributors to J. Paul (ed.), *Reading Nozick* (Totowa, N. J.: Rowman and Littlefield, 1981). The familiar position that citizens of national states have a right to use and control the resources of their country and should not be *required* to make a contribution to the good of outsiders has a close affinity with libertarianism.

4 Like many philosophical categories, 'communitarianism' lumps together theories which have different motivations and implications. I will concentrate on the views of M. Sandel and C. Taylor, philosophers who seem mostly closely to exemplify the views associated with communitarianism.

5 M. Sandel, *Liberalism and the Limits of Justice* (Cambridge: Cambridge University Press, 1982), pp. 15ff.

6 In J. Rawls, *A Theory of Justice* (Oxford: Oxford University Press, 1971), pp. 136ff, Rawls imagines that individuals making an agreement about the principles of justice that will govern their society remain behind a veil of ignorance which prevents them from knowing their race, class, idea of the good, or any other particular information about their relationships and abilities. He argues that these individuals would accept two basic principles: a principle which accords them equal liberty and a 'difference principle' which requires that inequalities in socially important goods must benefit the least well off.

7 C. Taylor, 'Atomism', in S. Avineri and A. de-Shalit (eds), *Communitarianism and Individualism* (Oxford: Oxford University Press, 1992), pp. 29–50. In C. Taylor, 'Politics of recognition', in A. Gutmann (ed.), *Multiculturalism: Examining the Politics of Recognition* (Princeton: Princeton University Press, 1994), he uses the term 'monological' to describe

the view of the self that he opposes. Our self-identity, he argues, is constructed 'dialogically', pp. 32ff.

8   Rawls insists on the priority of right when he forces individuals to choose principles of justice in ignorance of their ideas of the good. Another influential liberal philosopher, R. Dworkin, 'Liberalism,' in R. Dworkin, *A Matter of Principle* (Oxford: Clarendon Press, 1986), pp. 181–213, argues that principles of right should be neutral as far as individual objectives and ideals are concerned.

9   A. E. Buchanan, 'Assessing the communitarian critique of liberalism', *Ethics*, 99 (1989), pp. 853–4.

10   W. Kymlicka, *Contemporary Political Philosophy* (Oxford: Clarendon Press, 1990), ch. 6. He makes similar criticisms of communitarianism in W. Kymlicka, *Liberalism, Community and Culture* (Oxford: Oxford University Press, 1989), ch. 4.

11   Rawls argues for this view of his theory in 'Justice as fairness: political not metaphysical', *Philosophy and Public Affairs*, 14.3 (1985), pp. 223–39 (also in Avineri and de-Shalit, *Communitarianism and Individualism*, pp. 186–204), and later in J. Rawls, *Political Liberalism* (New York: Columbia University Press, 1995).

12   In *Political Liberalism*, lecture 4, Rawls regards principles of justice as the overlapping consensus of people who in their social life are committed to different communities. He insists that this consensus is not a political compromise but something that everyone from his or her own point of view can regard as fair. Rawls's concessions to communitarians make it even more crucial to answer the question of why people should subordinate the interests of their community to considerations of justice.

13   The communitarian critique, as I understand it, is similar to Bernard Williams's criticism in *Ethics and the Limits of Philosophy* (London: Fontana, 1985), ch. 4, of the idea that morality should take precedence over all other objectives. Williams also thinks that the kind of authority which morality is supposed to have depends on questionable Kantian metaphysical views about the self.

14   Sandel, *Liberalism and the Limits of Justice*, pp. 77ff.

15   Nozick, *Anarchy, State and Utopia*, ch. 7, section 2.

16   Rawls emphasizes in *Political Liberalism*, lecture 1, section 3, that justice is based on cooperation and the mutual benefits individuals get from cooperating. But this is not an adequate social basis for a principle of distributive justice. Redistribution required by the difference principle is above all meant to benefit those who are not able to contribute to a system of cooperation – the unemployed, the handicapped, the very young and the very old.

17   Sandel, *Liberalism and the Limits of Justice*, p. 80.

18   Rational choice theorists have pointed out that democratic participation is beset by paradoxes of rationality. A cost/benefit analysis would show that the inconvenience of participation for an individual will usually outweigh the benefits she can get from voting, since in most cases an individual has no reason to believe that her vote will make a difference. See A. Downs, *Economic Theory of Democracy* (Cambridge: Harvard University Press, 1957), pp. 260–74. Similarly, theorists have wondered how it can be

rational for an individual to accept a democratically arrived-at decision if she can best pursue her interests or uphold her values by ignoring it.

19 Rawls discusses international justice briefly in *A Theory of Justice* pp. 378ff. This time representatives of states are behind the veil of ignorance, and he imagines that they would agree that states should be equally entitled to determine their own affairs. In a later essay, 'The law of peoples', *Critical Inquiry*, 20 (Autumn 1993), pp. 36–68, he argues that this principle can be supplemented by a guarantee of basic individual rights, though what is acceptable will depend upon whether states are liberal or non-liberal.

20 This is the basis of C. Taylor's moral and political theory in *Sources of the Self* (Cambridge: Cambridge University Press, 1989), part 1.

21 Sandel, *Liberalism and the Limits of Justice*, pp. 31–2.

22 Sandel does recognize that individuals in a modern society are likely to be members of many different communities, see *Liberalism and the Limits of Justice*, p. 146. But he does not discuss how this is likely to affect individual identity.

23 This reaction is noticeable in the last section of Sandel's 'The procedural republic and the unencumbered self', *Political Theory*, 12 (1984), pp. 81–96 (also in Avineri and de-Shalit, *Communitarianism and Individualism*, pp. 12–28).

24 Taylor, *Sources of the Self*, ch. 3.

25 Taylor, 'Politics of recognition', pp. 59ff.

26 Valuing liberal ideals does not seem sufficient. W. Kymlicka in *Multicultural Citizen* (Oxford: Clarendon Press, 1995), pp. 187ff, points out that English and French Canadians have the same ideas about right and justice, and so do most Europeans in both the West and the East. But this does not necessarily result in political community.

27 Cf. Thompson, *Justice and World Order*, ch. 9.

28 Sandel, *Liberalism and the Limits of Justice*, pp. 147ff.

29 Taylor, 'Politics of recognition', p. 30.

30 Y. Tamir stresses this point in *Liberal Nationalism* (Princeton: Princeton University Press, 1993), pp. 20ff. An individual can't choose all of his ends at once, but there is no reason, she points out, why he can't change or remake himself in a piecemeal fashion.

31 One example is G. Clark and L. B. Sohn, *World Peace through World Law: Two Alternative Plans*, 3rd edn (Cambridge: Harvard University Press, 1966).

32 To replace Kant's metaphysical foundation for morality, I am adopting the contractual strategy of Rawls and J. Habermas which requires justifying moral claims in terms of a universal consensus among rational agents. Habermas's approach is presented in J. Habermas, 'Discourse ethics: notes on a program of philosophical justification', in S. Benhabib and F. Dallmayr (eds), *Communicative Ethics Controversy* (Cambridge: MIT Press, 1990), pp. 60–110.

33 Rawls, *Political Liberalism*, lecture 4. However, my account of the overlapping consensus differs from Rawls's in that he believes that the consensus will consist of *principles* of justice. I think that moral consensus will be about what I call 'ideals', not principles.

34 Held, *Democracy and the Global Order*, pp. 267ff.

10

Principles of Cosmopolitan Democracy

Daniele Archibugi

Cosmopolitan democracy is an ambitious project whose aim is to achieve a world order based on the rule of law and democracy. Politicians and diplomats, along with many students of political theory and international relations, tend to disregard such ideas. They are, they say, as noble as they are inconclusive. These sceptics do not deny that the desire to apply these values to international relations is valid in principle. But they do point out that there are other factors which really count in relations among states, such as the political clout of nations, the self-interest of governments, and unfathomable (often even for the proponents themselves) geopolitical interests. According to this argument, any effort which overlooks these hard facts is doomed for failure – sheer utopia, the stuff of dreamers oblivious of how world politics really works.

Yet this surfeit of realism underestimates the role projects play in defining the rules of political systems, world order included. Over the past few centuries, the global order has been informed by rules subscribed to by the leading players on the international stage. Although sometimes interpreted liberally, these rules set constraints on strategic decisions. The Peace of Westphalia (1648), the Peace of Utrecht (1712), the Congress of Vienna (1814), the Congress of Paris (1919), the Yalta Conference (1944) and the Charter of San Francisco (1945) all defined an international order. On each occasion the wielders of world power subscribed to rules which they were prepared to abide by – albeit only in part. Yet all these events were, directly or indirectly, influenced by thinkers who, often centuries in advance, had elaborated doctrines, laws or even projects and statutes which created bodies of opinion and influenced the politicians sitting at the negotiating tables.

The history of how utopian ideas influenced world politics has yet to be written. We do know, however, that the writings of Hugo Grotius and Émeric Crucé informed some of the ideas approved at Westphalia; that Saint-Pierre was physically at the gates of Utrecht; that President Wilson was acquainted with the peace projects of William Penn and William Ladd; and that Hans Kelsen prepared and circulated drafts for a new League of Nations statute long before governments agreed on the founding of the United Nations. Arguably more important was the role that these ideas played in spreading the belief that international life did not necessarily have to be a theatre for all-out war; it could also encompass institutional cooperation and generate political and social peacemaking movements.

There is general agreement that we are now experiencing the transition from one international system to another. We are well acquainted with the characteristics of the order we are leaving behind – the Cold War[1] – but the shape of the coming world order has still to be defined. The factors which will regulate the international system will depend, as in the past, on the balance of power between political actors. But this balance will also be determined by our ability to identify the objectives and strategies around which we intend to mobilize the forces at our disposal and over which different interests may clash.

Under the banner 'cosmopolitan democracy', we intend to build a political project for a different world order.[2] This chapter reasserts and outlines the main points on this agenda.

FOUR PREMISES FOR DEMOCRACY

The political project presented here is strongly linked to the concept of democracy. But what do we mean by 'democracy'? Defining the word is no easy matter, not least because of the virtually universal favour democracy enjoys today. However we look at it, theoretically and practically, democracy exists in a variety of substantially different systems.[3] In this chapter, I will apply the rather wide definition provided by David Beetham:

Democracy I take to be a mode of decision-making about collectively binding rules and policies over which the people exercise control, and the most democratic arrangement to be that where all members of the collectivity enjoy effective equal rights to take part in such decision-making directly.[4]

It is not the intention of this chapter to enter into the debate on the nature of democracy. Rather, I wish to point out that, so far, democracy has mainly been applied to the management of power within states. In order to extend democracy beyond the borders of individual political communities, four premises are required.

(1) Democracy is an unfinished journey   The journey towards democracy has not been completed in any country,[5] including those in which the principles of democracy are most consolidated and developed. In both democratic and autocratic states, there are struggles, admittedly of a very different nature, to extend or to obtain democracy.

(2) Democracy is an endless journey   Democracy is much more than just a set of norms and procedures. It ought, indeed, to be viewed as a fully fledged process of interaction between civil society and political institutions. In this sense, it may be more appropriate to speak not so much about plain democracy as about the *democratic route*,[6] that is, a progressive evolution of political systems to meet individuals' demands for participation. We can identify a number of milestones along the democratic route: among them, the majority principle, universal suffrage, minority rights, etc. Individual polities have met none or some of these milestones in different historical situations and not necessarily in the same order. As a journey, the democratic process is not only unfinished but also endless.

(3) Democracy has a meaning in its historical context   Since the democratic process is a historical one, the very notion of democracy needs to be viewed *comparatively* not *absolutely*. Ancient Athens was democratic compared to other city-states in the fourth century BC, yet it fails to meet most of the criteria commonly applied today. Its lack of suffrage for the vast majority of the population would make it a system very similar to the South Africa of apartheid. In the nineteenth century, Great Britain and the United States were exceptionally democratic nations, yet they barred the majority of their respective populations, women included, from voting. This is a crucial point for understanding the evolution of democracy at the international level: there will never be a point in history when all states will share the same procedures and values for the management of power. Even if all states embrace democracy, each will be characterized by its unique features and stage of development. The idea of a global democracy should therefore be based on the acceptance of a variety of models and stages.

(4) Democracy needs an endogenous fabric to work   The democratic route is an integral part and parcel of social dynamics and, as such, flows out of the day-to-day political struggle. Democracy is a conquest and, like all conquests, is the outcome of conflict. To be substantial and effective, the greatest part of the struggle for democracy should be based on endogenous, rather than exogenous, forces. This suggests that democ-

racy is achieved in a bottom-up manner and when the internal conditions are suitable to allow it to function. Even when democratic principles were imposed by external forces, as with Germany, Italy, Japan and other countries after the Second World War, they took hold only because the reconstruction of the social fabric within these countries ensured the acceptance of such principles.

The concept of cosmopolitan democracy outlined in this chapter heavily relies on these four premises. These premises will be applied to develop a process whereby independent but interdependent communities should search their own route to improve their political institutions.

HAS DEMOCRACY WON?

At the dawn of the twenty-first century, democracy is, of all political models, the undisputed winner. It was a moving experience in the 1980s and early 1990s to see millions of people forming orderly queues, sometimes for hours or even days, to take part in the 'holiest' rite of democracy – free elections. All over the world, from Chile and Nicaragua to Czechoslovakia, Russia and Poland as far as the Philippines, South Africa and many other countries still, citizens were at last allowed to exercise their right to choose their own rulers. Although the procedural aspects of democracy have not always (yet?) been matched to substantive outcomes,[7] it is significant that so many governments have decided to seek legitimacy in free elections.

In the academic community, the victory of democracy dates even further back – and has been even more overwhelming; these days, in fact, only a handful of dyed-in-the-wool conservatives are still prepared to come out explicitly against democracy. But what is the true essence of the model's victory? More important still, how much of it is rhetoric and how much is substance? It is possible to view democracy's triumphal march according to two parallel parameters:

- Geographical extension, or 'widening': how many countries are governed according to what we can refer to as democratic principles?
- Qualitative development, or 'deepening': what level of participation has been achieved in political communities inspired by democratic principles.

Although the geographical extension and qualitative development of a political system in the long run generally proceed in the same direction, in the short and medium terms they may diverge. Between the two world wars, for example, many European countries broadened the suffrage, extending it to the poor and to women, and introduced given economic and social rights for the first time. In other countries still – Italy, Germany and Spain, for example – liberal political regimes were overthrown by fascist ones. Europe thus experienced qualitative development on the one hand, and a slowdown in geographical extension on the other.

The number of democratic countries has notably increased over the last two centuries. While at the end of the eighteenth century, democratic principles were applied only in Swiss cantons, France and the United States, today there are as many as 107 democratic countries around the world.[8] They include several countries which have become democratic only recently. This new wave[9] encompasses both states which have *returned* to democracy after some form of interruption (especially in Europe), and states which are embracing a democratic system for the first time.

So much for the geographical extension of democracy, but what of quality? It does not seem that the new wave has yet fostered qualitative improvements in countries that were democratic in the first place. Economic rights have been eroded, while those of ethnic minorities remain undefined. In addition, achievements during the 1960s and 1970s such as the welfare state have been savagely undermined by the governments concerned. In many countries, the state's ability to hold together the various components of civil society is being tested. In some democratic states, such as Canada, Spain, Italy, Australia and Belgium, sharp conflicts have emerged among different ethnic groups, jeopardizing the very idea of national unity. In other states, such as the former Soviet Union, Yugoslavia and Czechoslovakia, the process of transition towards democracy has brought with it divisions between ethnic groups and the re-emergence of bloody civil wars.

The wave of democratization has in no way heralded the 'end of history' hoped for by the most optimistic observers (or perhaps those least conscious of the cyclical nature of history). The idea that the collapse of a wall – even if it happened to be the Berlin Wall – could bring history to an end was based on the basic misconception of democracy as a set of rules and procedures to which all states adhere rather than as a route, and as a static as opposed to an essentially dynamic phenomenon. It is not surprising, therefore, that while the end of the Cold War has cleared the path towards democracy, it has also caused new problems for which politicians and scholars were entirely unprepared.

We hear again predictions on the future of democracy, and they are by no means unanimous. Some observers maintain that all states will ultimately embrace this political credo, and go as far as to say that in the space of about a century virtually all countries will become democratic.[10] Others counter that the conditions which allowed the emergence of democracy do not exist in many parts of the world, and that it is thus unlikely to extend any further.[11] Democracy, it has been argued, is a Western-specific cultural value and there is little point in attempting to extend it outside its native cradle.

The conception of democracy outlined in the previous section suggests different answers. The struggle for democracy which has mobilized so many Western and non-Western populations does indicate that democracy has become a universal aspiration. It is striking that many Western scholars and politicians who strongly support their own democratic systems would deny other populations the right to be ruled according to the same principles.[12] Democracy has not become a universal principle of political conduct through the textbooks of a few scholars, but rather because an increasing number of populations aspire to it.

Moreover, the claim that democracy can be applied only within Western societies ignores the fundamental problems that these very countries are experiencing in defending and extending this system.[13] One of the problems is that it is increasingly difficult to be internally democratic in an increasingly interdependent world. What then are the hurdles to the democratic process raised by international factors? The next section attempts to answer this question.

DOMESTIC DEMOCRACY AND THE INTERNATIONAL SYSTEM

The international system influences domestic political life in many ways. In developing the arguments of cosmopolitan democracy, it is important to stress two types of influence: (1) those stemming from international conflict, and (2) those stemming from processes of economic, social and cultural globalization.

International conflict

Sharp international conflict hinders the attainment and development of democracy within states. Historically, the most significant example of the phenomenon is also the most recent: the Cold War, creating an incessant external danger that strongly limited political freedom within states. Democratic states felt almost besieged. In a world in which the majority of states were autocratic, many deemed it impossible to apply all the norms of domestic democracy. This lack of democracy was evident mainly in those policies most directly linked to the international framework: foreign and defence policies. These were often removed from the control of public opinion and dominated by oligarchic power groups which *de facto* deprived citizens of external sovereignty.

In addition, external threats were used to prevent any opposition to the established authorities, the assumption being that internal criticism would weaken the country's position. This was true – albeit at different levels of intensity – in both democratic and autocratic countries. Mary Kaldor has shown that the reasons underpinning the rivalry between the

United States and the Soviet Union were largely internal.[14] Although taking different shapes, external threats were used in both blocs for political ends: in the East to thwart the advent of democracy, in the West to prevent its development.

The conflict between the two blocs further limited the number of sovereign states. Only a handful of them, those equipped with nuclear arms, were *de facto* sovereign. The others were forced to accept interference in their domestic affairs and limitations on their own sovereignty. Interference took various forms, ranging from full-scale military invasion (the Soviet invasions of Hungary and Czechoslovakia, for example), to hostile interventions leading to the overthrow of regimes (CIA activities to topple the Allende government in Chile), to intrusions to prevent hostile parties from having access to government (the US *de facto* veto on the entry of Communist parties into the governments of various European countries). The dominant powers installed puppet regimes whose only merit was that they were loyal. In Indo-China, the Middle East and Africa the rivalry between the two blocs often overflowed into armed conflicts fought by third parties. The lack of external sovereignty thus ultimately compromises internal sovereignty.

The Cold War set precise limits on the endogenous development of democracy, making it possible only when compatible with global scenarios. Although the Cold War was a specific international regime and now belongs to the past, it laid bare a problem of much wider proportions: namely that domestic democracy cannot fully mature in a world marked by conflict. The project of cosmopolitan democracy should therefore be based on the control of international violence.

Globalization

The sovereignty of states has not been limited exclusively by a fiercely competitive international regime. It has also been eroded by the spontaneous but even more tenacious process of economic, political, social and cultural globalization. New information and communication technologies have made the various national communities increasingly interdependent. Structural changes have also implied substantial changes in the process of political decision-making: few decisions made in one state are autonomous from those made in others. A decision on the interest rate in Germany has significant consequences for employment in Greece, Portugal and Italy. A state's decision to use nuclear energy has environmental consequences for the citizens of neighbouring countries. Immigration policies in the European Union have a significant impact on the economic development of Mediterranean Africa. All this happens without the affected citizens having a say in the matter.[15]

It is difficult today to conceive of a political decision being taken in one state without its having consequences for others. Likewise, every aspect of a state's economic, social and political life is affected by political decisions taken in others. The idea that the citizens of a given community may autonomously determine their own destiny is thus an illusory one in a world increasingly characterized by interdependence.

The two points raised above lead to the following conclusion: either we accept that democratic systems are largely incomplete due to the lack of a congenial world order[16] or we attempt to extend democracy to international life as well. This means, on the one hand, ensuring a peaceful, non-violent international system and, on the other, developing methods of civilized coexistence to allow communities to democratically address problems that also involve others. The next section asks whether this option is desirable, and whether it is feasible.

IS A DEMOCRACY AMONG STATES POSSIBLE?

Although democracy is universally acknowledged today as the best system possible for the governance of states,[17] not everyone is prepared to address the question of global democracy. Some believe that such a scheme is impossible, others that it is undesirable, while still others feel it is a problem of the domestic life of states.

The critique of realist theoreticians

The realists posit that the main driving force of international politics is national interest. It is highly unlikely that a government will give priority to global rather than national interests. Greater coordination among states is possible only when there are explicit advantages, and when no one state can benefit from a situation of conflict. Whenever these conditions have existed, they have given rise to specific international regimes. Otherwise, it is impossible to achieve the climate of cooperation among states which is a *sine qua non* for a world order founded on the values of democracy. To overload the international system with expectations it is incapable of meeting is, the realists argue, counterproductive. Moreover, it would be wrong to assume that the internal political regime of a state has any influence on its foreign policy: 'A realist theory of international politics' stated Hans Morgenthau, the most articulate of its advocates, 'will also avoid the popular fallacy of equating the foreign policies of a statesman with his philosophic or political sympathies, and of deducing the former from the latter.'[18]

To maintain a world order it is also necessary to reduce the number of political actors. If the parties to the main strategic choices increase in number – as the democratization project implies – the resulting complexity would risk becoming ungovernable. The consequence might be world disorder, not order, and the number of conflicts may increase rather than decrease. Some realists have related the upheavals of the 1990s to the end of the superpower-dominated world order. For them the Cold War system was imperfect, but it did keep in check forces that were later to prove ungovernable.

Realists are right to stress the importance of national interests in determining political choices, especially international choices. But they also tend to underestimate the development of interests with global scope. The fact is that commerce, tourism, cultural and social exchanges and many other activities mobilize massive interests which rely on an international arena based on cooperation. It is therefore likely that these interests will lead to greater coordination in world politics; this already happened a few centuries ago when the enlargement of economic and social areas led to the making of nation-states. The growth in the number and role of international governmental and non-governmental organizations and other 'control mechanisms' is proof that such interests have already achieved significant results.[19]

There is, of course, no guarantee that greater coordination in world politics will be informed by the values of democracy. Democracy continues to be a contestable principle. The question which should therefore be posed to realist theoreticians is the following: should 'control mechanisms' in world politics be informed by the principles of democracy?

The objections of communitarians

Some argue that the very concept of democracy can only be applied within communities which are relatively homogeneous from a cultural point of view. Danilo Zolo, for example, warns that democracy cannot be exported.[20] Democracy requires the formation of a majority which must govern in the interest of the whole population. In excessively heterogeneous communities, it would be impossible to form a majority homogeneous enough to allow the formation of a government. And such a government would have to struggle to represent the very different minorities. Multi-ethnic states have proved too vast to be governed democratically without minorities perceiving the rules of the majority as unacceptable. Such difficulties confirm the problems involved in the working of democracy on too large a scale.

It may be possible to force the populations into a cultural and social relationship which would allow the formation of a socially and culturally homogeneous world community. According to communitarians, though, any gains in terms of democracy would be losses in terms of diversity, one of humanity's most precious assets and most worth preserving. Far from denying that the international system hinders the full development of democracy inside states (sometimes considerably), communitarians believe that we must be prepared to accept the fact and do what we can to allow states to override the ensuing constraints. Their standpoint is that international democracy is not desirable.

Communitarian theoreticians seem to underestimate the negative implications which the absence of international democracy implies for democracy inside single communities. Nonetheless, as we shall see below, the cosmopolitan democracy project sets great store by the communitarian suggestion that it is necessary to imagine a world order flexible enough to both meet the needs of different peoples and protect the political, social and cultural rights of minorities.[21]

Communitarians are right to point out, after Rousseau, that democracy works better on a small scale. But exactly what this scale should be is impossible to determine in advance. While Plato and Rousseau believed that it could not be greater than a city-state, today it has become possible in vast, diverse regions such as the United States. The European Union is inventing new constitutional forms. To date, the evolution of democracy has depended, at least in part, on the scale of the communities it has had to administer. Hence the progression from direct democracy (applicable on a small scale) to representative democracy. The open question is: which form of democracy should be applied on a global scale?

Reducing international democracy to a domestic problem

There is, finally, a third school of thought which, unlike the first two, believes that international democracy is both possible and desirable. But it adds the proviso that the attainment of such a democracy is not so much a problem of the international system as of single states. If all states were to become democratic, the international system would necessarily tend towards greater democracy. Bobbio formulates this hypothesis in the questions 'Is an international democratic system possible among solely autocratic states?' and, alternatively, 'Is an international autocratic system possible among solely democratic states?', concluding that 'the negative answer is automatic in both cases.'[22]

Working to achieve international democracy thus means, first of all, transforming autocratic states into democratic ones. If the entire international community were made up of democratic states, the world order would be informed by democratic values. Attaining international democracy is, therefore, not impossible but possibly pointless in so far as it would be the natural outcome of internal democracy.[23]

It is, in my view, simplistic to believe that the democratization of international relations would evolve exclusively as a result of states' domestic regimes. It is, first and foremost, difficult to establish a causal nexus between domestic regimes and the international system. Bobbio states that 'the vicious circle may be formulated as follows: states can become democratic only in a fully democratized international society, but a fully democratized international society presupposes that all states that compose it are democratic.'[24] If the existence of authoritarian regimes is a stumbling-block for the fully democratic regulation of international relations, it follows that a sharply hierarchical international system – like the one which prevailed throughout the Cold War – is, in turn, an obstacle to the development of democracy within nations.

We have seen how this international system has prevented democracy not only in areas dominated by authoritarian countries (the countries of Soviet Union-controlled Eastern Europe), but also in those dominated by democratic countries (Latin America, South Africa and states of southern Asia under the wing of the United States). We have also seen foreign policies which are 'incoherent'[25] with the conduct which inspires political systems inside countries. Authoritarian countries have often used cynical and brutal methods in foreign policy too: we might almost say that it is what we have come to expect. The Soviet Union, for example, used violence to defend its control over its satellite states – as the invasions of Hungary, Czechoslovakia and Afghanistan demonstrate. On other occasions, it acted 'incoherently' in supporting the process of decolonization or opposing the apartheid system in South Africa with greater firmness than many democratic countries.

The same 'incoherences' can be seen in democratic countries. In certain cases, they have effectively promoted the export of their own political system; after the Second World War the United States played a fundamental role in restoring democracy in Europe and introducing it for the first time in Japan. On other occasions, it was responsible for brutal displays of force contrary to international law, as with the invasions of Vietnam, Grenada and Panama. Elsewhere, democratic countries have perpetrated hostile actions – albeit not necessarily direct military intervention – against democratic countries, as in the case of US actions against Chile and Nicaragua.[26]

These facts confirm that there need be no correspondence between the nature of a country's domestic system and the actions it adopts in its foreign policy. As the realist school of international relations suggests, a nation's domestic political system is not wholly binding on its foreign policy.

In all likelihood, some of the unlawful actions of foreign policy carried out by democratic states may have depended on the fact that such states found themselves pitted against autocratic states. This takes us to a third question posed by Bobbio: 'Is it possible to be fully democratic in a non-democratic world?'[27] However much a conflictual international system has distorted the conduct of democratic states, it cannot be seen as the only reason for that conduct. It would be disingenuous to deny that whenever interests and principles have clashed, democracies have often opted for the first and forgotten the second.

THE AIMS OF COSMOPOLITAN DEMOCRACY

The relationship between democracy and international relations is not linear but ambivalent. Internal democracy helps but does not determine the rise of a democratic world order, just as a democratic international system would not necessarily generate democracy in all states. This suggests that to develop democracy further, it is necessary to operate on different complementary and self-sustaining levels. Cosmopolitan democracy is a project to build a world order capable of promoting democracy on three different but mutually supporting levels: (1) democracy inside nations; (2) democracy among states; (3) global democracy.[28]

In the cosmopolitan project, the notion of democracy may be applied differently in each of the three levels. Democratic procedures and norms need to be tailored according to the issues concerned: for example, what are the appropriate constituencies to settle problems involving two local communities of separate states but located on opposite sides of the same river, for problems involving regional settlements, or for problems of global concern? Quite clearly, the forum will be different in each of these cases.

Democracy inside nations

It is good news that democracy is emerging as a universal aspiration. An increasing amount of evidence shows that formal democracy is correlated to several substantive measures of welfare, ranging from environmental protection to economic development.[29] Although the causality is still uncertain, this evidence indicates that peoples' claim to be ruled according to democratic principles is based on sound expectations.

The cosmopolitan project, however, should not prescribe identical procedures in each national community. This is an issue which should be addressed by national communities and not by the international system; the norms, procedures and structure of democracy will be very different in Western, Asian or African societies. The concept of democracy outlined above suggests that this must be a basically endogenous, as opposed to exogenous, phenomenon. Robespierre warned against the mania of making peoples happy against their will. Paraphrasing him, it is necessary to adopt the same caution in making peoples democratic against their wishes. Empirical studies[30] show that three-quarters of democratic countries have become so due to internal rather than external forces. This confirms that we cannot do without endogenous development.

This does not mean that the world order has no influence on the development of national democracies. The main contribution that the world order can provide in support of internal democracy is to remove obstacles by providing peaceful international relations (see the discussion on pp. 203–4 above). For the development of democracy inside nations would be greatly helped by a favourable external environment. In many cases, obstacles to democratization come from internal forces, as in the case of authoritarian regimes which stay in power by repressing their citizens. This also happens to be one of the most problematic situations to address, since action may entail undue interference in a state's affairs, and inaction may entail connivance with its tyrannous government. A consensus is now emerging on the right to democracy and to elected government.[31] The shaping of an international legal framework is certainly a major support to the internal forces pressing to achieve democratization. But which methods should the international community use to 'interfere' in favour of democratization?

The traditional solution, namely military intervention promoted and managed by other governments, is unsatisfactory since in the majority of cases they pursue their own interests rather than the restoration of democracy. One of the aims of cosmopolitan democracy is therefore to identify alternative means of interference to the traditional ones. These include, on the one hand, the creation of new legitimate non-governmental authorities charged with pushing for democracy; and, on the other hand, the identification of new methods which minimize the use of violence.

In recent years, new forms of intervention have been tried. They include assistance from international organizations to organize, monitor and certify elections; enhanced diplomatic actions; economic and other sanctions; conditionality on economic aid; conditionality for participation in regional organizations such as the European Union, etc. The pressure of the international community on national governments has been helpful and many governments declare themselves democratic even if some basic principles of democracy, such as minority rights or freedom of expression, are not actually enforced.[32] This leads to the urgency that democratic procedures should somehow be assessed by external agents, as has already happened with electoral assistance. The role played by non-governmental organizations could be further expanded.

Democracy among states

Democracy among states must be seen as respect for reciprocal sovereignty and as a set of norms commonly shared and subscribed to by states. The juridical and largely formal norm of sovereignty should therefore be defended and enforced in cases of one state's interference in the domestic affairs of others. Sovereignty should however be matched to norms which states – unilaterally, bilaterally or multilaterally – are prepared to respect. The basic representative criterion in the interstate system should be based on the criterion of 'one state, one vote'.[33]

Democracy among states also implies strengthening ties between states by developing intergovernmental institutions to deal with specific regional and global problems. This may allow the creation of subject-specific institutions where the states more directly involved in selected issues have a greater weight. A large number of UN specialized agencies have already applied similar criteria. Similarly, interstate democracy is an area where the 'functional approach' to international organizations is more pertinent.[34] The more competences and functions are absorbed by problem-driven intergovernmental organizations, the less significance is left to the juridical state's external and/or internal sovereignty.

We speak of democracy among states, but states have often been defined arbitrarily. Examples abound of stateless peoples and of multi-ethnic states. In the event of a strong claim for the formation of a new state, it is necessary to find methods to achieve this without recourse to violence.

Global democracy

There are some problems, such as the environment question and, more generally, all problems concerning security and world survival, which transcend the authority of national governments. These problems can be named 'global' since they cannot be addressed effectively by intergovernmental bodies. Different forms of representation are made necessary by the fact that many of the governments concerned are authoritarian governments whose positions are often different from those of their populations.

Even in democratic countries, national public opinion is not generally consulted on such specific issues and notable differences might emerge between the positions of governments and those of civil society. For example, the French public probably took a different view from that of its government over nuclear experiments in the Pacific. In other cases, the choices of a people, even when made democratically, might be biased by self-interest. It may, for example, be in the interest of the French public to obtain cheap nuclear energy if they manage to dispose of radioactive waste in a Pacific isle under their control, but this will obviously be against the interests of the public living there.

If some global questions are to be handled according to democratic criteria, there must be political representation for citizens in global affairs, independently and autonomously of their political representation in domestic affairs. The unit should be the individual, although the mechanisms for participation and representation may vary according to the nature and scope of the issues discussed.

The discussion of the aims of cosmopolitan democracy shows that they can be served only by institutional arrangements which would link across and within the existing states. But which union of states can best serve the objectives stated? To answer that question, I will use as reference points the two principal models of existing state systems: confederations and federations,[35] describing them as ideal models which do not necessarily stem from specific historical experiences. My aim is to show the ways in which the cosmopolitan democracy model differs from both.

THE CONFEDERAL MODEL

A confederation is an association of sovereign states which, through an appropriate treaty, reach an agreement on given issues. Some confederations have arisen as coalitions pitted against states or unions of rival states; as such, their function has been essentially military. NATO and the Warsaw Pact belong to this category. Other confederations are virtually open to all the states in the world. They include organizations with very restricted aims, such as the Universal Postal Union and the World Intellectual Property Organization. But the confederations which are of most interest here are ones of universal scope whose main objective is to prevent war and guarantee peace. The prime example is one of the most ambitious, sophisticated confederations ever created – the UNO. The following is an analysis of the confederal model's capacity to fit the three levels of democracy presented in the last section.

Democracy inside nations

The confederal model may help indirectly to foster democratization to the extent that it overrides some of the hurdles which a conflict-ridden international system puts in the way of domestic political participation. It does not, however, envisage a channel of direct intervention to promote democracy within nations. The principle of non-interference prohibits the intervention of the confederation and its members in domestic affairs. Not even in blatant cases of violation of fundamental human rights – genocide, for example – is the confederation entitled to intervene in a state's domestic affairs. On the contrary, the very existence of mutual institutional acknowledgement between the governments of states might render external interventions for humanitarian reasons even more difficult. The problem of domestic democracy thus remains totally removed from the international system.

Democracy among states

In the confederal model, sovereignty should guarantee that all states have autonomy and equal rights. Democracy is, nonetheless, limited by the fact that democratic and authoritarian governments enjoy the same rights. It is possible to imagine a world order in which decisions are taken democratically by the various governments, even though all the governments are authoritarian. For that matter, the joint forces of rulers might even be used to repress the claims of subjects in a given state. The Congress of Vienna came very close to this model.[36] It is not surprising, therefore, that from Rousseau onwards democratic thought has been extremely suspicious of peace projects such as that of the Abbé de Saint-Pierre, which purported to set up a league of princes without questioning the domestic exertion of sovereignty.[37] Paradoxical as it may seem, democracy *among states* might end up being used as a tool for tyranny *within* nations.

Global democracy

Since the confederal model envisages no form of participation by individuals in international politics, any global decision choice is delegated to relations among states, represented by their governments. Global democracy is thus very limited and clearly defined.

It is important to stress that global democracy would be humbled in the confederal model, even if all of its members were to be democratic governments. The governments of states do not necessarily represent global interests. On the contrary, they tend to privilege the particular interests of their own political quarter. Inside the European Union, for example, the Council of Ministers, made up of the representatives of each of the national governments, is much less prepared to advocate 'European' solutions than a directly elected body such as the European Parliament.

The reason why the confederal model does not fit with global democracy resides in the fact that the civil societies in each of the states are separate from one another. They have no institutional channels to communicate through and have limited scope in so far as they are represented by national political parties on non-national questions.

THE FEDERALIST MODEL

The federalist model has a much more rigid constitutional structure than the confederal model. Its aim is to implement principles and norms valid for all members of the federal union. The model has been applied in a large number of contemporary states, including Switzerland, the United States and Germany. These three states emerged as confederations, and have progressively centralized their powers to become constitution-based federal states. Other early confederations, such as the Netherlands, have developed into unitary states.

A distinguished intellectual and political tradition maintains that the problem of world peace and democracy can only be solved by setting firm limitations on the sovereignty of states, and by giving life to a process of centralizing power which would ultimately lead to a world federal state. This tradition maintains that the subdivision of the world into national states is a surmountable historical heritage. Not only may the fundamental values of democracy be shared by all human beings, but the institutions which protect them may also share some common basic principles and be under the same authority. Let us now see if this organizational model is capable of meeting the three levels of democracy highlighted above.

Democracy inside nations

If the federal state is founded on principles of democracy, it is paramount for these principles to be extended to its component members. In the event of essential conflicts, the federal government has the authority and coercive means to impose respect of democratic principles in component states. There are well-known examples in which different bodies of the federation have expressed different opinions on specific norms, and this has often given rise to conflict. In some cases, conflict has in turn triggered civil war. The most obvious example was the American War of Secession which ended with the restoration of the union and the application in all states of a constitutional norm – the abolition of slavery – imposed by the federal government.

The concept of democracy I put forward here is one of internal conquest. It casts doubt on the idea that there is one model which is simultaneously applicable to all the regions of the world. The federal system presupposes the existence of a unity of norms among the various parties which is hard to reconcile with the world's cultural and anthropological differences. If we pay heed to communitarian arguments, this uniformity, albeit democratic, is undesirable among the world's communities.

Democracy among states

In a narrow sense, democracy among states is abolished in a federal state in so far as sovereign states are abolished. Relations between central and local power are – as the history of existing federal states teaches – regulated as conflicts of competences. The process of centralization which gave life to existing federal states shows, nonetheless, that the process which allowed different communities to accept a common sovereignty was the result of external conflict. The Swiss Confederation, the Dutch provinces and the United States were constituted in defence against attacks from other states. One wonders, therefore, whether the same experiment may be possible on a global scale where no external threats exist.

There is always the possibility that one party will gain control over the others through coercion, or, more precisely, that a sort of federal empire will arise. But if a means such as war is used to install this model, there is no reason to believe that, once it is operational, it will be inspired by the norms of democracy.

Global democracy

A central federal power would have the authority and competence to address global problems on the basis of democratic principles. It is, however, likely that some local problems would be dealt with to the detriment of the rights of component communities. A global government, no matter how democratic, would be the expression of a heterogeneous majority, while the minorities not participating in government would be even more heterogeneous. A government of this kind would be constantly tempted to look for technocratic solutions to global problems. It would, in short, resemble the government of guardians dear to Plato more than a genuinely democratic one.

THE COSMOPOLITAN DEMOCRACY MODEL

Is it possible to design a union of states midway between the confederal and the federalist models? Whereas the latter has acquired significant historical experience, cosmopolitan democracy has not. The few examples which have approached this third model have been the fruit of transitory experiences: confederations which during their transformation into federal states fleetingly assumed the essential characteristics of cosmopolitan democracy. Today this intermediate state can be seen in the European Union, already more than a simple confederation but not yet a federal system. At present it is uncertain whether the European Union will assume the shape of a federation, or whether, instead, it will preserve its distinctive characteristics.

Partisans of the cosmopolitan model believe that it is undesirable to go beyond a given threshold of centralization on a scale as vast as a global one. Applied on a global scale, the cosmopolitan democracy model is not intended as a transitional step towards a federal system, but rather as a more permanent organization. On the other hand, the existing system of 'global governance' is not suitable for cosmopolitan democracy as it lacks sufficient legal competence, and its decision-making is not necessarily guided by the principles of democracy.[38]

The adjective 'cosmopolitan' is used in its eighteenth-century sense as a notion of citizenship both of the state and of the European *res publica*.[39] For Mary Kaldor,

the term cosmopolitan, when applied to political institutions, implies a layer of governance that constitutes a limitation on the sovereignty of states and yet does not itself constitute a state. In other words, a cosmopolitan institution would coexist with a system of states but would override states in certain clearly defined spheres of activity.[40]

I have preferred to refer to a 'cosmopolitan' democracy rather than an 'international' or 'supranational' one because the former may be confused with an exclusively intergovernmental organization and the latter may conjure up a hierarchical relationship between central institutions and individual states. The term 'transnational' comes closer to the project described here, although it does not necessarily refer to a concept of politics founded on citizenship. The term 'cosmopolitan', instead, manages to capture the dual reference to citizens of the world and of existing states.

Cosmopolitan democracy is therefore a project which aims to develop democracy within nations, among states and at the global level, assuming that the three levels, although highly interdependent, should and can be pursued simultaneously. It stresses that different democratic procedures are needed for each of these levels. Such a project proposes to integrate and limit the functions of existing states with new institutions based on world citizenship. These institutions should be entitled to manage issues of global concern as well as to interfere within states whenever serious violations of human rights are committed.

World citizenship does not necessarily have to assume all the demands of national citizenship. The real problem is to identify the areas in which citizens should have rights and duties as inhabitants of the world rather than of secular states. In some cases spheres of competence may overlap, in others they would be complementary.

The cosmopolitan system envisages not only the existence of universal human rights protected by states, but also the creation of a mandatory core of rights which individuals may claim, as well as duties *vis-à-vis* global institutions. Rights ought to relate, in the first instance, to the sphere of survival and to issues which cross national boundaries. In relation to these rights, world citizens undersign certain duties which enable global institutions to perform a function of temporary replacement, subsidiarity and substitution *vis-à-vis* national institutions.

In the cosmopolitan model, the idea of sovereignty typical of the confederal and federal models is also profoundly changed. States, in fact, preserve their internal sovereignty *vis-à-vis* other states, but their sovereignty is eroded – including legally – by the transfer of functions to intergovernmental and non-governmental bodies. External sovereignty may also be eroded or, paraphrasing the young Kelsen, may become less 'dogmatic'.[41]

That internal and external sovereignty should be limited is an opinion shared by functionalism and by legal pacifism alike.[42] It is significant, however, that the two approaches diverge drastically when it comes to strategy. Functionalism champions a *de facto* erosion of sovereignty as a result of spontaneous processes, or at all events, without a general political design. On the other hand, legal pacifism aims basically for a *de jure* transfer of competences from government to supragovernmental authorities and to set up a unitary normative reference framework.

The two approaches have the same objective – the reduction of government authority – and they are thus highly complementary. In the cosmopolitan democracy project, however, the demands of both functionalism and legal pacifism are qualified. With respect to functionalism, the cosmopolitan model intends to accompany the spontaneous erosion of sovereignty with new forms of democratically legitimated political authority. With respect to legal pacifism, the cosmopolitan model does not necessarily intend to establish a single normative construction or a precise hierarchy of legal sources in which those at the national level are subordinated to those at the international level.[43]

The essential characteristics of the cosmopolitan model and its differences from the models presented earlier are discussed below. While the account of the confederal and federal models is mainly descriptive, that for the cosmopolitan model is prescriptive.

Democracy inside nations

Unlike the federal model, the cosmopolitan democracy model encompasses states with different political constitutions. This does not entail unquestioning acceptance of the dogma of non-interference, as is the case with the confederal model. On the contrary, the cosmopolitan model deliberately sets out to transmit and disseminate methods and tools of government to various political communities, and hence to gradually make all the member countries of the international community democratic. Nonetheless, the conception of democracy which underpins the cosmopolitan model suggests that differences between political systems will continue to exist in one form or another. Hence the need for international organizations which will allow this coexistence.

Since one state's intervention in the domestic affairs of another has no legal foundation and may be instrumental, the cosmopolitan model entrusts civil society as opposed to national governments with the task of 'interfering' in the domestic affairs of another state. The objective aim of this interference is to increase political participation in all states. The concept of democracy summarized in the four premises (pp. 199–201 above) suggests that all nations, albeit at very different stages in the democratic process, have something to gain by a critical analysis of their own political systems in relation to the experiences of others.

Democracy among states

Relations between states are managed by intergovernmental organizations. Multilateralism is the tool used to ensure non-interference and to prevent individual states from perpetrating acts which have harmful consequences for other members of the international community.

If the arbitration of intergovernmental institutions is not effective, disputes between states are passed on to international judicial institutions whose jurisdiction the states are compelled to accept. If a member of the international community refuses to obey the ruling of the judicial authority, the international community may adopt coercive measures, including economic, political and cultural sanctions. Military force is only the *extrema ratio* if all other political and diplomatic tools prove ineffective. The use of military force is controlled directly by the institutions of the union and must be *preventively* authorized in advance by the institutions of world citizens. States which participate in an armed conflict are dutybound to minimize the number of casualties on either side. The international community must also appeal to the citizens of the state which has violated international law to overthrow their government and replace it with one which abides by international law.

Global democracy

The management of essentially global issues such as the environment and the survival of humanity, including the rights of future generations, is delegated not only to intergovernmental institutions but also to transnational ones. Global civil society participates in political decision-making through new permanent institutions. These institutions may have both specific competences (such as the environment, population issues, development, disarmament, etc.) and broader political mandates (such as the defence of fundamental rights, the protection of future generations, etc.). Some of these issues may be addressed on a regional basis through specially created organizations. Others are entrusted to established global institutions. These institutions would supplement but not replace existing intergovernmental organizations. Their function would be essentially advisory and not executive.

The institutions of global civil society would exercise direct control in one essential area: the prevention and impediment of acts of genocide or democide. To do so they would be entitled to demand the immediate intervention of the governments of all states. An international criminal court would also be set up to try individuals responsible for acts of genocide and democide, crimes against fundamental human rights, aggression against other states, and war crimes. The fact that jurisdiction is individual means that the responsibilities of a people may be separated from those of its rulers, and it is therefore possible to punish the wrongdoers.

THE VEHICLES OF COSMOPOLITAN DEMOCRACY

This description of the cosmopolitan democracy model may appear somewhat puzzling. Even those convinced of the theoretical validity of the model put forward here will wonder how it is possible to achieve such a world order and how this conceptual model is related to the existing world order. Has such a model any direct implication for the real world? Has it something to say about everyday political behaviour? This section will stress some of the policy implications of the cosmopolitan democracy model which might be seen as normative prescriptions for international organizations, individual states and the nascent global civil society.

The European Union

The first international organization which begins to resemble the cosmopolitan model is the European Union. Its members are in fact sovereign states which have voluntarily transferred increasingly broad tasks (from coal and steel policy to human rights) to the Union. Furthermore Europe has displayed a notable centripetal force. Only six states originally signed the Treaty of Rome, but the number of EU members has now increased to fifteen (plus East Germany). The centripetal force of the European Union is even greater than that of the United States, which has extended geographically without absorbing culturally heterogeneous communities.

From the constitutional point of view, it is extremely significant that intergovernmental institutions such as the Council of Ministers are now backed by technical institutions such as the Commission, and even by a body directly elected by citizens, such as the European Parliament. The principle of subsidiarity has allowed European institutions to intervene in selected policy areas of member countries. Seen from a global perspective, the European Union is an experiment of great importance.[44] We can only hope that it will be imitated by other regional organizations, be it the Union of African Unity or the Organization of American States. At the same time, the European Union offers interesting cues for a possible reform of the United Nations and the setting up of new institutions.

It is certainly significant that an international example of cosmopolitan democracy such as the EU is undergoing a process of centralization which may, in the future, make it resemble more closely the federalist model. Today there is much discussion on the appropriateness of centralizing within European bodies the competences typical of sovereign states, such as monetary and defence policies. It is not my intention to discuss the prospects of the European Union,[45] but I would like to stress that, notwithstanding its prodigious capacity to integrate and expand geographically, it remains a substantially regional experience. And in so far as it has been joined by exclusively democratic governments, it is an organization of countries with homogeneous constitutions.

The United Nations

Unlike the European Union, the UNO has set no conditions on membership. It has accepted governments on the basis of their effective territorial control as opposed to their legitimacy. The UNO is thus the first intergovernmental organization which involves all the states of the world but which, until recently, was made up chiefly of non-democratic states. Although the UNO came into being as a confederation, from the beginning it has cultivated much broader ambitions. The approval of the Universal Declaration of Human Rights ratified the principle that, even domestically, all member states should undertake to respect given norms. This principle was of course a formality and never put into practice, nor was the UNO to enforce it. However, the Universal Declaration itself was a seed that was bound to grow.

Would it be possible today to reform the United Nations and make it the backbone of the cosmopolitan model? Some observers argue that the UNO as such cannot serve these purposes; that it is impossible to reform, given the prevailing interests of states and the excessive power of the permanent members of the Security Council.[46] I take the opposite view. I believe it is unrealistic to look for more finely tuned vehicles to achieve a democratic world order, and that we must mobilize forces to reform the UNO democratically.

The cosmopolitan democracy model has many points in common with the proposals to reform the organization.[47] The main reform proposals are summed up in table 10.1.[48]

Table 10.1 Reform of the United Nations

Institution	Present structure	Reform proposal
General Assembly	Five delegates appointed by governments.	Delegates must represent both government and opposition. Direct election of one or two delegates.
Security Council	Five permanent members with power of veto and ten members elected by the General Assembly.	Limitation and, in the future, abolition of the power of veto. Opening to regional organizations such as the European Union. Consultative vote to representatives of civil society.
International Court of Justice	Optional acceptance of jurisdiction by states.	Compulsory jurisdiction as consequence of UNO membership.
Peacekeeping	On the mandate of the Security Council, the Secretary-General asks states to supply soldiers.	Military and civilian peace forces set up and trained by states in collaboration with INGOs but at the disposal of the Security Council.
Civil society	Thematic forums (on environment, population, development, etc.) in which governmental and non-governmental organizations take part.	Elective parliamentary assembly with consultative powers.
Criminal jurisdiction	Special courts for situations of outstanding gravity (former Yugoslavia, Rwanda).	International criminal court with compulsory jurisdiction over crimes of genocide, aggression and violation of human rights.

The role of states

It is above all individual states which can begin to make cosmopolitan democracy materialize by adopting its principles in their domestic and foreign policies. States may unilaterally implement many of the norms suggested by this model without necessarily having to wait for a general consensus. There are a number of actions which are already taken by states in order to reinforce the principles of democracy at the three levels mentioned above. Extending internal democracy, for example, also implies granting to foreigners certain political rights, including the right to vote, as many states or even local governments already do. Governments willing to reinforce interstate democracy may take unilateral decisions, including accepting unilaterally the jurisdiction of the World Court, banning the production of and trade in weapons, and promoting and participating in intergovernmental organizations. Governments can also provide a substantial contribution to democracy by providing resources, such as economic aid or peacekeeping forces, in areas of global concern.

The list of these prescriptions is much longer and is not unique to the project presented here. Andrew Linklater, for example, has already addressed the question of which states should be considered good citizens of the international society.[49] There are many specific actions which governments already take or could take to extend democracy within nations, among states and at the global level. Any state could be a micro-example of cosmopolitan democracy.[50]

Civil society

This chapter has placed great emphasis on the involvement of citizens as agents of global change. This is based on the development of a nascent global civil society which is transforming the political landscape.[51] Citizens and their organizations can play a fundamental role at the three levels of democracy described here. Besides the perennial struggle to extend democracy in their own polity, civil societies can induce their governments to adopt policies conducive to peaceful and lawful interstate relations. They can also play a direct role in the management of global issues. Experiences of these types abound. This does not mean that there is a massive movement to extend democracy beyond the state level. On the contrary, it should be recognized that such a movement is small in the light of such ambitious goals. Still, there is sufficient evidence that citizens can play an important role in the process of democratizing the global society, as they have already done in the struggle to achieve democracy in their own communities.

CONCLUSIONS

'Would you tell me, please, which way I ought to go from here?' Alice asked the Cheshire Cat. 'That depends a good deal on where you want to get to,' came the reply. We should always remember this simple but illuminating lesson when we address the broader political problem of the world order. We know that one world order – the Cold War – has come to an end, and that we are now experiencing a phase of political and theoretical uncertainty in which those steering states must devise new rules for an as yet unfinished game, and academics must attempt new interpretations and propose new strategies.

The cosmopolitan democracy project points to a way out of the present uncertainty: the democratization of the international system as a political course parallel to the domestic democratization of states. Democracy has made great progress in recent years, but it is still a long way from outright victory. To be able to claim that, it must also assert itself in international relations. Today the conditions are more favourable than ever before.

States must, first of all, be ready and willing to form a society of societies. The typical forms of international organization, exemplified here in the confederal and federalist models, do not seem to meet the prerequisites of a democratic world order. It is thus necessary to design a system of states different from the existing one. This is the ambition of the cosmopolitan model.

The feasibility of this, as with any other political project, depends in the final analysis on the forces that are prepared to come out into the open and actively support it. The forces which oppose it are relatively easy to identify: they range from opponents of democracy to those who favour domestic democracy but who are sceptical about its extension to international affairs. It is, above all, the concept of world politics as the exclusive realm of states which is against any form of international integration based on cooperation and legality.

There are, however, strong tendencies in civil society towards a democratic world order. Forces which promoted democracy inside states to meet extremely tangible needs are now approaching the world framework with the awareness that domestic democracy on its own is incomplete. Although this awareness is still the preserve of relatively restricted circles, there are also historical trends which draw individuals towards a global society. This is by no means the first time that economic and social processes have moved faster than institutional innovations. Sooner or later, however, society always manages to create organs capable of serving its vital needs.

What is needed now is the participation of new political subjects. According to the cosmopolitan project, they should be world citizens, provided with the institutional channels to take part and assume duties *vis-à-vis* the global destiny. If citizens had not been capable of assuming this responsibility directly, democracy would never have enjoyed such great success in so many countries. It is no vain hope, therefore, to believe that in time the citizens of the world will take upon themselves the responsibility of managing this small planet of theirs democratically.

NOTES

Norberto Bobbio, Luigi Bonanate, Marina Calloni, Paola Ferretti, Richard Falk, Barry Holden, Mathias König-Archibugi, Mario Pianta, François Rigaux, Bruce Russett and the participants in the workshops on Transnational Democracy held in Rome (April 1995) and in Cambridge (March 1996) have provided detailed and useful comments on various drafts of this chapter. My greatest gratitude is to David Held and Martin Köhler for their on-line, just-in-time and off-the-record comments.

1 Cf. M. Kaldor, *The Imaginary War* (Oxford: Blackwell, 1990).
2 See D. Archibugi and D. Held (eds), *Cosmopolitan Democracy: an Agenda for a New World Order* (Cambridge: Polity Press, 1995); D. Held, *Democracy and the Global Order: From the Modern State to Cosmopolitan Governance* (Cambridge: Polity Press, 1995); R. Falk, *On Humane Governance: Toward a New Global Politics* (Cambridge: Polity Press, 1995).
3 According to G. Sartori, *Democrazia. Cosa è* (Milan: Rizzoli, 1994), there is a single model of democracy which can take different forms. Other scholars have convincingly shown that there are various theoretical models of democracy. See C. B. Macpherson, *The Life and Times of Liberal Democracy* (Oxford: Oxford University Press, 1977); and D. Held, *Models of Democracy*, 2nd edn (Cambridge: Polity Press, 1996) and the classification of democratic countries proposed by A. Lijphart, *Democracies: Patterns of Majoritarian and Consensus Government in Twenty-One Countries* (London: Yale University Press, 1984).
4 See D. Beetham, 'Liberal democracy and the limits of democratization', in D. Held (ed.), *Prospects for Democracy* (Cambridge: Polity Press, 1993), p. 55.
5 J. Dunn (ed.), *Democracy: the Unfinished Journey, 508 BC to AD 1992* (Oxford: Oxford University Press, 1993).
6 By democratic route I refer to the evolution of the political system. The concept is therefore different from Robert Dahl's notion of democratic process, which describes the formulation of decisions in a democratic society, see his *Democracy and its Critics* (New Haven: Yale University Press, 1989), ch. 8.
7 See the appraisal of the new democracies by J. Linz and A. Stepan, *Problems of Democratic Consolidation: Southern Europe, South Africa, and the Post-Communist Europe* (Baltimore: Johns Hopkins University Press, 1996).
8 I draw these data from the annual reports of Freedom House Survey Team, *Freedom in the World: Political Rights and Civil Liberties 1995–96* (New

York: Freedom House, 1996). These data are controversial and it has been argued that some of these countries are just facade democracies. Still, it is undisputable that Western democracies have extended considerably.

9   S. Huntington, *The Third Wave: Democratization in the Late Twentieth Century* (Norman: University of Oklahoma Press, 1991) dates the beginning of the third wave of democratization to 1974, when the remaining fascist regimes in Europe were overthrown. Observed from the point of view of the world order, however, it would appear that the main change came with the fall of the Berlin Wall in 1989.

10   M. W. Doyle, 'Kant, liberal legacies and foreign affairs', parts 1 and 2, *Philosophy and Public Affairs*, 12.3 and 12.4 (1983), pp. 205–35, 323–54.

11   This is the thesis of Dahl, *Democracy and its Critics*, ch. 22, and Huntington, *The Third Wave*, ch. 6.

12   See S. Huntington, 'The West: unique, not universal', *Foreign Affairs*, 75.6 (1996), pp. 28–46.

13   These problems are dealt with in a vast and growing body of literature. For an overview of problems, see N. Bobbio, *Il futuro della democrazia* (Turin: Einaudi, 1984); Dahl, *Democracy and its Critics*; Held, *Prospects for Democracy*.

14   Kaldor, *The Imaginary War*, pp. 112ff.

15   The effect of globalization on democracy is at the heart of Held, *Democracy and the Global Order*; see also chapter 1 above. Cf. also Y. Sakamoto (ed.), *Global Transformation: Challenge to the State System* (Tokyo: United Nations University Press, 1994).

16   For a discussion, see K. Goldmann, 'Democracy is incompatible with international politics', in K. Goldmann, S. Berglund and G. Sjöstedt (eds), *Democracy and Foreign Policy* (Aldershot: Gower, 1986).

17   Where possible, the term 'nation' is used to define a political-ethnic community and the term 'state' an institutional structure with specific control over a given territory. The distinction is necessary since nation-states are *de facto* only a minority of states.

18   H. J. Morgenthau, *Politics among Nations: the Struggle for Power and Peace*, abridged edn (New York: McGraw-Hill, 1993), p. 6.

19   The 'control mechanisms' of world politics are defined and described by J. Rosenau, chapter 2 above, and the body of literature he cites. See also J. Rosenau and E.-O. Czempiel (eds), *Governance without Government: Order and Change in World Politics* (Cambridge: Cambridge University Press, 1992).

20   D. Zolo, *Cosmopolis. La prospettiva del governo mondiale* (Milan: Feltrinelli, 1995), p. 173, trans. as *Cosmopolis: Prospects for World Government* (Cambridge: Polity Press, 1997). For a discussion of the communitarian arguments, see Janna Thompson, 'Democratic communities', in J. Thompson, *Justice and World Order* (London: Routledge, 1992), ch. 7, and chapter 9 above.

21   In dealing with specific institutions such as the European Community and the United Nations, Bellamy and Castiglione, in chapter 8 above, and D. Bienen, V. Rittberger and W. Wagner, in chapter 14 below, stress that international and supranational organizations should somehow accept and recognize the reasoning of communitarians.

22   N. Bobbio, 'Democracy and the international system', in Archibugi and Held, *Cosmopolitan Democracy*, pp. 17–18.

23   Although with some caution, this seems to be the thesis supported by B. Russett, 'A neo-Kantian perspective: democracy, interdependence, and international organizations in building security communities', in E. Adler and M. Barnett (eds), *Security Communities in Comparative and Historical Perspective* (forthcoming), and N. P. Gleditsch, 'Democracy and the future of European peace', *European Journal of International Relations*, 1.4 (1995), pp. 539–71.

24   Bobbio, 'Democracy and the international system', p. 39.

25   'Incoherence' is defined as acts of foreign policy which do not conform to the nature of the domestic political system. Cf. L. Bonanate, 'Peace or democracy?' in Archibugi and Held, *Cosmopolitan Democracy*, p. 52.

26   D. P. Forsythe, 'Democracy, war, and covert action', *Journal of Peace Research*, 29.4 (1992), pp. 385–95, has documented the covert actions undertaken by the United States against elected governments in Iran (1953), Guatemala (1954), Indonesia (1955), Brazil (1960s), Chile (1973) and Nicaragua (1980s).

27   Bobbio, 'Democracy and the international system', p. 18.

28   It is highly significant that the former Secretary-General of the United Nations, Boutros Boutros-Ghali, stressed the organization's action precisely on these three levels: 'The United Nations must act to promote democracy not only within states and among states, but also within the global society in which we shall be living. These are three levels of the policy of democratization pursued by the UN.' From 'Secretary General reflects on global prospect for United Nations', address to annual meeting of the World Economic Forum, Davos, 24 Jan. 1995. Boutros-Ghali released *An Agenda for Democratization* (New York: United Nations, 1996) which was the complement to his previous and successful *An Agenda for Peace* (New York: United Nations, 1992) and *An Agenda for Development* (New York: United Nations, 1994). Unfortunately, the latest *Agenda* was only published in December 1996, when the General Assembly did not confirm his position. The document therefore received very little attention.

29   For a summing up of this evidence, see N. P. Gleditsch, 'Democracy in International Affairs', paper presented at the Transnational Democracy workshop, Cambridge, Mar. 1996.

30   Cf. T. Vanhanen, *The Process of Democratization: a Comparative Study of 147 States, 1980–88* (New York: Crane Russak, 1990).

31   See T. Franck, 'The emerging right to democratic governance', *American Journal of International Law*, 86.1 (1992), pp. 46–91. These issues are discussed at length by Crawford and Marks, chapter 4 above. See also Crawford, 'Democracy and international law', *British Year Book of International Law* (1993), pp. 113–33.

32   See Linz and Stepan, *Problems of Democratic Consolidation*.

33   'One state, one vote' does not necesarily imply that the votes of all states should count as equal. It might be agreed that the votes of individual states are weighted by their size. But this is quite different from the notion that the members of a state might support different views. This issue is further discussed in Bienen, Rittberger and Wagner, chapter 14 below.

34 D. Mitrany, 'The functional approach to world organization', *International Affairs*, 24.3 (1948), pp. 350–63.

35 A classic account of the legal differences between confederations of states and federal states is provided in H. Kelsen, *The General Theory of Law and State* (Cambridge: Harvard University Press, 1945), section 5D. An excellent theoretical and historical overview of state unions is found in M. Forsyth, *Unions of States: the Theory and Practice of Confederation* (Leicester: Leicester University Press, 1981). Cf. also the suggestive essays of M. Wight, *Systems of States* (Leicester: Leicester University Press, 1977).

36 H. Köchler, *Democracy and the International Rule of Law* (Vienna: Springer-Verlag, 1995), and Zolo, *Cosmopolis*, have argued that after the Gulf War, the world order took on the characteristics of a new Holy Alliance.

37 I demonstated in 'Models of international organizations in perpetual peace projects', *Review of International Studies*, 18 (1992), pp. 295–317, that this was the fear of many democratic thinkers *vis-à-vis* a league formed of sovereigns.

38 E.-O. Czempiel has defined governance as 'the capacity to get things done without the legal competence to command that they be done'; see 'Governance and democratization', in Rosenau and Czempiel, *Governance without Government*, p. 250. See also chapter 2 above.

39 I highlighted the Kantian derivation of the cosmopolitan democracy model in 'Immanuel Kant, cosmopolitan law and peace', *European Journal of International Relations*, 1.4 (1995), pp. 429–56.

40 M. Kaldor, 'Proposal to the Economic and Social Research Council for a seminar on Cosmopolitan Democracy', University of Sussex, Brighton, 1993.

41 Cf. in particular H. Kelsen, *Das Problem der Souveränität und die Theorie des Völkerrechts* (Tübingen: Mohr, 1920).

42 For paradigmatic expositions of these two approaches see D. Mitrany, *The Functional Theory of Politics* (London: Martin Robertson, 1975) and N. Bobbio, *Il problema della guerra e le vie della pace* (Bologna: Il Mulino, 1984).

43 This idea of sovereignty is compatible with T. Pogge's notion of 'vertical dispersal of sovereignty', see his 'Cosmopolitanism and sovereignty', in C. Brown (ed.), *Political Restructuring in Europe: Ethical Perspectives* (London and New York: Routledge, 1994), pp. 103ff. See also A. Linklater, chapter 6 above.

44 U. Preuß, chapter 7 above, and Bellamy and Castiglione, chapter 8 above, discuss at length the significance of the European experience for the cosmopolitan project.

45 Two possible scenarios for Europe, the first a traditional one based on the creation of a European superstate, and another congruent with the cosmopolitan model presented here, are outlined by M. Kaldor, 'European institutions, nation-states and nationalism', in Archibugi and Held, *Cosmopolitan Democracy*, p. 86. Bellamy and Castiglione, chapter 8 above, review the current debate on the European Union's future.

46 This is the thesis of, *inter alia*, Zolo, *Cosmopolis*.

47   I discussed the prospect of reforming the United Nations on the basis of the cosmopolitan project in 'From the United Nations to cosmopolitan democracy', in Archibugi and Held, *Cosmopolitan Democracy*, and *Il futuro delle Nazioni Unite* (Rome: Edizioni Lavoro, 1995). Similar proposals are discussed in Held, *Democracy and the Global Order*, pp. 278ff., and *Models of Democracy*, pp. 358–9, as the prescriptive part of his exposition and defence of the cosmopolitan democracy project. The most significant UN reform proposals are discussed in E. Childers and B. Urquhart, *Renewing the United Nations System* (Uppsala: Dag Hammarskjöld Foundation, 1994); Commission for Global Governance, *Our Global Neighbourhood* (Oxford: Oxford University Press, 1995); Independent Working Group on the Future of the United Nations, *The United Nations in its Second Half-Century* (New York: Ford Foundation, 1995). Bruce Russett, 'Ten balances for weighing UN reform proposals', in B. Russett (ed.), *The Once and Future Security Council* (New York: St. Martin's, 1997), discusses the pros and cons of these proposals.

48   Bienen, Rittberger and Wagner, chapter 14 below, and Falk, chapter 15 below, address the implications of some UN reform proposals for political theory.

49   A. Linklater, 'What is a good international citizen?' in P. Keal (ed.), *Ethics and Foreign Policy* (St Leonards, New South Wales: Allen and Unwin, 1992).

50   J. Thompson, 'Cultural rights and political obligation', paper, La Trobe University, Bundoora, 1995.

51   M. Köhler, in chapter 11 below, considers the role of civil society in global change. A specific case study of the impact of transnational activities is also provided below by G. Prins and E. Sellwood, see chapter 12 below.

Part III

The Prospects of Cosmopolitan Democracy

11

From the National to the Cosmopolitan Public Sphere

Martin Köhler

With 'globalization' becoming an important issue in social and political research, the notion of an emerging 'global civil society' is carving out a niche for itself in the study of international relations, as well as in the self-understanding of social actors and movements. At the same time, conceptions of an emerging 'global polity' are being ventured which challenge traditional interpretations of the processes and structures of international affairs.[1] Both ideas reject the vision of a world order based exclusively on competitive interstate relations, and conjecture instead a world developing as a single whole thanks to the social activity and the deliberate political will of a population sharing common values and interests, such as human rights, democratic participation, the rule of law and the preservation of the world's ecological heritage.

There is an abundance of evidence to support the thesis of an emerging global civil society[2] and the formation of a global polity. In many issues of public concern – economic development, peace, social policy, environmental issues, consumer concerns and civil liberties, to name but a few – interest groups are engaged in undertakings which extend beyond borders, building transnational networks to disseminate knowledge, raise consciousness, develop common viewpoints and influence the arena of intergovernmental decision-making in global affairs. Their number has grown at an astonishing rate over the last three decades.[3] During the latest round of UN-sponsored intergovernmental conferences on the environment (Rio), human rights (Vienna), social development (Copenhagen), population policy (Cairo), women (Beijing) and urban habitats (Istanbul), tens of thousands of people[4] attended the parallel forums of civil society organizations (CSOs).[5] The practical and detailed knowledge of CSOs has made these forums a valuable resource for government actors. Vice versa, CSOs have managed to gain far-reaching influence over the agendas and outcomes of official conferences, so that it is now accepted UN policy to grant CSOs access to intergovernmental 'preparatory committees' and follow-up working groups.[6]

Though they have received no formal mandate from any political community or authority, CSOs and their transnational networks are increasingly recognized by governments as legitimate representatives of a global sphere of public interest which acts on its own behalf. For former UN Secretary-General Boutros-Ghali they are 'a basic form of popular representation in the present-day world. Their participation in international relations is, in a way, a guarantee of the political legitimacy of those international organisations.'[7] CSOs, especially those which have been granted consultative status by UN agencies, frequently see themselves as direct partners of the UN system, demanding that the transnational civil society they represent should join forces with UN agencies to act as a counterweight to the narrow economic, social and political interests of governments and economic interest groups.[8]

These examples support the claim that a transnational public sphere is emerging through which social interest groups are able to participate in international affairs beyond the traditional limits of state-confined politics. A closer look, however, reveals that this claim needs to be differentiated. First, not all agencies of intergovernmental cooperation are equally open to the influence of non-state actors. Some of the most important, such as the UN Security Council and the World Trade Organization, are explicitly off-limits for CSO participation. The Bretton Woods institutions only recently started to bow to the strong CSO demand for participation, which they are attempting to confine to the policy implementation phase. Secondly, even where access is granted, states have a variety of means of limiting the participation of non-state actors. A survey of the reasons why CSOs took part in the recent UN world conferences showed that more than half felt restricted by their governments and UN procedures in getting a hearing for their opinions.[9] Thirdly, another finding of the same survey is that the state continues to be a central focus for CSOs, even at UN world conferences. CSOs, in fact, are primarily concerned with influencing their own governments and, by fostering close relations with state officials, with increasing the domestic importance of their organization. The transnational realm is seen as offering a better opportunity than the national one for achieving these goals. To this end, most CSOs primarily demand better access to or even integration with the delegations of their governments.

It is thus misleading to conceive of the transnational public sphere as an arrangement independent of the dynamics governing the realm of national politics. While the transnationalization of the activity of civil society suggests that the traditional intrastate confinement of the public sphere no longer exists, an orientation towards domestic politics still persists. Albeit increasingly influenced by the dynamics of the transnational public sphere, the national one remains a focal point for interest aggregation and policy formulation. Yet the transnational public sphere itself cannot be conceived of simply as the extension of the national one. The very concept of the public sphere is intrinsically bound up in structures of authority and accountability which do not exist in the transnational realm.

In this chapter, I suggest that it is necessary to relate the phenomenon of the evolving transnational public to the functions and requirements of national public spheres, which are changing as a result of globalization. I argue that the transnationalization of civil society activities is intrinsically related to the state's increasing commitment to intergovernmental cooperation. Both phenomena broaden the base for the development of a global society and a global polity. Yet as long as the state continues to be the only site of political authority in international relations, it is impossible for a transnational public sphere – in which a global politics would have to be embedded – to emerge. Although it is assuming a cosmopolitan dimension, the public sphere remains basically a national arrangement. The term 'cosmopolitan public sphere' at once reflects the ongoing centrality of the state for civil society actors, and acknowledges that state politics is the result of transnational coalition-building and interest aggregation. These coalitions are not restricted to the actors of civil society. The specific novelty of the cosmopolitan public sphere is that it envisages the possibility for interest aggregation both between and across different groups of people and states. Directly, through financial support, or indirectly, as a result of easier international contacts, state actors may choose to side with civil society actors in other states to obtain changes in the policies of the latter. Likewise, civil society actors may choose to side with other states in order to obtain changes in their own state's policies.

The shift from the national to the cosmopolitan public sphere is by no means an automatic process. The impact of forces from outside community boundaries challenges the state's control over society and may *de facto* undermine its political sovereignty. To various degrees states, according to their size and resources, their internal organization and openness to the influence of civil society, are thus inclined to restrict this process.[10] On the other hand, it is the state itself which, as a result of the need to adapt to processes of globalization and by increasing involvement in intergovernmental cooperation, provides the impetus for the cosmopolitan enlargement of its own public sphere. This chapter seeks to explain this tension and how it affects the development of a cosmopolitan public sphere. In the next section, I look at the dynamics which induce civil society actors to transcend state borders, and interpret them as the consequence of a changing function of the public sphere caused by globalization and related state adaptation strategies; Ulrich Beck's concept of 'risk society'[11] will guide me along the way. In the following section, I look at the changes which the extension of the national public sphere implies for the state's loyalty requirements and the concept of the political in international relations.

GLOBALIZATION, STATE ADAPTATION AND THE CHANGING ROLE OF THE PUBLIC

The process of globalization has been described as the stretching and deepening of social relations and institutions across space and time so that, on the one hand, day-to-day activities are increasingly influenced by events happening on the other side of the globe and, on the other, the practices and decisions of local groups or communities may have significant global reverberations.[12] In manifold dimensions, social, cultural, economic and political activities cross the spatial boundaries of the state-centric political organization and interconnect states and societies in new political practices. Policies of individual states increasingly have to cope with transnational coalitions of interest and the framing conditions of transnationally evolving structures and institutions, which are reflected in the internal political process and its institutional structures.

Globalization is, however, an erratic, asymmetric historical process. It involves state institutions and societies to different degrees, in different forms and at different times, and thus produces profound differentials in the way state political systems adapt to the external environment.[13] On the one hand, the process of globalization blurs the distinction between the inner and outer spheres of social relations; on the other, it highlights the distinction *vis-à-vis* the political organization of social relations. Especially in the democratic industrialized societies most deeply involved in the process of globalization, internal order responds, by and large, to social demands and enjoys a high degree of political loyalty and social acceptance. The external environment, on the contrary, is characterized by non-accountable and rapidly changing transnational coalitions of interest, for whom loyalty to the rules of individual states or questions of social acceptance are at best arbitrary. The gap between the two spheres is considerably less marked for underdeveloped, authoritarian societies, where the social base for the internal order is often not much greater than it is for the external environment. As a result the political requirements for state adaptation are also less marked.

Strategies of state adaptation and their limits

Adaptation to the external environment means, first of all, coping with the pressures brought to bear by a structurally interdependent world economy, with its high cross-border mobility of capitals, goods, labour and services.[14] It is impossible to identify where such pressures arise in terms of inner and outer spheres. Nowadays, almost all societies are – albeit to different degrees and at different stages – involved in the global system of industrial production and consumption, or, more generally speaking, in a global cycle of industrial resource transformation. This cycle influences, inside and outside communities, the social base of reproduction in all its different dimensions, from gender relations and cultural patterns to the way in which societies are organized. Societies may benefit from this cycle in terms of increasing wealth, social cohesion and material freedom, but they are also confronted with the social costs inherently associated with it elsewhere, such as social displacement, resource depletion and disruptive changes in sociocultural habits. Pressures arise from the spatial separation across borders of the social benefits and costs connected with the process of *globally* interconnected resource transformation. With the globalization of the industrial system, social benefits in one place may be related to the production of costs in another; it may be that the costs are felt by the original actor, or by a third party, only much later, or in a form which has lost any visible connection to the initial accumulation of benefits, and so the costs lose their link with those responsible for them.

In this context, the state adapts to the external environment by seeking to shift the global social cost/benefit ratio to the optimum advantage of its own community. On the one hand, this means gaining an edge over other states by preventing the repatriation of external costs associated in one way or another with the production of internal benefits. On the other hand, since this strategy has objective limits precisely because of the cross-border nature of globalization and the rapidly changing transnational coalitions of interests, it means increasing the capacity of the state to accommodate returning costs internally and as smoothly as possible. There are structural constraints to this strategy, however, since any advances in cost accommodation are, at the same time, an incentive for other political communities to offload or redirect returning costs. Thus a seemingly unconstrained third adaptation strategy comes to the fore, complementary to the others: accelerating the production of benefits in order to make the balance positive. Gaining locational advantages over others is the social aspect of the worldwide thrust towards technological progress and the development of the productive forces which promotes the economic globalization process.

With the globally competitive race to accelerate social benefit production, a new constraint emerges: in fact, due to the finiteness of ecological resources and, increasingly, to unexpected collateral synergies in the transformation of resources,[15] unhampered technological and economic progress produces systematically – and, at a certain stage of its development, exponentially – not only socially determinable costs but also socially indiscriminate risks. Toxic agents and contaminants in air, water and food and changes in the climate devalue social benefits in a different way from collateral costs in so far as they are not spatially separated off. They take their toll of even the immediate producer of wealth, a fact that clashes with the interest of profit and property that fuels the industrialization process.[16] The social demand for risks to be brought under political control puts considerable pressure on the state's role as a competent regulator between society within and the outer environment; this is especially true of democratic states, which are required to respond to social demands in order to receive political loyalty in return. Conceptually speaking, however, risk management differs from the management of the above constraints. In fact, risks are not susceptible to political influence and intrastate decision-making, and the job of controlling them thus extends beyond the options for adaptation available to the individual state. Moreover, the technological and economic progress whose unhampered course is responsible for generating risks eludes the intrusion of political intervention. It even evades any attempt to define it as the problem. Here we touch on a set of questions lying yet deeper, centring around the concept of the political in democratic industrial society, on the role of the public sphere in political decision-making and its change in so-called 'risk society'.[17]

The changing function of the public sphere

The term 'public sphere' denotes not so much a theoretically coherent concept as an organizing principle for the legitimacy of political order which has prevailed in liberal pluralist Western democracies since the Second World War.[18] Within this historical understanding, it is the function of the public sphere to articulate and aggregate social demands. This continuously produces conflicts of interest which require authoritative choices as to the allocation of collective resources and the appropriate institutional setting in which this task has to be performed. Influencing such choices is the essence of democratic political conduct. Yet another function of the public sphere is to facilitate the implementation of choices and to generate loyalty to the decisions of the political authority to such an extent that the opposing losing interests (the interests, that is, that have failed to become state choices) accept defeat and respect limits on conflict. The degree of required loyalty and permitted conflict is expressed in rights and duties by which both society and state authority are held accountable. In the last instance, it is this framework of accountability which integrates the two diverse functions of the public sphere and generates its political character.

While the notion of the political is generally closely linked to interactions in the public sphere, there is much debate as to which types of social interaction should be considered public, and hence political. In the prevailing liberal view, the sphere of the political public is seen as distinct from the sphere of the unpolitical private by the reach of social interaction stopping short of primordial groups, such as the family and religious affiliations, and by the associative nature of interaction excluding the sphere of individual economic activity. The citizen is thus split in two. He or she participates in the public sphere only as the good *citoyen* who, equal among equals, formulates social interests and legitimizes the decisions of the political administration, providing for social and political cohesion in order to maintain the postulate of equality. Since the social evidence of class-related inequality threatens this postulate, the basis of cohesion includes provisions of social welfare, that is the consensual redistribution of economic benefits to the degree that nobody is excluded from the chance to participate in public activities. The idea of the equality of the *citoyen* in the public sphere is thus linked to the idea of social progress. This is all the more important since, like the good *bourgeois*, the same citizen remains not public but private. As such, private person against other private people, he or she produces wealth and technological and economic progress which, in the modern industrial society, is *a priori* equated with social progress and thus does not require public legitimization. The *citoyen* is derived from the *bourgeois*, the political public from the unpolitical private, not the other way around.

Historically, the depoliticization of the technological and economic sphere has proved decisive for the unleashing of productive forces and, by means of public redistribution of the benefits, for social progress – which, together, have strengthened the postulate of social cohesion and equality in modern industrial democracy. Not that productive progress and social progress necessarily follow a parallel course. Indeed, since they follow different dynamics and rationales, their relationship is one of tension. This tension increases, moreover, with processes of economic globalization. The technological and economic sphere, ever more globally oriented because new technologies and productive means require global sourcing and marketing, continues to generate economic progress; but its local social benefits are increasingly outweighed by globally determined social costs and risks which, channelled back to the local in various forms such as displacement, health hazards or ecological degradation, threaten the social cohesion of political communities.[19]

While the tension between the interests of the *bourgeois* and those of the *citoyen* was open to political influence as long as both were members of one and the same political community, the globalization of the industrial system has changed things. As a *bourgeois* the citizen has become global, as a *citoyen* he or she remains confined within national boundaries. In the former role the citizen expands the costs and risks connected with the production of technological and economic progress to the global level; in the latter he or she has no political voice to decide which of the costs and risks produced by the *bourgeois* of other political communities may be deemed acceptable. For the citizen, the pursuit of private global interests threatens to destroy the conditions for exercising public interests at home. This changes one of the premises on which the development of modern industrial society was built: namely, that technological and economic progress is politically neutral, merely providing the material base of a social progress distributed by means of public choices with a view to maintaining social and political cohesion. When it is not publicly legitimized procedures but the private application of technological innovation which shape the social and political cohesion of a society, then 'the political becomes unpolitical and the unpolitical becomes political.'[20]

With accelerated technological progress at a global level, the distinction between the political and the non-political is blurred, a fact which challenges our traditional understanding of the role of the public, of legitimate procedures and required loyalty and permitted conflict. Signs of change are empirically visible at very different levels. Three of them – observable in advanced, Western democratic states but increasingly also in newly democratized societies with strong industrial bases, such as those of the Asian region – seem especially significant with regard to a changing function of the public sphere.

1   Indicators such as electoral turnout and party membership show that interest in community institutions of political representation is decreasing. At the same time, according to opinion polls, interest in forms of direct political participation, in issue-oriented citizen initiatives and broad-based social movements, is increasing.[21] Such activities are not directed at gaining political power through large-scale interest aggregation around competing values, but represent a new political culture in which citizens directly claim civil interests and entitlements. The mediating agencies for such claims tend to be the media and courts and the appeal to a common civic sense rather than the institutions of the political system. Their decentralized and evolving dynamics give action at the individual, local, national and transnational levels equal political meaning in terms of the aims of participants. The borders of the political community become meaningless in the traditional political sense of

mobilization for specific goals. The new borders are differences of language and political culture, and they do not necessarily coincide with community borders.

2   The *a priori* equation of technological and economic with social progress is losing social acceptance. Scientific activity is not only enhancing technological and economic capacities, but also providing the means to evaluate publicly the direction and the results of technological change. On this basis, a public awakened to the increasing collateral social costs connected with industrial production starts to oblige economic entrepreneurship to legitimize its activity and choices at the public level. The attempt to hold technological and economic activity politically responsible is not mediated primarily through the institutions of the political system but by influencing consumer behaviour and lifestyles. With the existence of global markets and transnational corporations, community borders are more or less irrelevant in this respect. Inducing changes in economic behaviour does not depend on a community's majority decisions but on the use of the media to produce what Prins and Sellwood call 'informed consent',[22] inside and outside borders.

3   With the dismantling of the dynamics of technological and economic change and the public interpretation of its loci, conditions and synergies – especially since the nuclear meltdown at Chernobyl in 1986 – a new dimension of public conflict has gradually appeared.[23] Broadly speaking, it is conflict over what is to be regarded as risk and the definition of its scale and urgency. Influencing this conflict of definition depends to a large extent on communication skills and access to science and the media. As Prins and Sellwood show in chapter 12 below, access to political power and means of production is not necessarily decisive in determining outcomes. What is more important still, this new type of conflict transcends the role of the public sphere. So far the function of the latter has been to mediate between claims in the public distribution of social benefits. This is possible because issues of benefit distribution relate to stages in national economic development. Now the public sphere increasingly generates rival visions of private security from the fall-outs associated with global economic development. Public benefit distribution and private security concerns enter into a contest over how to redefine social priorities, any attempt to mediate being in vain since security has – in terms of survival – absolute connotations. Moreover, under conditions of globalization, this conflict cannot arrive at a lasting balance within the political community. The conflict between wealth and security interests is transnational in nature, so classical strategies of interest aggregation to obtain political power within community institutions are inadequate to meet the problem.

The signs outlined above suggest that political institutions and community borders lose their central role in the formation of the political and the shaping of conflicts, diminishing the state's classical function as arbiter and, as a consequence, its normative competence in establishing the limits of permitted conflict and required loyalty. At the same time, however, the state's role as an authorized mediator *vis-à-vis* the external environment increases as social demands of a transnational nature also increase. Here the state acquires new opportunities to reconfirm the political loyalty of the community – and even to gain a new normative competence.

Intergovernmental cooperation, global society building and the role of new actors

With the process of globalization, international cooperation is a rapidly developing means for states to implement their foreign policies; it can be measured in terms of the number of specialized international governmental organizations (IGOs), which has increased exponentially over the last few decades.[24] IGOs not only boost the number of people involved in intergovernmental affairs way beyond the classic teams of foreign ministry diplomats, but also change styles of working and the dynamics of intergovernmental cooperation and decision-making.[25] It is typical for IGOs to elaborate common norms and procedures specific to their tasks and operate with shared visions of their function. These elements of community building have considerably influenced the theory of international relations. The divergence between statist and universal interpretations which concerns us here emerges broadly in the question of whether the orientation of IGOs to maintain their global functions – in response to a transnational range of social demands – supersedes their members' orientation towards their entity of origin, namely, state institutions. In other words, the issue is that of the actor structure of the emerging international society.

In a statist interpretation, Hedley Bull and Adam Watson envisage the transformation of the international system into an international society in which states, nonetheless, continue to be the only actors:

By an 'international society' we mean a group of states (or more generally, a group of independent political communities) which not merely form a system, in the sense that the behaviour of each is a necessary factor in the calculation of the others, but also have established by dialogue and consensus common rules and institutions, and recognize their common interest in maintaining these arrangements.[26]

This aspect of the growing socialization of the international system has been further elaborated by the functionalist approach to regime analysis. Regimes are seen as issue-specific arrangements in the maintenance of the international system which do not depend *a priori* and solely on the state. They may be constitutively based on interactions between state and non-state actors.[27] Developing this approach further in a universalist direction, Martin Shaw defines Bull and Watson's international society of states as an 'institutional component'[28] of an emerging global society:

From the point of view of global society, the development of what is called international society is the *development of the institutions and the institutional culture of the state system* in the direction of greater coherence and consensus. Redefining international society in this way, we look at it as a development specific to the state system, but one which reflects this system's role in global society. It is the product not only of developments within the system, but also of the system's articulation with the structures, culture and other institutions of that society.[29]

In this perspective, transnationally operating interest groups are legitimate 'intruders'[30] into the intergovernmental realm. Irrespective of their status, they provide the input needed to develop global society, as well as feedback on the interstate system, which enables the latter to maintain a world order that is increasingly building a social base. Other universalists, arguing from a perspective of a global *civil* society – an expression closely related to the concept of the non-state realm[31] – emphasize the lack of formal accountability of the interstate system to the emerging global society and, thus, regard non-state transnational cooperation as a 'parallel arrangement of political interaction' which challenges the interstate system 'from below'.[32]

What both arguments manage to do is to point out the growing horizontal and vertical actor differentiation in the international realm, which results in an increasingly broad social base of intergovernmental cooperation. Yet they tend to refrain from answering the question of how the emerging social construction of the world order alters the dynamics and the structure of the international system, and how this, in turn, changes the role of the public sphere inside or outside states. Universalist interpretations emphasize the role of non-state actors in international affairs, primarily in terms of the dynamics of global community building.[33] The evocation of 'an international people'[34] responsibly tending to the preservation of global common goods, such as the environment, or the role attributed to global 'opinion communities' in the definition of 'mutually agreed upon values that guide the daily lives of people'[35] points to the role of non-state actors in conflating international relations with compulsory ethical norms and values. The transnational activity of CSOs is interpreted as evidence that an all-inclusive ethical base of world politics exists from which it is possible to appeal to governments as a supplementary element in the world community.[36] In such a vision, the question of what exactly constitutes the political in the international system remains unclear. Accountability is replaced by shared responsibility towards common ethical imperatives. The requirements of loyalty and conflict limitation are thus set *a priori*; they do not, that is, result from political discourse. Conflicting interests seem to disappear together with the political dimension of any transnational public sphere.[37]

The statist interpretation poses problems of an opposite kind. It would not deny that the emerging social construction of world order alters political dynamics in the international system but, since its international society remains an arrangement among states, it would disagree that this concerns the system's basic actor structure. It would not deny either that non-state actors and institutions are acquiring new roles in providing feedback on the international conduct of states' behaviour, hence indirectly in the maintenance of the interstate system, but it would disagree that this concerns a change in the functions of the public sphere or accounts for its transnationalization. Referring to the predominant role that states undeniably play in decisions about the institutional settings of intergovernmental cooperation, the functions and resources available to UN agencies and so on, statist interpretations insist that it is still, first and foremost, the society of states which influences the degree of international community building.[38] Consequently, the state and the national public sphere remain the focal point for the formation of what constitutes the political in international affairs.

Framed like this, the problem is more than a mere scientific skirmish. It is instead part of a lively debate among transnationally operating CSOs about how to define their role.[39] Some advocate that the increasing recognition of the individual as a subject of international law – in human rights covenants, international criminal law and regional settings such as the EU – is the first step towards a framework of direct accountability between individuals and global institutions which is not bounded by states, and which might eventually lead to a global public sphere. Hence, they regard it as the role of non-state actors to enlarge the competences of the UN agencies. Others argue that since political accountability still lies mostly inside the state-segregated global system, the main role of non-state actors is to monitor states' international conduct and feed back information to the political process in the national public sphere in order to make states more responsive to social demands for increased intergovernmental cooperation and international community building.

Mediating between the two positions, the role of non-state actors can be defined more specifically by referring back to our initial assumption that intergovernmental cooperation responds to burgeoning social demands for the regulation of conflicts between national benefit production and global security concerns.[40] While any solution to this conflict might eventually lead to structures of global authority and direct accountability, in the meantime it remains the task of non-state actors to help the state to commit itself more wholeheartedly to intergovernmental cooperation over a variety of pressing issues for global security, such as climate control, persisting interstate violence, global social displacements and consequences of the increasing gap between rich and poor. Most of these issues are not being adequately addressed at the moment, one of the reasons for this being that it is hard to reconcile intergovernmental cooperation in such fields with the state's task of generating community loyalty. This leads us back to the discussion of the strategies states implement to adapt to processes of globalization.

Seen from the perspective of state adaptation, intergovernmental co-operation is a highly sensitive strategy for regulating the distribution of benefits and costs and managing the risks deriving from global techno-logical and economic activities. First, it constrains the state's autono-mous strategies, such as the rechannelling of costs to third parties and the freedom to foster unlimited wealth production despite the accompanying risks. Secondly, it stresses differences in structures of political order to the detriment of those most responsive to internal social demands – that is, democratic states – since these are more constrained by public scrutiny and the need for accountability.

This accounts for a paradox in the dynamics of conflict. Industrialized democracies are the most deeply involved in the process of globalization and, politically speaking, are thus highly sensitive to evolving costs and risks at a global level. Democratic states have to respond to the social demand for global regulations and are thus objectively more interested in cooperative arrangements than other political systems. Moreover, at least the OECD countries boast a degree of material freedom that allows them to negotiate limits on benefit production to accommodate security concerns. Conversely, the democracy gap between states impedes coop-erative agreements – in issues such as climate control, for example – containing serious limitations on benefit production.[41] First, the more democratic an internal order is, the more the effects of far-reaching limitations will generate social conflicts with immediate and unfavour-able political repercussions for incumbent political rulers. Secondly, democratic rulers will find it difficult to question the legitimacy of such social conflicts, while other, more authoritarian rulers are less compelled to react to social criticism. In sum, global cooperation over the rebalancing of national benefit production and global security concerns is constrained by the fact that it may, for some states, lead to a loss of community loyalty, while in others it may not.

In terms of James Rosenau's ideal-types of state conduct to adapt to the external environment, the democratic state would appear to have a choice of two possible approaches to this kind of conflict: either it rejects the cooperative strategy and optimizes the alternatives, or it embarks, through cooperation, on a long-term process of democratization of the external environment to obtain more equal conditions for implementa-tion constraints.[42] The former course stems from the primacy of national benefit production and responds to immediate community requests; the latter stems from global security concerns and long-term community loyalty. In terms of the internal conditions for external conduct, neither approach suffices in itself to solve the internal political conflict between benefit interests and security concerns. Thus the cooperation strategy of democratic states tends to contain both a rejection of steps which could substantially limit autonomous action, and an interest in enhancing democratic norms and procedures beyond borders in order to secure fairness. This dual strategy of democratic states has been largely confirmed during the latest round of UN conferences on the environment, human rights, social development, population policy, urbanization control and food security. The demand for transparency, the rule of law, good governance and respect for human rights has by far outweighed proposals to achieve tangible results.

While the worldwide democratization of states would significantly improve the conditions for international cooperation on achieving a balance between national benefits and global security interests, the cooperation strategy will be ambivalent for the state as long as political accountability remains segregated and the upholding of community loyalty a state task. Hence the demands of transnationally operating CSOs for structures of global authority and direct accountability embedded in a global public sphere are sensible ones. However, the first step in this direction remains the worldwide democratization of states.[43] Here non-state actors can achieve a role not in contrast with but complementary to the state system by providing or stimulating transnationally extended support for democratic forces and states – irrespective of whether it affects their own political community or others – to enable their own and other states to establish cooperation on global security issues. While the segregation of accountability and loyalty structures remains a permanent fixture in the interstate system, the dynamics of national public spheres will change as they are extended transnationally: they will assume a cosmopolitan character.

POLITICAL LOYALTY IN THE COSMOPOLITAN PUBLIC SPHERE

If, on the one hand, national civil societies are increasingly involved in conflicts over security interests which can only be mediated through international cooperation, and if, on the other, for the democratic state engagement in international cooperation depends on the bridging of the 'democracy gap' between the inner and outer spheres, then both share a common interest in bringing about democracy beyond the borders of the political community. The extent of the democratic state's engagement in intergovernmental cooperation on global security issues thus depends on its *and* its civil society's ability to foster transnational coalitions in this direction. Different coalitions between state institutions and CSOs can be established to work on interconnected issues of democratization, such as human rights, the rule of law, increased levels of political participation, transparency and accountability in decision-making and so on. First, CSOs may support societal actors in another state who demand more democratic freedom from their government. Secondly, a state may seek the support of its civil society in implementing its foreign policies *vis-à-vis* another state. Thirdly, a state may appeal to CSOs abroad or support them indirectly in their efforts to influence the policies of their state. Fourthly, CSOs may seek the assistance of their own state in furthering activities in other states.

Inducing democracy beyond borders is, however, only a means of allowing for an enhanced level of international cooperation to serve different ends. For the state, the ultimate end of cooperation is to serve in the upholding of the political loyalty of its community. For its civil society, instead, international cooperation serves to foster global decisions on conflicting visions of how to redefine social priorities in terms of the production of wealth and the concern for collective security. Albeit transnational in nature, this conflict is already present within each community. The transnational realm of coalition building also helps CSOs to obtain transnational support for conflicting positions at home, both among national CSOs and between civil society and the state. Thus a fifth possible coalition, not outward bound but inward bound, has to be added to the list: more specifically, societal groups may seek the assistance of CSOs in other countries or of foreign states in furthering their specific goals at home. As two of the organizers of the civic forum at the Rio Conference on Environment and Development (UNCED) observed: 'Even though UNCED was mostly enacted on the international stage, it gave NGOs a chance to test their clout by trying to sway their national delegations. Some lobbied their own delegations directly, while others enlisted allies from foreign delegations to help them pursue their causes internationally.'[44]

This fifth cross-border coalition option evidences the difficulty with which the cosmopolitan extension of the national public sphere is confronted. While in the four outward-bound dimensions a state and its civil society participate equally in the development of a cosmopolitan public sphere in which CSOs obtain a role largely independent from the state, in the fifth inward-bound dimension the civil society remains dependent on the loyalty requirements set by its state:

This partial dependence of civil society on the state, together with continuing national loyalty, provide the basis of the state's ability to affect the patterns of transnational activity. Through conscious policies and the operations of their internal structure, states can both funnel transnational interactions by determining the extent to which local societal actors can form autonomous transnational ties, and provide or close off particular pathways by which foreign societal actors can use contacts with local societal groups or the state apparatus. In the immediate term, then, domestic state structures appear very solid, able to withstand and channel transnational impulses.[45]

In political practice, the outward-bound and inward-bound dimensions of the cosmopolitan public sphere are, of course, intertwined. It is hardly conceivable that coalition building directed outwards does not have repercussions internally, and vice versa. The very term 'coalition' suggests a situation of some form of reciprocal benefits. The reciprocality inherent in coalition-building efforts, together with the inequality of state and non-state actors because of state-imposed loyalty constraints, mark the specific conflict of the cosmopolitan public sphere. Broadly speaking, the conflict is between the state's interest in upholding community loyalty and channelling transnational impulses, and the interest of its civil society in optimizing the political effects which transnational coalitions may achieve within the community. The latter depends on the willingness of the state to recognize transnational coalitions and to grant them political legitimacy: that is, to acknowledge forces acting from outside community boundaries and, hence, from outside the sphere of established loyalty rules. Without some degree of state-granted legitimacy and recognition, for CSOs transnational coalition building remains, politically, an arbitrary effort.

This conflict posed by the cosmopolitan extension of the public sphere goes to the very base of the state's sovereignty to regulate, through loyalty rules, the political life of the community. Once legitimacy and recognition are granted to transnational coalitions, interest aggregation and policy formulation would cease to be *national* affairs, subject to indivisible loyalty requests by the state. Moreover, since the state or state agencies take part in transnational coalition building, the very concept of the political would change. Traditional forms of national, horizontal interest aggregation encompassing competing sets of demands and values would be complemented by forms of vertical networking which would cross levels of authority and territorial boundaries. These new forms of vertical networking would centre around competing sets of social and political institutions in local, national, regional and global governance. The establishing of cross-level coalitions with converging goals could become decisive in determining political outcomes not only at state level but at all levels involved.

Such cross-level coalitions would strain yet another principle of state sovereignty: that is, its upholding of institutional coherence in relation to the outside. Different agencies of one and the same state might find themselves in opposed transnational coalitions. For example, the pressure of a rural southern CSO on its agricultural state ministry would receive additional strength if supported by, say, an education ministry of a northern state and the World Health Organization. At the same time, opposed CSOs of the same southern state could align with their industrial ministry, the defence ministry of the northern state and the World Bank against the former alliance. The arising institutional conflicts would, to different degrees, have to be dealt with not only at state level but at all levels involved. Such intrainstitutional competition would, moreover, give added meaning to the development of reciprocal recognition and political legitimacy in transnational coalition building, since these principles underpin the identification and political processing of common goals across different levels.

This picture is not as futuristic as it looks. State level apart, it is possible to observe that cross-level coalition-building components have started to influence the orientation of social and political institutions. For example, the UN Environment Programme and the World Bank have long operated with different non-state constituencies and, in certain respects, built coalitions running counter to each other. In order to involve state agencies in this coalition building between local and global levels more fully, hence enhancing equality in their legitimacy and reciprocal recognition, the cosmopolitan public sphere is confronted with the task of reconciling the changing meaning of political loyalty with the ongoing sovereignty interest of the state. But how far can the state uphold its competence to protect itself from outside interference and to determine required community loyalty and the limits of conflict in key areas which touch on its sovereignty in representing all of its institutional parts? And how far can coalitions representing transnational cultural, social, political or environmental interests override the state's interest of institutional coherence?

The development of the cosmopolitan public sphere may thus be marked by a situation of changing and unstable loyalty arrangements between the state and its civil society. The very meaning of loyalty might change in the course of this conflict to include compliance with, on the one hand, a set of globally shared values which affect coalition building, such as human rights, democratic participation and the rule of law, and on the other, standards to limit the scope of transnational coalitions and the conflicts they may produce, such as respect for social and cultural self-determination. Hence the shared interest of a state *and* its civil society in inducing democracy beyond its borders, which originally accounted for the development of the cosmopolitan public sphere, may ultimately produce repercussions which require a realignment of the national with the evolving global standards of democracy.

It seems clear from these last remarks that the development of the cosmopolitan public sphere is a continuous project without an ultimate, definitive stage. As the project progresses – and as the political legitimacy of institutions, including all the various state agencies, in representing sets of interests aggregated across all levels increases – it may well lay the foundations for an integrated global public sphere in which the distinction between state and non-state actors may eventually be overridden.

However, if this global public sphere is to have a *political* character, it must be founded on a consolidated cosmopolitan public sphere.

NOTES

I am indebted to Franck Amalric for fruitful discussions, to David Held and Mario Pianta for constructive criticism of first drafts, to Daniele Archibugi for encouragment, to John Irving for correcting my English, and to Renata Del Papa for her infinite patience.

1   See, for example, M. Shaw, *Global Society and International Relations* (Cambridge: Polity Press, 1994); R. D. Lipschutz, 'Reconstructing world politics: the emergence of global civil society', *Millennium*, 21 (1992), pp. 389–420; M. Walzer (ed.), *Toward a Global Civil Society* (Oxford: Berghahn Books, 1995).

2   Definitions of 'civil society' differ widely, though theorists of different orientations basically agree with Hegel's three-part model in which civil society is the autonomous sphere of social interaction between the family on the one hand and the agencies of the political administration on the other. See G. W. F. Hegel, *Elements of the Philosophy of the Right*, ed. A. W. Wood (Cambridge: Cambridge University Press, 1991). Contemporary controversy is mainly concerned with which activities are included in this model. Liberal and realist theorists focus primarily on freedom from state influence and, hence, regard economic activity as a central element of civil society. Critical theorists focus on the functions of civil society in generating political opinions and social goals and, hence, on the public sphere civil society represents. According to Cohen and Arato, only the organizations which represent economic interests in the public sphere, such as labour and employers' unions, should be considered part of civil society. See J. Cohen and A. Arato, *Civil Society and Political Theory* (Cambridge: MIT Press, 1992). Here, I follow this interpretation.

3   According to UN estimates, the number of international non-governmental organizations (NGOs) grew from roughly 1,300 in 1960 to over 36,000 in 1995. NGOs are – at UN level – defined as 'self-governing, private institutions engaged in the pursuit of public purposes outside the formal apparatus of the State'; see B. Boutros-Ghali, *An Agenda for Democratization* (New York: United Nations, 1996), p. 34. The estimates do not include international informal and ad hoc activities of individuals or interest groups, which would make the number much higher.

4   During the Fourth UN Women's Conference in Beijing in 1995, 40,000 people attended the CSO forum compared to 11,000 during its predecessor in 1990 in Nairobi. See R. Krut, 'Globalization and civil society: NGO influence in international decision-making', paper presented at the Globalization and Citizenship conference of the United Nations Research Institute for Social Development, Geneva, 9–11 Dec. 1996, p. 18.

5   In the self-definition of public social interest groups, the term civil society organizations is increasingly replacing the term non-governmental organiza-

tions to include new forms of autonomous organization such as informal alliances, social movements and ad hoc networks which are not necessarily recognized by governments, and to exclude the sphere of economic enterprises.

6   See Y. Kakabadse and S. Bruns, 'Movers and shapers: NGOs in international affairs', in *International Perspectives on Sustainability* (Washington, D.C.: World Resource Institute, 1994).

7   Quoted in Krut, 'Globalization and civil society', p. 19.

8   R. Dumelie, 'A forum for NGOs: a proposal', *Development Journal of the Society for International Development* (1993), pp. 51–3.

9   Benchmark Environmental Consulting, *Democratic Global Governance: Report of the 1995 Benchmark Survey of NGOs* (Oslo: Royal Norwegian Ministry of Foreign Affairs, 1996).

10   Empirical observation suggests that small democratic states with federal elements of political organization and a high degree of political cohesion are most open to allow and actively engage in cosmopolitan coalition-building. Most prominent are the Netherlands, Canada and the Scandinavian states.

11   U. Beck, *Risk Society: Towards a New Modernity* (London: Sage, 1992).

12   See David Held, chapter 1 above.

13   For the approach which focuses on state adaptation to the global environment see J. N. Rosenau, *The Study of Global Interdependence: Essays on the Transnationalization of World Affairs* (London: Frances Pinter, 1980); and J. N. Rosenau, *The Study of Political Adaptation* (London: Frances Pinter, 1980).

14   See I. Wallerstein, *The Politics of the World Economy* (Cambridge: Cambridge University Press, 1984).

15   See Gwyn Prins and Elizabeth Sellwood, chapter 12 below.

16   Beck, *Risk Society*, esp. ch. 1.

17   The following section is largely based on Beck, *Risk Society*, ch. 8.

18   See H. J. Laski, *A Grammar of Politics* (London: Allen and Unwin, 1948).

19   Some authors put in parallel the thermophysical laws of entropy – which make increasing costs of economic reproduction inevitable – and forms of social entropy, that is a constant and inevitable decrease in social cohesion in the global industrial production system. See H. Henderson, *Creating Alternative Futures: the End of Economics* (New York: Putnam, 1980).

20   Beck, *Risk Society*, p. 186.

21   For the member states of the European Union, see H. Scheer, *Zurück zur Politik. Die archimedische Wende gegen den Zerfall der Demokratie* (Munich: Piper, 1995). For the OECD states, see K. Armingeon, 'Gründe und Folgen geringer Wahlbeteiligung', *Kölner Zeitschrift für Soziologie und Sozialpsychologie*, 46 (1994), pp. 43–64.

22   See chapter 12 below.

23   See for this paragraph particularly Beck, *Risk Society*, ch. 1.

24   The number of global IGOs increased from 37 in 1909 to about 300 in 1989. See D. Held, *Democracy and the Global Order: From the Modern State to Cosmopolitan Governance* (Cambridge: Polity Press, 1995), p. 108. If regional and subregional IGOs are included, the number rises to about 2,000. See Union of International Associations (ed.), *Yearbook of International Organizations*, 32nd edn (Munich: Saur, 1996), vol. 1.

25 See more specifically on international actor structures and decision-making, Held, *Democracy and the Global Order*, ch. 5.

26 H. Bull and A. Watson (eds), *The Expansion of International Society* (Oxford: Clarendon Press, 1984), p. 1.

27 M. Zürn, 'Bringing the second image (back) in: about the domestic sources of regime formation', in V. Rittberger (ed.), *Regime Theory and International Relations* (Oxford: Clarendon Press, 1993), pp. 282–311. See also James Rosenau, chapter 2 above.

28 Shaw, *Global Society and International Relations*, p. 131.

29 Ibid., p. 130, emphasis in the original.

30 Ibid., p. 131.

31 See Cohen and Arato, *Civil Society and Political Theory*.

32 Lipschutz, 'Reconstructing world politics', pp. 390, 391.

33 B. Buzan, 'From international system to international society: structural realism and regime theory meet the English school', *International Organization*, 47 (1993).

34 B. Holden, 'Democratic theory and global warming', in B. Holden (ed.), *The Ethical Dimensions of Global Change* (London: Macmillan, 1996), p. 150.

35 R. A. Coate et al., 'The United Nations and civil society: creative partnerships for sustainable development', *Alternatives*, 21 (1996), p. 93–122, at p. 117.

36 See, for example, E. Boulding, *Building a Global Civic Culture: Education for an Interdependent World* (Syracuse: Syracuse University Press, 1990).

37 For a sharp critique on the avoiding of the question of the political in ethical readings of international relations, see R. B. J. Walker, 'Social movements/ world politics', *Millennium*, 23 (1994), pp. 673–4.

38 For a good synthesis of statist approaches to international actor structures, see K. J. Holsti, *The Dividing Discipline: Hegemony and Diversity in International Theory* (Boston: Allen and Unwin, 1985).

39 See Krut, 'Globalization and civil society'.

40 Global security concerns are defined not as security concerns which are perceived globally, but as security concerns whose origins derive from global factors. They may be perceived only by a limited number of persons, groups or political communities as threatening security. The term thus corresponds to private security. It is introduced here to mark the difference from national benefit production and to come into line with the concept in chapter 12 below.

41 According to the International Climate Commission, we have global CO_2 emissions of 20 billion tonnes a year (1990) which need be reduced to 10 billion tonnes by the year 2050 to comply with criteria of sustainability. One billion people in the developed northern part of the globe produce 16 tonnes per head/year, while 4 billion people in the underdeveloped southern part produce 1 tonne per head/year. By the year 2050 the northern population will have grown to 1.5 billion people, the southern one to 8.5 billion people. If parity were achieved, each person would be allowed to produce 1 tonne per year. This would mean a reduction in the north from 16 to 1 tonnes. Such a tremendous reduction would require completely different patterns of consumption and social relations in the north. See R. Kurz, 'Nachhaltige Entwicklung und Nord-Süd-Problematik', *WSI-Mitteilungen* (1995), pp. 272–7.

42 In Rosenau's four-type model of state adaptation strategies, the former would correspond to the intransigent, the latter to the promotive type, seen as the extreme variants for states with a strong internal base of political loyalty. See Rosenau, *The Study of Global Interdependence*.
43 For a discussion of the relation between state democratization and global democracy see Daniele Archibugi, chapter 10 above.
44 Kakabadse and Bruns, 'Movers and shapers', p. 4.
45 M. J. Peterson, 'Transnational activity, international society and world politics', *Millennium* (1992), pp. 371–88, at p. 386.

12

Global Security Problems and the Challenge to Democratic Process

Gwyn Prins and Elizabeth Sellwood

What rights, and under what conditions a person shall be allowed to exercise over any portion of this common inheritance cannot be left undecided. No function of government is less optional than the regulation of these things, or more completely involved in the idea of a civilised society.

John Stuart Mill

WHY GLOBAL SECURITY PROBLEMS MATTER FOR COSMOPOLITAN DEMOCRACY

Global security problems are already some of the most politically intractable in contemporary affairs, and are set to bulk larger in the future. They are of special importance to any project of cosmopolitan democratic reform both because they attach to fundamental material and cultural aspects of the common inheritance of humankind and because, unresolved, they are among the most prominent obstacles barring the gateway to political transformation. No function of government is less optional or more completely involved in the idea of a civilized society.

What are global security problems? Underpinning the idea of a civilized society, including any putative global society, is that of a shared sense of community; underpinning any functioning community is a common material inheritance. In a crowded and globally interactive world, these interlinked fields are the terrain of global security problems. Such problems are not satisfactorily defined by subject categories, as we are accustomed to do, but rather by certain shared characteristics. They are not simply the security implications of environmental stress or the switch in emphasis from inter- to intrastate violence in the conduct of war; nor are they what some call the problems of 'structural violence' alone – gross wealth differentials leading to curtailment of health and life or the burdens of living in failed states. What makes global security problems distinct is that wherever they occur within these areas (and they do occur within all of these areas), it is not possible to get a grip on them through conventional state-derived and democratic institutions.

All are cross-cutting. From the perspective of cosmopolitan democracy, two characteristics are especially important: global security problems are *transnational* – not just geographically, but in the sense that borders are irrelevant to them – and they exhibit *unexpected and unpredictable synergisms* which make it very difficult to foresee the consequences of individual actions in a fundamentally more interactive world. Clear examples of such interactions unhappily proliferate.

One of the first to capture public attention was the 'ozone problem'. This is the unpredicted interaction of chlorofluorocarbon gases (which are used in refrigerators and as aerosol propellants) with stratospheric ozone, leading to its depletion, with consequences as various as skin cancer, cataracts of the eye or damage to phytoplankton at the base of the oceanic food chain, by virtue of increased rays of UV striking the earth's surface. The phenomenon of global warming will provide one of the most extensive, worrying and fundamental examples of such synergisms. The British BSE crisis in the cattle population is another, more recently noticed, example. Interestingly, one part of that trail also starts with climate change. An unanticipated and strange web of causation is still being uncovered. It appears to start with relaxation of the regulations requiring high temperature processing of sheep's offal by renderers. Motives may have included a desire to reduce processing costs and to increase profit, or may have been part of a concern to reduce fuel use nationally, or may simply have been a belief that previous high temperatures were unnecessary. Coupled with this was a reduced use of solvents at a time of rising 'ozone awareness' as these were seen to give off ozone-destroying gases. Whatever the motives, the unanticipated result was that 'prions', carrying bovine spongiform encephalopathy, survived in offal which entered cattle through feed. The meat from parts of these cattle, when consumed by humans, may have a causal connection with the human version of BSE – Creutzfeldt-Jakob disease (CJD).

Global security problems are chaotically cross-linked politically as well as physically. If unexpected linkages, such as those just illustrated, and to be illustrated further in other case materials later in this chapter, are typical, they pose formidable problems in the framing of effective political action. Ozone depletion, global warming and BSE all show that. Just as they defy the pigeon-holes of academe (are these questions of politics? of international relations? of chemistry? of ethics?), so they make it less possible to anchor a problem in one or other substantive area of policy, or jurisdiction, or country. The issue is not just a problem of the environment, of health or drug regulations, not just a problem of interstate security, not just a problem of civil rights, but contains elements of all these.

In logical consequence, the interactions characteristic of global security problems force a series of questions about agency and institutions, the resolution of which is vital to the viability of any project of cosmopolitan democracy. The traditionally legitimate agents of the modern state are the legal institutions of statute or custom and they cannot cope well – or well enough to satisfy citizens – with cross-cutting issues. So many actors are involved in the creation of these problems that we have no clear culprits on whom to pin blame, resulting in what Ulrich Beck calls 'organized irresponsibility'.[1] But we must also consider that the failure to tackle them is a consequence of the specific design of our democratic institutions, not solely of the new tasks that they face. The central question is therefore *what would produce effective action that can be given democratic legitimacy in a new way?* This is an issue of the recasting of governance. It is framed by a paradox and two dilemmas.

The paradox is that, on the one hand, since the collapse of Communism liberal and democratic forms of government have emerged with vigour around the world, but on the other hand, disappointingly few of our most serious political problems have been solved by this upsurge of liberal democratic impulses. Even the more optimistic expectations about the likely degree of climate change that has been brought about suggest that it may pose threats to territory and economies quite as devastating as those posed by invading armies.[2] In other areas which are regarded as crucial for *national* security, it is considered prudent to prepare for the worst-case scenario; yet hitherto this has not commensurately been the case where global threats are concerned. So long as no theory provides a satisfactory answer, capable of being implemented in practice, to the question of how to revive democratic institutions, the situation gives rise to what Will Hutton describes as a 'do it yourself' culture of politics, and will continue in this vein.[3] In this chapter, we investigate an episode in the operation of this DIY culture. We then seek to understand how it works, and suggest what we see as the implications of global security threats for future democratic processes.

Beyond the framing paradox, two dilemmas loom, both of which may be simply stated. The first is that in the eyes of some constituency more knowledgeable or more sensitized to the issue than the general population, global security problems are judged to be urgent enough for the activist constituency to be convinced that a start must be made on addressing them; but by their nature the problems are not generally agreed to be visible enough as a threat for a traditional democratic consensus to coalesce (what Ronald Dworkin has called 'statistical democracy').[4] Therefore the only way for action to be begun ahead of the achievement of such a democratic mandate seems to be by inherently undemocratic means. The pressure for change from agitating, dissenting minorities (what James Madison called the 'mischiefs of faction')[5] has usually been the engine of change in democracies. Ways have been found to manage them by strategies of limitation, insulation or accommodation.[6] This is not a new type of challenge, although it may be new in scale and speed of onset. If an impasse over global security problems is to be avoided, the issue here is how to create informed consent, which, in common with others in this book, we believe to be the essential underpinning of any new democratic form.

The second dilemma follows directly. Often the general public is vaguely and quite widely uneasy about the consequences of a global security threat (like global warming) where the existing democratic structures are unable or unwilling to act. The failure to alleviate effects and the appearance of powerlessness serve to erode confidence in established institutions and produce either passivity, manifested in falling voter turnouts (among the majority), or Hutton's DIY politics (among the active minority). The issue here is therefore one of political structure. Together these two dilemmas compose the global security challenge to democratic process. Together they identify the two key requirements in a prescription for successful cosmopolitan democracy: *consent* and *institutional structure*.

David Held has argued that central to a project of cosmopolitan democracy, including resolution of the two dilemmas just posed, must be the preservation of the individual's autonomy of action. He is careful to explain what he does (and does not) mean by this, and since we share his anxiety not to be misunderstood, we reproduce his formulation here:

The principle of autonomy, entrenched in democratic public law, ought to be regarded, therefore, not as an individualistic principle of self-determination, where 'the self' is the isolated individual acting alone in his or her interests, but, rather, as *a structural principle of self-determination* where 'the self' is part of the collectivity or 'the majority' enabled and constrained by the rules and procedures of democratic life.[7]

The importance of achieving appropriate structures is a refrain in Held's work. Freedom, he thinks, is indissolubly linked to structure:

'individuals are equally free when they can enjoy a common structure of political action.'[8] How then shall such structures be formed? Not by philosopher kings *ex cathedra*, but by the informed consent of citizens. Nor can this be Dworkin's 'statistical democracy'. Held launches a stream of pregnant rhetorical questions:

Whose consent is necessary and whose participation is justified in decisions concerning, for instance, AIDS, or acid rain, or the use of non-renewable resources, or the management of transnational economic flows? What is the relevant constituency: national, regional or international? To whom do decision-makers have to justify their decisions? To whom should they be accountable? Further, what are the implications for the idea of legitimate rule of decisions taken in polities, with potentially life-and-death consequences for large numbers of people, many of whom might have no democratic stake in the decision-making process?[9]

Here his worries coincide exactly with ours; for in this chapter we argue that the achievement of informed consent is the precondition to the necessary institutional reconstructions that will facilitate new personal freedoms, which alone may underpin cosmopolitan democracy.

If informed consent can be achieved, how will that be, and what will be the *nature* of that consent? For there is a world of difference between active participation in democratic decision-making and the passive consent of *nihil obstat*. Or, in other words, what, in Andrew Linklater's felicitous phrase, gives fibre to a concept of 'thick citizenship'? This is at the nub of our present dilemma and our potential tragedy. What best motivates thick citizenship, which we take to mean an active, engaged public life, is belief in a better – physically and morally better – future. Then, like all utopians before, we are faced, in Linklater's poignant phrase, 'with the weakness of strong moral duty'.[10]

Legitimacy is in important part a product of performance: nothing succeeds like success (and nothing fails like failure!). So the challenge is not just to produce an alternative vision but to produce such a vision in a form *which can generate effective action*. That requires a redefinition of what represents a mandate, and an evaluation of different ways to achieve a mandate. We shall return to these questions in the final section. Held describes this grounded, performance-related approach to political ideology as 'embedded utopianism'. 'If utopia is to be embedded, it must be linked into patterns and movements as they are,' he observes, but adds that this must not be at the price of immobility. Movement is imparted by constantly measuring present performance against future aspiration; and this is utopianism defined by the principles of cosmopolitan democracy.[11] Held has no qualms in identifying the political theorist as advocate under such a prescription; but in so doing he raises difficult questions of standing and of legitimacy which he does not fully resolve.

Having identified the problem, much can be learned from the practice of 'DIY' politics as it actually exists. Recognizing their ineffectiveness as agents in the existing democratic process, activists have attempted – with some success – to influence it through unconventional means. Does their success in action represent a violation of the democratic principles inherent in the established institutions of government? Or are the actions of the protesters evidence of the shortcomings of institutionalized democracy, and a legitimate attempt to push further the *degree* of democracy within the states concerned? Do they represent an attempt to coalesce a transnational constituency to address problems that cannot be confined to the domestic affairs of particular states? Crucially, what form of mandate do they claim to construct, and how should we assess this claim?

None of these questions can be answered without examining a case. In the following section, we describe a specific instance – the Brent Spar affair – in which a transnational coalition of activists effectively reversed a decision taken by a democratic government.

THE BRENT SPAR AFFAIR

The Brent Spar is a very large floating oil storage and loading buoy, 141 metres in height and weighing 14,500 tonnes. During operations the buoy was used in the North Sea by the oil company Shell UK to store oil from the Brent 'A' oil rig, and also acted as a tanker-loading facility for the whole Brent oil-field.

After the Spar ceased to operate in 1991, Shell commissioned studies, including one by the University of Aberdeen, to determine the Best Practicable Environmental Option (BPEO) for its disposal. It was decided that deep-water disposal – literally sinking the buoy after towing it to an approved place – was the safest and least damaging way to dispose of the Spar. A further £1 million was spent surveying alternative deep-water sites for the sinking and a site was chosen in the North Atlantic, 240 kilometres from the west coast of Scotland, where the sea is over two kilometres deep. In 1994 formal consultations were carried out on the deep-water disposal option with a number of organizations, including the Scottish Fishermen's Association, Scottish Natural Heritage and the Joint Nature Conservation Committee. A formal submission was accepted by the British government.

Late in the day, Greenpeace noticed the impending disposal. Opposition to this chosen deep-water disposal plan was expressed, based on the principle that industries, like individuals, should clear up and if possible recycle their rubbish, rather than simply discard it: the disposal of a used oil storage buoy was governed by the same code of behaviour as the disposal of a used car, refrigerator or tin can. Greenpeace chose to focus on Brent Spar because it believed that deep-water disposal of the structure would set a precedent and lead to the future littering of the seabed with the 400 other oil installations which are currently in use in the North Sea. This, they claimed, would threaten life in the seas and on the coasts of Northern Europe.

The Greenpeace campaign began on 30 April 1995, when climbers and activists boarded the Brent Spar from the Greenpeace vessel *Moby Dick*, amid gale-force winds and huge seas. This act of protest immediately attracted enormous media attention, an outcome actively sought by the campaign organizers. Shell UK turned immediately to legal means to try to end the campaign. The company obtained orders of the Court of Session in Edinburgh which required those on board the Brent Spar to leave and not to impede any future action necessary to implement the disposal plan for the installation. Shell UK was then granted a court order for the trespassers to be evicted; on 23 May the twenty-three protesters were removed from the Spar by Sheriff Officers and Grampian police. The company also stressed in press releases the scientific evidence it had compiled, suggesting that deep-water disposal would effect minimal environmental damage. However, having gained a high level of public awareness of the issue through the drama on the North Sea, Greenpeace continued its campaign, advertising in national newspapers, leafleting petrol stations in Germany, hanging a banner on the Brent Spar to highlight the issue for the start of the North Sea ministers' conference at Esbjerg, and displaying a 1.5 tonne model of the installation outside the conference. The strategy was to attract a high level of media attention and to encourage consumers across Europe to boycott Shell products.

Greenpeace did not initiate the campaign expecting Shell to reverse the decision to dump the Brent Spar. By 30 April, when Greenpeace activists first boarded the Spar, all the important decisions had already been taken by the authorities in the UK, and a reversal of these decisions would inevitably cost both Shell UK and the government a great deal in terms of both embarrassment and money. The aim was to use the Brent Spar as a symbol, to draw public attention to the abandonment plan, in an attempt to ensure that *in future* such littering of the seabed would be considered unacceptable.

However, the campaign was so effective that on 20 June Shell UK announced that it had decided to abandon deep-water disposal of the Spar. The company felt that its position had become 'untenable' as a result of the 'opposition of some European governments' – on 16 June Chancellor Helmut Kohl of Germany, under pressure from vociferous press and public protests, had asked the British Prime Minister to rescind the British government's approval of the sinking of the Spar. Shell also explained that the 'increased safety threat from actions on the Continent and Greenpeace activists interfering with the disposal operation'[12] had forced the reversal of its position. The announcement occurred as the Prime Minister, John Major, was reiterating in the House of Commons his government's support for the Shell decision to dump. Shell UK had effectively turned its back on the recommendations of the British government, which had stood by its original decision throughout the affair, despite considerable pressure from its European neighbours.

The scale of the public reaction to the campaign took even Greenpeace by surprise.[13] Why did this 'single issue' evoke so much public outrage? How did David defeat Goliath? Greenpeace is an organization with 1,200 employees, ships, helicopters, a couple of hot air balloons, an income of £89 million and (in this case) demonstrably inaccurate scientific data. Yet it defeated Shell, with its 106,000 employees, 100 supertankers, an annual turnover of £84 billion and the support of the elected British government. Certain aspects of an answer stand out as being especially important: loss of confidence in established institutions, including their relative evaluations of evidence; the ability of the issue to be projected beyond itself, to resonate with wider value judgements; and the hermeneutic double role of new means of communication in both facilitating and stimulating 'DIY culture' political mobilization, all leading to a cumulative effect of what might be described as 'protective democratic' action.[14]

LOSS OF CONFIDENCE IN ESTABLISHED INSTITUTIONS

Two of the key protagonists in the Brent Spar affair offer initial bearings to identify their position on their shared battlefield. Chris Rose of Greenpeace writes: 'There is now a widely observed loss of faith and confidence in Western countries in institutions and processes (political parties, trade unions, local authorities) which formerly enabled people to feel that they had social agency (influence).'[15] He stresses that what is important is to find new ways of working rather than new issues, because he is principally impressed by the limits on the effectiveness of the provision of 'proof'. Indeed, he suggests that since 1990 there has been a surplus of 'media' proof and a deficit of real change.[16] For him, the question of how to produce effective or timely action is paramount, which is hardly surprising.

John Wybrew, representing Shell UK, the owners of the redundant oil storage platform which was the focus of the dispute, shares one point in common with Rose, but then stands in sharp distinction.[17] 'The real debate – and it is a vital one – centres on the role of *emotive, single issue campaigning* in a democratic process and on how, within a democratically established framework of *reasoned discussion, painstaking evaluation, and thoughtful consultation* the best practical environmental solutions can truly be reached.'[18] What both agree on is that there has been a loss of faith in established institutions. In the box (provided by Shell UK and used in discussions within Shell about changing public

THEN	NOW
• trust-granted	• mistrust-institutionalized
• ownership	• stewardship
• freedom, within law	• 'licence to operate' *responsibly*
• economies of scale valued	• disaggregation and market test
• confidentiality respected	• transparency demanded
• government's problem	• industry's problem

Source: J. Wybrew, Shell UK.

perceptions of the industry) the nature of this transformation is schematized in a way with which many in the environmental movement would not disagree.[19]

While both sides agree that there has been a breakdown of trust, there still exists quite profound disagreement between industry and environmentalists over one of the central concerns of this chapter, namely *what forms of information and argument may legitimately be allowed to support the granting of a mandate to act?*

Industrialists have often attempted to marginalize criticism from environmentalists by representing such criticism as emotional and unreasoning. In the Brent Spar case, Shell UK employed this old-established discourse, contrasting the 'science' of the Shell case for disposal of the installation with the 'emotion' of the Greenpeace campaign. The 'reasoned discussion, painstaking evaluation and thoughtful consultation' was by implication contrasted with the 'emotionalism' of the Greenpeace case. 'Well-informed' and established industry was contrasted with the 'ill-informed' and, in this case, demonstrably (scientifically) wrong campaigning organization. Science was contrasted with fear; reason with emotion; dialogue with direct action; responsibility with power with power without responsibility. In the past, such tactics have been very successful.

In consequence, constructive discussions between industry and environmental campaigners have been rare: the opposing sides have based their respective arguments on quite different premises, making dialogue almost impossible. As a result, campaigning organizations have resorted to direct action as the best and most effective means of conveying their side of the argument.

Some are doubtful that a constructive partnership between industry and environmentalists can ever be built. In his robust attack on the world-view of the Greens, Richard North excoriates the abuse of science by environmental movements.[20] And, indeed, a dispute over scientific fact was an important feature of the battle over Brent Spar. But at the end of the day, the striking thing is that the general public does *not* appear to share North's opinion, or to conform to the Shell analysis of how to react to 'new democracy'. In fact, opinion polls repeatedly find that campaign groups are more trusted on environmental matters than government scientists or the media.[21]

This, of course, fits with the earlier and shared view that a fundamental breakdown of trust is occurring. In this there may be a legacy from the most powerful earlier example of the fracturing of trust in official reassurance which concerned the threat from nuclear accidents. The fall-out from the explosive fire at Chernobyl in 1986 included a shower of deeply corrosive scepticism in the minds of many aware and intelligent people who were usually politically passive, about official statements made by the National Radiological Protection Board and other official bodies. This scepticism has not been alleviated by subsequent revelations about radiation-related accidents – for example, information about an American nuclear bomber which caught fire at Greenham Common in 1958 and probably released radiation to the local environment, an accident denied until 1996. Earlier reassurances from government ministers of the safety of eating British beef have now given way to evidence that a variant of the fatal human Creuztfeldt-Jakob disease may be passed from cattle to humans. It cannot be demonstrated, but it seems inherently likely that it is as a cumulative consequence of such earlier episodes that public opinion seems little dented even when Greenpeace makes a mistake.

THE ABILITY OF AN ISSUE TO PROJECT BEYOND ITSELF

Not all direct action campaigns can capture the public imagination and provoke enough outrage to affect political decisions made within well-established bases of power. Greenpeace chose the Brent Spar exactly because it was seen to have the potential to project a message beyond itself. The Brent Spar 'was the perfect *symbol* of sea pollution', said Cindy Baxter of Greenpeace International. 'It was clear and simple, and we were confident it would capture the public's imagination.'[22] Shell chose to respond by attempting to draw its critics on to ground not of their own choosing. This ground was called 'science'.

When the chairman of Shell announced the decision to postpone the disposal, he stressed the enormous amount of independent scientific research that had gone into selecting the 'Best Practicable Environmental Option' for the disposal of the Brent Spar. Scientific opinion remains divided over the best way to dispose of the Spar – clearly one debate that the affair did not settle in Northern Europe was that between scientists over the environmental consequences of deep-sea dumping.[23] However, as it developed, scientific arguments were not the sole, nor even the main, basis for the campaign: 'Old newspapers, empty bottles, used drink cans.

You know exactly what to do with them. Shell also knows what should be done with its waste, but is opting for a different course of action. It is taking the easy way out: dumping it in the North Sea.'[24]

One aspect of Greenpeace's campaign did develop a scientific case (ultimately with little success, because due to technical operator mistakes in measuring the amount of residual sludge in the Spar, one of the figures on which Greenpeace based their 'science' attack was very inaccurate). But the organization refused to be drawn on to Shell's narrow definition of the terrain of science. It stressed that it objected to Shell's decision-making process because 'both scientific information and *value judgements* were hidden from wider scientific and public scrutiny.'[25] While Shell sought to pull the campaigners into a struggle for *specific* scientific proof of the best environmental option for disposal of the Spar, Greenpeace tried to place the emphasis of the campaign on the fundamental questions of Shell's responsibilities to society as a whole.

This is an important distinction. Opponents of this and similar campaigns consistently describe the debates as being over 'single issues': the sinking of a particular oil storage buoy, the building of a new motorway through prized countryside to reduce traffic through one particular town, the specific siting of a nuclear power plant, a toxic waste dump or a sewage outlet. The implication behind these 'single issue' accusations is that the protesters are selfish, monomaniac and politically naive, whereas central government (or the directors of a multinational company) can see the whole picture and weigh the environmental costs against the benefits of economic growth, employment for more people and international competitiveness. The protesters' aims are portrayed as unrealistic, utopian, out of touch with the realities of modern governance and the pressures of international business. Local opponents of environmentally damaging schemes are accused of demonstrating self-interested 'NIMBY' consciousness ('not in my back yard'): enjoying the comforts of modern living and economic growth, they are, however, selfishly unprepared to put up with the environmental sacrifices that necessarily come with them.

Environmental campaigners would describe the 'single issues' on which they concentrate as fulcra for a broader ethic of stewardship and environmental responsibility. Their aim is to find a concrete issue, capable of graphic representation, which can then be used to project beyond itself to illustrate a broader idea. In the case of Brent Spar, the public arguments in continental Europe, particularly in Germany, ranged far wider than the 'sludge content/radioactive waste/Best Practicable Environmental Option' discussion specific to the oil storage buoy in question. The publication by Greenpeace of the erroneous calculation, which severely dented the credibility of the purely scientific aspect of their campaign, was made five days before the Shell decision to abandon the dumping, yet it did not materially affect the public outcry, which was already enormous.[26] Clearly, scientific arguments were less important to the broader public than the *principle* of environmental responsibility, and the proposed dumping of the Brent Spar had become symbolic of the violation of that principle.

THE ROLE OF THE MEDIA AND OF INFORMATION

Visual images have been important in some of the most successful direct action campaigns: in the American civil rights movement, scenes of marching, confrontation and police violence broadcast on national television ensured that a badly funded, minority movement generated broad public support and substantial political impact. Now campaign groups have a broader range of media through which to publicize their causes, and a much wider national *and transnational* audience on whom to work. Many are clearly aware of the importance of shaping and projecting a set of images through the public broadcast media as an integral aspect of the generation of a mandate. Anti-roads protesters at Newbury (England) produced their own film footage and photographs, organized 'photo opportunities' that would make good television and portray the movement in a favourable light, and tried to emphasize in representations to the media the inclusive nature of the campaign, stressing business involvement and the support of the more conservative as well as the radical environmentalists. At a mass walk at Newbury, media celebrities (such as Johnny Morris, David Bellamy and Maggie Philbin) lent their public support to the cause, bringing important press coverage to campaign events. Johnny Morris, the far-from-radical eighty-year-old zoologist and children's television presenter, was at the centre of the press conference organized at the start of the march.

Greenpeace recognizes, perhaps more than any other group, the importance of generating favourable and exciting media coverage. The boarding of the Spar – a traditional protest action of political theatre – was presented in all its drama by the Greenpeace publicity machine. The organization used satellite transmission and advanced computer and telecommunications techniques to transmit live video footage and photographs from the dramatic North Sea operation to a media base in Frankfurt. From here, Greenpeace distributed high quality, edited footage of the drama to national and international television news channels. The Greenpeace product was simply broadcast by editors in their news programmes: when we saw Greenpeace helicopters dodging the fire hoses of the Brent Spar's escort tugs, we were looking through a Greenpeace director's lens. The Brent Spar thus quickly became a political issue that concerned public and politicians across Europe. Greenpeace consistently uses this tactic to draw public attention to its campaign issues: at a Greenpeace action in the South Pacific aimed at preventing

French nuclear testing, the alarming spectacle of French commandos breaking their way into the cockpit of the MV *Greenpeace*, with the sound of splintering wood and the screams of those inside, was filmed by a Greenpeace camera operator and then broadcast around the world from national and global television stations.

The development of communication media based on print played an important role in the emergence of new forms of public life, giving rise to the articulation of a new kind of 'public opinion' which was distinct from, and often critical of, the policies and doctrines of the state. Communication and public debate was no longer linked to the sharing of a common locale.[27] Now the wide availability of high-quality communication media has stretched this public sphere further. This has strengthened both the functions that the media perform – that of facilitating independent and uncontrolled communication, and that of creating the phenomenon of 'virtual' (and then suddenly, actual) DIY political communities, both within and beyond national borders.

With the increasing number of communications media – local, national and global television and radio stations, newspapers, magazines and the Internet – campaign groups can broadcast their message more cheaply, frequently and to a wider audience. Modern media are by their nature beyond state control, even in authoritarian states. With the push for ratings forcing editors to search hard for exciting news stories, campaign groups have a great incentive to direct their limited resources to the generation and broadcast of dramatic images rather than to the direct lobbying of governments. In the early 1980s, Russell Hardin noted that group politics was worthwhile because a relatively small effort was leveraged through government into a large effect.[28] Now, in contrast, lobbying effort is more likely to be focused on the media.

These movements depend critically on information to form, maintain and legitimate their mandate. In the Brent Spar affair, the success of the campaign to boycott Shell petrol demanded mass action – albeit at a brief, but strategic moment. The media, in reporting the issue and the campaign in action and detail, play a role crucial to initial mobilization: without media involvement too few people would know about the campaign for it to have any impact. The independent media provide the public with information about the issues and the activities of campaign groups, governments and industries in a way that public authorities simply cannot do. Without them, mass participation in democratic politics of any kind, including direct action campaigning, is hardly possible. But the media alone cannot determine whether people think 'terrorists' or 'heroes' when they see the footage of the action in the North Sea. Most recent research into the interpretation of mediated information has demonstrated its hermeneutic nature: the same information broadcast to different audiences provokes very different reactions. Individuals' opinions and conceptualizations of events are influenced by background knowledge and political context as well as by the immediate information they are receiving.[29] The boycott of Shell petrol in June 1995 was the result of many individuals' private decisions about whom to trust. Favourable broadcast media coverage is *necessary but not sufficient* to turn an issue such as Brent Spar into a campaign of transnational mass action.

Once people are sensitized, media can play another role in the modes of mobilization. Through the use of new communications media those who are participant in the protest are able to coordinate their activities. Here the role of narrow-cast media – fax machines, telephones, photocopying machines and e-mail – consolidates the transition from being informed to being active.

THE CUMULATIVE EFFECT OF WIDESPREAD DIRECT ACTION CAMPAIGNING

Most people will only participate in political actions if they think that through their participation they can make some real difference to the outcome. As direct action movements are seen to be successful, more people join, and other groups follow their example. Particular organizations such as Greenpeace and Amnesty International gain respect and credibility through success in action, and their influence carries them from one campaign to the next. Furthermore, the examples given by these groups prompt others to take direct action to draw attention to the issues that concern them most. Through better broadcast and narrowcast communications, both national and transnational, campaign groups learn about and are able to contact other similar groups, to share networks and strategies of resistance. People now feel empowered to confront the elected government through direct means because they have witnessed other groups gain favourable publicity and occasional success, both within their own national boundaries and elsewhere.

People are attracted to events which they perceive might be changing their own lives or the course of their history, in however small a way. All over the country, schools, colleges, parks and town halls exist as the legacy of previous generations' willingness to do good public acts locally; under current political arrangements it is harder for people to make their own decisions and participate directly at a local level. The excitement of the mass march or protest, combined with the widespread feeling of alienation from the established decision-making process, compel many people to attend these mass action events out of a desire for self-fulfilment and self-determination as well as out of principle.

According to Robert Goodin, this general sense of *the possibility* of involvement in decision-making and self-determination is an important component of 'green' political theory: not genuinely 'participatory democracy' in the now unworkable Athenian sense, but 'protective democracy'. It is an opt-out version: if you agree with X, do nothing; if you disagree with X, act.[30] This is clearly more than just a theory: increasingly the citizens of democratic states are exercising their right to withhold consent to specific aspects of government policy, and – whether they are granted 'legitimacy' or not – are effecting concrete changes in the practices of democratically elected governments. This leads us to consider directly the nature of the mandate that is constructed in this way, and to assess to what extent it answers the requirements for a legitimated cosmopolitan democracy.

THE NATURE OF THE MANDATE

The Brent Spar case illustrates the two problems which typically face those seeking action on transnational issues. It also provides an example of how 'DIY' politics seeks to overcome them and to construct a political campaign that is capable of attracting broad public support and generating action *in practice*, in the real world.

The first and central problem which issues such as the Brent Spar present to proponents of 'protective democracy' is the difficulty mentioned earlier of producing large constituencies in support of decisive action *before* there is incontrovertible evidence of damage. In this case, unusually, and in the ways described, this was done. A second problem then appeared, for the legitimacy of the constituency was challenged not only on 'science' grounds, given earlier, but also on the grounds that Shell had UK government approval and Greenpeace did not. In the end, the anti-dumping constituency did gain government backing through German Chancellor Helmut Kohl's intervention with British Prime Minister John Major. So in relation to the demand often found in the wider, disengaged public – a passive penumbra beyond the active constituency – that legitimacy must be externally endorsed by some elected power, both sides, Shell and Greenpeace, stood equal.

The mandate was legitimated in both cases by a modern form of Anglo-Saxon oath swearing. Both sought and attracted a range of endorsements from a variety of public figures and private individuals. This source of legitimation for the mandate of action by an organization like Shell or Greenpeace goes directly to the representation of power. It asks a question rather like Stalin's about the Pope ('How many regiments has the Pope?'). For, manifestly, the Pope's power does not come from regiments, nor does the power of Shell or of Greenpeace come from presenting the organization through formal and traditional and democratic processes at the ballot box.

Each claimant has an inner core and an outer casing. Shell's mandate is the explicit endorsement of the shareholder in the stock exchange (the inner core) and the implicit endorsement of the consumer in the market-place (the outer casing). The legitimacy of its influence over government policy is derived from the *public* goods that it helps to provide: economic growth and the creation of jobs.

Greenpeace's core mandate is the size of its membership list and the 'votes' and freedom of action which their membership subscriptions provide. Interest groups such as trade unions also enjoy some freedom of action provided by the combination of the efforts and resources of individuals whose interests converge. These are associations formed with the explicit purpose of defending and furthering the interests of particular groups, often to the detriment of other groups. This criticism is hardly applicable to Greenpeace: organizations which include a wide variety of social and economic groups within their memberships have little incentive to pursue policies which systematically favour particular interests and exclude or damage others.

The outer casing of the Greenpeace mandate is provided by what one might call the 'Tinkerbell effect'.[31] The participation of thousands of individual motorists, who received no personal recognition for their decision to boycott, and who would gain nothing directly from the reversal of Shell's decision to dump the Brent Spar, gave Greenpeace a kind of legitimacy. This was derived from the impression that the principles behind the protest – the defence of the *public* good of a clean environment – were supported by a significant proportion of the general public, not just in one country but across Europe. This broadly based defence of the transnational public good was contrasted by the protesters and their supporters with the apparent motives of Shell and the British government, both of whom, it was claimed, were prepared to disregard the good of all to further their own economic interests. The legitimation of protesters such as we studied comes from performance in generating the broad and diverse mandate detailed above, and is reinforced by success in performance. This stands in strong contrast to the *a priori* legitimation of other bodies.

Each party obtained the backing of elected representatives in very different ways. Shell were 'insiders' and worked by familiar means, through government departments, ministers and committees, riding the forces of bureaucratic momentum and exploiting their considerable economic influence. The working assumption between the partners in such relationships is that industry and officialdom inhabit the same established political domain; therefore trust is granted. The presumption is that permission will be granted unless good reason can be shown – in the terms established in this political domain – not to do so.

The protesters do not have such a relationship. Outside this established political domain, they face a double task. The burden of proof is set against them, so they have either to climb into the domain established by government and industry, and defeat the proponents in these terms, or to marshal irresistible force outside.[32] In the Brent Spar case, Greenpeace tried to do both. Its success in mounting a scientific challenge was inconclusive. Its success in exerting economic pressure on Shell and political pressure on Chancellor Kohl (and consequently on Prime Minister Major) was decisive.

In the final section we return to the questions about the nature of consent and democratic legitimacy with which we began, to consider what lessons this study has to teach us there.

LESSONS FOR THE ACHIEVEMENT OF
COSMOPOLITAN DEMOCRACY

The case study shows that within the group of committed activists, active support of dissent is clearly given and there is a manifest belief in the legitimacy of the mandate. The accounts of the Brent Spar occupiers show individuals who justify their actions and the discomfort to which they put themselves in terms of a higher purpose. The Brent Spar activists faced considerable personal danger, not in the expectation of turning back the oil platform, but in order to make a point about humanity's relationship to the natural world. The antecedents for such symbolic acts are old. Beside anti-road protesters in the treetops stands St Simon Stylites on top of his pillar in the desert. Next to the Brent Spar occupiers are George Fox and the early Quakers witnessing Truth against Power. The activists feel mandated in two ways: both by being sensitized to the interactions and synergisms which make disposal of an oil installation emblematic of and part of the wider agenda; and secondly by the presence of an aura of public acclaim. The first sort of affirmation is grounded in a belief that the case is supported by two types of information deriving respectively from an ethic of global responsibility and from a worst case analysis of contemporary environmental science. The second is the 'Tinkerbell effect'.

Active support of dissent stands in contrast to the other extreme, which is one of rejection of the bases of a legitimacy grounded in this way. That was most explicitly clear in Shell's response to the irresistible pressure exerted by a combination of activist catalysts, consumer boycott and government disapproval in key countries (notably Germany). The response, as exemplified by the Shell UK chairman's strained television interview on the night of the reversal of Shell's decision over Brent Spar, was simultaneously to reiterate rejection of both the knowledge-based credibility of the protesters' case and their claim to any form of legitimate democratic mandate, and to accept that give their ability to make trouble they had to be engaged and to propose a strategy to deflect them on the basis of that view. That strategy of discussion with 'stakeholders' was elaborated by John Wybrew and in the Shell advertisements in the German press. However, yielding to *force majeure* must not be confused with anything else.

Towards the camp of those who reject dissent stand those who are apathetic but inclined to believe that those in power have both a right to act for the general good, and a self-interest in doing so. Chancellor Kohl's intervention was particularly important in reconciling this group to the change in policy on dumping. Towards the boundary with active support of dissent stand those who are equally personally disengaged, but whose view of the world is informed by a general unease – by a sense that all is not well, that all that should be told is not told – and whose consciences are pricked by a sense of wider obligation beyond the inward-looking core of the individual and family.

Some of the most interesting findings from research on the subject relate to the mobilization of people in this middle category (Bavarian motorists and the like). What divides them is their willingness to trust established authority and received information. The cases show that increasing mistrust of established institutions has tended to enlarge that part of the middle category prepared to grant assent to the dissenters.

The Brent Spar affair is an example of the cross-boundary and cross-linked issues described in the introduction to this chapter. The media can now ensure that a transnational audience becomes aware of such issues. This case was a source of concern for a body of people significant enough to sway the decisions of elected national governments (in this case, notably the British and the German, although other European governments under public pressure also voiced protests). In the absence of effective transnational institutions, protesters chose to make their case through direct action campaigning. These means, while unconventional, are no less democratic than the means by which Shell exerts influence on government – 'democratic' politics is often still largely a game of resources and their effective employment. The lesson for cosmopolitan democracy is of the way in which, in the absence of suitable established political structures, DIY politicians set about erecting a rough and ready substitute structure.

Was the influence that Greenpeace exerted over the British government and Shell UK illegitimate? A broadly based mandate – an imperfect kind of democratic legitimacy – emerged *as a consequence* of the success of the core in mobilizing a wider constituency: the 'Tinkerbell effect'. Greenpeace's success came from the expert application of leverage, largely operated through the international mass media. This leverage gave the transnational 'constituency' a *choice* about whom to believe: accusations levelled against protesters of manipulation of 'public opinion' through media representation must be balanced by a recognition that respect and trust of governmental or industrial authority has been deeply ingrained in people's consciousness and cannot easily be erased.

The Brent Spar affair demonstrates the potential of a spontaneous transnational democratic forum to focus political energy and thereby to enable people to consider themselves effective agents in the process of policy formation. Can this political energy be channelled into what citizens can trust as *responsive* and *responsible* transnational democratic institutions? We must assess the shortcomings of existing democratic institutions – both national and transnational – and recognize that such manifestations of DIY politics might be a valid and necessary attempt to increase the *degree* of democracy in states where theoretically it already exists as a form of government.

Before transnational democratic institutions can be built, it is crucial to establish why growing numbers of the citizens of democracies are turning away from conventional democratic politics and using more direct means to exert their influence over national and transnational affairs. While in some areas government and industry operate comfortably together without interference from 'outside', the tacit assumption that industry or government is acting responsibly is being slowly eroded by a sense of mistrust, a loss of faith in established institutions, which puts an increased burden on these previously accepted authorities to demonstrate that their position is well founded.

We have suggested that without more empirical evidence and more grass-roots research it is not likely that we can advance our understanding much further. Where to look? Examples proliferate. J. Vidal writes:

The European consumer boycotts of Shell following its decision to dump the Brent Spar and of French goods following President Chirac's Pacific intransigency mark a rejection of business and establishment *values* as much as any direct protest against environmental damage; the felling of a tree in East London to make way for an urban motorway was easily interpreted by locals as the remote state bulldozing aside the community; when a native American can visit South Wales miners and be applauded for calling them 'indigenous peoples', and 'tribes' of homeless motorway protesters identify with Zapatistas in Mexico, then something is happening.[33]

In this chapter we have attempted to begin to discover what, how, and with what implications.

NOTES

We wish to acknowledge particular debts to Daniele Archibugi and Martin Köhler for constructive criticism of Gwyn Prins's Rome paper, from which sprang important aspects of the present project, to staff of Greenpeace and Shell UK for interviews and assistance with access to materials on Brent Spar, to George Monbiot for permitting Elizabeth Sellwood access to his cuttings collection, to Alison Suter and Chris Williams for help and criticism on the various drafts of this paper and to David Held for practical help in facilitating the project.

Epigraph from J. S. Mill, *Principles of Political Economy: With Some of their Applications to Social Philosophy* (London: Routledge and Kegan Paul, 1965).

1   U. Beck, 'Global risk society and global sub-politics: the Shell case', lecture given at Cambridge University, Mar. 1996.
2   See J. Leggett (ed.), *Climate Change and the Financial Sector* (Munich: Gerling Akademie Verlag, 1996).
3   Will Hutton, 'It is broke, and it needs fixing', *Observer*, 30 June 1996.
4   R. Dworkin, *Taking Rights Seriously* (London: Duckworth, 1977).
5   J. Madison, Federalist Paper 10, in *The Federalist* (New York: G. P. Putnam, 1907), pp. 51–60.
6   J. Cohen and J. Rogers, *Associations and Democracy*, vol. 1 of the series The Real Utopians Project ed. E. Olin Wright (London and New York: Verso, 1995), pp. 11–33.
7   D. Held, *Democracy and the Global Order* (Cambridge: Polity Press, 1995), p. 156, emphasis added.
8   Ibid.
9   Ibid., p. 18.
10   See A. Linklater, chapter 6 above.
11   Held, *Democracy and the Global Order*, p. 286.
12   Shell press release, 20 June 1995.
13   U. Jurgens, who coordinated the campaign from the Shetlands, said, 'I thought it would be our biggest action this summer, but not *that* big,' see *The Guardian*, 21 June 1995, p. 4.
14   This expression was used by C. B. Macpherson, *The Life and Times of Liberal Democracy* (Oxford: Oxford University Press, 1977).
15   Chris Rose (Programme Director, Greenpeace UK), 'Beyond the struggle for proof: factors changing the environmental movement', *Environmental Values*, 2.4 (1993), p. 29.
16   Ibid.
17   G. Prins and E. Sellwood, interview with John Wybrew at Shellmex House, London, 6 Feb. 1996.
18   John Wybrew (Director of Public Affairs and Planning, Shell UK), 'Brent Spar – a "public relations disaster"?', *Journal of the UK Institute of Public Relations*, 14.2 (1996), p. 2.
19   Neither would two social theorists: Ulrich Beck and Anthony Giddens in their complementary work on the transformation of risk in modern society offer schematic frameworks which harmonize well with the Shell UK *Weltanschauung*, see U. Beck, *Risk Society: Towards a New Modernity* (1986; London: Sage, 1992) and A. Giddens, *The Consequences of Modernity* (Cambridge: Polity Press, 1990).
20   'Greenpeace's scientists are not challenged because the most distinct and powerful of Greenpeace's remarks are made on the hoof to the media and are matters of policy and opinion rather than pin-pointed risk-assessment or strict science. The scientific specialists in the field seem to think that there is not much point in trying to engage Greenpeace in an ordinarily scientific conversation because that is not what Greenpeace is about': see R. North,

Life on a Modern Planet: a Manifesto for Change (Manchester: Manchester University Press, 1995), p. 109.

21   R. M. Worcester, 'Public and elite attitudes to environmental issues', *International Journal of Public Opinion Research*, 5.4 (1993).

22   'Brent Spar climbdown', *The Guardian*, 22 June 1995, p. 5, emphasis added.

23   An article by Ewan Nisbet and C. M. R. Fowler, 'Is metal disposal toxic to deep oceans?', *Nature*, no. 375 (June 1995) and an 'Opinion' article in the same issue argued that dumping the Brent Spar in the sea was the best environmental option, because 'the environmental effect on deep-sea life of dumping the Brent Spar would be minimal or even beneficial.' These remarks elicited extensive correspondence in subsequent issues of the journal from scientific establishments and universities (including the departments of Earth Sciences at Cambridge, of Oceanography and Geology at Southampton and of Biochemistry at University College London), both attacking and defending this and Greenpeace's opposite contention. The Scottish Association for Marine Science agreed with Greenpeace that Shell's research was incomplete; the National Environment Research Council agreed with Shell that deep-water disposal would be best.

24   Greenpeace advertisement, *Financial Times*, 1 June 1995.

25   Greenpeace publicity leaflet, Aug. 1995, emphasis added.

26   In Britain, where throughout the campaign the scientific debate had been more prominent than the ideological one, the public outcry and the boycott of Shell petrol was not so effective as in continental Europe. Shell Germany lost up to 70 per cent of its trade at some stations, and overall sales fell by 20–30 per cent. Douglas Parr of Greenpeace UK reflected afterwards that the UK wing of the organization should have stuck to its original argument – that it is wrong to dump toxic rubbish in the sea – rather than being dragged by Shell experts into the scientific struggle for proof (interview with Elizabeth Sellwood, 30 Jan. 1996).

27   See P. Burke, *Popular Culture in Early Modern Europe* (New York: New York University Press, 1978), ch. 9.

28   R. Hardin, *Collective Action* (Baltimore and London: Johns Hopkins University Press, 1982).

29   See for example A. Crigler and K. Bruhn Jensen, 'Discourses on politics: talking about public issues in the United States and Denmark', in P. Dahlgren and C. Sparks (eds), *Communication and Citizenship: Journalism and the Public Sphere in the New Media Age* (London: Routledge, 1991).

30   Robert E. Goodin, *Green Political Theory* (Cambridge: Polity Press, 1992), p. 127.

31   When Peter Pan's fairy friend Tinkerbell lies poisoned by the evil Captain Hook, the only way that she can be restored is by Peter Pan appealing to all the children in the world who believe in fairies to clap. When the faint sound of much clapping is heard, Tinkerbell is restored to life. J. M. Barrie, *Peter Pan* (London, 1928).

32   As President Richard Nixon's White House aide Chuck Colson once immortally observed, 'When you have them by the balls, their hearts and minds soon follow.'

33   J. Vidal, 'Localism versus globalism', *Guardian*, 15 Nov. 1995, pp. 4–5.

13

Refugees: a Special Case for Cosmopolitan Citizenship?

Pierre Hassner

In an oft-quoted passage, Hannah Arendt has called statelessness 'the newest mass phenomenon in contemporary history', and stateless persons 'the most symptomatic group in contemporary politics'.[1] By the same token, the refugee could be said to embody, more than anyone else, the problems of cosmopolitan citizenship and of transnational democracy.

What makes these twin notions so promising is that each of them indicates a tension which is at the heart of the contradictions in today's world. Can citizenship be truly cosmopolitan, or is it necessarily linked to a particular community, whose citizens have rights and duties which distinguish them from those of non-citizens? Can democracy be separated from the nation-state, or is it related at least to a political community which, to the extent, precisely, that it is political, cannot avoid an exclusionary dimension? Yet we are all aware that in our time the individual and the planet, the universality of human rights and the solidarity of mankind have acquired a more immediate and more visible relevance, that the status of all intermediary collective identities and organizations, from class to nation, from state to international institutions, is more open to challenge and to debate.

No situation is more illustrative of these contradictions and uncertainties than that of the refugee. If the world were ruled by a single authority, there would be no refugees; nobody would have, nor indeed would be able, to go into exile. Conversely, if the world were made of nation-states which were perfectly integrated either through force, making it impossible to flee, or through consent or satisfaction – making emigration possible if it was wanted but less desirable or at least less necessary – there would also be no refugees. What creates them is the fact that on the one hand nation-states are divided from within, by tensions, persecutions and exclusions, and that on the other hand they are not hermetically closed to the outside world, that immigration, whether legal or clandestine, frequent or rare, is nevertheless possible, and that transnational links – whether ethnic, religious, ideological, professional or humanitarian – are binding individuals or groups to their respective counterparts beyond borders. The refugee phenomenon is based on the double nature – interstate and transnational – of the world system.

But it would not raise a real theoretical or practical problem if all refugees could find a refuge or, conversely, if they were all sent back to their home countries. A Holy Alliance of tyrannical states based on mutual extradition would bring us back to world tyranny. Conversely, a bipolar situation where refugees from one side were greeted as heroes or allies, as honorary citizens or as natural members of the opposite camp would also be manageable. The Cold War came close to that situation. The real problem which turns the refugees into the witnesses and victims of the international system and its contradictions is the more and more frequent case of 'refugees without refuge', or of 'refugees in orbit', wandering on the roads or as clandestine passengers of trains and boats and planes, sent back and forth from one airport or provisional camp to another without any state accepting them physically or, even less, as full citizens.

It is precisely because they are citizens of nowhere that they are potential citizens of the world. It is to the extent that nobody can deprive them of their rights as men and women but that no community is ready to guarantee them these rights, let alone to enable them to exercise the responsibilities of citizens, that the question is raised whether citizenship can be based on universal rights alone and, conversely, whether a community based on political citizenship alone, without any particularistic identity, is possible.

We shall return to these ultimate questions. But first we must show the deadlocks and the contradictions which the recent crisis has revealed in the international refugee regime itself, in the current theories of the nation, of transnational trends and of international relations, and finally in the attempt at creating a European Union, a new world order, and a conception of citizenship which should be compatible with both.

A SHATTERED REGIME

The spokespeople of the United Nations High Commissariat of Refugees (UNHCR) have been second to none in describing their disarray in the face of the worsening of the problem after the end of the Cold War, and their powerlessness in the face of its change as compared to the conditions at the time when their institutional system was created. 'We can't cope,' said Sylvana Foa, spokeswoman for the refugee agency. 'We used to be a bunch of lawyers working on protection. Our function was legalistic. Now it's emergency response.'[2] The problem, obviously, does not lie just in the transition from 2.4 million refugees in 1974 to 10.5 in 1984 and 23 million in 1994, or in the acceleration of the rush carried to an extreme in the case of Rwanda. It lies in the very definition of the refugees which the international regime is supposed to protect, in the powers of the international organization which is supposed to manage it and of the states which are supposed both to finance and to implement it. The central problem is that the regime is collapsing under the opposing pressures of the avalanche on the ground, which breaks apart the conceptual distinctions the regime was based on, and of the increasingly restrictive attitude of the host countries, which are less and less ready to accept the constraints of common rules. Between a demand which is becoming more and more abundant and global and an offer which is becoming more and more restricted and reluctant, the specialized organizations can only try to limit the damage by running – inevitably, since they are financed only from project to project – from one catastrophic emergency to another.

The most paradoxical result of this situation is that every humanitarian organization wants to broaden the definition of refugees, while every host country government wants to narrow it. The definition adopted by the Geneva Convention of 1951 on the Status of Refugees, which has been in force since 1954, is the following:

A refugee is one who, owing to a well-founded fear of being persecuted for reasons of race, religion, nationality, membership of a particular social group or political opinion, is outside the country of his nationality, and is unable, or owing to such fear is unwilling to avail himself of the protection of that country.[3]

It has been interpreted as being based on four distinctions, which were as many restrictions: (1) between victims of man-made and of natural catastrophes; (2) between persons displaced outside or within their country; (3) between political refugees, victims of persecutions, and economic refugees who try to escape poverty or unemployment; (4) between victims of individual persecutions and of collective ones. Within each of these pairs, only the first category could be accepted. But these distinctions are more and more obviously untenable both from a practical and a moral point of view.

How can one stick to the first distinction in the case of famines produced by civil wars, as in Somalia, or used by governments in order to starve or chase away part of their population, as in Ethiopia or in Sudan? How can one apply the second in the case of civil wars where the stakes, as indicated by the notion of ethnic cleansing, consist precisely in deciding who will or will not belong to the same country? What is the status of those who take refuge in safe havens or security zones in Kurdistan, Bosnia or Rwanda?

In the case of the third, how can one defend a strict distinction between political and economic refugees when governments themselves vary their implementation of asylum rights along with their immigration policies, which are themselves heavily and legitimately influenced by economic conditions? Of course in a case like that of Germany, which remains exceptionally reluctant to see itself as an immigration country and was until recently exceptionally open in its asylum policy, a great proportion of asylum-seekers were simply would-be immigrants, in search of a job. But how can one justify the position of the United States, which until recently was automatically considering Cuban refugees as political and Haitian ones as economic, while denouncing the oppressive character of the Haitian regime and worsening its economic situation through an embargo which was prompted, precisely, by its political nature?

Finally concerning the fourth distinction, which is arguably contrary to the letter of the Geneva convention itself but has increasingly been applied by governments, what about populations, belonging or not to minorities, who are persecuted for racial, ethnic or just national reasons? Can, must or should a member of the Albanian community in Kosovo, a Tutsi who has narrowly escaped genocide, or a Hutu exposed to Tutsi vengeance prove the danger he or she is running individually? The answer to these questions is never quite obvious, witness the changing and contradictory verdicts, within the same country, of German courts on the refugees from Kosovo.

In general one can see that the plight of refugees from war and civil war and the necessity of offering them a temporary asylum or a protected zone are more and more impossible to ignore, even by the most reluctant governments, but that all, even the most open ones, insist on not tying their hands by a general or constraining regime. Hence the voluntary maintenance of a legal vacuum which allows governments to adapt their behaviour to their political and economic sympathies, interests or fears – for instance the French government, while denying refugee status both to Bosnians and Algerians, is even less hospitable towards the latter than the former (although, under Prime Minister Jospin, it has corrected some of its harshest policies) – and, individually or collectively, to shift the burden to their neighbours, especially the so-called 'first safe countries', that is, the first country entered by a refugee where he or she is supposed to be free from persecution.

The other side of this maximum freedom of action for governments is a maximum of precariousness for the individuals concerned, who are subject to a tolerance which is always provisional and liable to be cancelled. Various formulas have been used by different governments to this effect: in France refugees from Bosnia are granted residence for three months at a time; the Dutch government has put into practice a so-called 'B status', also characterized by its precariousness – these are two versions among many of what has been called 'territorial' or 'black market' asylum whereby governments are prefering to encourage an illegal situation which they feel better able to control than a juridical one. The UNHCR and even the European Commission are trying in vain to promote a status of war or civil war refugees or of temporary but guaranteed asylum. By contrast, European governments have not only come up with a series of measures which have effectively discouraged applications, but have bribed neighbouring and fragile countries, or in some cases the countries of origin, into accepting refugees they did not want.

In more recent moves, the same governments have added to the four restrictive conditions of the Geneva Convention a fifth exclusion: that of being persecuted by a state,[4] thereby making victims of Algerian fundamentalists or of Serbian militias ineligible. The protests of international organizations, above all of the High Commissariat for Refugees, serve only to underline the extent to which they are excluded from a decision process which takes place essentially at the intergovernmental level and in an atmosphere of secrecy, that is, in exactly the opposite conditions to those one could have expected from the institutionalization of an international regime for refugees. While, on the ground, the role of international and non-governmental forces has grown enormously, the opposite happens as far as admission and exclusion are concerned: there, the role of states, and in particular of governments, is more and more decisive, not to say exclusive.

THEORIES IN A QUANDARY

Does this not raise some interesting and troubling problems for the current debates about the nature and the evolution of international relations? Two discussions seem relevant here: first an ideological and moral one about the respective importance of principles and interests, of solidarity and egoism; and second a historical and structural one about the trend towards the unity of the planet through interdependence or its growing division between centre and periphery, between North and South or between 'the West and the rest'.

The most immediate observation seems to show that the universalistic principles based on the rights of man which gave rise to an impressive set of institutional measures after the Second World War ceased to carry much weight once they no longer served Western strategic interests in the framework of East–West rivalry, and, above all, in the face of fears that the number of refugees and their cultural features might threaten the economic and social stability of host countries or their 'societal security'.[5] However, one should not forget that the efforts of organized solidarity – including those concerning the acceptance and protection of refugees – in spite of their tragic inadequacy, go a long way beyond anything practised before. But today states and silent majorities tend to lean towards retrenchment; solidarity is represented, rather, by active minorities, acting through non-governmental organizations and sometimes backed by broader opinion movements mobilized by the new perception of 'distant suffering', thanks to television.

Yet this notion too must be qualified because of the new character of 'state humanitarianism' – to use a term which originates in the French discussion around the initiatives of former Minister for Humanitarian Action, Bernard Kouchner[6] – which is for the first time an element of international politics and presents itself as a temporary substitute, an advanced detachment for an international community which is supposed to do the real job. And it is this international community which is desperately absent when what is needed is to replace isolated initiatives with permanent structures, particularly as far as asylum is concerned.

There is room for another dialectical reversal, however. Immigration movements, particularly when they are a result of forced emigration, may well be, along with transnational mafias and financial institutions, the last obstacle to the structural fragmentation of the international system, the last link between two worlds about to separate.

Among the various prophecies about international evolution, more than Fukuyama's 'end of history' or Huntington's 'clash of civilizations', those which seem most to accord with present trends are those of Jean-Christophe Rufin[7] or of Max Singer and Aaron Wildavsky.[8] For them, there is an increasing contrast between the developed part of the world, where war seems to have been made obsolete by interdependence and democracy, and the periphery, which is plagued by ethnic and religious, national and social strife, by poverty, revolution and war. The first world more and more sees the second either as a threat or as a Pandora's box of insoluble problems, for whom nothing much positive can be done but from which one should above all be isolated, so as not to sink into its quicksands or be contaminated by its illnesses.

But are this isolation and this quarantine possible? Yes, to some extent, as shown by the effectiveness with which Western Europe has managed to close its doors to asylum seekers. Are they viable in the long run? Yes again, economically, for in this respect it seems that, on balance, the developed world may well do without its periphery. But on the one hand the circuits of arms dealing, of drugs, of nuclear materials controlled by national, subnational and transnational mafias challenge the borders between the two worlds just as much as those between states; on the other hand, the more poverty and conflicts are raging in the periphery, the more their victims tend to flock towards the centre. The latter can repel them only within certain limits, including material ones; while it can only admit them by riding a wave of xenophobia and security anxiety which endangers social peace, the rule of law and democracy, in other words, precisely the good features it would like to preserve at home.

For better or worse, the two worlds are linked by a social and cultural interpenetration which does look irreversible, short of a generalized ethnic cleansing. The role of diasporas – which go from boat people and suffering refugees to effective lobbyists in their host countries for or against their native lands – is an illustration of the many roads transnationalism can travel.

The real problem, from a theoretical point of view, is that of the nature of the actors on the world scene and of the relations between them. One can distinguish two great simplifying approaches, that is, the classical interstate one and the modern transnational one, and two attempts at overcoming their opposition – through concepts like 'the global community' or the 'world system' – or at finding a compromise – through concepts like 'international society' or 'regimes'. All of them seem embarrassed by the refugee problem and its increasingly unmanageable dimensions.

Realist theory has no difficulty in explaining the behaviour of states where refugees are concerned, with states' preference for interests over principles, and for special short-term interests over collective long-term ones. For instance, a realist stance would have predicted that a common immigration policy would consist in common exclusion rather than in burden-sharing. But the problem is that apart from the logic of competition, of alliances and of equilibrium among states, it does not explain much else. It does not have much to say on their internal divisions and their transnational ties, or on anything having to do with societies. But that is precisely the dimension which is most relevant to the problem of refugees. Realist theory postulates an arrangement of nation-states, and it feels more and more comfortable the closer one gets to the 'billiard balls model', involving maximum unity within and maximum separation between the various actors. But, as we have seen, refugees exist precisely because of heterogeneity and conflict within countries and of special ethnic, ideological or simply geographic ties between certain groups and other countries. To put it another way, realist theory emphasizes domestic stability and interprets change primarily in terms of diplomatic flexibility or military conquest. It is relatively silent in the face of revolutions or the disintegration of empires and the birth of new units. But these are just the phenomena which are the most liable to produce refugees.

It is hardly surprising, then, that refugees should have been cited as an important argument in favour of the opposite school, that of trans-nationalism. In their preface to Leon Gordenker's book, *Refugees in International Politics*, Thomas G. Weiss and David Pitt write: 'With the possible exception of trade, refugees provide perhaps the best illustration that the behaviour and narrow self-interest calculations of sovereign nation-states have been significantly influenced by transnational forces.'[9] Conversely, Bertrand Badie sees in migrations an essential element of the crisis of the state and of citizenship through 'the extreme atomization of migration choices' which illustrates the 'individualization of the world' and its deterritorialization.[10]

One may wonder, however, whether these remarks are not valid essentially for migratory movements other than those of refugees, and whether the latter do not precisely expose their limits. When the 'pull' effect is more important than the 'push' one, when emigrants are at-tracted by the hope of a better life or by 'city lights', one certainly can disaggregate their movements into individual strategies which are unpre-dictable because they are so decentralized. But for the masses who are fleeing genocide, or civil war, or famine, is it very enlightening to point out that each individual within them is following a survival strategy which can be described in terms of rational choice? If there is a rational strategy, does it not belong to those who have the power – more often than not state power – to expel or to reject, rather than to those who are thrown back and forth like ping-pong balls?

The present fate of refugees could thus be seen as a terrifying regres-sion concerning the individual freedom of choosing one's residence, hence of living in a place or leaving it, or settling in another, and as a no less terrifying reaffirmation of territory, nation or state, in sum of all the realities which the transnational turn of the world had relativized. It is precisely those who are most deprived of them – the stateless, the 'refu-gees in orbit', those who, by lack of a community, are deprived of what Hannah Arendt calls 'the right to have rights'[11] – who would bear witness to the persistence and the importance of those realities. The nation has lost its coherence, the state its authority, their territory is both frag-mented and penetrable, and yet, as Gil Loescher points out, 'refugees are usually created as the direct result of political decisions taken by sover-eign states, with consequences that extend beyond national borders' and 'national states remain the decisive actors in refugee affairs.'[12] As the French geographer Marie-Françoise Durand put it, 'migration does not deterritorialize but it sharpens the tensions between territoriality and its opposite.'[13]

One could say as much for the relations between the interstate and the transnational dimensions, or more generally, between power and legitimacy; increasingly legitimacy, at least according to the Western consensus, is on the side of the individual and the universal, but more often than not, power is in the hands of particular state or non-state, military or financial, religious or ethnic collective forces.

This is the tension, both theoretical and practical, encountered by all those who are trying to understand or organize international relations today. Clearly the refugee problem, like that of genocide, or of the environment, or of nuclear proliferation, can be seriously handled only by going beyond the monopoly of states towards a more universal perspective, such as that of human rights, or a more global one, such as that of the collective interests of the planet. The question is whether this point of view remains, as Hegel would have said, 'in the dimension of the ought', or whether the real evolution, particularly through economic interdependence, global communication and transnational flows is beginning to delineate an effective synthesis of the global and the local, the universal and the particular.

Marie-Françoise Durand wonders whether migrations are not accelerating the genesis of a 'world society'. Analytically one can only follow her when she calls for an 'articulation of territories and networks more than an opposition between a world of states and a world of flows'.[14] But one cannot help injecting a note of scepticism even about her tentative optimism.

First, while the migratory situations of communities constituted by developed liberal societies which are economically, politically and culturally close to each other support the diagnosis of 'more movements, and more fluidity, but fewer reasons to migrate', the situation of the refugees forced to flee the catastrophes of the periphery and rejected by the centre or parked in camps is exactly the opposite: more reasons to migrate but less movement and fluidity.

In these cases, and more generally, while society is global, communities are particular. The contradiction between a modern society which is universal in principle through economics, technology, communications, etc., and a politics which is fragmented in the dimension of power as well as of solidarities is more present than ever. The notion of the 'international community' so often used in official speeches, as well as that of 'the new world order', which today is discredited at least in its promise of peace and justice, relies on the highly debatable equation between world society, international organization, the United Nations, the Security Council, and the permanent members of the latter.

Of course, in the gaps of interstate relations, there does exist a growing presence of the universal dimension. I tried to indicate it elsewhere through the slogan 'Conscience, experts, concert',[15] by which I meant, first, the beginnings of a feeling of planetary solidarity within public opinion confronted with crimes and catastrophes; secondly the existence of impartial organisms endowed with some technical or moral authority, whose opinions are not necessarily followed by states but cannot be totally ignored by them; and finally the convergence, by no means automatic or permanent, between the interests and policies of great powers in some circumstances – like the Gulf War – on certain issues – like nuclear non-proliferation. But the last word, when it comes to butter or guns, to financial resources or to the use of force, belongs either to states or to actors who are even less respectful of universal imperatives.

It is tempting, then, to settle for the compromise represented by the English theory of 'international society' or by the American theory of 'regimes'. They strive to overcome the opposition between the unique emphasis on power rivalries characteristic of realist theory and the revolutionary hope for a world political authority characteristic of idealistic or universalistic theories; hence they insist on the possibility for states to organize anarchy, that is, to cooperate without a superior authority or an external arbiter on the basis of converging interests and of common or reciprocal values, rules, practices and institutions.

We have seen that such a regime has been progressively instituted, since the interwar period, for the international management of the refugee problem. But we have also seen that this regime has been jeopardized by the proliferation of demands, by the inadequacy of resources, and above all by the tendency of states, in times of crisis, to increasingly put their immediate interest and their freedom of action ahead of common rules. But this is precisely the more general weakness of solutions like 'international society' or functional regimes. They tend to be fair-weather arrangements which function satisfactorily in normal times but collapse or get stuck in times of crisis when every state follows its own priorities and emergencies and considers cooperation as a desirable but unaffordable luxury. The effort of organizations whose function it is to propose a common line of action is either rejected or used as an alibi for not acting. Institutions based on intergovernmental cooperation risk, in times of crisis, oscillating between paralysis and anarchy. At any rate, a minimum agreement will be more easily reached for a defensive and conservative position than for innovative and positive initiatives. And this is illustrated by the refugee problem better than by any other, including even that of peacekeeping.

THE CONTRADICTIONS OF POLITICAL PROJECTS

More important and more obvious still than the crisis of international relations theories is that of the political projects which, after two world wars and two totalitarianisms, have tried to avoid a return to the same old logic of military and economic power relations between states. The first, of course, is the United Nations, which has briefly inspired renewed hopes in the aftermath of the Cold War. The other is European integration, probably more realistic and more irreversible, as it is based on a more homogeneous and more inextricably interdependent region. The crisis is linked to the relations of the central states with the institutions of the organizations they have created, to their own mutual relations, and last but not least, to their relations with their periphery, inside and outside these organizations.

In the case of the treatment of refugees by the United Nations, we have already mentioned the outstanding work and the increasing plight of the United Nations High Commission for Refugees. Suffice it to add that currently one of its main activities is to protest against the decisions of its member states, whether in terms of the new requirement of persecution by a state or in terms of forced repatriation, for instance in the case of the German decision about refugees from Bosnia. A recent publication of the UNHCR itself raised the question of whether states were in the business of protecting refugees or of protecting themselves against refugees.[16]

Many non-governmental organizations, national or international, aimed specifically at refugees or more generally at immigrants, try to fill the gaps created by the negative stance of governments. They are among the first signs of the tentative beginnings of a cosmopolitan society or of a transnational solidarity which would be the positive counterpart of the networks created by forced migrations or by transnational crime. Yet they, too, have to resort to immediate humanitarian relief or to lobbying public opinions and governments.

Perhaps, then, the most promising level, halfway between the international community and the nation-state, would be the regional one, and more particularly that of the European Union. The latter has a double originality, expressed by the two complementary and rival perspectives of deepening and broadening: that of being a political entity in the process of being built, and yet of having no fixed and definitive borders. Not only the mutual relations of its member states – in particular through the new notion of European citizenship – but also the relationship of the Community as such with its periphery, particularly through the association agreements, or the role of the Union (imperfect as it is) in former Yugoslavia point to a solidarity and a co-responsibility which go beyond classical international relations.

Ulrich Preuß has shown the differences between European and national citizenship and has pointed out, in particular, that the former would be necessarily more partial, more complex and more flexible, that it would not be meant as a substitute for the latter, but that, nevertheless, a direct European citizenship which would not have to be mediated by a particular nation-state was conceivable. When studying the relation of complementarity rather than identity between nationality and citizenship, he points out, too, that citizenship in terms of rights, in terms of belonging and in terms of participation do not always coincide totally. Finally, he indicates the direction a European citizenship could take as a first step to a European *societas civilis sive politica* enabling the citizens of a European country to 'feel at home' in the others and to overcome for the citizens of each state what, borrowing a formula from the United States Supreme Court, he calls 'the disabilities of alienage in the other states'. He refers explicitly to the American context, to the role of American citizenship as a protection against slavery in the states of origin.[17] One could, hence, venture the notion that the idea is to overcome not only 'the disabilities of alienage in the other states' but also 'the disabilities of alienation' in one's own. On the other hand, the European institutions have constantly affirmed that encouraging peace and the respect of human rights on the whole continent is part of their role.

Pulling all these threads together, would it be too idealistic to envisage that European citizenship should be extended not only to the citizens of the member states of the Union, but also to those Europeans who do not, or no longer, have a territorial state within the framework of which they may have access to the rights and duties of citizens? Representative organizations of gypsies have claimed 'direct access' to European citizenship for their people. Could not and should not this apply equally to refugees, giving a community to those who no longer have one? The European Union could then play, for persecuted Europeans, the same role as Israel for the Jewish diasporas. Would this not be the best demonstration that the future of European integration is not that of Fortress Europe?

We should not, however, be blind to the obstacles faced by such an idea, making its implementation more than unlikely for the time being. To the extent that the European Union is not about to become a federation, let alone a unitary state, the question arises of who would select the genuine refugees among the immigrants and distribute them among the various states.

The Commission of the European Union has not tried to play that role, but it did try to present proposals for a common immigration policy, for a permanent resident status coming close to citizenship, and for a coordinated strategy towards refugees. The states which have been admitting the greatest numbers of refugees, such as Germany, Austria and Sweden, have appealed to their partners for a more equitable distribution either of refugees, through quotas, or at least of the costs. Nothing doing. As we have seen, states exercise a strict control over policies towards refugees, and they do so essentially in the light of the economic needs of their own countries or of the reaction of their respective public opinions. What they agree on is to send them back to 'the first safe third country', that is, to peripheral countries whose difficulties are even greater than their own and who hasten, in turn, to reproduce the race to self-closure with their own neighbours. The priorities of states include first and foremost, by a wide margin, their own national interests; then those of the Union; and finally, far behind, those of the other Europeans and of human rights in general.

We are back, then, to square one, that of nation-states. It would be a mistake, however, to think that they are entirely self-closed. Particularly in our time, each modern state cannot help having some kind of relationship to something beyond it and this relationship may lead to an opening to improve the fate of refugees, or at least of some of them.

The nature of this opening depends on the character of the respective nation-states. Here Bikhu Parekh's analysis may be useful. He has examined the attitudes of states towards immigration in the light of a distinction between three types of national identity: that of the liberal state, that of the communitarian state and that of the ethnic state.[18]

The communitarian state is probably the one which is least prone to accept and integrate refugees. The ethnic state tends to welcome one type of refugee, that is, people of the same national origin. Parekh sharply criticizes the 'right of return' for ethnic diasporas. One may find him too negative and deem it a legitimate solidarity, in the case of Germans as well as of Jews, as long as it does not serve as an alibi for expansionist policies. But it is true that no state can concretely, in conditions of scarce space and jobs, sign a blank cheque for an unlimited immigration. The question, then, is that of the criterion for choice. The unconditional access of *Aussiedler* as opposed, for instance, to the victims of ideological or political persecution raises the problem of the definition of the nation and of the nature of the state. Here Parekh has the last word when he states, speaking of the liberal state: 'The humanitarian admission of refugees and asylum seekers is best defended as an integral part of the moral culture of the receiving country. It not only helps the needy but also tests, reinforces and deepens the spirit of humanity and universality of the host society.'[19] And this leads us straight to a conception which seems more relevant every day, that of the cosmopolitan situation as perceived by Kant.

It is well known that the three definitive articles of Kant's *Project for Perpetual Peace* have to do with the republican character of states, with their organization as a confederation, or at least as an alliance against war, and with cosmopolitan law as distinct from the law of nations. This law, which constitutes Kant's most original contribution, concerns individuals as members of the human race or as inhabitants of the planet Earth, irrespective of the state they belong to. Its imperative is that of universal hospitality. Taken strictly, this hospitality is limited to the right of visit, or to the right of being greeted peacefully everywhere. It does not imply a right to permanent residence or to citizenship. But for Kant himself the main point is the cosmopolitan spirit, which must inspire the general behaviour of states not only towards all men, not only towards other states, but just as much towards their own citizens. Perhaps the last word belongs to Reflection 8077: 'To consider oneself, according to internal civil law, as an associate member of a cosmopolitan society is the most sublime idea a man can have of his destination. One cannot think of it without enthusiasm.'[20]

NOTES

1   H. Arendt, *The Origins of Totalitarianism* (Cleveland: Meridian Books, 1977).
2   J. Darnton, 'UN swamped by a world awash with refugees. We can't cope with the crisis', *International Herald Tribune*, 9 Aug. 1994.
3   Quoted in A. Dowty, *Closed Borders: the Contemporary Assault on Freedom of Movement* (New Haven and London: Yale University Press, 1987).
4   See S. Helm, 'Europe to slam door on asylum seekers', *Independent*, 22 Nov. 1995.
5   See O. Waever, B. Buzan, M. Kelstrup and P. Lemaître, *Identity, Migration and the New Security Agenda in Europe* (London: Pinter, 1993).
6   See, for example, the debate in 'Ingérence: vers un nouveau droit international?', *Le Débat*, 67 (1991), special issue with contributions by M. Bettati, P. Hassner, J.-C. Rufin and B. Kouchner.
7   J.-C. Rufin, *L'Empire et les nouveaux barbares* (Paris: J. C. Lattès, 1991).
8   M. Singer and A. Wildavsky, *The New World Order: Zones of Peace, Zones of Turmoil* (Chatham, N.J.: Chatham House Publishers, 1993).
9   T. G. Weiss and D. Pitt, 'Foreword', in L. Gordenker, *Refugees in International Politics* (London: Croom Helm, 1987), p. 1.
10   B. Badie, 'Flux migratoires et relations internationales', in B. Badie and C. Wihtol de Wenden (eds), *Défi migratoire. Questions de relations internationales* (Paris: Presses de la FNSP, 1994), ch. 1, p. 27.
11   Arendt, *The Origins of Totalitarianism*, p. 29.
12   G. Loescher, 'Introduction', in G. Loescher and L. Monahan (eds), *Refugees and International Relations* (Oxford: Clarendon Press, 1990), p. 26.
13   M.-F. Durand, 'Entre territoires et réseaux', in Badie and Wihtol de Wenden, *Le Défi migratoire*, pp. 141–58.
14   Ibid., pp. 154–5.
15   See P. Hassner, *Violence and Peace* (Budapest: Central European University Press, 1996), ch. 10.
16   Quoted by I. Vichniac, 'L'ampleur des déplacements de population oblige le HCR à réajuster sa mission', *Le Monde*, 16 Nov. 1995.
17   See chapter 7; see also U. Preuß, 'Two challenges to European citizenship', *Political Studies*, 44 (1996), pp. 534–52.
18   B. Parekh, 'Three theories of immigration', in S. Spencer (ed.), *Strangers and Citizens: a Positive Approach to Migrants and Refugees* (London: IPPR/ Rivers Oram Press, 1994), pp. 91–111.
19   Ibid., p. 109.
20   Quoted by M. Castillo, 'L'idée de citoyenneté cosmopolitique chez Kant', *Cahiers de Philosophie Politique et Juridique*, 14 (1988) p. 175.

14

Democracy in the United Nations System: Cosmopolitan and Communitarian Principles

Derk Bienen, Volker Rittberger and
Wolfgang Wagner

CHANGE IN THE INTERNATIONAL SYSTEM AND ITS IMPLICATIONS FOR DEMOCRACY

The issue of democracy has in recent years been affected in fairly contradictory ways by two principal developments. First, processes of democratization in the former Soviet Union culminated in the collapse of 'real socialism', the end of the Cold War and the transition of most East European states and former Soviet republics to democratic systems of rule. As a further consequence, a number of non-socialist authoritarian regimes in Africa, Asia and Latin America lost their strategic importance to the United States and the West and thus their external support, which has made it increasingly difficult for them to maintain themselves domestically. Moreover, 'strategic-military conditionality' was at least partly replaced by a 'new political conditionality' within a 'good governance agenda': foreign aid has increasingly become tied to the practice of 'good governance', especially to regular and genuine elections and the rule of law. Heightened 'democratic consciousness' in hitherto non-democratic countries, and cross-national demonstration effects, delegitimized repressive institutions and practices because their justification as a response to alleged external threats rang increasingly hollow. Thus the pressure for change on authoritarian systems of rule resulted in the 'third wave of democratization', which had begun in the 1970s but which reached a peak after 1989–90.[1]

It has to be borne in mind, moreover, that the increase in the number of democracies was preceded and paralleled by the establishment of democracy as a universal political value after the Second World War. Today even authoritarian states often feel forced to excuse obvious deviations from democratic practices with reference to difficulties in transforming their states into democratic systems of rule or with reference to particular national traditions.[2]

The second major development, in contrast, has affected both the idea and the actual practice of democracy far more negatively. The foundations of national democracies have changed dramatically: the high (and growing) degree of interdependence makes states susceptible, even vulnerable, to developments within the international system.[3] The exercise of state sovereignty is undermined by processes of internationalization and globalization, most notably in the economic and ecological realm. At the same time, state sovereignty is permeated by activities of international governmental and non-governmental organizations in a wide variety of issue areas, which again reduce the scope of national control over public policy-making. As a result, the national control over the authoritative allocation of values within a society has been significantly reduced.

This loss of national control conflicts with the implicit assumption of national democracy that the authoritative allocation of values is based on the consent of the affected political community.[4] Thus, as the elected rulers themselves are no longer able to control the authoritative allocation of values which is deemed to be in the responsibility of public policy-makers, the basic idea on which democracy as a system of rule rests is no longer empirically valid: the fundamental concept of democracy, the congruence between the rulers and the ruled, ceases to exist.[5] Thus, as Norberto Bobbio has pointed out, it is no longer possible for democratic states to be fully democratic in a non-democratic international system.[6] But it is not only philosophers and political scientists who are concerned about these developments. The national referenda on the Maastricht Treaty in Denmark and France have demonstrated how the reach of international integration might become restricted if the electorate fears the loss of congruence mentioned above.

The question of democracy at the international level becomes crucial under two assumptions. First, substantively more national control over public policy-making, if at all possible, cannot be regained without impairing desired outcomes. If it is true that 'on the one hand, day-to-day activities are increasingly influenced by events happening on the other side of the world and, on the other, the practices and decisions of local groups or communities can have significant global reverberations,'[7] the scope of national (democratic) decision-making will diminish further in the future.

The second assumption is that only democratic legitimacy will be accepted in international policy-making, at least in the long run. This assumption is based on two arguments. The first is that a causal relation exists between legitimacy and effectiveness: 'Institutions that lack legitimacy are seldom effective over the long run.'[8] Thus the legitimacy of international institutions has to be enhanced. Second, with democracy having evolved as a universal norm, any institution in which substantive decisions are made faces demands for democratic decision-making procedures. In sum, 'as the role of international institutions in global governance grows, the need to ensure that they are democratic also increases.'[9] Therefore, important though they are, reforms of international organizations that merely seek to enhance effectiveness are to be complemented by democratic reforms.

Therefore the question of democratic governance arises at the international level, to which the authoritative allocation of values in many issue areas has already been transferred.[10] This chapter attempts to contribute to the conceptualization of democracy at the international level, focusing on the United Nations system as the institutional core of global governance. In the next section we take the characteristics of governance at the international level as our point of departure, and in the following section elaborate on a working definition of democracy at the international level. Then we present and review current proposals for reform of the United Nations. By drawing on both cosmopolitan and communitarian arguments, we finally elaborate on the criteria necessary for evaluating the reform proposals from the perspective of democratic theory.

CHARACTERISTICS OF GOVERNANCE AT THE INTERNATIONAL LEVEL

When we speak of governance above the national – and particularly at the global – level, we have to deal with several issues unknown in the national context. We consider four characteristics of governance at the international level to be of major importance.

(1) Governance without government At the international level we cannot refer to a particular constitutional system of rule. There is no world state with a world government to be democratized. However, to a large extent international politics does take place within international institutions. A network of international organizations and international regimes enables states to overcome collective action problems that are inherent in the anarchical structure of the international system. By coordinating their policies and thereby performing 'governance without government'[11] states are able to achieve benefits that would not be

possible if they relied on unilateral self-help strategies. Most importantly, people are significantly affected by international regimes and decisions made in international organizations. In this sense they are governed by international institutions. Within this network the United Nations is certainly the most important institution. It is endowed with far-reaching powers regarding the authoritative allocation of values, especially in the realms of peace and security. Because of its prominent status we want to explore how and to what extent the concept of international democracy can be rendered applicable to the United Nations.

(2) Distance between the rulers and the ruled   The appearance of the modern nation-state changed the meaning of governance as compared to governance in the ancient city-states, because the distance between decision-makers and the people affected by their decisions increased substantially. In democratic nation-states, a system of representative government was devised to deal with this distance (and was largely substituted for direct participation). Governance at the international level has resulted in an even greater distance, in fact the maximum distance possible. It is not clear whether direct electoral representation, familiar from the modern democratic nation-state, can be extended to the global scale, at least in more than a symbolic way. As a consequence, alternatives to the traditional concept of representation have to be considered.

(3) Heterogeneity and lack of consensus   The heterogeneity of those 'governed' is also at its maximum. Governance at the global level concerns all known political, social and cultural groups. Hence collective identity, that is, shared values and experience, will be minimal, if it exists at all. At the national level, a minimum of shared values has generally been regarded as indispensable to attain the consensus necessary for legitimate governance. For governance at the international level, however, the required minimum of collective identity is certainly lower than at the national level because a large part of the authoritative allocation of values will remain under national control.[12]

(4) Dual subject status   As the institutional core of a complex system of international governance, the United Nations can be conceived of as the top layer of a multilayered system of rule. In this sense, it comprises two categories of subjects affected by decisions taken: states and individuals. From the viewpoint of democratic theory, they are both eligible to be considered the subjects of democracy in the United Nations, subjects of democracy being the bearers of rights and duties in a democratic system of rule. It is their preferences which are to be aggregated in the decision-making process and it is they who are to be (at least collectively) responsible for the decisions taken. Thus these dual subjects of democracy have to be represented in the major decision-making arena(s). Including states as subjects of democracy involves the principle of territorial representa-

tion ('one state, one vote'), whereas electoral representation ('one person, one vote') applies when individuals are considered to be the subjects of democracy. Dual subject status, therefore, produces a debate about territorial versus electoral representation.[13]

The present United Nations conceives only of states as subjects of democracy. As an international organization, the United Nations is based on a treaty signed by member states. In the major decision-making bodies, only states are allowed to articulate their interests and only states' preferences are taken as a basis for bargaining and the taking of decisions. Though permanent members of the Security Council are certainly 'more equal' than their fellow states, the General Assembly's work is based on the 'one state, one vote' principle which is but the institutionalized version of territorial representation.[14] In the General Assembly, every state, irrespective of its size or other properties, is endowed with the same voting power.

However, since interdependence has blurred the distinction between domestic and international politics, politics in the international system cannot be conceived of as an interstate affair only. Thus critics of territorial representation argue that, being a layer in a system of complex governance, the United Nations should be accountable not only to the governments of the member states but also to their populations, that is, to individuals. Accountability to individuals, however, can only be ensured by granting the populations of the member states some representation at the United Nations, by 'giving them a voice' in the decision-making process.

Our enumeration of four major characteristics of international governance also represents challenges which the concept of democracy must cope with if it is to be extended to the international level. The lack of a constitutional system of rule makes transparency difficult, and the maximum distance between rulers and ruled makes direct participation, perhaps even representation, difficult to achieve, if possible at all. The heterogeneity of those governed increases the difficulties of attaining a basic consensus about the rules of democracy at the international level. Finally, the dual subject status implies that two sets of claims and demands – those of states and those of individuals – have to be taken into account.

DEMOCRACY AT THE INTERNATIONAL LEVEL: A WORKING DEFINITION

The concept of democracy was introduced in ancient Greece when formerly non-democratic systems of rule were transformed. A second major transformation of governance took place when a new concept of democracy had to be invented to fit the framework of the modern nation-state instead of the ancient city-states. Largely replacing direct participation, representative democracy completely altered the concept of democracy. While both systems of governance can certainly be regarded as meeting the normative demands of democratic theory, neither the Greek *polis* nor modern representative systems can be considered the exclusive models for democracy. Consequently, a 'third transformation',[15] which alters the concept of democracy once again and adapts it to the specific features of the international system, can be regarded as generally possible. However, given the many differences between the ancient *polis* and the modern nation-state, it seems difficult to determine essential criteria of democratic governance which both ancient and modern democracies meet and which democracy at the international level can also be measured against. For example, turning back to the four characteristics of governance at the international level already mentioned, both the vast heterogeneity of the governed and the maximum distance between the rulers and the ruled are unknown issues for traditional concepts of democracy.

Many definitions of democracy advanced in the literature on democratic governance in fact refer exclusively to modern representative systems, such as those by Lipset and Sartori, which focus on 'regular constitutional opportunities for changing the governing officials',[16] or define democracy as 'a political system in which the influence of the majority is assured by elective and competitive minorities to whom it is entrusted'.[17] They both presume the existence of an elaborate, constitutional system of rule. Other definitions are broader and thus better for our purposes, such as John Plamenatz's statement that a 'political system is democratic if it operates in such a way as to ensure that makers of law and policy are responsible to the people'[18] or Dahl's notion that democracy implies 'processes by which ordinary citizens exert a relatively high degree of control over leaders'.[19]

The definitions by Plamenatz and Dahl can easily be applied to the *polis* as well as to the representative democratic system in modern nation-states. If we leave unspecified the question whether 'the people' is comprised of individuals or states, or whether an individual or state is considered as 'the ordinary citizen', they also meet our understanding of what democracy in all likelihood means at the international level. A first core feature of all definitions of democracy is the 'rule by the many', or majority rule, as opposed to the 'rule by the few' or even the 'rule by the single one'.[20] The rule by the many is based on a concept of equality of the citizens, which in turn is guaranteed and institutionalized in constitutional law.[21] Thus the rule by the many and the second core feature of democracy, the rule of law, are closely intertwined with each other. The two features constitute a very general definition of democracy and therefore are a suitable point of departure for elaborating a concept of democracy not tied to the nation-state. In sum, we consider the concept of the 'rule by the many according to the law' to be the essential feature of democracy.

Because modern political theory has been conceptually tied to the nation-state,[22] concepts of international governance and democracy are still underdeveloped. Thus it remains one of the most difficult tasks to adapt the concept of democracy to the above-mentioned conditions of distance and heterogeneity. In contrast, our fourth characteristic, dual subject status, has been a familiar issue in both political theory and practice. A balance between territorial and electoral representation has been institutionalized in the world's federations and in some of its multi-ethnic states, as well as on an international scale in the European Union. Furthermore, the question of democratic representation has a forerunner in international law in the controversy about the subject status of states and of individuals at the international level. From the perspective of classical international law, states, not individuals, were the exclusive subjects of international law. On the other hand, a gradual change of this interpretation has been occurring since the end of the Second World War. A considerable number of international conventions and declarations are binding on a state's conduct towards its population. Thereby individuals' rights have been indirectly acknowledged.[23] Thus the status of states as the only subjects of international law has not been left unchallenged.[24]

The issue of the dual subject status is not an entirely academic matter; instead it has occasionally played a role within the United Nations itself. Although scepticism might well remain regarding claims that 'we are witnessing in the UN . . . but another of the eternal struggles . . . between the principles of territorial representation and representation by population [electoral representation],'[25] the debates on reforming the United Nations have regularly made reference to the issue of dual subject status. In the remainder of this chapter we focus on some recent reform proposals which have paid attention to the issue of states and individuals as the subjects of democracy in the United Nations.

REFORM PROPOSALS REGARDING THE UNITED NATIONS

An intense debate on reforming the United Nations has accompanied the organization's work for at least a decade, reaching a recent peak on the occasion of its fiftieth anniversary in 1995, when a significant number of reform proposals were submitted. Though many reform proposals have presented themselves as, among other things, detailed contributions to a more democratic United Nations, a theoretical debate has not yet taken place. As a consequence, the very meaning of democracy at the international level has hardly been explored, let alone elucidated. Regarding the characteristics of international governance mentioned above, the issues of the distance between the rulers and the ruled as well as the heterogeneity among the ruled have not been addressed by any reform proposal.

However, almost every reform proposal has, implicitly or explicitly, taken a position on the issue of dual subject status.

In the following review of reform proposals, we will distinguish between those which aim at a democratic order based on the rule by the many with states as subjects of democracy, and those which focus on a democratic system of governance grounded in the notion that individuals are the subjects of democracy. The review of reform proposals will demonstrate that the issue of the dual subject status can indeed be taken as a base-line for further discussion. Since the ultimate task of this chapter, as of any critical review of reform proposals, should be a theoretical evaluation of particular reform proposals, we will go on to elaborate criteria for evaluation in the section which follows.

Proposals with states as subjects of democracy

If states are taken as the subjects of democracy, their equality, reflected in the 'one state, one vote' principle, serves as a general guideline: just as individuals in national democratic systems of rule dispose equally of their vote regardless of their economic well-being, physical strength, etc., states are considered to be equal regardless of their population size, economic or military strength, their internal system of rule, etc. In this sense, an analogy is drawn between individuals and states on the one hand, and a national democratic system of rule and the United Nations, on the other.[26] But the analogy must not be taken too far: as described above, in contrast to governance at the national level, international governance is possible even though there is only a minimum of collective identity among its subjects. However, decision-making by simple majority, as the analogy with decision-making in Westminster-type democracies suggests, may not be appropriate at the international, let alone global, level. For authoritative decision-making by simple majority to be accepted by the outvoted minority, a strong sense of collective identity is indispensable. As a consequence, the missing collective identity among states should be reflected in formal and informal rules aiming at achieving a broad consensus and at protecting states from being in a permanent minority. Thus consociational rather than Westminster-type democracy serves as a model of democracy if states are taken as the subjects of democracy.[27]

Our discussion of reform proposals focusing on states as the subjects of democracy centres on two issues. First, the obvious deviation from the principle of equality in Security Council decision-making, the permanent members' right of veto, has to be discussed. Second, assuming that the veto is likely to remain, we review some proposals that approach the problem of privileges in the Security Council by strengthening other UN organs in relation to the Security Council.

(1) Reform of the Security Council The right of veto of the five perma-nent members most obviously contradicts the idea of the equality of states – and thus of democracy at the international level – because it establishes what could be called an oligarchy among states. Consequently, the extension of the veto to more and new permanent members, as proposed by Germany and Japan and supported by the Interaction Council,[28] would merely change the composition of the oligarchy, not promote a democratic reform. In any case, the general abolition of the veto would be a significant step towards a democratic international system and will be indispensable in the long run if the United Nations is to attain democratic legitimacy.[29] In the short run, however, any change regarding the preroga-tives of the five permanent member states is very unlikely.

Another set of proposals argues that 'the Security Council must become more representative of diverse perspectives if its actions are to command full respect in all parts of the world,' and consequently focuses on the extension of membership of the Security Council by increasing the number of permanent members without the veto as well as the number of non-permanent members.[30] Again, these proposals would neither change the present oligarchical structure of the Security Council nor would they strengthen the position of members not possessing the veto.

(2) Reform of the relation between the Security Council and other main organs of the United Nations Reform proposals aiming at a different relationship between the Security Council and other main organs – and thus trying to establish a system of 'checks and balances' – have two foci: the relationship between the Security Council and the General Assembly and the relationship between the Security Council and the International Court of Justice. All these proposals are based on the assumption that the permanent five will prevent a significant reform of the Security Council itself. Of course, the veto powers can prevent any change of the Charter. However, the General Assembly can be strengthened without changing the Charter. Furthermore, Charter amendments are more likely to pass if they leave the Security Council unaffected.

Reform proposals directed at the relationship between the Security Council and the General Assembly are primarily concerned with enhanc-ing the Security Council's accountability.[31] For example, the second Conference on a More Democratic United Nations (CAMDUN) pro-posed to establish 'a standing committee of the General Assembly of 15 rotating, geographically representative members, not at the same time members of the Security Council, to report to the Assembly on the adequacy of efforts made by the Council'.[32] Another proposal in the same vein was set forth by the Commission on Global Governance in 1996. Taking the historic example of the Uniting for Peace resolution in 1950 which enhanced the General Assembly's weight *vis-à-vis* the Security Council by giving it the power to deal with the latter's functions in situations of deadlock, it urges 'the revitalization of the General Assembly as a universal forum of the world's states'.[33] Specifically, the Commission proposes that the General Assembly institutionalize in-depth discussions of reports from the Security Council and consultations and briefings with the Security Council, as well as put forward suggestions to the Security Council concerning non-military peace operations and humanitarian action.[34]

A problem that is being addressed by proposals focusing on the relationship between the Security Council and the International Court of Justice is whether some kind of (judicial) review of the Security Council can be institutionalized within the UN. Decisions made by the Security Council are binding on all states (article 25 UN Charter) but these decisions must not be arbitrary: the Security Council 'shall act in accordance with the Purposes and Principles of the United Nations' (article 24(2)). The problem is that the Charter itself does not say whether the International Court of Justice, the 'principal judicial organ' (article 92), is entitled to review whether decisions of the Security Council are indeed in accordance with UN purposes and principles.[35] At the San Francisco founding conference, 'it was preferred that each organ would interpret its own competence.'[36] It would have been possible for the International Court of Justice to become the supreme organ of judicial review, that is, to attribute to itself 'the power to determine whether a political organ has acted *ultra vires*'.[37] Dealing with the *Case Libya v UK/USA*, however, the International Court of Justice decided implicitly that it is not entitled to supervise the Security Council acting under Chapter VII, and it leaves it unclear whether the Security Council can be supervised if it is not acting under Chapter VII.[38] Even the Commission on Global Governance does not 'recommend at this stage a right of review of all Security Council decisions in the World Court', but encourages the Security Council to make greater use of the International Court of Justice as a legal adviser.[39]

Both the General Assembly and the International Court of Justice so far have preferred not to interfere with matters of the Security Council. However, the concentration of power in the Security Council and particularly in the hands of the permanent members has been criticized on various occasions. Thus it seems that the legitimacy of Security Council decisions has already been damaged. Therefore, the extension of institutionalized control of the Security Council through other main organs of the United Nations is a necessary first step to strengthening the democratic legitimacy of its decisions.

Proposals with individuals as subjects of democracy

As we elaborated above, states are certainly not the only candidates for bearing rights and duties in a democratic system of rule. It is a truism that all present-day national democracies have individuals as their subjects.

The reform proposals that we discuss in the following paragraphs do not intend to replace states with individuals. Rather, they take their point of departure from the present United Nations which consists exclusively of states as its constituent parts and seeks to 'democratize' this state-centric system of rule by giving 'the peoples of the United Nations' (preamble of the UN Charter) a voice in the decision-making process of the United Nations. We focus our attention on two specific proposals: the creation of a United Nations second assembly and a change of the voting powers in the General Assembly that would balance the 'one state, one vote' principle with the 'one person, one vote' principle.

(1) A United Nations second assembly Proposals for a United Nations second assembly[40] most obviously aim at an increased representation of individuals at the UN level. Contrary to the present diplomatic representation at the United Nations, members of a second assembly would not be accountable to their governments but to their electorates. Furthermore, any national group of deputies would represent their polity in its political, social and cultural diversity. The representation of a country's societal groups and forces is also an important means for recognizing societal as well as intersocietal conflicts at an early stage.[41] The proposals differ regarding both the electoral mode[42] and the general tasks of such a second assembly, but they all share the aim of giving societal actors a voice at the United Nations. Therefore we will limit our description to just one pre-eminent example of such a proposal, the creation of a United Nations parliamentary assembly as elaborated by Erskine Childers and Brian Urquhart.

Childers and Urquhart take the European Parliament as a model of how a parliamentary assembly could be established, and indicate which functions and powers it should be given.[43] As in the early stages of the European Parliament, that is, before its members were directly elected, the UN parliamentary assembly would be established as a subsidiary body of the General Assembly (under article 22 UN Charter), and parliaments of member states would, in proportion to their populations, select a number of representatives to this first UN parliamentary assembly. The assembly would then develop proposals for its conversion into a directly elected world parliamentary assembly. After several years of wide-ranging public debate, the Charter would be amended to create the UN parliamentary assembly as an additional principal organ.

The functions of this parliamentary assembly, according to Childers and Urquhart, would consist of the following: it would be consulted by the General Assembly and by the ECOSOC; the major draft resolutions would be read before it before they were voted on by the General Assembly; it would convey opinions and have a procedure for questioning the principal organs; and, finally, it could request that policies adopted by the General Assembly be extended or amended, or it could propose new policies. Childers and Urquhart anticipate that any attempt to endow this assembly with budgetary powers, traditionally a genuine function of any parliament, will meet with too much opposition to have a reasonable prospect of success.

The issue of representation in the second assembly has been discussed extensively.[44] A broad consensus can be found regarding the necessity of balancing two tasks. On the one hand, a state's voting power should be dependent on the size of its population. Hence a large state's voting power should be bigger than that of a small state. On the other hand, the political, social and cultural diversity of even the smallest states should be represented. Differentiated voting powers can be achieved by either weighting representation or weighting votes. While the former refers to endowing states with different numbers of representatives, the latter means that equally sized delegations are equipped with different numbers of votes. In order to represent the political, social and cultural diversity of each state, representation rather than voting has to be weighted, because only the former ensures the representation of a state's diversity.

One major problem of a United Nations second assembly derives from the second characteristic of international governance considered above, the distance between the rulers and the ruled: if the second assembly is intended to represent the political, social and cultural diversity of each state, the total number of delegates would easily reach several thousands. The more differentiated the representation is intended to be, the more delegates the assembly would have to comprise. Also, the costs and technical problems of such an assembly are likely to be enormous.

(2) Voting in the General Assembly   The 'one state, one vote' principle leads to distortions between the representation of large and small countries – at present 0.5 per cent of the world population dispose of more than 25 per cent of General Assembly votes[45] – which contradicts the understanding of democracy which takes individuals as the subjects of democracy. Under this assumption, the General Assembly would become more democratic if the voting power of member states varied according to their population size. In a strict meaning of democracy based on individuals as subjects, every person's vote would have to have exactly the same weight. None of the known proposals, however, supports such a strict interpretation, because the inequalities between the voting powers of states would be extreme, with just four countries – China, India, the United States and the former USSR – together disposing of an absolute majority.[46] Most proposals based on individuals as subjects of democracy draw on mathematical methods such as the so-called Penrose method to mitigate this inequality of voting powers.[47] We will return to the issue below.

Many proposals also employ further indicators to give states different voting strengths, such as GNP, financial contributions to the UN, and share in world trade.[48] Obviously, these indicators contradict the basic equality of persons and cannot be derived from any concept of democracy based on the individual as the subject of democracy. Therefore, these proposals will not be discussed further here.

There is another weakness in weighting votes in the General Assembly in order to give individuals a voice in the United Nations. While a country's political, social and cultural diversity could in principle be represented in a UN second assembly, with a system of weighted voting in the General Assembly only countries' governments are represented.

COSMOPOLITAN AND COMMUNITARIAN PRINCIPLES OF INTERNATIONAL DEMOCRACY

This review of reform proposals has been descriptive in character. We now turn to an elaboration of criteria in order to evaluate the reform proposals on a theoretical basis. We first turn to the so-called 'statist paradigm' as a relevant strand of political theory which considers states as the only subjects in international affairs. Within this line of thought, states are conceptualized as largely self-sufficient entities, and the international system is depicted as a state of nature. In this sense, the statist paradigm draws on an analogy between states and persons. The sovereignty of states corresponds to the equal liberty of persons. Regarding democracy at the international level, states are the only possible subjects of democracy.

The analogy between persons and states is central to the statist paradigm. However, the analogy suffers from several shortcomings: Beitz has argued that 'the conception of international relations as a state of nature is empirically inaccurate and theoretically misleading.'[49] Above all, the state–person analogy is incorrect because 'states are not sources of ends in the same sense as persons.'[50] According to this viewpoint, individuals have to be the subjects of democracy at the international level because the individual is the only possible bearer of rights. Most importantly and in sharp contrast to the statist paradigm, individual rights must not be abrogated by states' rights. From this perspective, the universal validity of human rights renders state borders meaningless. Thus we can call this line of thought represented by Beitz the 'cosmopolitan' paradigm. The cosmopolitan principle of democracy at the international level states that the subject of international democratic governance is the individual whose rights must not be abrogated by states' rights.

From the viewpoint of democratic theory, cosmopolitan liberals are expected to demand a democratic world state with a single world parliamentary assembly. In this strict sense, cosmopolitan liberals are hard to find. Even Immanuel Kant, allegedly the most influential cosmopolitan liberal, searches for a constitutional international order in which both individual rights and the sovereignty of states are respected.[51] In his 'Perpetual peace', Kant presents a federation of sovereign republics as a solution. Kant's proposal has rightly been criticized for being inconsistent with his cosmopolitan point of departure. Habermas has pointed out that Kant's cosmopolitan point of view is incompatible with his notion of the state as an immediate bearer of rights.[52]

Habermas's criticism also applies to the reform proposals which we discussed under the heading of 'democracy with individuals as subjects of democracy'. If individuals are indeed the subjects of democracy and if human rights do render political borders meaningless, then the representation of states at the United Nations cannot be justified from a cosmopolitan point of departure. Like Kant in 1795, today's proponents of cosmopolitan democracy do not intend to replace states by individuals. Instead, they seek to complement the present state-centric decision-making procedures of the United Nations by giving individuals an increased representation. However, as Kant did two hundred years ago, today's cosmopolitans suffer from their inability to justify why states should continue to be important actors in international affairs and thus remain represented at the United Nations.

We argue that the cosmopolitan principle has to be complemented by a communitarian principle of democracy in order to resolve the inconsistency of strict cosmopolitan democracy. Because communitarianism is anything but a consistent school of thought, we first have to explain what line of thought in contemporary communitarianism we refer to. In general, communitarianism has become a label for a variety of arguments of which the opposition to modern liberal political theory is the most salient common feature. Corresponding to two threads of liberal thought, there are two lines of communitarian criticism. On the one hand, there are communitarians who reject the liberal claim of universally valid human rights. Instead, from this communitarian point of view, values are exclusively defined within, and dependent on, cultures and civilizations. Accordingly, there is no common ground of shared values either with respect to human rights or regarding good governance. Communitarians strongly disagree with Fukuyama's thesis of 'the end of history'[53] and instead describe the post-Cold War international system as a 'clash of civilizations'.[54] With regard to this chapter's topic, communitarians conceive of democracy as a Western idea which does not apply to non-Western cultures and civilizations. Hence proponents of this line of thought already disagree with our point of departure, that is, the establishment of democracy as a universally valid norm.

We do not intend to discuss here the universal validity of democracy as a norm of governance in any detail. The empirical question of whether there is an adequate set of shared values among the world's cultures and civilizations will not be addressed either. It is important to note, however, that it is impossible to reconcile this line of communitarian criticism with our task of developing a concept of democracy at the international level. Thus we are left to emphasize that we strongly disagree with the kind of communitarianism presented by Huntington and others. As we have indicated above, we conceive of the vast heterogeneity of those governed as a challenge for international theory but, as we made explicit in the first section, we adhere to the concept of democracy as a universally valid norm against which international governance, too, should be measured.

In order to elaborate criteria for evaluating the competing claims of individuals and states to be the subject of international democracy, we follow another line of communitarian thinking which can be found in the work of, among others, Charles Taylor and Michael Walzer.[55] This version of communitarianism is compatible with our point of departure that democracy is a universally valid norm of governance.

This communitarian point of view also takes individuals as a point of departure. In contrast to liberal theories, however, the individual is not depicted as an 'unencumbered self'[56] with given aims and preferences. Instead, communitarians stress the social ties of any individual who, from this point of view, cannot become a moral being ouside his or her given community. It is within a specific community that individuals learn which goods are valued and which norms are to be respected. It is important to note, however, that the way of acquiring norms and values is independent from their validity. This is why this line of communitarian theory may well disagree with Huntington's vision of irreconcilable norms and clashing civilizations. But even though individuals in different communities may be introduced to similar values and norms and may be socialized, at a very abstract level, into a single world community, it still remains a specific community which is valued by its citizens because it is within this community that they have become the moral beings they are. Because of the function a community performs in socializing the individual, the community's persistence is desirable and deserves respect, if not protection, by outsiders.

Since communitarians are concerned with the functions and, as a consequence, with the rights of communities, how can we derive a communitarian principle in respect to states? Certainly a given state and a specific community do not always share the same territory. On the contrary, many states comprise more than one community, and members of the same community often live in several states. In the end, however, it is the state that claims a right to be respected or even protected. States may claim to have a right of non-intervention because they are the actual sovereigns responsible for external defence and internal peace and wealth. However, we are concerned with the functions of a community and not with the tasks of states. The latter might even come to be partly replaced by international institutions, while it seems hard to substitute for the role of communities as places of socialization. At the same time, it does not seem feasible to discuss communities instead of states as subjects of international democracy. Thus we suggest regarding a state's rights as being derived from the rights of a community. The state is certainly the most important arena for communities in fulfilling their functions, to the extent to which the state guarantees domestic peace.

In contrast to the statist paradigm, communitarians do not endow the state with a special (Hegelian) dignity. Instead, the state's rights are derived from the needs of individuals. Not to respect the peculiarities of a specific community means to ignore basic human needs; to eliminate peculiarities means to endanger the development of individuals as moral human beings. In the communitarian perspective,

> there is a general principle, which we can think of as the expression of democracy in international politics. What is at stake is the value of a historical or cultural or religious community and the political liberty of its members. . . . They ought to be allowed to govern themselves – insofar as they can do that given their local entanglements.[57]

It is the preservation of given communities and states that the communitarian principle of international democracy is concerned with.

Since communitarians derive states' rights from individuals' rights, the communitarian principle of international democracy is compatible with the cosmopolitan principle. Furthermore, the proponents of cosmopolitan democracy have tacitly respected the communitarian principle, as their reform proposals for the United Nations indicate. The constitutional order proposed by cosmopolitans leaves states intact and wants them to be represented at the United Nations. At the same time, however, cosmopolitans criticize the status quo for keeping to the statist paradigm, that is, endowing states alone with democratic rights. Cosmopolitans claim that democracy at the United Nations could be enhanced in two ways. One possibility is to give individuals a representation of their own, that is, a second assembly of the United Nations should be established. Another way to strengthen democracy at the United Nations is to give states with a large population more weight in the decision-making process than smaller states, that is, by introducing weighted voting in the General Assembly. Though both reform proposals respect existing states, they stress the priority of individuals' rights.

In sum, the concept of democracy at the international level has to incorporate a cosmopolitan and a communitarian principle. The cosmopolitan principle rightly claims that individuals are the primary subjects of democracy at the international level and that any institutional order must be justified on the basis of individuals' rights. The cosmopolitan criterion, therefore, asks whether a reform proposal ensures that individual rights are respected. The communitarian principle complements the cosmopolitan principle by pointing to a state's right to be preserved and thus to be represented as such in collective decision-making. The communitarian criterion leads to an examination of whether the preservation and representation of states in collective decision-making is guaranteed. Every reform proposal should be evaluated on the basis of these two criteria.

CONCLUSION

The present United Nations system consists exclusively of states as its constituent units. The communitarian principle is well institutionalized in the General Assembly. Every state disposes of the same voting power in the General Assembly. Hence any community's common way of life, as represented by a state, enjoys equal representation. However, within the framework of international democracy based on the communitarian principle, the 'rule by the many according to the law' could still be enhanced by strengthening the General Assembly's position *vis-à-vis* the Security Council and by establishing judicial review of Security Council decision-making.

However, our discussion of dual subject status suggests that democracy at the international level could primarily be enhanced by complementing the communitarian principle of international democracy with a cosmopolitan principle that pays more attention to the democratic rights of individuals. Cosmopolitans want individuals to be represented at the United Nations in order to have the decisions taken at the United Nations to be accountable to a majority of individuals. To realize that task, the 'one state, one vote' principle of territorial representation has to be complemented by a 'one person, one vote' principle of electoral representation. As demonstrated above, the 'one person, one vote' principle is unlikely ever to be realized in its strict meaning because smaller communities would cease to be represented. Strictly implemented, the electoral principle would contradict the communitarian principle. However, there is no single reform proposal, at least in the present debate on the reform of the United Nations, that aims at the implementation of the 'one person, one vote' principle in its strict sense. Since even the cosmopolitan reform proposals respect the communitarian principle of democracy at the international level, the best way to strengthen democracy in the United Nations is indeed to strengthen the cosmopolitan principle of international democracy.

Basically, there are two ways to institutionalize the 'one person, one vote' principle at the United Nations: Either a new institution based on some kind of electoral representation (such as a second assembly) may be created, or an existing institution like the General Assembly may be reformed in the spirit of the 'one person, one vote' principle (by introducing weighted voting or representation).

The creation of a United Nations second assembly, however, presupposes that the member states themselves have a democratic system of rule. Otherwise the election of parliamentarians, and even their delegation from national parliaments, does not seem to make much sense. Furthermore, if a large number of states have a non-democratic system of rule, the weighting of votes in the General Assembly may also yield results which have to be seen as undesirable from a democratic point of view. Under the assumption that considerable numbers of states do not have democratic systems of rule, a paradoxical situation emerges: a strengthening of procedures of democratic decison-making at the international level leads to a weakening of democracy at the national level where democracy is already firmly established. Thus our argument confirms Bobbio's thesis that democracy at the international level is not possible if its subjects – that is, states – are not democracies themselves.[58] After all, it can hardly be considered democratic if a majority of representatives from non-democratic states is able to outvote the representatives from democracies.

As a consequence, the debate on reform proposals for the United Nations has to take into account the systems of rule of its constituent units. The 'third wave of democratization'[59] has yielded a multitude of democratic states, especially in Eastern Europe, Latin America and Africa. According to the 1995 Freedom House Report, 117 out of 191 states can be considered democratic, with 54 per cent of the world population living under democratic regimes.[60] Thus the non-democratic states are still in a strong position, partly due to more than one billion people living under an authoritarian regime in China. Furthermore, many states are most adequately labelled 'semi-democracies' and thus should not be counted on either side.

If democracy is indeed the only legitimate form of governance, as we have presumed, history is still far from its end. Change in the international system has challenged the democratic idea at the very time that its acceptance has spread. A significant proportion of the authoritative allocation of values has already been transferred to the international level. Therefore the struggle for democracy must also follow this path. At the same time, however, the active assistance to, and insistence on, democratic governance at the national level is the most important strategy to attain the preconditions for democratic governance at the international level.

NOTES

The authors wish to thank Andreas Hasenclever for helpful comments on an earlier version and Dirk Peters for assistance with the preparation of the manuscript.

1   S. P. Huntington, *The Third Wave: Democratization in the Late Twentieth Century* (Norman and London: University of Oklahoma Press, 1991).

2   For instance, East Asian autocratic states point to an alleged national culture which is unfamiliar with the idea of conflict and thereby try to legitimize the suppression of political opposition. Cf. M. Alagappa, *Democratic Transition in Asia: the Role of the International Community* (Honolulu: East-West Center, 1994); M. Mols and C. Derichs, 'Das Ende der Geschichte oder ein Zusammenstofl der Zivilisationen? Bemerkungen zu einem inter-kulturellen Disput um ein asiatisch-pazifisches Jahrhundert', *Zeitschrift für Politik*, 42 (1995), pp. 225–49.

3   Cf. D. Held, *Models of Democracy*, 2nd edn (Cambridge: Polity Press, 1996), pp. 335ff.

4   In a strict sense, this has certainly never been the case: collective decisions may always have external effects.

5   D. Held, 'Democracy: from city-states to a cosmopolitan order?', *Political Studies*, 40 (1992), pp. 10–39.

6   Cf. N. Bobbio 'Democracy and the international system', in D. Archibugi and D. Held (eds), *Cosmopolitan Democracy: an Agenda for a New World Order* (Cambridge: Polity Press, 1995), pp. 17–41.

7   D. Held, *Democracy and the Global Order: From the Modern State to Cosmopolitan Governance* (Cambridge: Polity Press, 1995), p. 20.

8   Commission on Global Governance, *Our Global Neighbourhood: the Report of the Commission on Global Governance* (Oxford: Oxford University Press, 1995), p. 66.

9   Ibid.

10 Cf. M. Zürn, 'Jenseits der Staatlichkeit: Über die Folgen ungleichzeitiger Denationalisierung', *Leviathan*, 20 (1992), pp. 490–513.

11 J. N. Rosenau and E.-O. Czempiel (eds), *Governance without Government: Order and Change in World Politics* (Cambridge: Cambridge University Press, 1992); see also P. Mayer, V. Rittberger and M. Zürn, 'Regime theory: state of the art and perspectives', in V. Rittberger, with the assistance of P. Mayer (eds), *Regime Theory and International Relations* (Oxford: Clarendon Press, 1993), and V. Rittberger, with the assistance of B. Zangl, *Internationale Organisationen – Politik und Geschichte. Europäische und weltweite zwischenstaatliche Zusammenschlüsse*, 2nd edn (Opladen: Leske and Budrich, 1995).

12 Cf. Held, *Democracy and the Global Order*, p. 282.

13 It is also possible to conceive of societal actors, i.e. (international) non-governmental organizations, as democratic subjects, cf. B. Boutros-Ghali, *An Agenda for Democratization* (New York: United Nations, 1996). Though a complete discussion of democracy at the international level would certainly have to include them, we will restrict ourselves here to the 'traditional' subjects of democracy, that is, states and individuals.

14 Within a system of territorial representation, existing polities are the subjects that are to be represented. Most importantly, the territorial units are considered to be of equal importance (irrespective of size and population). Thus every territory is endowed with the same voting power. In contrast, a system of electoral representation is based on the notion that individual citizens are the subjects to be represented. As a consequence, within a system

of territorial representation a certain majority of territories (e.g. states) is required to take a decision while in a system of electoral representation a certain majority of voters (across the entire system of rule) is needed.

15 R. Dahl, *Democracy and its Critics* (New Haven and London: Yale University Press, 1989).

16 S. M. Lipset, *Political Man: the Social Bases of Politics* (London: Heinemann, 1960), p. 45.

17 G. Sartori, *Democratic Theory* (Detroit: Wayne State University Press, 1962), p. 126.

18 J. Plamenatz, *Democracy and Illusion* (London: Longman, 1973), pp. 69f.

19 R. Dahl, *A Preface to Democratic Theory* (Chicago: Chicago University Press, 1956), p. 3.

20 M. I. Finley, *Politics in the Ancient World* (Cambridge: Cambridge University Press, 1983), p. 9.

21 Of course, the question of who is to be regarded as a citizen has been answered differently over time.

22 Cf. M. Jachtenfuchs and B. Kohler-Koch, 'Einleitung: Regieren im dynamischen Mehrebenensystem', in M. Jachtenfuchs and B. Kohler-Koch (eds), *Europäische Integration* (Opladen: Leske and Budrich, 1996), pp. 15–44.

23 Cf. T. M. Franck, 'The emerging right to democratic governance', *American Journal of International Law*, 86 (1992), pp. 46–91, and Held, *Democracy and the Global Order*, pp. 101ff.

24 O. Kimminich, *Einführung in das Völkerrecht*, 5th edn (Tübingen: Francke, 1993), p. 215.

25 J. E. Trent, 'Foreign policy and the United Nations: national interest in the era of global politics', in C. Alger, G. Lyons and J. Trent (eds), *The United Nations System: the Policies of Member States* (New York: UNU Press, 1995), p. 472.

26 An extreme example of this analogy is given by Otfried Höffe, who argues – comparing the United Nations with democratic systems of rule at the national level – that 'all (supranational) power emanates from the (supranational) people, i.e. the member states', see O. Höffe, 'Die Vereinten Nationen im Lichte Kants', in O. Höffe (ed.), *Immanuel Kant: Zum ewigen Frieden* (Berlin: Akademie Verlag, 1995), p. 252.

27 Consociational democracy can be found in political systems which comprise a heterogeneous society. The task of consociational democracy, which is 'essentially a system of compromise and accommodation', is to 'accommodate a variety of groups of divergent ideas in order to achieve a goal of unity', see D. Apter, *The Political Kingdom in Uganda: a Study in Bureaucratic Nationalism*, (Princeton: Princeton University Press, 1961), pp. 24f. Cf. also A. Lijphart, 'Typologies of democratic systems', *Comparative Political Studies*, 1.1 (1968), pp. 3–44.

28 Interaction Council, *Report on the Conclusions and Recommendations by a High-Level Group on the Future of the Global Multilateral Organisations* (The Hague: Interaction Council, 1994), p. 8.

29 Cf. the proposal of the Second International Conference on a More Democratic United Nations (CAMDUN 2): 'Abolishing the Security Council "veto", by instituting nondiscriminatory voting powers, or failing

this, by permitting a non-concurring vote of permanent members to be overridden by a concurring vote of the non-permanent members', see J. J. Segall and H. S. Lerner (eds), *CAMDUN 2: The United Nations and a New World Order for Peace and Justice* (London: Conference on a More Democratic United Nations, 1992), p. 20; cf. also Commission on Global Governance, *Our Global Neighbourhood*, p. 239, as well as D. Archibugi, chapter 10 above.

30 Independent Working Group on the Future of the United Nations, *The United Nations in its Second Half-Century: the Report of the Independent Working Group on the Future of the United Nations* (New York: Office of Communications, 1995), p. 15.

31 An exception, however debatable, is Boutros Boutros-Ghali's *Agenda for Democratization*, which calls for a revitalization of the Economic and Social Council in order to give it more weight *vis-à-vis* the Security Council.

32 Segall and Lerner, *CAMDUN 2*, p. 19. Another way to enhance the accountability of the Security Council is the extension of reporting mechanisms. According to article 15 (1) UN Charter, the Security Council has to report to the General Assembly about its activity. However, this provision has in practice been transformed to a mere matter of routine, with the Security Council presenting an annual report of its work that is not even discussed in the General Assembly. This could be transformed into an annual statement of accounts without any change in the UN Charter. In contrast to the present practice of reporting, the statement of accounts would be debated in public. The effect would be that the Security Council would be forced to justify its actions.

33 Commission on Global Governance, *Our Global Neighbourhood*, p. 250.

34 Ibid., p. 248–50.

35 T. M. Franck, 'Editorial comment: the 'powers of appreciation': who is the ultimate guardian of UN legality?', *American Journal of International Law*, 86 (1992), pp. 520f.

36 R. Higgins, *The Development of International Law through the Political Organs of the United Nations* (London: Oxford University Press, 1963), p. 66.

37 Franck, 'Editorial comment', p. 520.

38 Cf. M. Reisman, 'The constitutional crisis in the United Nations', *American Journal of International Law*, 87 (1993), pp. 83–99, and T. M. Franck, *Fairness in International Law and Institutions* (Oxford: Oxford University Press, 1995), p. 243.

39 Commission on Global Governance, *Our Global Neighbourhood*, p. 321.

40 Cf. D. Archibugi, 'The reform of the UN and cosmopolitan democracy: a critical review', *Journal of Peace Research*, 30 (1993), pp. 301–15, and Archibugi, chapter 10 above; F. Barnaby (ed.), *Building a More Democratic UN: Proceedings of the First International Conference on a More Democratic UN* (London: Frank Cass, 1991); E. Childers with B. Urquhart, *Renewing the United Nations System* (Uppsala: Dag Hammerskjöld Foundation, 1994); E.-O. Czempiel, *Die Reform der UNO: Möglichkeiten und Mißverständnisse* (Munich: Beck, 1994); Interaction Council, *Report*, p. 4; for a move sceptical position with regard to a second assembly, cf. Commission on Global Governance, *Our Global Neighbourhood*, pp. 257f.

41   Cf. Czempiel, *Die Reform der UNO*, p. 158.
42   Cf. the contributions to the working group on Representing 'We the Peoples' in Barnaby, *Building a More Democratic UN*, pp. 83–148.
43   Cf. Childers with Urquhart, *Renewing the United Nations System*, pp. 176–81.
44   Cf. Barnaby, *Building a More Democratic UN*.
45   Cf. M. C. Ortega Carcelén, 'La reforma de la carta de Naciones Unidas: Algunas propuestas institucionales', *Revista Española de Derecho Internacional*, 43 (1991), p. 401.
46   H. Newcombe, 'Democratic representation in the UN General Assembly', in Barnaby, *Building a More Democratic UN*, p. 227.
47   Cf. J. Segall, 'A UN second assembly', in Barnaby, *Building a More Democratic UN*, pp. 108f.
48   Cf. P. C. Szasz, 'Ein Staat, eine Stimme? Aufwertung der UN-Generalversammlung durch Gewichtung der Stimmen', *Der Überblick*, 30.3 (1994), pp. 54ff.
49   C. R. Beitz, *Political Theory and International Relations* (Princeton: Princeton University Press, 1979), p. 179.
50   Ibid.
51   I. Kant, 'Perpetual peace', L. W. Beck (ed.), *Kant on History* (New York: Bobbs-Merrill, 1974).
52   J. Habermas, 'Kants Idee des Ewigen Friedens – aus dem historischen Abstand von 200 Jahren', *Kritische Justiz*, 28 (1995), pp. 293–319.
53   F. Fukuyama, 'The End of History?', *National Interest* 16 (1989), pp. 3–18.
54   S. P. Huntington, 'The clash of civilizations?', *Foreign Affairs*, 72.3 (1993), pp. 22–49.
55   Cf. C. Taylor, 'Cross-purposes: the liberal-communitarian debate', in N. L. Rosenblum (ed.), *Liberalism and the Moral Life* (Cambridge: Harvard University Press, 1989), pp. 159–82; C. Taylor, *Reconciling the Solitudes: Essays on Canadian Federalism and Nationalism* (Montreal: McGill-Queens University Press, 1993); M. Walzer, *Just and Unjust Wars: a Moral Argument with Historical Illustrations* (New York: Basic Books, 1977); M. Walzer, 'The moral standing of states: a response to four critics', *Philosophy and Public Affairs*, 9 (1980), pp. 209–29; M. Walzer, 'The communitarian critique of liberalism', *Political Theory*, 18.1 (1990), pp. 6–23; M. Walzer, 'The new tribalism', *Dissent*, 39 (1992), pp. 164–71.
56   M. Sandel, *Liberalism and the Limits of Justice* (Cambridge: Cambridge University Press, 1982).
57   Walzer, 'The new tribalism', p. 165.
58   Bobbio, 'Democracy and the international system', pp. 17f.
59   Huntington, *The Third Wave*.
60   Cf. Freedom House Survey Team, *Freedom in the World: the Annual Survey of Political Rights and Civil Liberties, 1994–95* (New York: Freedom House, 1995).

15

The United Nations and Cosmopolitan Democracy: Bad Dream, Utopian Fantasy, Political Project

Richard Falk

Richard Falk

THE UNITED NATIONS AND THE DEMOCRATIZATION OF STATES

The United Nations, despite the wide-ranging language of the UN Charter, was mainly founded to prevent the recurrence of large-scale war and to protect weaker states against aggression. It was, unavoidably, shaped by the atmosphere of its founding, which was dominated by the perceived realities of the Second World War and by the sort of social learning that was associated with the earlier, generally failed experience of international institutions in the domain of peace and security, the experience of the League of Nations.

The realities of the Second World War meant that the most important states within the United Nations were exactly those that had been the major allies in the struggle against the Axis powers. It also meant that the views and outlook of the United States, and its leaders, would exert a particularly strong influence on the formation and initial operations of the United Nations. This influence was reinforced by the widespread belief that the failure of the United States ever to participate in the League, along with the withdrawal of Germany, Japan and Italy, as well as the expulsion of the Soviet Union after its invasion of Finland in 1940, was one major explanation of why the League was unable to stem the tide of Axis aggression that culminated in the recurrence of world war. Another line of explanation, complementary rather than as an alternative, emphasized the constitutional and behavioural failure of League organs and procedures to distinguish between so-called 'great powers' and ordinary states, thereby failing to take explicit hierarchical account of the special peacekeeping roles played in international political life by major states.

This latter concern was supposedly addressed by the United Nations through its vesting of the exclusive power of decision in the Security Council composed of only a small number of states that always included those deemed most important, and by giving permanent tenure and the right of veto only to these five geopolitical players.[1] The identity of the original five permanent members has not been altered in over half a century despite far-reaching changes in the power structure and composition of international relations. The five permanent members owe their initial selection to the outcome of the Second World War. If the United Nations Organization had been recreated from zero fifty years later, the only way the original five could have validated their retention of a select permanent status in the Security Council would have been by a reliance on purely militarist criteria: that is, being the only five declared nuclear weapons states and the five leading arms exporting countries. Other criteria based on size, population, economic scale and geographical or civilizational representativeness would have resulted in a different make-up for the five permanent members, excluding the United Kingdom and France in all likelihood, and a more general sense that the Security Council represented the peoples of the world. It is quite probable that a Security Council constituted *de novo* in 1995 would have adopted a different formula for permanent representation and veto rights, possibly combining the idea of leading states (for example, United States, China, Russia, India and Brazil) with regional representation (Europe, Africa, Middle East, South Asia) based on some system of rotation. It is also likely that the availability of a veto would have been more restricted substantively, possibly limited to enforcement activities and connected with a range of voting changes (such as requirements for four-fifths majorities in the context of peacekeeping and budgetary assessments).

Every attempt to add new permanent members has been blocked so far by North–South disagreements and by certain intraregional tensions, as well as by efficiency concerns, namely, the contention that if the Security Council were to be significantly enlarged it would become an unwieldy body that would perform badly in crisis situations. The failure, however, to agree on a formula for expansion threatens to make the Security Council appear more and more as a geopolitical instrument available to implement US foreign policy goals, which may involve either a reliance on the UN (Gulf War) or its avoidance (Middle East 'peace process'). Such perceptions reinforce the impression that the Security Council is an unrepresentative anachronism, reflecting an illegitimate structure of authority that bears the stigmas of being both outdated and Eurocentric. A principal UN organ of this sort can have no claim to democratic legitimacy on the basis of its representational relationship either to the power structure of the world or to its distribution of peoples, and their civilizational identities. This circumstance at the very centre of operations, as the UN is understood by public opinion, is deeply discrediting to the overall image of the United Nations, and erodes citizen and media support for strengthening the Organization.

It was this Organization set up more than fifty years ago that has evolved over time into the current reality of the United Nations, giving rise at various stages both to a series of disappointments and to a number of pleasant surprises, both to hopes raised too high and expectations fallen too low, as the Organization has seemingly alternated between periods of effectiveness and futility. Such an ebb and flow of appraisal is magnified by the complexity and manifoldness of the United Nations system as a whole. Evaluating the UN has often been distorted by the prominence accorded in media reports to extremist and sensationalist ideological views of tiny minorities, especially in the United States, pitting world federalists whose fervent wish would be to transfer many sovereign rights to the UN against ultranationalists whose most dire fear is that this was indeed happening as a project of a conspiratorial cabal.

Meanwhile, the mainstream governmental elites have fashioned over time a greatly enlarged and continuously shifting UN agenda of commitments and goals that has reflected the changing moods and challenges besetting international society during the historically distinctive period of decolonization and the Cold War that dominated this first half-century of United Nations history.[2] It is evident that every academic assessment of the UN reflects the priorities and preoccupations of the evaluator, as well as the specific institutional arena being mainly considered (was it the Security Council or UNICEF or the IMF?). From the perspective of public opinion, and the media, the sense of UN success or failure has been far more focused, relating to the big issues of war and peace, especially where there was a sense of UN engagement, and hence responsibility. Thus the UN has been bitterly blamed for the dark sides of Somalia, Rwanda, and most of all, Bosnia, while not being viewed nearly as responsible for the comparable tragedies that have befallen Sudan, Liberia, East Timor and Tibet.[3]

Democracy was never made a condition for participation in the United Nations at the level of the sovereign state, and for good reason. Most states could not have qualified as genuine democracies even in the minimal sense of governing on the basis of some genuine show of consent by the citizenry, periodic contested free elections, and a generalized adherence to the rule of law.[4] Furthermore, with the sharp divide on a global level between socialism and capitalism as the foundation of political legitimacy that dominated the political landscape during the Cold War years, any effort to insist that one or the other political system was alone entitled to claim the mantle of 'democracy', although both deployed the rhetoric, would have produced ideological controversy quite inconsistent with the central idea that a primary role of the United Nations was to provide a forum hospitable to such differences. Even in this period of relative ideological homogeneity, the United Nations, as such, has refrained from formally specifying what is meant by democracy, although its recent practices associated with electoral assistance suggests an acceptance of the view that democracy, at the very least, presumes a constitutional model of government operating in an atmosphere of political pluralism.

The domestic jurisdiction exception to the authority of the United Nations has been generally understood to mean that the choice of the domestic public order system was a matter of sovereign right, and was never to be subject to interventionary action under the auspices of the United Nations.[5] This idea of deference was reinforced by the way in which the right of self-determination was generally interpreted within the United Nations, especially achieving the status of a norm of international law as the common article I of both human rights covenants, which were opened for ratification in 1966. Although state practice in the 1990s appeared to validate a series of self-determination claims of a state-shattering variety (the CIS states, the successor states in Yugoslavia, Eritrea), the main doctrinal idea behind self-determination, aside from the former colonial setting, was one of according respect to the outcome of the play of internal social forces, whether democratic or not, provided some adherence to human rights and international law was maintained.[6]

The Charter also failed to include any reference to democracy as a precondition for membership or as a basis for suspension of rights or expulsion. Article 4 of the Charter refers to membership being open to 'peaceloving states' that accept 'the obligations contained in the present Charter and . . . are able and willing to carry out these obligations.'[7] Here again it is evident that in the Cold War era the idea of maximizing participation within the Organization was to be accorded an invariable priority over any assessment of whether the internal public order of a state satisfied criteria associated with some agreed notion of democracy or capacity and willingness to carry out Charter duties. Such an orientation is strongly confirmed by the failure ever to expel countries whose internal political structure was deeply offensive to world public opinion and to the majority of the membership of the Organization. And from the angle of the members, the same priority prevailed. Except for the special case of Switzerland, which never joined, and Indonesia, which withdrew briefly in the early 1970s, all states have deemed it advantageous to remain within the purview of the United Nations, no matter how much the government of a member finds itself at odds with the Organization on fundamental matters. The principle of universality has been achieved and sustained despite many tensions in international life during the last several decades, lending support to the view that despite all the criticisms of the Organization even its most dissatisfied members would rather be inside than outside. Arguably, one of the roles of the United Nations, especially of the General Assembly, is to provide a framework for discussion of common concerns that facilitates communication between governments of widely divergent ideological persuasions, including the spectrum of political systems embedded in the governing structures of the memberships, covering a range of democracies and non-democracies.

Even direct censure of a sovereign state for anti-democratic internal practices has been a rarity in the annals of the United Nations. The General Assembly did condemn Zionism in its notorious resolution of 1975, but in an effort to win back credibility in the North, especially with the United States, it repudiated its own resolution in 1991, and the defining concern related to the refusal of Israel to allow the Palestinian people an opportunity to exercise their right of self-determination in territory *external* to pre-1967 Israel. The anti-apartheid campaign was a different matter, being credited with mounting part of the pressure on South Africa that induced a peaceful transition to a democratic public order, but even here the characterization of apartheid as being a violation of the United Nations Charter and of international law was based on charges of racism and crimes against humanity, and was not premised on the absence of democracy, although among the wrongs attributed to apartheid was its systemic denial of rights associated with democratic participation to the majority of its population.

Some academic writing in the Cold War era did emphasize the differences between the democratic public order systems of the Western alliance systems and the totalitarian character of public order in the Soviet bloc, suggesting that it was important to draw this distinction in global arenas in relation to claims involving the use of force, insisting that actions by democratic countries were inherently defensive and entitled to a presumption of legality, while those of their totalitarian rivals were by their nature aggressive and were to be properly regarded as challenges to law and stability.[8] But even in these writings that are intended to embolden leading democratic governments in their international roles, there was no claim that the United Nations should, as such, require that its members adhere to the precepts of democracy as understood in the West or else face censure or even intervention in some form.

Perhaps what came closest, but mainly by indirection, was the UN role in providing auspices, encouragement and procedures for the promotion of human rights as ingredients of the international legal order. This normative architecture, abetted by the emergence of a powerful network of transnational civic initiatives in the form of independent human rights organizations, has been an important continuing achievement of the United Nations. Implicitly at least, but not by name, many of the elements of a democratic public order system were affirmed as morally and legally mandatory for states from the time that the Universal Declaration of Human Rights was adopted in 1948. But it needs to be appreciated that although the Universal Declaration and the two covenants of 1966 incorporate East/West priorities, as between social, economic and cultural rights and civil and political rights, they refrain from any direct attempt to prescribe the constituent elements of a legitimate public order system of a state or to insist that the implementation of human rights depends on the establishment of democracy in the form of a non-authoritarian political order.[9] Nevertheless, the question persists as to whether the effective and comprehensive realization of human rights is not virtually synonymous with a wider move in international political life towards the affirmation of democracy as the only legitimate system of governance in the contemporary world, and increasingly, the democratization of its membership has been adopted as an explicit and formal goal by the United Nations.[10]

However, even within this consensus that increasingly gives credence to claims of democratic entitlement for all peoples, there remains considerable interpretative space as to the range of political arrangements that qualify as 'democracies', and the extent to which this interpretation is dependent on cultural factors as well as political ones. Most of the literature on democratization issues from the West and is heavily oriented towards conceptualizations that stress constitutionalism rather than the duties of government to satisfy the basic needs of their inhabitants. Non-Western discourse on democracy to make this point more explicitly has started to introduce its own terminology, such as positing its normative goals in relation to the achievement of 'substantive democracy' to encompass economic, social and cultural aspects as well as political and legal features.[11]

The role of the United Nations in relation to human rights is both dominated by unintended effects and organically linked to laying the foundations for the evolution of cosmopolitan democracy as an emergent global political culture. At the outset, the formulation of human rights norms, as with the Universal Declaration, was treated very much as a sideshow with no real expectation of taking seriously the challenge of implementation. Indeed, the programme of action that would be called for if the entirety of the Declaration were to be taken seriously would come very close to resembling a scenario for the attainment of a transformed world order that embodied the chief precepts of cosmopolitan democracy.[12]

The covenants, being in the form of international treaties, represent a step forward and backward if their normative horizons are measured against those of the Universal Declaration. They are a step forward formally as governments that sign and ratify are specifically accepting the norms as obligatory, and rendering them potentially relevant in domestic political discourse and legal arenas. But the covenants are also a step backward to the extent that the splitting of economic, social and cultural rights from political and civil rights reflected the influence of ideological factors that were so dominant in the Cold War period, and tended to validate for each side a posture of benign neglect towards that portion of a previously unified conception of human rights that failed to correspond with its primary belief system. Also, the growing importance of human rights was less attributable to any stiffening of the political will to seek implementing procedures than it was a realization that the language of human rights was useful for propaganda purposes.

Turning now to unintended consequences, what was unexpected and only appreciated subsequently was that the authoritative creation of human rights norms under UN auspices created an instrument available for social forces in civil society as well as for governments and official elites. The emergence of human rights associations, independent from the state and funded by citizens and members, created a new constituency that was, above all, dedicated to the implementation of human rights. The main energy associated with these initiatives originally came from the West where traditions of activism and liberal sentiments prevailed. As a result, this stress on human rights was somewhat selective, expressive of Western priorities and values, and thus focused on governmental abuses in the political domain, especially the practice of torture and the detention of political dissenters. In recent years, civil initiatives in the South have been far more active, but also selective, concentrating more energy on economic and cultural issues than on governmental abuses of political authority.[13]

It is also important to appreciate the extent to which this emphasis on human rights altered state–society relations in conditions of oppression. Political oppositions were encouraged both to proclaim the legitimacy of their demands for reform by an appeal to external norms and to interpret the championship of leading states (for example, the United States in the early years of the Carter presidency) as a signal of support, or at least acquiescence, in the event that a government was directly challenged by a revolutionary movement. This interaction was especially relevant to the relations between the United States and its Third World authoritarian strategic allies, and often produced an unintended flow of consequences. Perhaps the most spectacular instance occurred in relation to Iran during the period of the Shah when Iranian opposition forces wrongly construed US advocacy of human rights as a green light for their revolution.

What it is important to appreciate is that the legitimizing of human rights norms generated many consequences, among the most significant being the erosion of statist control over territorial political life. Both internal oppositional tendencies and transnational normative challenges subverted notions of unconditional sovereignty that had earlier insulated governments from such pressures. Once external accountability moves from the realm of lip-service to that of practical politics, the Westphalian system of world order is threatened in a very basic way.

It is this process of subverting unconditional sovereignty that points world order in the direction of cosmopolitan democracy. Such an outcome is far from inevitable, as contradictory market forces and the dynamics of statist backlash politics point in the direction of an oppressive type of globalization, but it is the normative implication of a human rights culture. Cosmopolitan democracy is thus not a utopian project superimposed by way of the political imagination, but is rooted in the evolving norms and patterns of practice in the life-world of political behaviour.[14]

But there have been important ideological developments in the course of the last decade that seem to bring the United Nations closer to an explicit avowal of democracy as an element of political legitimacy for a sovereign state. First of all, the diplomatic ascendancy of the United States has also resulted in its ideological hegemony. Ever since the Reagan presidency the United States has insisted that democracy, as understood in a Western way, particularly as interpreted by American leaders to imply a strong private sector and a major role for property rights, was the only reliable basis for peace and prosperity in the world. This insistence has been maintained in the Bush and Clinton presidencies, with the latter pushing hard in its early months a foreign policy doctrine of 'enlargement' as the basis of its post-Cold War foreign policy, with enlargement referring to the spatial domain embraced by market-oriented democratic countries, and thus any extension of 'democracy' meaning the enlargement of that geographical domain. And even though the language of enlargement has been backgrounded by US officials in the mid-1990s, the Clinton presidency continues to base its assessments of progress in world order almost exclusively by way of the assertion that more people than ever before live in democracies, and on the desirability of spreading democratic governance to the entire world. This American version of 'democracy' is not generally accepted, with the prevailing conceptions stressing consent of the governed and human rights.[15]

Of course, there are many ironies associated with any systematic application of the American version. For instance, China combines a Leninist state with a remarkable record of market-oriented achievements in the last two decades, while Yeltsin's Russia is nominally democratic and a champion of neoliberalism, yet it is pervaded by crime and corruption, and its commitment to constitutionalism is very fragile and inconsistent. These Russian moves towards democracy, and their encouragement, have not until very recently – and even then indirectly, through

IMF and World Bank pressures – been seen as part of the proper work of the United Nations.

But three developments have brought the United Nations into the picture in a significant way. The first is the abandonment of military dictatorship by several important countries in Latin America during the 1980s, followed by the formal embrace of constitutional democracy by the republics that once composed the former Soviet Union and the countries of Eastern Europe. These developments reinforced an overall empirical and prescriptive trend towards multiparty electoral politics and the democratization of state–society relations throughout the world. This liberal conception of democracy seems expressive of a normative consensus that enjoys support at a rhetorical level from most of the membership of the United Nations.[16] The second development is the widespread dissemination and endorsement of the 'democratic peace' argument that democratic countries are highly unlikely to wage war against one another, suggesting that if regions and the world could be fully democratized, then the problem of war, the original *raison d'être* of the UN, would be solved.[17] Third is the extension of UN peacekeeping to embrace post-conflict peace-building undertakings in countries such as Cambodia and Haiti that have generally included high-profile efforts to institutionalize democracy, involving the organization of free elections, education in human rights and the encouragement of civic associations as the essential tests of UN success and effectiveness. These developments have been given an articulate and coherent form by Boutros-Ghali, while he was still Secretary-General, in his extended essay *An Agenda for Democratization*, published as a UN document towards the end of 1996.[18]

It is worth observing that *An Agenda for Democratization* has received almost no media attention since its publication in late 1996, a fact that is in sharp contrast to the interest and discussion generated by *An Agenda for Peace* soon after its release in 1992. Whether this reflects the diminished status of Boutros-Ghali as Secretary-General or reflects the temporary decline of the United Nations as a political actor it is difficult to say at this point. It also may be that unlike peace and development, the subject-matter of democratization raises a mixture of appropriate concerns about new pretexts for post-colonial intervention by the North in countries of the South and opportunistic objections to any UN pressure so as to better insulate cruel and oppressive patterns of governance from international scrutiny.

I think it is possible to conclude that the question of democratization has been explicitly posed in UN contexts so far mainly at the level of the state, and that the United Nations, being partly a forum for the interaction of all states, whether democratic or not, has been reluctant to pass judgement on domestic public order issues. At the same time, it can be concluded too that the promotion of human rights has become an important activity of several parts of the Organization, and is widely regarded as one its achievements, with the effect at the very least of calling into question the most abusive practices of undemocratic states. However, geopolitical pressures limit this aspect of the UN role, since a powerful member such as China can inhibit scrutiny of its human rights abuses, while a weak country such as Cuba is subject to undue scrutiny. Also, through the Bretton Woods institutions there has been some recent efforts to encourage the strengthening of civil society in countries receiving loans and economic assistance, with the goal of achieving a better equilibrium between state and society, thereby making the latter less vulnerable to the exercise of arbitrary, unaccountable power by the former.

The remainder of this chapter seeks to extend the inquiry into the democratic potential of the United Nations in two directions: first of all, with respect to democratizing the internal workings of the United Nations itself with respect to participation, transparency, accountability and adherence to the rule of law; and secondly, in relation to the interplay between the United Nations and the undertaking associated with the advocacy of cosmopolitan democracy, and whether to consider such a prospect as an appropriate normative horizon in the setting of UN reform.

DEMOCRATIZING THE UNITED NATIONS AND THE DEMOCRATIZING AGENCY OF THE UNITED NATIONS

There has always been a democratic spark within the United Nations, which was given a textual encouragement in the opening, oft-quoted words of the preamble: 'We the peoples of the United Nations . . .' to achieve international peace, security, and economic and social progress '. . . have resolved to combine our efforts to accomplish these aims.' But the Charter is essentially a statist framework, and the Organization over the course of its existence has been shaped almost exclusively by the participation of governments, whether representative of their citizenry or not, and in most crucial respects, by the geopolitical leaders of the world system.[19] Whether several changes in the global setting, including the rise of non-state actors, will erode the statist character of the United Nations is difficult to tell at this point, but what is clear is that the world order as a totality is moving away from a strictly statist framework. If the UN does not alter its structures and processes to reflect this changing character of international society, its role is likely to remain marginalized, especially in relation to the various dimensions of globalization, especially those concerned with the activities of financial markets, transnational corporations and international banking and media operations.

In the run-up to the fiftieth anniversary, undoubtedly encouraged by the spread of democracy that accompanied the end of the Cold War, there was an optimistic sense that the time had arrived to democratize the United Nations as well, and that this objective was a crucial part of any successful attempt to position the Organization to be an important actor in the twenty-first century. Such an emphasis converged with widespread discussions of global governance as the next step in world order, implying both stronger functional institutional frameworks to address global problems and the normative procedural innovations needed to incorporate the main strands of transnational social and political initiatives. Proposals looked to the development of means for NGOs to take part more actively within the UN by way of a people's assembly, some sort of forum for civil society, and endowing individuals and groups with a right of petition.[20]

In *An Agenda for Democratization*, Boutros-Ghali refers to 'a growing interest among the Member States themselves in the democratization of the United Nations itself'.[21] The essay aptly identifies 'a clear need towards intergovernmental machinery that is less fragmented, better able to deal with global forces and more open to civil society'.[22] What is contemplated is a more effective role for the General Assembly and the Economic and Social Council, a more representative membership of the Security Council, an extension of the jurisdiction of the World Court, and an overall strengthening of the institutional foundations for the application of the rule of law, especially the establishment of a permanent international criminal court moving forward from the experience of the ad hoc tribunals established in relation to the former Yugoslavia and Rwanda. All these initiatives assume a more constructive UN atmosphere than exists at the present time, or is likely to be present until there is either a change of heart on the part of the United States government or an indication of alternative leadership for the Organization that can give crucial support to reformist energies and provide the added resources that would be needed to make the UN more effective. As matters now stand, the UN is operating precariously and unreliably with a frozen budget and with a demoralizing primary mandate to carry out downsizing reforms that are likely to accentuate the role of non-democratic operating procedures and to align the substantive priorities of the Organization with the geopolitical priorities of leading member states. That is, without strong, democratizing countervailing trends taking shape, the United Nations is highly unlikely to promote internal democratization within its own organization or to make the activities of its principal organs more accessible to qualified representatives of global civil society.

For several centuries the dominant outlook of political theory and international law was to conceive of order and justice by reference to the conditions pertaining *within* territorially bounded sovereign states, or by reference to various types of formal and informal imperial arrangement. World order in the modern period was generally conceived of in these Westphalian terms, and to the extent that democracy and democratization were prescriptive at all, their impact was mostly aspirational and was exclusively associated with the internal political relations between state and society.[23] The United Nations was formed within this framework as essentially an extension of statism, not as an alternative to it, and it has in most respects preserved this character by being a club of states, but with various levels of membership that express geopolitical realities. Even so conceived, the Organization can be seriously faulted in not adapting to the changes in geopolitical structure that have occurred between 1945 and the end of the twentieth century. This is most evident by reference to the unchanged cohort of permanent members of the Security Council.

As might be expected against this background, and as suggested in the previous section, the United Nations role was problematic with respect to democratization, in this modernist sense, at least until very recently. But now the scope and character of democratization is itself being extended by a radical, not yet by any means established, mutation in political theory, to the effect that from now on democracy has to be conceived of in relation to the generality of governance processes and structures, and not exclusively in relation to governance at the level of the sovereign state, and that this generality includes the United Nations itself.[24] One expression of this emergent, as yet unnameable, framing of politics is the significance and salience of political actors other than the sovereign, territorial state.[25]

Such a mutation as it evolves should produce a major modification in the manner in which the United Nations is linked to the subject-matter of democratization, but such a politics of adaptation is likely to be resisted by a statist backlash, states seeking to retain the formal trappings of their former pre-eminence even as they lose their capacity for control and problem solving, and are less able to claim the full loyalty of their citizens. The United Nations is almost certain to become a site of struggle between two sets of actors other than states: by transnational banks and corporations seeking to define the agenda and priorities of the Organization by primary reference to economistic criteria such as maintaining growth, profit margins, capital flows and trade expansion; and by transnational social forces concerned about normative issues such as human rights, environmental sustainability, unemployment and work, poverty and disarmament. At its best, over the course of its existence, the United Nations has struck something of a balance between these generally opposed orientations, even institutionally, providing both the Bretton Woods arenas and the UNCTAD and UNDP arenas to deal with economistic concerns, while evolving a series of new institutional arenas to respond to the transnational social agenda (such as the Human Rights Commission, UNEP, UN world conferences and summits on global policy issues). Until recently, this tension between economistic and humanistic conceptions of the UN role was expressed in a minor key, the major key being provided by the geopolitical struggles between East and West on matters of war and peace, and the related processes of decolonization. But with the Cold War over and decolonization almost completed, the rise of these other actors, agendas and world pictures are central to the reshaping of the United Nations.

The dynamics of this reshaping involves a struggle for the very soul of the Organization. Note that this struggle is now seemingly under the control of geopolitical actors in coalition with global market forces, and is expressed partly by the 'downsizing' approach to restructuring and reform and partly by squeezing the more South-oriented economistic arenas, while giving added resources and authority to the North-oriented Bretton Woods institutions. That is, reshaping can involve 'reforms' that reaffirm the statist character of the United Nations, or it can involve a grass-roots effort that exerts enough pressure to reassert transnational humanistic claims.

The multidimensional character of democracy is an important aspect of this struggle. By and large, market forces are seeking to instrumentalize the state in this era so that it serves their purposes, one of which is to prevent the extension of democracy to new international arenas, including the United Nations. To a degree, transnational social forces also seek to instrumentalize the state so as to promote their goals, but are in a far weaker position to do so given elite structures, media orientations and financial resources. This assessment of a looming struggle can be considered in relation to two sets of important developments that have strongly influenced the way these opposed perspectives view the United Nations: global conferences and peacekeeping.

From the outset, the use of UN auspices to host global conferences on large policy issues was an innovative, controversial, unpredictable and potentially radical phenomenon. The initial event, the Stockholm Conference on the Human Environment (1972), was conceived in traditional intergovernmental, formal terms, with the objective of raising consciousness within governmental bureaucracies and the media, but cautiously, being deferential to transnational business interests and having the appearance of a Northern-oriented exercise that was insensitive to the developmental imperatives of the South. What made Stockholm more than a pedestrian diplomatic occasion was the unexpected and uninvited presence and militancy of grass-roots and transnational environmental groups that created a vivid presence that could not be ignored by the assembled media, bored by the official proceedings and hence ready to treat the more spontaneous and alive 'counter-conference' of the NGOs as real news.

This activist engagement with a UN activity initiated a new era in global policy, giving rise to an appreciation that political participation could no longer be successfully reduced to governments acting on behalf of people as defined by state–society interactions. Of course, transnational environmental and human rights activism outside the Organization was also beginning to occur at that time as rudimentary signs of the emergence of global civil society.[26] In these substantive areas, important governments in democratic societies also became engaged to varying degrees with the promotion of normative goals, establishing a synergistic relationship that produced impressive adjustments by way of public policy and societal awareness. The United Nations was especially prominent and effective in relation to the effort by women to transnationalize their movement, holding major conferences every five years from 1980 onwards until 1995. As a result of these developments, women became a powerful presence, which in turn added to their influence within national political spaces.

What ensued in the 1980s represented a series of adjustments on all sides, with varying tactical efforts to exert influence on the Organization, culminating in the series of UN conferences of the 1990s: Rio Earth Summit (1992); Vienna Conference on Human Rights and Development (1993); Cairo Conference on Population and Development (1994); Copenhagen Social Summit (1995); Beijing Conference on Women and Development (1995); Istanbul Conference on Human Settlements (1996). What became evident was the increasing importance of this new type of conference format, not only for transnational activists, but also for states and business interests. The Rio Summit was particularly notable in this regard. An unprecedented number of heads of state appeared; regular facilities were set aside for the non-governmental participants, who for the first time far outnumbered the governmental delegations; the concerns of the South and of the marginalized, especially those associated with indigenous peoples, were given more attention; and governments were to varying degrees coopted and struck bargains with leading environmentalists, even attaching some NGO experts to their delegations. Also, the NGO participants were a resource at these occasions, self-consciously providing information and alternative initiatives that were widely used in the formal intergovernmental sessions, especially by smaller countries from the South. In effect, this transnational, populist presence diminished the inequality among governmental delegations, particularly the knowledge gap.

Finally, a strong business presence added a dimension to Rio: business interests financed part of the conference, a Business Council was formed and given a status that exceeded that accorded to environmental NGOs, and an explicit tug-of-war occurred between business and transnational social forces with regard to the exertion of influence and appropriate orientation, with business arguing for reliance on market signals to achieve sustainability rather than for working towards the establishment of regulatory regimes to take on the task of environmental protection.[27]

What was evident from Rio onwards was that these UN arenas were adding a multifaceted dimension to democratic politics on some of the most contested policy issues confronting the peoples and the governments of the world. Inevitably, the result was to expand the scope of debate and reshape the agenda, partly through efforts by governmental sectors to minimize tensions between statist and grass-roots approaches to global policy by incorporating more radical perspectives into the context of discussion, and partly by access to the media afforded by the occasion of the conferences. Transnational participation in such events was engaging the political commitments of activist individuals and associations throughout the world in a manner that rivalled, or exceeded, the energies devoted to national political parties and elections. As the state appeared to decline, particularly with respect to the global policy agenda, and the political space available to leaders diminished, the UN arenas took on added value, not only to achieve substantive goals, such as the negotiation and ratification of treaties, but also to build various networks of activists that became, in many instances, imaginative programmes of empowerment that went far beyond the confines of this or that conference. An aspect of this new turn towards democratization within the United Nations framework was the disclosure of significant diversity and controversy among those initiatives that as a totality constituted 'globalization from below'.[28]

There is a danger of romanticizing these expressions of transnational civic energy. It is necessary to realize that such transnational manifestations can be reactionary as well as emancipatory, as is equally true of grass-roots initiatives of a local and territorial character. There are contradictory normative tendencies at work at all levels of social organization. Not only were women's groups committed to feminist goals active at the Cairo Conference on Population and Development, but so also were religious groups that were determined to reinforce patriarchal standards and privileges. Also, even at the height of civic militancy, the forces of global civil society could do little to challenge the supremacy of the Bretton Woods institutions and their economistic orthodoxy or to penetrate the Security Council, the decisive arena for war–peace issues. In other words, the democratizing pressures could not touch the top levels of the global policy agendas, and even at lower levels, where their activism has had some impact, the enduring results are questionable. What happens *after* the global conferences is often indicative of the persisting role of geopolitics and statism in the implementation phases of the global policy process. UN conference 'plans of action' that read impressively are cast aside or selectively applied.

The major point here is that the rudimentary glimmering of global civil society is not sufficient to ensure the realization of substantive democracy either within states or in relation to the United Nations. The democratizing structures must be deepened and extended laterally so as to encompass the realities of complex interdependence, and so it is the imperative of cosmopolitan democracy that must be heeded so as to ground specific efforts to promote world order values associated with peace, economic well-being, social and political justice, and environmental quality.

In the neoliberal climate of economism that has prevailed since the collapse of the Soviet Union, the United Nations has so far managed to keep alive the global social agenda, especially by way of UNICEF and UNDP (especially the annual Human Development Report), and through the agency of its global conferences. This agenda, addressed to the needs of those who are not beneficiaries of market operations, is itself an expression of a democratic character, providing attention to the concerns of peoples not otherwise adequately represented. The Social Summit, held in Copenhagen, was the climax of this democratizing effort to compensate for the narrowing, and even the closure, of governmental and intergovernmental arenas previously receptive to the voices of those who were being most victimized by current world order arrangements: the poor, the jobless, the unprotected and insecure, and traditional peoples.

At the same time it was itself an intergovernmental occasion that needed to thread the needle of social democracy with the greatest care. As a result, the official conference documents refrained from direct criticism of market logic and even paid deference to a growth-led world economy, while simultaneously seeking to advance the case for the reallocation of resources on bases other than the efficient and profitable return on capital. Meanwhile the NGO presence at Copenhagen that was deliberately encouraged by the main conference organizers advanced a more coherent set of claims based on societal and people-oriented priorities, subordinating economistic criteria. In a sense, this division of effort reflected the political realities: neoliberal ideological discipline and control over intergovernmental arenas within the United Nations all but precluded any direct attack on global market forces, but the opening of this arena to social democratic transnational forces embodied in the NGO community highlighted a set of human concerns that was interpreted by market-oriented perspectives as almost 'socialistic' in content and spirit. Taken together with the highlighting of radical variants of feminism at the subsequent Beijing meetings, the statist reactions to Copenhagen, especially by the geopolitical gatekeeping states (that is, permanent members of the Security Council), seemed to spell the end, at least temporarily, of this creative role for the United Nations in the opening up of democratic spaces.

It is difficult to give a persuasive account of this backlash as it is rarely acknowledged as such, but rather concealed behind a preoccupation with budget reductions, alleged wasted expenditures of money on junkets and 'talking shops' that accomplish nothing tangible and by a supposed emphasis on the essential peace, security and development functions of the Organization. The backlash in this disguised form will only be challenged if there is sufficient pressure within the broader domain of global civil society to induce governments and their UN representatives to take new democratizing initiatives that will revive the use of these conferences with their capacity to raise consciousness and mobilize the grass-roots. It is possible that certain marginal opportunities for transnational democratic forces will be maintained within the UN framework in the years ahead, partly as a result of the momentum of earlier conferences, which looked towards an implementing process, including smaller follow-up conferences. For instance, 'Rio + 5' was held at UN headquarters in June 1997. This possibility exists in the area of the environment and human rights, the two clusters of issues that enjoy the strongest level of governmental support and are not perceived at this time as consistently challenging globalization from above.

Also, it is possible that certain specialized activities that are not perceived as expensive or mobilizing in any serious respect will be sustained, like the Informal Working Group on Indigenous Populations that has been meeting for some weeks each year in Geneva, and is itself a project of the Subcommission on Racial Discrimination and Persecution, under the aegis of the Human Rights Commission. The network building and the evolution of a normative framework on behalf of indigenous peoples that have taken place over the course of the last fifteen years are suggestive of the democratizing roles and potential of the United Nations, conceiving of democratization as modes of meaningful participation, influence in relation to norm creation and norm implementation, and the dynamics of legitimizing claims for special identity and resources.

Unfortunately, it is also confirmatory of the limits of such action. After a decade of effort by indigenous peoples, a Declaration of the Rights of Indigenous Peoples was agreed on, but can become 'official' only to the extent that it passes through the statist filters of the Human Rights Commission, and eventually the General Assembly. Indications are that the version of the Declaration submitted on behalf of indigenous peoples, with its expected stress on the right of self-determination, will be reconfigured in such a way as to nullify this most fundamental claim of right. If so, it is necessary to consider whether the UN provides anything more than consolation and illusion to indigenous peoples, who are doomed to subordination, and even extinction, unless in their specific circumstances as they exist now they are able to mobilize an effective campaign of resistance. There is no doubt that the Informal Working Group has increased the global awareness of the grievances held by indigenous peoples, and has created links between these peoples that approaches a kind of solidarity, but can it provide real protection? This remains a challenge to the claimants on behalf of an emergent global culture of human rights and democracy.

The analysis of the wider ideological and structural global setting at this historical moment suggests a process of contraction of these highly visible political spaces in the UN system, especially those with an explicit commitment to aspects of the social agenda and perceived to be vehicles for critical thought about neoliberal advocacy of privatization, fiscal austerity, minimal regulation and free trade. The great majority of governments within the UN have been substantially instrumentalized, or at least intimidated, by these global market forces, and will insist that the UN adhere to the neoliberal consensus as a precondition for financial solvency, although not, of course, in this explicit ideological fashion. The gatekeeping will be done by way of proposals for financial solvency. During this period, the UN will not be perceived as contributing to the growth of global civil society or to the formation of cosmopolitan democracy, although certain limited positive results may still be achievable within the Organization.

For instance, the UN is likely to continue to provide assistance in facilitating transitions to constitutional democracy on the level of the state in the form of electoral assistance, human rights training and, through the World Bank, some degree of aid in the task of economic reconstruction. By reference to the modernist view of democratization, as statist in essence, the appropriate role for the United Nations is to provide technical assistance in setting up and monitoring elections at the national level, a means by which to realize human rights as preconditions for the exercise of democracy and as elements in a democratizing polity, and as an ethical justification for the application of the norms of self-determination. A postmodernist view of democracy and democratization, what is called here cosmopolitan democracy, or even transnational democracy, suggests that the United Nations must be concerned in the future with the authority structure of all governance structures that make up the totality of political life and that this must include a reflexive concern with its own varied arenas of action and decision.

The argument of this chapter has been that the statist view of democratization (as the political dynamics of public order within existing sovereign states) will itself not be viable unless reinforced by the extension of democracy to all arenas of authority, those of a societal character (family, workplace, place of worship) and of an institutional character, including the family of organizations that constitute the United Nations itself. In this regard, the global village dimensions of social, economic and cultural reality can only be addressed within bounded space if they are also addressed in relation to unbounded space. Post-Westphalian world order depends on comprehensive democratization (widening as well as deepening) if it is to achieve either functional stability or normative legitimacy.

THE PROSPECT OF COSMOPOLITAN DEMOCRACY

The future of the United Nations as a positive force in the political life of the planet depends on internal restructuring of the Organization and a consequent adjustment of its external role. What is proposed as a goal, and asserted as a necessity, is the substantial emancipation of the United Nations in its various aspects from control by a combination of geopolitical and global market forces. Such a 'liberated' United Nations would, in turn, be far more responsive than is currently the case to pressures from transnational social forces expressive of global civil society. Although not free from dangers of its own, such a transforming mandate will be both the cause and effect of the gradual strengthening of those tendencies that are shaping cosmopolitan democracy.

At present, clouds on the horizon make such expectations appear utopian. The economistic climate tends to dominate most arenas of decision, and when it is challenged at all, it is usually from the perspective of geopolitics and statism in their most regressive forms, often as a crude defence of ethnic, gender and class privilege within a particular polity, which itself is clearly delimited. Both such contending forces, globalization versus geopolitics, are generally resistant to democratizing claims that over time could build a constituency in favour of cosmopolitan democracy.

But there are chinks in the armour. To construct suitable economistic strategies on the level of the state for gaining market shares in the global marketplace, it may seem advantageous from governmental perspectives to construct a regional political community that rests on a strong affirmation of individual and group rights *vis-à-vis* those who administer the region and its resources. By fits and starts such a process has gone forward in Europe since 1945, giving human rights an override in relation to sovereignty, as in the case of the European Court of Human Rights. Such initiatives, with their ethos of accountability on the part of those acting with the authority of the state, is a potentially revolutionary move. From its acceptance flows a whole idea of accountable governance. More relevantly, such a tendency suggests that societal forces are participating in democratizing arenas outside the control of the state, although their creation and persistence depends on state action.

And positive, also, are the several claims of humanitarian intervention mounted from within the United Nations, with highwater experiences involving Cambodia, Somalia, Bosnia. These experiences suggested two diametrically opposed realities: first of all, the reluctance of states to push hard on behalf of these claims to a common humanity; and secondly, the legitimation of such humanitarian undertakings as falling within the mandate of the United Nations.

Such initiatives have yet to attain cumulative weight of the sort that would testify to the emergence of a global civil society inclined towards cosmopolitan democracy. But such a potentiality exists at least to the extent that the statist, territorial character of international society is being decisively superseded by a large variety of technological, economic and cultural trends.

As a result, it seems inappropriate to dismiss as utopian the prospect of cosmopolitan democracy as the basis for a dynamic world order. Yet it would be foolhardy to be optimistic about its real transformative impact unless present intimations are bolstered by currently unforeseen developments. In this regard, the globalizing trends could indeed eventuate in a dystopia, a kind of bad dream come true. What is proposed, then, is to posit a sense of uncertainty about the future, but to note that this doubt will be removed by the play of contending aspirations, and that to the extent that cosmopolitan democracy is accepted as the most beneficial future for humanity, then it contributes to this possibility by an engagement in a struggle to bring it about.

This analysis pertains directly to the United Nations, which offers an array of arenas within which differing images of the future are being promoted. Whether civil society perspectives can gain and hold a sufficient foothold within these arenas is itself unclear. At present, a backlash against earlier attempts to shift the United Nations away from its geopolitical priorities is in full steam, especially in the form of the budget crunch (which is not about money, or even power, but about whose priorities will determine what the UN does and does not do). Will this last, or will it engender a backlash against the backlash?

What is evident is that for global civil society to gain enough capabilities to challenge geopolitics and economic globalization within the United Nations, it will be necessary to emphasize the centrality of cosmopolitan democracy, in both its deepening and widening aspects, to the accountability of those with the power of decision, participation by those who are subject to governance structures, transparency of governance operations, adherence to established procedures and rules with means for redress in the event of perceived deviance, and the advocacy of nonviolence as a core value with respect to security and development policy.

If the United Nations can be transformed in these directions by conscious redesign, then the rest of the project is likely to fall rather easily into place. Thus, at the very least, for those who believe that cosmopolitan democracy is part of a humane future for the peoples of the world, the United Nations is not a sideshow but quite possibly the stage on which the defining struggle will be waged. As a result, despite the UN being discredited and precarious, its intimate connection with the clash of globalizing, geopoliticizing and democratizing forces makes it a site of vital importance in working out the constitutive structures of global governance for the twenty-first century.

NOTES

1 The size of the Security Council is one of the few changes made in the structure of the Organization by formal amendment, enlarging the membership from an original nine to the current number of fifteen. This adjustment took some account of the greatly expanded membership that resulted mainly from decolonization.

2 For an assessment see Falk, 'Appraising the UN at 50: the looming challenge', *Journal of International Affairs*, 48 (1995), pp. 625–46; Tom Barry (with Erik Leaver), *The Next Fifty Years: the United Nations and the United States* (Albuquerque: Resource Center Press, 1996); Phyllis Bennis, *Calling the Shots: How Washington Dominates Today's UN* (New York: Interlink, 1996).

3 See the devastating indictment of the UN role in Bosnia of David Reiff, *Slaughterhouse: Bosnia and the Failure of the West* (New York: Simon and Schuster, 1993).

4 It should be noted that even this minimal sense of democracy is far from being universally accepted. Mikhail Gorbachev in a short essay about China recalls a question put to him by Zhao Ziyang: 'Can a one-party system ensure the development of democracy?' Gorbachev believed evidently that the notions of democracy and a one-party state were compatible provided there was enough space for diversity of viewpoint to be safely expressed. In Gorbachev's words: 'Even within a one-party state greater pluralism is necessary.' See M. Gorbachev, 'Our different paths', Time, 3 Mar. 1997, p. 34.

5 Reference is being made here to the key phrasing of article 2(7) of the UN Charter that reads as follows: 'Nothing contained in the present Charter shall authorize the United Nations to intervene in matters which are essentially within the domestic jurisdiction of any State or shall require the Members to submit such matters to settlement under the present Charter.'

6 The language here is also indicative of the intention to leave matters of the domestic public order system to the dynamics of self-determination; see the influential formulation contained in the Declaration on Principles of International Law concerning Friendly Relations among States, UNGA Res. 2625 (XXV), 24 Oct. 1970. But as soon as there is an acknowledgement of 'humanitarian intervention' the line is blurred and effectively assigned to political processes.

7 Even this level of scrutiny was formalistic in application and rendered meaningless by the so-called package deal between East and West on the matter of admission, an approach that won endorsement by the World Court in The Conditions of Admissions of a State to Membership in the United Nations, 1948 *ICJ Reports* 57–115.

8 For two notable expressions of this outlook see Myres S. McDougal and associates, *Studies in World Public Order* (New Haven: Yale University Press, 1960) and the views of Jeane Kirkpatrick that became so influential during the Reagan presidency, especially the distinction between authoritarian regimes that could evolve in more humane directions (and were aligned with the West) and totalitarian regimes with no potentiality for reform (and were part of the Communist world). Kirkpatrick's views were ideologically

useful and were never discredited even though the Gorbachev phenomenon demonstrated them to be empirically suspect.

9 Recent significant explorations of human rights have reaffirmed the distinction between upholding human rights and democracy, that it is possible to be a decent polity, yet non-democratic. See, in particular, John Rawls, 'The law of peoples', in Stephen Shute and Susan Hurley (eds), *On Human Rights: the Oxford Amnesty Lectures, 1993* (New York: Basic Books, 1993), pp. 41–82. Of course, such a view contrasts with the views that observance of human rights (by way of its endorsement of free expression, political participation, and dissent) implies adherence to democracy in some form, or even a distinct emergent right to democratic governance. See Thomas M. Franck, 'The emerging right to democratic governance', *American Journal of International Law*, 86 (1992), pp. 63–77. See also David Beetham, chapter, 3 above.

10 Perhaps, a partial exception should be noted. Indigenous peoples, by their insistence on their own formulations of human rights in the draft Declaration on the Rights of Indigenous Peoples emphasize their rights to sustain, and even revive, traditional identities and practices, including those that are not democratic in conception or execution. Arguably, such traditional societies embody different approaches to relations between individuals and communities that imply distinctive forms of participation and accountability that deserve to be acknowledged, in their essence, as democratic, or as acceptable instances of 'the law of peoples' in Rawls's usage.

11 See Walden Bello, 'Substantive democracy and real security for the Asia-Pacific region', Conference of Forum Asia, Bangkok, 27–30 Mar. 1997.

12 See Universal Declaration on Human Rights, articles 25(a) and 28, calling for a standard of living sufficient to meet basic human needs for everyone, in the former case, and for 'a social and international order' capable of realizing the rights set forth, in the latter instance.

13 This is very contested terrain. See S. Kothari and D. Sheth (eds), *Rethinking Human Rights* (New York: New Horizon, 1989); Chandra Muzaffar, *Human Rights and the New World Order* (Penang: Just World Trust, 1993).

14 See D. Archibugi and D. Held (eds), *Cosmopolitan Democracy: an Agenda for a New World Order* (Cambridge: Polity Press, 1995); D. Held, *Democracy and the Global Order: From the Modern State to Cosmopolitan Governance* (Cambridge: Polity Press, 1995); D. Archibugi, chapter 10 above.

15 For a more flexible approach see Thomas Carothers, 'Democracy without illusions', *Foreign Affairs*, 76 (1997), pp. 85–99; for the range of arrangements qualifying as 'democratic' in different types of polities see David Held, *Models of Democracy*, 2nd edn (Cambridge: Polity Press, 1996).

16 See Thomas M. Franck's argument on an emerging norm of democratic entitlement, note 9; the Swedish NGO Institute for Democracy and Electoral Assistance (IDEA) proceeds on the assumption that the essence of democracy consists of periodic, free and contested elections.

17 The most fundamental work arguing this thesis remains that of Michael Doyle, see his 'Kant, liberal legacies, and foreign affairs', *Philosophy and Public Affairs*, 12 (1983), pp. 205–35, 323–53.

18 *An Agenda for Democratization* (New York: United Nations, 1996) should be read in conjunction with Boutros-Ghali's earlier two documents, *An Agenda for Peace* (New York: United Nations, 1992) and *An Agenda for Development* (New York: United Nations, 1995) as setting forth a relatively comprehensive view of the normative guidelines.

19 For a more supportive view of the relation of the UN to democratic ideals see the report of the Commission on Global Governance, *Our Global Neighbourhood* (Oxford: Oxford University Press, 1995), pp. 225–33. For a survey of proposals, see Bienen, Rittberger and Wagner, chapter 14 above.

20 Such reforms are discussed in *Our Global Neighbourhood*, pp. 257–63.

21 Boutros-Ghali, *An Agenda for Democratization*, p. 3.

22 Ibid., p. 47.

23 See a collection of essays which mainly argue that Westphalian notions hold if the critical question is whether 'intervention' by the organizing international community for the protection of the common good is being effectively achieved: Gene M. Lyons and Michael Mastanduno (eds), *Beyond Westphalia? State Sovereignty and International Intervention* (Baltimore: Johns Hopkins University Press, 1995).

24 By far the most comprehensive recasting of this statist prism is to be found in the work of David Held, see esp. his *Democracy and the Global Order*; for a less normative, comprehensive interpretation see James N. Rosenau, *Turbulence in World Politics* (Princeton: Princeton University Press, 1990).

25 E.g. David Korten, *When Corporations Rule the World* (San Francisco and West Hartford: Barrett-Koehler and Kumarian Press, 1995).

26 See Falk, *Explorations at the Edge of Time: Prospects for World Order* (Philadelphia: Temple University Press, 1992).

27 Compare R. Falk, 'Environmental protection in an era of globalization', in *Yearbook of International Environmental Law*, vol. 6 (Oxford: Oxford University Press, 1996), pp. 3–25, with Stephan Schmidheiny and the Business Council for Sustainable Development, *Changing Course: a Global Business Perspective on Development and the Environment* (Cambridge: MIT Press, 1992).

28 For further explication see R. Falk, 'The making of global citizenship', in Jeremy Brecher, John Brown Childs and Jill Cutler (eds), *Global Visions: Beyond the New World Order* (Boston: South End Press, 1993), pp. 39–50; for a more comprehensive approach see R. Falk, *On Humane Governance: Toward a New Global Politics* (Cambridge: Polity Press, 1995). The subject is also well discussed in Sonia E. Alvarez, 'Latin American feminisms "go global": trends in the 1990s and challenges for the new millennium', paper presented at Princeton University, Mar. 1997.

Index

absolutism
  and citizenship   143
  and organized violence   92–4
accountability
  and democracy   4, 11, 39–40,
    327–8
  and European Union   153, 170
  and human rights   67
  of INGOs   39, 42, 48–50, 106
  and international law   83, 120
  and multinational
    corporations   40
  to civil society   64, 237, 241–2,
    244
  transnational   7, 12, 22–4, 48
  and United Nations   24, 48, 291,
    295, 303, 316
action, direct   34, 53 n.13
  cumulative effect   265–6
  and global security   255, 257–63,
    265–6, 323
  and mandate   256–7, 259–61,
    263–4, 266–8, 269

  and the media   263–5, 269, 321
  on-line   46
  single-issue   259, 262
*Aerial Incident at Lockerbie
  Case*   90 n.62
African Charter on Human and
  Peoples' Rights   75, 87 n.15
aid, and conditionality   65, 210, 287
AIDS epidemic   12, 22, 31, 35
alienage, and citizenship   129, 146–
  8, 284
Allott, Philip   83
Alston, Philip   62
American Convention of Human
  Rights   75, 89 n.53
Amnesty International   43, 155, 265
  and human rights
    implementation   63
anarchy
  and disaggregation of
    authority   32
  and new wars   103
  organized   282

apartheid 200
  opposition to 6, 43, 208, 313
Arato, A. 248 n.2
Archibugi, Daniele 1–8, 164, 174
  n.9, *181*, 198–224
Arendt, Hannah 273, 280
Aristide, Jean-Bertrand 78
arms trade 101–2, 110 n.13, 222
assembly, freedom of 74, 79, 81
assimilationism, and the nation-
  state 123, 129
association, freedom of 74, 79,
  81
associations, transnational 194
Atlantic Charter, and democracy 73
Austria, and refugees 284
authoritarianism
  and democracy 2, 11, 29, 207–8,
    210, 211, 213, 287–8, 304
  and globalization 234–5, 243
  and organized violence 94, 109
    n.6
authority
  crises of 31, 182
  disaggregation 32–3, 40–1, 45–6,
    51, 130, 156, 157
  relocation 34–6, 38–9, 40–1, 44,
    48, 217
  transnational 189–90, 193
autonomy
  ethnic minorities 179
  individual 255
  state: erosion 3, 91, 101, 103,
    108–9, 114, 243, 288–9;
    preservation 158

Badie, Bertrand 280
Balibar, E. 128
Bamy, David 263
Barry, B. *181*
Bauman, Zygmunt 102
Baxter, Cindy 261
Beck, Ulrich 120, 234, 254, 271
  n.19
Beetham, David 4, 58–68, 105,
  149, 199
Beijing Conference on Women
  (1995) 20, 24, 63, 232, 322,
  324

Beitz, C. R. *181*, 299
Bellamy, Richard 5, 152–73, 225
  n.21
Bentham, Jeremy, and
  non-violence 91
Berlin Wall, collapse 2, 6, 11, 202,
  225 n.9
Best, G. 110 n.19
Bienen, Derk 7, 225 n.21, 287–
  304
Bobbio, N. 207–9, 288, 304
Bodin, J. 129
Bosnia, elections 78
Bosnian war 64, 102, 311, 327
  and civilian deaths 96
  and civility 103
  and organized crime 99
  and refugees 96, 276–7, 283
boundary, state 117–18, 125
  and global security 253
  and globalization 21–2, 24–6,
    239–40
  and governance mechanisms 35,
    38, 43
  and pollution 19, 26, 35
Boutros-Ghali, Boutros 78, 226
  n.28, 232, 307 n.31, 317, 319
boycotts, economic 43, 47
Brent Spar affair 6, 257–9, 260,
  261–5, 266–70
Bretton Woods institutions 232,
  318, 320–1, 323
Britain
  and Brent Spar affair 258–9,
    266–9
  and citizenship 124–5, 143
  and European Union 158, 159,
    166
  and human rights 63
Brunner, Manfred 169–70
Bruns, S. 245
BSE (Bovine Spongiform
  Encephalopathy) 6, 22, 253–4,
  261
Buchanan, Allen 183
Bull, H.
  on the European state 66, 114,
    117, 120, 121, 124, 132, 134
    n.15

334   *Index*

Bull, H. *cont'd*
  and neo-medievalism   21, 115–16,
    128, 129
  and statism   240–1
Bush, George   316

Cairo Conference on Population and
  Development (1994)   24, 232,
  322, 323
Cambodia, and elections   77, 327
Camilleri, J. A.   43
capital, cultural   118
Cappelletti, M.   171
Carr, E. H.   125, 127–8, 131
Case Libya v UK/USA   296
Case Paul v Virginia (US Supreme
  Court)   151 n.30
Case Toomer v Witsell (US Supreme
  Court)   151 n.31
Castiglione, Dario   5, 152–73, 225
  n.21
centre and periphery
  and refugees   277–9, 281, 283
  and war   278–9
change, social, and
  cosmopolitanism   193–4
Chechen war   102
Chernobyl incident   19, 239, 261
Childers, Erskine   297–8
China
  and democracy   304, 316
  and human rights   64, 65, 155,
    318
  and the Internet   19, 47
citizenship   12, 124–9, 139
  and communitarianism   185, 186,
    188
  cosmopolitan: and human
    rights   66, 108, 114, 124–5,
    130–1; and refugees   6–7, 273–
    86; and sovereignty   5, 113–33,
    216; and world
    citizenship   179–80, 190, 193
  European   5, 138–49, 167–9,
    283–4: and alienage   145–9,
    284; consciousness of   167–8;
    and exclusion   145, 158, 168;
    meanings   140–4; and
    nationality   148, 149, 167, 283;

    as non-national   145; and
    refugees   284
  global   126–8, 131, 179–94, 223–
    4
  as moral duties   126
  and the nation-state   118–23,
    124–6, 145, 148
  post-military   126
  supranational   138, 139, 140, 145
  'thick'   130, 256
  'thin'   5, 130
  world   179–94, 216–17
  see also human rights
city
  as functional equivalent of
    democracy   43–6
  and independent foreign
    policies   31
city-states
  and citizenship   141–3
  and democracy   44, 200, 207, 291
civil society
  and cosmopolitan democracy   6,
    25, 164, 218, 222, 231–48,
    328
  definition   248 n.2
  and democracy   82, 200, 202, 211
  European   140, 148, 284
  and global democracy   213, 223,
    318, 319–23
  and the nation-state   92–3
  and war and peace   103, 104
civil society, international   3, 6, 24,
    231–48, 322–7
  and citizenship   130, 218–19
  and environment   6, 218, 252–71,
    322
  and human rights   58, 64, 315,
    327–8
  and international law   83
  and war and peace   5, 219
  see also organizations, international
    non-governmental
civil war   5, 95, 102, 202
  and federalism   214
  and human rights   64
  and refugees   276–7
civility, and perpetual peace   103,
    106, 109

Clausewitz, Karl Marie von 95, 97, 99–100, 102, 105, 106–8
climate change 19, 242–3, 253–4
Clinton, Bill 316
Clough, M. 45
Cohen, J. 123, 248 n.2
Cold War
 and balance of power 95
 and democracy 202, 203–4, 206, 208, 287, 319
 and disaggregation of authority 32, 34
 ending 1–2, 12, 39, 69 n.4, 179, 199, 223
 and international law 73, 79
 and modern wars 95, 97–8, 101, 102, 103
 and refugee problem 275
 and United Nations 73, 311–13, 315, 321
command systems, and governance 29–30, 98
Commission on Global Governance 295–6
communications
 and environmental issues 263–5
 and globalization 12, 13, 18–19, 155, 204, 281
communitarianism
 and citizenship 185
 cosmopolitan 154, 162–5, 172–3
 and cosmopolitanism 5–6, 152–3, 154–65, 182–6, 191–4
 critique 5–6, 186–90
 and European Union 153–69, 170–2
 and global democracy 206–7, 214, 299–303
 and human rights 171, 188–9, 300
 and justice 180–2, *181*
 and middle way 5, 172–3
 and the right and the good 188–9
 and rights and democracy 159–62
 and state sovereignty 157–9, 301–2
 and world citizenship 180, 182–6
community
 borders 238–40

and citizenship 141–4, 273
and cosmopolitanism 192–3
and democracy 193–4
dialogic 121, 122, 123, 124
empowerment 50
of fate 21–2, 24–6, *25–6*, 82, 141, 189–90
global cosmopolitan 154, 206–7, 253, 279
and identity 5–6, 182, 186–7
international 280–1
international security 117, 253
non-territorial 46, 164
post-Westphalian 93, 113–14, 117–20, 124, 128, 129–32, 316, 320, 326
and rights 157, 160–1, 185
as subject of democracy 301–2
and war 119
computers, access to 47
confederation, and cosmopolitan democracy 6, 65, 154–7, 212–13, 215, 217, 220, 223, 285–6
Conference on Security and Cooperation in Europe 77, 117
conflict
 interethnic 76–7
 international 2, 203–4: *see also* peace; war
 public 239–40, 243–4
consensus
 and citizenship 127
 and discourse theory of morality 122, 197 n.30
 and global security problems 255
 and heterogeneity 290, 292, 293
 and organized violence 104
 and peace 91–2, 104, 106–8, 191–2
 value 188–9, 191–2
consent
 informed 239, 255–6, 288
 and legitimacy 22, 33
 withholding 266
Conservative Party, UK
 and communitarianism 162–3
 and Maastricht Treaty 63
consociationalism 129, 165

constitutionalism
  and democracy   314, 316, 326
  supranational   140, 172
constraint, alternative systems   47–50
contract theory   123, 193, 197 n.32
control
  alternative systems   47–50
  and governance   4, 29–30, 31, 32, 33, 34, 35, 36–8, 37
  and non-governmental organizations   41–2, 206
  regional   44–5
  and social movements   42–3, 47
Cooper, Michael   46
cooperation,
  intergovernmental   205–6, 240–4, 245
Copenhagen Social Summit (1995)   232, 322, 324
Corbett, R.   140
corporations, multinational (MNCs)
  and democracy   12, 39, 40, 41
  and globalization   3, 17–18, 28, 155, 157
  and social movements   43, 239
  and United Nations   320
cosmopolitanism
  communitarian   154, 173
  and communitarianism   5–6, 152–4, 162–5, 182–6, 191–4, 207
  and European Union   153–67, 170–2
  globalism and federalism   154–7, 159, 162, 165, 167–8, 172
  and human rights   154–5, 157, 159–62, 171
  and international democracy   299–303
  and justice   180, 181
  and middle way   5, 172–3
  and political loyalty   244–8
  and post-nationalism   162, 168
  and public sphere   236–40, 244–8
  and refugees   273–86
  and rights and democracy   108, 159–62
  and world society   179–80, 182

  see also citizenship, cosmopolitan; democracy, cosmopolitan
Council of Europe
  and democracy   74
  and minority rights   77, 117
Council of Rome   29
Crawford, James   4–5, 72–85
Creutzfeldt-Jakob disease (CJD)   253, 261
crime, organized   12, 36
  and warfare   98–9, 105
critical theory   120, 121–3, 124, 132
  and civil society   248 n.2
Crucé, Émeric   199
CSCE see Conference on Security and Cooperation in Europe
culture
  civic   164
  and diversity   118, 119–20, 122–4, 128–9, 133
  and effects of globalization   18–19, 155, 206
  and identity   189–90
  military   93
Curtin, D.   140
Czempiel, E.-O.   227 n.38

Dahl, R.   224 n.6, 292
decision-making, transnational   12, 18, 20, 22–3, 31, 39, 49, 113, 162, 231, 294–303
  in European Union   153–4, 168–9, 170
  and individuals   160, 193, 199, 256, 265–6
  and international law   73, 82, 83, 85
  in multinational corporations   40, 262
  and nation-states   11, 156, 204–5, 288–9
  NGOs   40, 42
  and the public sphere   236, 240
  see also European Union; United Nations
defence, collective   20–1, 162
democracy
  among states   2, 205–9, 210–11, 215, 218, 222

and communitarianism 154–65,
185–6, 207–9, 299–303
confederal model 6, 65, 154–7,
212–13, 215, 217, 223
consociational 294
cosmopolitan: aims 82, 198, 209–
12; and changes in international
system 2, 198–224, 287–9; and
citizenship and sovereignty 5,
113–33; and civil society 6,
222, 231–48, 252–70; and
community 193–4; and
European Union 116, 215–16,
219–20; four premises 199–
201, 218; and global
conflict 203–4; and global
democracy 28, 207–9, 211–12,
213, 215, 218–19; and global
governance 25, 50; and global
security 252–70; and human
rights 4, 58–68, 73, 78, 106,
159–60; and international
democracy 299–303; and
international law 3, 73–85;
model 215–19; principles 6,
24–6, 25–6, 198–224; prospect
of 327–8; and role of states 4,
24, 222; and United Nations 7,
220–1, 309–28
deficit 67, 72–85, 166, 168, 243,
244
deliberative 67
domestic, and international
system 4, 198–9, 203–5
as endogenous development 209–
10
European models 152–73
federalist model 6, 162, 214–15,
216, 217, 223
functional equivalents 40–7, 51,
156
global: and
communitarianism 206–7; and
cosmopolitanism 205, 211–12,
213, 215, 218–19; as domestic
problem 207–9; federalist
model 215; and realism 198,
205–6
and global governance 38–51

and globalization 1–2, 4, 11–26,
28–51, 82, 204–5, 243
and human rights 66–7, 202
individuals as subjects 7, 212,
294, 296–9, 300–1
inside nations 82, 85, 209–10,
212–13, 214, 217–18, 287–
8
and judicial review 160–1, 176
n.27
liberal 22, 69 n.6, 81–2, 123,
183, 254, 317
and the nation-state 21–4, 82–5,
288, 290, 291–3
protective 259, 266
representative 59, 69 n.6, 75, 81,
207, 290–1, 292
states as subjects 7, 290–1, 293,
294–6, 301
'statistical' 255, 256
supranational 140
transnational: and
communitarianism 186; and
cosmopolitanism 193–4, 216;
and critical theory 121–4; and
European Union
citizenship 138–49; and
libertarianism 180; and
organized violence 102–9; and
the refugee 273
in United Nations system 287–
304
victory 2, 201–3, 287–8
demos 59
and European Union 139, 160,
163, 167, 169, 170
Denmark, and European
Union 166, 288
desertification 19
Deutsch, Karl 117
devolution
and citizenship 131
and European Union 166
dialogue, and discourse theory of
morality 121–4, 130
diaspora
and external support for
warfare 101, 105
and refugees 279

dictatorship, in Latin America   63,
    317
difference
    and equality   60, 123, 128–9
    and universality   121, 122–4,
        129–30, 132–3
disaggregation
    as functional equivalent of
        democracy   40–1, 51, 156
    and global governance   32–3, 38–
        41, 45–6, 130
distance between ruler and
    ruled   131, 290, 291, 292, 293,
        298
Doerge, D.   45
Doyle, M. W.   *181*
Drozdiak, W.   44
drug trade   12, 31, 35
Durand, Marie-Françoise   280–1
duties
    and communitarianism   152, 185,
        187
    and European Union   139, 140–1
    and global citizenship   126–8,
        131–2, 217, 224
    and rights   60–1, 128
Dworkin, Ronald   180, *181*, 196
    n.8, 255, 256

Earth Summit, Brazil (1992)   19, 20,
    24, 232, 245, 322–3
East Timor Case   90 n.61
ecological movement   42–3
economism   320–1, 323–4, 327
economy
    and climate change   254
    as constraint system   48–9
    and cosmopolitan democracy   25
    economic rights   58–9, 64, 125,
        130–1, 201–2
    global underground   102
    and globalization   12, 13–14,
        35, 119, 162, 235–6, 237–8,
        288
    and new wars   100–1
    and regional control
        mechanisms   45
    world   17–18, 48–9, 194 n.1, 235,
        324

    see also corporations,
        multinational; finance; market,
        global; sanctions; trade
Edwards v UK   89 n.52
egalitarianism, and citizenship   124
elections
    and international law   79–80, 85
    monitoring   30, 77–8, 79, 210,
        326
    and participation   168, 196 n.18,
        201
Elias, Norbert   102
elite, cosmopolitan   14, 67–8, 120
embeddedness, social, and
    citizenship   142–3
English, as dominant language   18
environment
    and civil society   6, 7, 252–71,
        322
    and democracy gap   243
    and global governance   37, 211
    and global security   253
    and globalization   19–20, 31, 158,
        162, 204, 218–19
    and mandate to act   259–61, 263–
        4, 266–8
    and post-military citizenship   126
    and single issues   259, 262
    see also Brent Spar affair;
        pollution, transboundary
equality
    and citizenship   124, 126–9, 131–
        3, 143–4, 145, 237
    and difference   60, 123, 128
    and human rights   66
ethnic cleansing   96, 102, 276,
    279
Europe
    and asylum-seekers   276–7, 278
    citizenship and sovereignty   113–
        33
    of the regions   116
European Charter of Regional
    and Minority Languages   77,
        117
European Commission   156, 220,
    277, 284
European Convention on Human
    Rights   62, 171

Eleventh Protocol 85
First Protocol 74, 75
Ninth Protocol 84–5
European Court at
    Luxembourg 62–3
European Court of Human
    Rights 62–3, 74, 75, 84, 89
    n.52, 327
European Court of Justice 157,
    165–6, 169–72
European Economic
    Community 138
    see also European Union
European Monetary Union 166
European Parliament 156, 165–6,
    168–9, 213, 220, 297
European Union
    bill of rights 171
    as civic nation 164–5, 168, 173
    Committee of the Regions 116
    and Common Agricultural
        Policy 158
    and cosmopolitan democracy 7,
        23, 67, 116, 215–16, 219–20
    and cosmopolitanism and
        communitarianism 5, 152–3,
        154–73
    Council of Ministers 165, 170,
        213, 220
    and direct effect 138–9, 157, 165
    and globalization 158, 167–8,
        204
    and judicial competence 161,
        165–7, 169–72
    models of rights and
        democracy 152–73
    peacekeeping role 106
    political structure 153, 207
    and refugees 283–4
    and sovereignty 5, 119
    supremacy of Community
        law 138–9, 146, 157, 165,
        171–2
    and trade 15
    see also citizenship; human rights;
        law; Maastricht Treaty
European Union Treaty *see*
    Maastricht Treaty
Everson, M. 145

exclusion
    and citizenship 121–4, 125–6,
        128–9, 133
    and European citizenship 145,
        158, 168
expression, freedom of 74, 79, 81,
    210

Falk, Richard 7, 83, 309–28
fate, identity as 189–90
federalism
    and citizenship 146
    and cosmopolitan democracy 6,
        154–7, 159, 162, 165, 166, 167–
        8, 172, 223
    and democracy among states 215
    and democracy inside
        nations 214, 217
    and European Union 215–16,
        220
    and global democracy 215, 300
    territorial/personal 147
feminism, and universalism 122
finance, and globalization 15–16,
    26, 35, 119, 155
foreign policy
    and civil society
        organizations 245
    and domestic democracy 207–9
Fox, Sylvana 275
France
    and citizenship 143, 145, 159
    and Maastricht Treaty 288
    and nuclear testing 43, 211, 263–
        4, 270
    and refugees 276–7
Franck, Thomas 79–80, 83
freedom, individual 191
Fukuyama, F. 278, 300
functionalism
    and regime analysis 240–1
    and sovereignty 217
fundamentalism, rise 23

Geneva Conventions 104
    on the Status of Refugees
        (1951) 275–6
genocide 64, 212, 219, 280–1
Georgia, war 97, 98

Germany
  and Brent Spar affair   258, 266,
    268–9
  and Maastricht Treaty   167, 169–
    72, 173
  and refugees   276, 283, 284
Giddens, Anthony   271 n.19
Gilligan, Carol   136 n.48
Glassman, J. K.   46–7
global warming   19, 250 n.41, 253–
    5
globalism, and
    cosmopolitanism   154–7
globalization   1, 12–14, 234–44
  and cosmopolitanism   155–6,
    157–8, 161–2, 165, 327, 328
  cultural and communication
    trends   18–19, 155, 206
  and democracy   1–2, 4, 11–26,
    28–51, 82, 204–5, 243, 288
  and the environment   19–20, 158,
    162, 204
  and European Union   158, 167–
    8
  and finance   15–16, 26, 35, 119,
    155
  and global society   240–4
  and governance   28–51
  and international law   82, 85,
    120, 156
  and mechanisms of
    governance   36–8
  and multinational
    corporations   17–18, 28, 39,
    40–1, 155, 157
  and politics, law and security   19–
    20, 239
  and the public sphere   234–44
  and state adaptation   2–3, 118,
    119–20, 233–4, 235–6, 243
  and trade   1, 14–15, 26, 35, 120,
    158, 206
  see also economy
Goizueta, R. C.   42
Goodin, Robert   265–6
Gorbachev, Mikhail   329 n.4
Gordenker, Leon   280
governance
  and cities and micro-regions   43–6

  and electrical technologies   46–7
  and global security issues   254
  'good' and foreign aid   287
  self-government   4, 42, 76
governance, global   3–4, 20–1, 289–
    93
  characteristics   289–91, 292, 293,
    298
  and command and control   4, 29–
    30, 31, 32, 33, 34, 35, 40–2
  and constraint systems   47–50, 51
  and cosmopolitan democracy 25,
    50, 194, 216
  and disaggregation and
    innovation   32–3, 34, 38–41,
    45–6, 51
  emergence and evolution   33–4,
    36–8, 44
  and globalization   2, 16, 17–18,
    24, 28–51
  and the individual   299
  and interdependence   30–1, 33,
    35, 37, 161–2
  and international law   79–80
  mechanisms   28, 35–8
  and non-governmental
    organizations   41–2
  and proliferation of
    organizations   31–2
  and relocation of authority   34–6,
    39, 40–1, 44, 48, 289
  and social movements   24, 35, 42–
    3
  see also United Nations
government, and global
    governance   289–90
*Grand Chief Donald Marshall v
    Canada*   89 n.51
Gray, J.   69 n.8
Greenhouse, S.   41
Greenpeace
  and accountability   48
  and Brent Spar affair   257–9,
    260–3, 266, 269–70
  and globalization   155
  and mandate   266–8, 269
  and nuclear testing   43, 263–4
  and use of media   263–5, 269
Grotius, Hugo   199

Gulf War 1991 97, 155, 282, 310
gypsies, and European
  citizenship 284

Habermas, Jürgen 67, 114–15,
  121–2, 124, 197 n.32, 300
Haiti, and elections 77–8
Hardin, Russell 264
Hassner, Pierre 6–7, 149, 273–86
hazards, export of 126
Heater, Derek 126, 127
Hegel, G. W. F. 187, 248 n.2, 281
Held, David 1–8, 50, 66–7
  and cosmopolitanism 164, *181*,
    194, 255
  and democracy and
    globalization 4, 11–26, 174
    n.9, 288
  and institutional structure 255–
    6
  and international law 82–3, 84
  and nation-states 145
heterogeneity, and consensus 290,
  292, 293
Hettne, B. 44
Hewson, M. 34
hierarchy
  and globalization 14
  and governance 29–30, 32, 36–7,
    40
Hirst, P. 157
Hobbes, Thomas 66, 94
Höffe, Otfried 306 n.26
human rights
  assessment 66–8
  and citizenship 66, 108, 114,
    124–6, 128–31, 139, 140–1,
    144, 148–9, 274, 283
  civil 74–5, 81, 85, 124–5
  and civil war 5
  and communitarianism 152, 159–
    62, 188–9, 300
  conflicting 157
  and cosmopolitan democracy 4,
    58–68, 106, 108, 194, 216–17
  and cosmopolitanism 154–5,
    157, 159–62, 171
  and countervailing logics 64–5
  cultural 124

and democracy 66–7, 73, 78,
  159–60, 299
economic 58–9, 64, 125, 130–1,
  201–2
and European Union 139, 145–6,
  152–73, 284, 327
informal regime 63–4, 105
and international law 73–5, 79–
  81, 83–4, 104, 114, 120
international regime 4, 61–3, 66,
  105, 313–18, 326
legal 124, 125
and minority groups 76–7, 114,
  117, 119, 128–9, 131–2, 171,
  179, 202, 210
normative basis 60
and organized violence 104–5
political 74–5, 85, 124–5, 130
and refugees 6, 274, 278, 281
social 64, 124, 125, 130–1, 201
and universalism 4, 58, 59–64,
  66–7, 163, 216
welfare rights 125, 127–8, 131,
  133, 202
see also justice
humanitarianism 278, 283, 327
Huntington, S. P. 225 n.9, 278, 301
Hutton, Will 254, 255

identity
  and citizenship 142, 148, 190,
    274
  civic 168
  collective 294
  community 5–6, 118, 142, 179–
    94
  convergence 159
  as fate 189–90
  global 159
  multiple 130, 132, 148, 156, 164,
    187–90
  national 92–3, 120, 123, 130–1,
    148, 168
  and new wars 98, 103
  as one-dimensional
    relationship 187–8
  as oneness with a
    community 186–7
  as value consensus 188–9, 290

Ignatieff, Michael   127
IGOs *see* organizations, international governmental
immigration   125, 276, 278–80, 283, 285
and European Union   204, 284
impartiality, and neutrality   107–8
indigenous peoples
and citizenship   123, 129, 179
and United Nations   90 n.64, 325, 330 n.10
individuals
and communitarianism   162, 164, 182–5, 186–90, 191, 193–4, 300–2
and cosmopolitanism   154–5, 159–60, 162–3, 191, 255–6, 299
and European Union   145–9
and globalization   13–14, 40, 156
and international law   242, 293
and society   144, 182–5, 186–90, 191–4
and statist paradigm   299
as subjects of democracy   7, 212, 294, 296–9, 300–2
as subjects of law   156
as subjects of rights   159–60, 180
Indonesia, and human rights   64
industry, and environmentalism   236–8, 259–61, 266–70
information technology
as functional equivalent of democracy   46–7
and globalization   12, 13, 155, 204
INGOs *see* organizations, international non-governmental
innovation, and governance   32–3
institutionalism, new   52 n.3
institutions
and global security issues   254, 255–7, 259
loss of confidence in   259–61, 269–70
integration, European   5, 12, 165–6, 168, 171, 282–3, 288
and citizenship   140, 147, 167

Inter-American Court and Commission of Human Rights   81, 84, 89 n.53
interdependence
and democracy   203, 204–5, 288
and European Union   168
and governance   30–2, 33, 35, 37
and human rights   61, 62, 161–2
and refugees   277, 281
and United Nations   291, 324
intergovernmentalism
and democracy among states   211, 217, 218, 234, 282
and European Union   157, 159, 165–6, 172–3
and United Nations   220, 277, 324
see also organizations, international
International Bill of Rights   58
International Commission of Jurists, and human rights implementation   63
International Court of Justice   83–4, 222, 295, 296, 319
International Covenant on Civil and Political Rights   74–5, 76, 85, 89 n.51, 314–15
international criminal court   83, 84, 219, 319
International Monetary Fund, and accountability   48, 156
International Nestlé Boycott Committee   43
International Union of Free Syndicats   156
internationalism, liberal   78
Internet
as functional equivalent of democracy   46–7
and national culture   19
Iraq, and human rights   65, 155
Ireland, and European Union   166
Istanbul Conference on Human Settlements (1996)   232, 322

judicial review   160–1, 167, 176 n.27
judiciary, independence   81, 161

justice
  and communitarianism 152, 180–
    1, *181*, 182–6, 187–8, 190, 195
    n.6
  and cosmopolitanism 180, *181*,
    182, 191–2

Kakabadse, Y. 245
Kakonen, J. 54 n.18
Kaldor, Mary 5, 91–109, 203–4,
  216
Kant, Immanuel
  and cosmopolitanism 6, 180, *181*,
    186, 195 n.2, 227 n.39, 299–
    300
  and the nation-state 113, 285–6
  and non-violence 91
Kantianism, and international
  law 78
Keane, John 102, 103
Keegan, John 93
Kelsen, Hans 199, 217
Kirkpatrick, Jeane 329 n.8
Kohl, Helmut 258, 266, 268, 269
Kohlberg, Lawrence 136 n.48
Köhler, Martin 1–8, 231–48
Kouchner, Bernard 278
Kymlicka, W. 123, 137 n.71, *181*,
  183, 197 n.26

Labour Party, UK, and financial
  policy 16
Ladd, William 199
Lahteenmaki, K. 54 n.18
Latin America, and dictatorship 63,
  287, 317
law, international
  and cosmopolitanism 285–6
  and democracy 4–5, 73–9, 80–2,
    210, 292
  and elections 77–8, 79–80, 85
  European Union 138, 141, 145–
    6, 153, 157, 165–7, 170–2
  and globalization 82, 85, 120,
    156
  and human rights 5, 58, 75, 79–
    81, 83–4, 104, 114, 120
  humanitarian 104–5, 106–7
  and the individual 242, 293

and *jus in bellum* 108
  and liberalism 80–2
  limits 4–5, 79–85
  and minority groups 76–7, 120
  and organized violence 104–5
  progress narrative 79–80
  reform of 83
  and self-determination 76, 77,
    79–80
  state-centric focus 3, 82–5, 118,
    120
  and UN resolutions 83, 84
law, national, and international
  law 72
League of Nations 309–10
legitimacy, democratic
  and consent 22
  and cosmopolitanism/
    communitarianism 152, 164,
    190
  and elections 201
  and European Union 153, 168–9,
    173
  and global security issues 254,
    256, 266–8, 269
  and human rights
    enforcement 105, 106
  and international law 73, 78, 81
  and nation-state 92, 93–4, 106,
    156, 188, 289
  and transnational issues 22–4,
    39
  and United Nations 295, 315–16
  and war 98
liberalism
  and civil society 248 n.2
  and communitarianism 182–6,
    189–90, 191, 300–1
  and consent 22
  cosmopolitan 299–300
  and human rights 59, 61, 182
  and international law 80–2
  and non-violence 91, 102
  and public and private
    spheres 237–8
  welfare *181*
libertarianism 180–2, *181*, 184–5
liberty, right to 59
Lijphart, A. 165

Linklater, Andrew   5, 66, 113–33,
148, 149, 222, 256
Lipset, S. M.   292
localization, and globalization   35,
39, 51, 133
Loescher, Gil   280
loyalties, political   113, 114, 118
community   184
conflicting   187–8, 190, 234
multiple   115–16, 118, 121, 128,
129–32, 148, 187–8, 191
and the public sphere   234, 236–
8, 240, 241–8

Maastricht Treaty   63
and citizenship   130, 139, 140,
146, 149, 165–7
and German ruling   167, 169–72,
173
tensions   166, 168, 288
McGrew, A. G.   34
Machiavelli, Niccolò   94
Macpherson, C. B.   271 n.14
Madison, James   255
Major, John   258–9, 266, 268
majoritarianism, and
democracy   75–6, 160, 215, 292
Mancini, G. F.   171
mandate
and civil society
organizations   232
and global security issues   256–7,
259–61, 263–4, 266–8, 269
Mandela, Nelson   11
Mann, Michael   92
Maragall, P.   44–5
market, global   15, 28, 40–1, 45,
155, 158
as alternative system of
constraint   48, 239
capital   15–16, 17–18, 22, 119,
155
and United Nations   320–1, 322,
324, 326, 327
Markoff, J.   46
Marks, Susan   4–5, 72–85
Marshall, T. H.   124–5, 130–1, 143
*Mathieu-Mohin & Clerfayt v
Belgium*   75–6, 89 n.52

media
and global security issues   258,
259, 261, 263–5, 269
and globalization   12, 13, 18–19,
155
and human rights   61, 278
and social movements   238, 239,
321, 323
Meehan, E.   140, 143
migration, mass   119, 125
*Military and Paramilitary Activities in
and against Nicaragua*   84
Mill, John Stuart
and global security   252
and non-violence   91
Miller, David   164
Milward, Alan   158
minority groups
and communitarianism   160, 171,
206
and cosmopolitanism   179, 207
and democracy   202, 206–7, 210
and global security problems
255
in international law   76–7, 114,
120
and liberalism   184
and state sovereignty   116–17,
119–20, 123, 124, 128–9, 131–2
MNCs *see* corporations,
multinational
mobilization of publics   30, 238–9,
259, 263–5, 269, 278, 325
morality
communitarian   163–4, 180, 182,
185–6, 187, 191
cosmopolitan   154–5, 162–3, 165,
180, 191–3
discourse theory   114–15, 120,
121–4, 132, 197 n.32
thick, thin   163–5
Morgenthau, Hans   205
Morris, Johnny   263
multiculturalism   119–20, 184, 189
municipality, and citizenship   149

nation-states
and citizenship   2–3, 5, 118–23,
124–6, 145, 148–9, 273–4

and democracy 12, 21–4, 82–5,
290, 291–3: among states 205–
9, 210–11, 215, 218; inside
nations 82, 85, 209–10, 212–
13, 214, 217–18
and European Union 158–9
and globalization 11–12, 13, 19,
118, 119–20, 156
and human rights 58, 59, 64–5,
66, 114, 120
and international law 72–3, 118,
120, 132
and political community 21–2
and refugees 277–82, 284–5
and regional control
mechanisms 45
state-building and political
community 117–18, 160, 168
and transnationalism 280
and war and peace 2, 5, 91–6,
103–4, 106, 108, 118–19, 153
see also autonomy; sovereignty;
state, European; states
nationalism
civic 159, 162, 164–5, 168
and cosmopolitanism 163–4, 179,
181
economic 125
and European citizenship 167–
9
and European Union 157–9
post-nationalism 162, 168
nationality
and European Union
citizenship 148, 149, 283
see also supranationality
NATO
and collective security 156
as confederation 212
Coordination Council (NACC)
103–4
peacekeeping role 106
Naylor, R. T. 102, 110 n.13
Nelson, Benjamin 117
neo-medievalism, and Bull 21, 115,
128, 129
neoliberalism 179, 195 n.3, 324,
326
and human rights 61

and libertarianism 180–1
Netherlands, and refugees 277
neutrality, and impartiality 107–
8
Nicaragua, United Nations Observer
Mission 77
Nigeria, and human rights 65
non-governmental organizations, as
functional equivalent of
democracy 41–2
non-violence *see* peace; peacekeeping
North, Richard 260–1
North American Free Trade
Agreement (NAFTA)
and alternative systems of
constraint 48
and trade 15
Nozick, R. 69 n.10, *181*, 195 n.3
nuclear technologies 1–2, 6, 22,
103, 204
testing 43, 211, 263–4, 270
Nuremberg Convention 127

Ohmae, K. 45
Oppermann, T. 140
organization, *see also*, civil society,
international
Organization of African Unity 220
Organization of American States 74,
75, 77, 220
Organization for Security and
Cooperation in Europe 77, 78,
106, 117
organizations
and democracy 12, 210–11, 218,
222, 288–9
and environment 19
and global governance 289–90,
319, 321
and individuals 130, 133
international governmental (IGOs)
20, 156, 206, 240–1
international non-governmental
(INGOs) 83, 206, 231–2, 248
n.3: and accountability 39, 42,
48–50, 106; and election
monitoring 77; and global
governance 41–2; and human
rights 59, 61–4, 67, 105; and

organizations *cont'd*
    international law   83–4; issue-
    based   37, 269–70;
    proliferation   20, 31–2, 63; and
    refugees   278, 283; *see also* civil
    society, international
  and peace and war   102, 103
  proliferation   31–2, 33
  and sovereignty   3, 288
  see also United Nations; World
    Bank
OSCE *see* Organization for Security
    and Cooperation in Europe
Oxfam   43
ozone depletion   19, 253–4

pacifism, legal   217
Paine, Thomas
  and non-violence   91
  and representative democracy   69
    n.6
Parekh, Bikhu   285
Paris, Congress (1919)   198
Parr, Douglas   272 n.26
participation   2, 131, 143, 159–
    60, 168, 223–4, 238, 291–
    2
  and citizenship   12, 124–7, 131–
    2, 143, 193, 196 n.18, 199
  and confederation   212–13
  and cosmopolitan democracy   24,
    218
  and global governance   38
  and global security issues   256,
    265–6
  and the media   264
  in transnational structures   130,
    133, 212, 232, 321–5, 327–8
  see also civil society
Partnership for Peace   103
peace
  and civility   103
  and confederations   212–13
  consensus on   91–2, 104, 106–8
  and democracy   2, 210, 317
  and federalism   214
  and globalization   119
  and human rights   105, 191
  movements towards   199

  and the nation-state   5, 92–6,
    118
  see also violence, organized; war
peace movement   42–3
peacekeeping, transnational   92,
    103, 104, 105–6, 155, 222, 290,
    310, 311, 317, 321
  second-generation   106–8
Penn, William   199
Peres, Shimon   28
Peterson, M. J.   245–6
Philbin, Maggie   263
Phillips, A.   129
Pitt, David   280
Plamenatz, John   292
Plato, and democracy   207
pluralism, and liberalism   183–4
Pogge, Thomas   164, 227 n.43
polis
  and citizenship   141–3, 145, 168
  and democracy   292
politics
  and citizenship   142–3, 152
  'DIY'   254–7, 259, 263–4, 266,
    269–70
  and global economy   16, 17–18,
    29
  and globalization   2–3, 4, 14, 20–
    1, 24, 40
  and human rights   59
  of identity   98, 103
  and interdependence   291
  and new forms of
    community   117–18
  and participation   124–5, 127,
    131, 159–60, 168, 199, 238
  of recognition   119, 128–9, 131,
    148
  and relocation of authority   34, 45
  and role of civil society   6, 231–48
  see also governance; United
    Nations
polity
  and citizenship   144, 145, 148,
    163–4
  global   231, 233
pollution
  transboundary   19, 26, 35
  see also Brent Spar affair

polyarchy, and global
 governance 51
population
 density 31
 displacement 96, 99, 125
power
 access to 14, 21, 239
 balance of 94, 95
 devolution 131
 economic 17–18
 and political community 117–18
Preuß, Ulrich K. 5, 138–49, 283–4
primitivism, and new wars 99–100,
 103, 105
Prins, Gwyn 6, 239, 252–70
progress
 social 239
 technological 237–8
proliferation, and governance 30–2
property rights 61, 69 n.10, 316
public sphere
 changing function 236–40
 and the media 263–5
 national and cosmopolitan 231–
 48
 and political loyalty 244–8
 see also civil society

rational choice theory, and
 participation 168, 196 n.18
Rawls, John 180, *181*, 182–6, 192,
 195 n.6, 196 nn.8,11,12,16, 197
 nn.19,32,33
Reagan, Ronald 316
realism
 and civil society 248 n.2
 and global democracy 78, 198,
 205–6, 208
 and refugees 279–80, 282
 and war and peace 94–5, 105
recognition, politics of 119, 128–9,
 131, 148
refugees
 and civil wars 276–7
 and cosmopolitan citizenship 6–7,
 273–86
 definition 275–6
 and ethnic cleansing 96
 and European citizenship 284

 and human rights 6, 274, 278
 international refugee regime 274,
 275–7, 282
 and new wars 96–7, 105
 and political projects 282–6
 political/economic 275–6
 and theories of the nation-
 state 277–82, 285
regime, international, analysis 240–
 1
regionalization 11, 12, 23–4
 and human rights 62–3, 65, 327
 and international law 84–5
 and the nation-state 114, 115–16,
 327
 see also European Union
regions
 and economic integration 67
 Europe of the regions 116
 and European Union 170, 283
 and growth in trade 15
 macro 43, 44
 micro 43–6
repatriation, forcible 96, 283
representation
 and democracy 39–40, 49, 292
 electoral 2, 81, 211–12, 290–1,
 293, 303
 territorial 211, 290–1, 293, 303
 in United Nations 290–1, 298,
 303, 305 n.14, 310–11
residence, right of, in European
 Union 148
resources, global
 and cosmopolitanism 180, 191
 and state adaptation 235–6
Rio Earth Summit (1992) 19, 20,
 24, 232, 245, 322–3
risk society 119, 120, 234, 236–43
Rittberger, Volker 7, 225 n.21,
 287–304
Robespierre, M. M. I. de 209
Rose, Chris 259
Rosecrance, R. 119
Rosell, S. A. et al. 30
Rosenau, James N. 4, 28–51, 243
Rousseau, Jean-Jacques
 and democracy 207, 213
 and non-violence 91, 94, 109 n.6

Rufin, Jean-Christophe   278
rule systems   30, 33–9, *37*, 40–1, 52
    n.3
  as alternative systems of
    control   47–50
  in NGOs   42
  regional   44, 45
Russia, and democracy   316–17
Rwanda, civil war   64, 275, 276,
    311, 319

Saint-Pierre, Abbé de   91, 94, 199,
    213
San Francisco Charter (1945)   198,
    296
sanctions   43, 47, 62, 65, 78, 210,
    218
Sandel, M.   *181*, 182, 184–5, 195
    n.4
  and identity   187, 189–90, 197
    nn.22,23
Sartori, G.   292
Schemo, D. J.   41
Schmidt, V. A.   49, 50
science, and environmentalism   259–
    63, 266, 268
security, global   7, 20–1, 156, 211,
    252–70
  and Brent Spar affair   257–9
  and civil society   242–4, 250
    n.40
  and cosmopolitan
    democracy   252–7
  and direct action
    campaigning   265–6
  and globalization   158, 239
  lessons   268–70
  and loss of confidence in
    institutions   259–61
  problems   253–7
  and role of the media   263–5
security, national   20, 254, 278
self *see* individuals
self-determination   42, 121, 265–6
  and cosmopolitanism/
    communitarianism   159, 161–2,
    191, 255
  and international law   76, 77, 79–
    80

and United Nations   312–13, 325–
    6
Sellwood, Elizabeth   6, 239, 252–70
Shaw, Martin   104, 126, 241
Shell UK
  and Brent Spar affair   257–9,
    260–5, 266, 268, 270
  and mandate   266–8
Shevardnadze, Edward   98
Shue, Henry   60, 126
Singer, Max   278
skill revolution   34, 50, 53 n.13
social movements   24, 35, 155
  as functional equivalent of
    democracy   42–3
  increased involvement   238
  and perpetual peace   103
  as system of constraint   47
socialism
  collapse   254, 287
  and communitarianism   162–3
society
  civilized   252–3
  and individuals   144, 182–5, 186–
    90, 191–4
  international   282
society, global   3, 13, 179
  and cosmopolitanism   152, 179–
    80, 182, 188, 190, 191–4, 283
  and global security   253
  and multiculturalism   119–20, 184
  and nation-state   118, 120
  and the public sphere   233, 240–4
  statist view   240–1
society, world   3, 179–94, 194 n.1
  and refugees   281
Soja, E. W.   52–3 n.6
solidarity, and refugees   278, 281,
    283
Sollenberg, Margareta   96
Somalia, civil war   64, 107, 276,
    311, 327
sovereignty
  and civil society   233, 246–7
  and communitarianism   157, 172,
    173, 301
  and confederation   212–13, 217
  and emerging states   116–17
  and European Union   5, 119

and federalism 214–15, 217
and human rights 58, 63, 64–5,
114, 159, 316, 327
internal/external 203–4, 211, 217
and international law 72, 85
in modern state 3, 5, 20, 21, 24,
92, 93–4, 113–33
and organized violence 94
pooling 23, 173
popular 81, 153, 160, 170
reciprocal 210–11
and relocation of authority 35, 54
n.18, 156, 288
unitarian conception 129–30, 132
and United Nations 312–13, 316,
320
Space, Globalized 38–42
and alternative systems of
constraint 47–50
and cities and regions 44, 45
and information technologies 46
Spain, and European citizenship 147
state, European
Bull on 21, 114, 115–16, 117,
120, 121, 124, 128, 132
citizenship and sovereignty 2–3,
5, 113–33, 148
critical theory and transnational
democracy 121–4
current developments 116–20
State, Global 104
states
adaptation to globalization 2–3,
39, 233–4, 235–6, 243
and boundary problems 21–2,
24–6, 117–18
and city states 44
and collective security *see* security,
global
communitarian 285
and democracy: among states 2,
82–3, 205–9, 210–11, 215, 218;
cosmopolitan 24, 115, 222;
democratization 198–224,
244–5, 304, 309–18; inside
nations 82, 85, 209–10, 212–
13, 214, 217–18; as subjects
of 7, 290–1, 293, 294–6, 299,
301

democratization 304, 309–18
ethnic 285
liberal 285
multi-ethnic 206, 211
new 116–17
and rights 301–2
and statist paradigm 299–300
see also nation-state; politics;
sovereignty
statism
and the public sphere 240–2,
315–16
and United Nations 232, 318,
320–1, 323–6, 327–8
statist paradigm 299, 302
Stauder v Ulm 177 n.60
Steiner, H. 69 n.10
Stockholm Conference on the Human
Environment (1972) 321
Strange, S. 48–9
subgroupism
and global governance 34–5, 36,
38, 54 n.14
and international law 120
and self-determination 76
and state sovereignty 114, 133
subjecthood
and citizenship 145
dual subject status 290–1, 293,
294, 303
subsidiarity
and cosmopolitan democracy 217
in European Union 166, 170, 220
supranationality
and European Union 138, 139,
140, 145, 156–7, 162, 165, 172–
3
and globalization 157–8
supremacy of Community law 138–
9, 146, 157, 165, 171–2
Sweden, and refugees 284

Tamir, Y. 197 n.30
taxation
and libertarianism 184
and the nation-state 118, 119,
132
Taylor, C. *181*, 182, 187, 188,
189–90, 195 n.4, 301

telecommunications
  as functional equivalent of
    democracy   46–7
  and globalization   18, 155
  and trade   15
  see also information technology
territoriality
  and citizenship   147
  and democracy   40–50, 328
  and federalism   147
  and the nation-state   3, 113, 133,
    280
  and organized violence   91–3, 104
Thompson, G.   157
Thompson, Janna   5–6, 164, 179–
  94
'Tinkerbell effect'   267, 268, 269,
  272 n.31
torture   61, 63
tourism, increase   18, 206
trade
  and external support for
    warfare   101–2
  and globalization   14–15, 24, 35,
    120, 155, 158, 206
transnationalism, and refugees   280
Trent, J. E.   293
tribalism, rise   23
Turner, B.   128, 144

unevenness, and globalization   14
United Nations
  and accountability   24, 48, 291,
    295, 316
  as alternative rule system   49
  Charter   73, 78, 309, 312–13, 318
  and civil society
    organizations   231–2, 315, 318,
    319, 321–6
  Committee on Economic, Social
    and Cultural Rights   62
  as confederation   212, 220
  Convention on the Elimination of
    All Forms of Discrimination
    against Women   63
  Convention on the Rights of the
    Child   63
  and cosmopolitan democracy   7,
    23, 158, 193, 220–1, 309–28

  Declaration and Convention
    against Torture   63
  Declaration on . . . National,
    Ethnic, Religious and Linguistic
    Minorities   77
  Declaration on the Rights of
    Indigenous Peoples   90 n.64,
    325, 330 n.10
  Declaration on Violence against
    Women   63
  and democracy   186, 211, 287–
    304, 318–26
  and democratization of
    states   304, 309–18
  and domestic jurisdiction   312,
    317
  Economic and Social Council   319
  and election monitoring   77–8,
    326
  Environment Programme   247
  General Assembly   74, 84, 291,
    295–6, 303–4, 313, 319, 325
  and global governance   29, 289–
    304, 319
  and human rights   65, 66–7, 313–
    18, 326, 327: covenants   61–2,
    63–4, 312, 314–15
  Human Rights Committee   85,
    320, 325
  and individuals as subjects of
    democracy   293, 297–9, 300
  Informal Working Group on
    Indigenous Populations   325
  intergovernmental conferences   20,
    24, 63, 232, 244, 320–5
  and international law   83, 84
  peacekeeping role   92, 106, 107,
    110 n.21, 290, 310, 311, 317,
    321
  reform proposals   7, 25, 220–1,
    221, 228 n.47, 293–303
  and refugees   275, 277, 282–3
  Resolution on Minorities   60
  and second assembly   83, 297–8,
    302, 303–4, 319
  and statism   232, 318, 320–1,
    323–6, 327–8
UNDP   62, 320, 324
UNESCO   158

UNICEF 62, 324
see also Universal Declaration of Human Rights
United Nations High Commissariat of Refugees 62, 275, 277, 283
United Nations Security Council
  and civil society 232–3, 324
  and International Court of Justice 84, 295, 296, 319
  and other UN organs 295–6, 303
  and peacekeeping 107, 310
  and right of veto 294, 295, 310
  and sanctions 78
  structure 62, 319–20
  and superpowers 158, 220, 309–11
United States of America
  and aid conditionality 65
  and democracy 208, 316
  and disaggregation of authority 32
  and human rights 315
  and local government 52–3 n.6
  and media control 18
  and monopoly of organized violence 104, 208
  and multinational corporations 17
  and national citizenship 146–7, 284
  and peacekeeping 107, 291
  and refugees 276
  Supreme Court 146, 151 nn.30,31, 176 nn.27,28
  and United Nations 65, 309–11, 313, 316, 319
United States Constitution, and alienage 146–7, 284
Universal Declaration of Human Rights 74, 75, 220, 314–15
universalism
  and citizenship 142, 274, 282
  and communitarianism 152, 157, 165, 180, 182, 186, 190
  and cosmopolitanism 191–2
  and democracy 202–3, 209, 301–2
  and difference 121, 122–4, 129–30, 132–3

  and feminism 122
  and human rights 4, 58, 59–64, 66–7, 163, 216, 273, 278
  and international organizations 241
Urquhart, Brian 297–8
utilitarianism, and justice 184
utopianism, embedded 256
Utrecht, Peace (1712) 198–9

values
  allocation 288–9, 290, 304
  consensus 188–9, 191, 193, 300
  plurality 169, 183
Vidal, J. 270
Vienna Conference on Human Rights and Development (1993) 63, 70 n.21, 322
Vienna, Congress (1814) 198, 213
Vienna Convention on the Law of Treaties (1969) 85 n.1
violence, organized 91–109, 118–19
  changing patterns 96–102
  consensus on 104
  and democracy among states 218
  and international law 104–5
  intrastate *see* war, new
  and nation-state 153
  and transnational democracy 5, 102–9, 132, 204
Vogler, J. 35

Wagner, Wolfgang 7, 225 n.21, 287–304
Wallensteen, Peter 96
Walzer, Michael 163, 301
war
  and centre and periphery 278–9
  Clausewitzean 95, 97–8, 97, 99–100, 102, 105, 106–8
  economy 100–1
  and external support 101–2, 105
  goals 98–9, 103
  increase in number 96
  interbloc 95–6, 97, 103, 204
  and mode of warfare 99–100, 103
  and the nation-state 2, 5, 92–6, 108, 118–19

war *cont'd*
  new   97–102, 97, 103–7, 253
  and war crimes   104–5, 106, 107,
    156, 219
  see also Cold War; nuclear
    technologies; peace; violence,
    organized
Warsaw Pact, as confederation   212
Watson, Adam   240–1
Weber, Max   92, 142
Weiler, J. H. H.   169, 172
Weiss, Thomas G.   280
welfare
  and democracy   209
  rights   125, 127–8, 131, 133, 202
Western European Union   103
Westphalia, Treaty (1648), and
    modern nation-state   93, 113,
    129–32, 198–9, 316, 320, 326
Wight, M.   113
Wildavsky, Aaron   278
Williams, Bernard   196 n.13
Wilson, Woodrow   79, 199
women
  and ethic of care   136 n.48
  and United Nations   20, 24, 63,
    232, 322–4

women's movement   24, 63
World Bank   12, 247, 326
World Court *see* International Court
    of Justice
world order
  and communitarianism   206–7
  and cooperation   205–6, 240–4,
    245
  and cosmopolitan
    democracy   198–224, 231
  democratization   198–224, 244–5
  and domestic democracy   4, 198–
    9, 203–5, 207–9, 210, 212–13
  and refugees   281
world system   279
World Trade Organization   232
Wright, A.   133
Wybrew, John   259, 269

Yalta Conference (1944)   198
Yugoslavia (former), civil war   5, 64,
    96, 99, 101–3, 202, 283, 319

Zolo, Danilo   206

Compiled by Meg Davies

- begs w/out addressing/while evading question Answers ambiguous. But conversation has to take place

- § literature on rising transnational loyalties

- In principle, easy to support transnational (though not everyone does) loyalties In practice, much harder, esp. for left.

- Linklater this volume, p. 119: Globalization "reduces the value of national citizenship for the victims of growing ec. inequalities."

→ Good norm. reasons having to do w/ democratization to support cosmopolitan order. When norm. concern is distrib. equality, is the outcome different? justice, See Linklater at 121 for democracy & recognition based arguments:

- Expanding rts of citizenship: wider vs. deeper?